FINANCIAL ANALYSIS
FOR EFFECTIVE
MANAGEMENT DECISIONS

TABLE OF CONTENTS

Brief profile of the Author

B D Chatterjee is a Chartered Accountant with CS, CMA qualifications and a diploma holder in IFRS from ACCA UK having over 35 Years of rich experience in overall business and finance function.

He possesses expertise in CFO solutions especially in areas like, Merger & Acquisitions, financial due diligence, business strategy, business restructuring & strategic planning including development of business plan and budgetary control, implementation of global best practices, ERP- Implementation and Project Management, Audit & Change Management, Financial Analysis & Business Valuations, Enterprise Risk Management, Value added management consulting and has extensive knowledge and experience in the fields of industrial gases, chemicals, dairy and FMCG businesses.

Before launching into practice, he has held key high profile positions working as Group CFO for Mother Dairy and Director Finance India for Kelly Services, US and various other senior positions like Director Finance/ Vice-President/Finance Controller with other large global MNCs like DuPont and BOC Gases and large Indian conglomerates like Max India.

Apart from his consulting assignments, he also teaches IFRS as visiting faculty with an international institute and has authored books on International Financial Reporting Standards, Financial Reporting, Indian Accounting Standards and Accounting Standards for finance professionals and students.

Preface to the book

We know that financial statements with all its details and complex reporting requirements sometimes become very difficult to read and comprehend. They say "Devil is in the details". Hence it is imperative to decipher the details of numbers:

a) to understand what these numbers want to convey,

b) arrive at conclusions as to the performance of the entity under review and

c) draw broad perceptions as to the direction the organisation is moving, which means whether it is growth centric, whether it is drifting or whether there are chances that it can fail owing to certain inherent risks

To make this study meaningful, the reader needs to have a fair understanding of some simple tools like, comparative analysis, ratio analysis and tools related to strategic cost management.

To assist the readers to get a hang of these concepts, an attempt has been made to explain these financial analysis tools in very elementary terms with as many practical illustrations as possible. Chapter one to six have been devoted on these topics.

In Chapter 7, the results of these financial tools have been assimilated into integrated Management Reporting in the form of Dash Boards. A lot of illustrations have been provided which will help the reader to create his own Executive Information System (EIS) or Financial Dash Board.

Chapter 8,9 and 10 provides as logical extension to the above concepts, an overview on financial modelling, explains Internal Rate of Return (IRR), Net present value (NPV), economic value added (EVA) and business valuation techniques.

Chapter 11 has been devoted to inorganic business growth through Merger & Acquisition and the relevant concepts have been explained in lucid form with lot of illustrations.

Finally Chapter 12 provides a window which discusses decision making tools through Strategic Cost Management.

In summary, the objective of this book has been to simplify the concepts and tools of financial analysis to make it readable, understandable and implementable with ease.

I would like to take this opportunity to mention that while considerable care has been taken to ensure that the contents of the book are accurate, a few errors and omissions might have crept in, for which I seek with all humility to my readers to bear with me.

I would like dedicate this book to my loving parents without whose constant inspiration this would not have been possible. I would also like to thank my wife who stood by my side to ensure that the book saw the light of day.

B D CHATTERJEE
121/ 105 SILVER OAKS APARTMENTS
DLF PHASE I
GURGAON 122002
INDIA
Dated 29th January 2017
Email: bdchatterjee105@gmail.com
LinkedIn: in.linkedin.com/pub/biswajeet-chatterjee/2/5a9/b6/

Chapter 1 : Financial trend Analysis

1.1. Financial Analysis

Financial Analysis is the art and science of analysis of statutory financial statements and come up with deterministic and predictive inferences for management decision making. Financial Analysis is professed to provide the users of financial statements the following:

a) understanding of the strengths and weaknesses of the business
b) highlight the possible pitfalls and business risks that may hit the business in the foreseeable future
c) come up with clear action plan how to redress the financial weaknesses and avoid the pitfalls and business risks

The other term for it is business analytics (both financial and non-financial) and this is supposed to work as a lighthouse function, to ensure the business ship is guided safely through hostile business waters and moored to safe havens.

Areas where business / financial analysis have major impact on business decision making have been listed below. This list is by no means exhaustive and can be extended according to business needs.

Capacity utilisation analysis:	**pacity Utilization Analysis along with estimated impact on costs and profitability** (Product-wise, Product Group-wise and Unit-wise) • Under-utilization of Capacities • Idle Capacities • Non-Productive Assets • Trend Analysis • opportunity Analysis • Outsourcing/Sub-Contracting Vs. Internal Capacities • Plant Break-down hours with impact on productivity, costs and profitability • Scope of Expansion and likely cost-benefit analysis
Productivity analysis:	Productivity Analysis along with estimated impact on costs and profitability (Product-wise, Product Group-wise and Unit-wise) • Production/Operations/Process Cycle Time and Productivity • Input-Output Analysis compared with Budgets or Standards or Industry Norms • Conversion Efficiency Analysis • Cost of wastages in operations
Utilities / energy efficiency analysis:	**Utilities/Energy Efficiency Analysis** (Utility-wise, Unit-wise, Product-wise, and Product Group-wise) • Utility Productivity compared with Budgets or Standards or Industry Norms • Input-Output Efficiency – impact on costs and profitability • Energy Conversion Ratio highlighting wastage & inefficiency • Energy Consumption Ratio for each product/operation and each product/ activity group compared with Budgets or Standards or Industry Norms
Cost and Contribution analysis:	Key-Expense Ratios vs. Cost of Production / Cost of Sales • Abnormal & Non-Recurring Costs – impact on profitability • Key Costs Trend Analysis indicating estimated impact on future profitability • Cost-effectiveness Analysis: Cost of Operation/Process vs. Benefits • Cost of Management vs. Net Turnover or Gross Margin or Net Margin • Cost Variance Analysis vs. Standards or Budgets – impact on profitability • Volume Variance Analysis vs. Standards or Budgets – impact on profitability

	• Marginal Cost and Contribution Analysis for each product/activity, each product/activity group, each market segment, each customer segment, etc. • Service Department-wise cost trends (element-wise)
Product / service profitability:	**Product/Service Profitability (for key products/services only)** • Product, • Turnover, % to Total, • Capital Employed, % to Total CE, • Gross Margin, % to Total, • Gross Margin as % of Turnover, • Gross Margin as % of Capital Employed, • Net Margin, % to Total Net Margin, • Net Margin as % to Turnover, • Net Margin as % to Capital Employed,
Market / customer profitability:	**Market/Customer Profitability – similar analysis as above** • Market Distribution – Indigenous vs. Overseas broken into smaller geographical divisions/segments • Customer Distribution – in order of percentage share in each product/ activity and in each product/activity group • Indicate cost of servicing each market/customer and its efficiency in terms of business, contributions, gross/net margins, scope of sustainability, etc. • Indicate cost of each supply chain vs. benefits • Indicate impact of FTAs and Dumping on each product, product-group or each market/customer.
Working capital analysis:	Movement of Debtors vs. Credit Sales • Days Debtors Analysis – impact on cash flow and profitability • Overseas Debtors – impact of likely FE Variations • Movement of Creditors vs. Credit Purchases • Days Creditors Analysis – impact on supplies and product-line • Inventory Turnover • Cash Flow Turnover – impact on profitability
Inventory analysis:	Inventory Analysis - Basis of valuation & Consistency • Turnover efficiency: Cost of Goods Sold/Average Inventory • Return on Inventory: GM/Average Inventory, NM/Average Inventory • Slow-moving or dead inventory • ABC analysis; Period holding analysis • Policy for Insurance Spares; Inventory Holding due to changes in technology, changes in production process, obsolescence, etc.
Manpower Analysis	**Manpower Analysis** (Function-wise, Unit-wise, Product-wise, and Product Group-wise) • Manpower Productivity vs. Returns compared with Budgets or Standards or Industry Norms • Manpower Pyramid – Ratio of Top Management to Middle Management to Officers to Workmen to Contract Labour • Idle Man-hours to Total Man-hours with reason-wise analysis and impact on productivity, costs and profitability • Manpower Absenteeism Vs. Total paid Man-days • Cost of Manpower Pyramid Analysis – broken into broad categories (including contract labour) • Cost of Training to Total Employee Cost
Application of Management	**Management Accounting Tools** – use of modern management accounting tools and techniques such as :- • Activity Based Costing,

Accounting Tools	• Target Costing • Lifecycle Costing • Quality Costing • Value Engineering • Supply Chain Management • Balanced Scorecard • Performance Pyramid • Lean Accounting • Theory of Constraints • Throughput Accounting • Kaizen Costing • Customer Valuation • Strategic Cost Management, etc. and benefits availed, if any.

In this Chapter we have discussed relatively simpler financial analytics which are depicted as under:

a) Comparative financial statements
b) Common size statements
c) Trend ratios
d) Forecasting techniques

1.2. Comparative Financial Statements

When the financial statements of current year and previous year are recast for comparison of all the elements of financial statements and the comparison is in absolute numbers as well as in percentages, it is called comparative financial statement.

The statement is constructed by
a) using absolute numbers represented by monetary values in the years / periods under consideration and
b) calculating the increase or decrease in monetary values in absolute numbers
c) calculating percentage increase of the monetary values by using the following formula:

$$\frac{\text{(Current period figures – Previous period figures)}}{\text{Previous period figures}} \times 100$$

d) the results of the aforesaid comparison are then analysed and interpreted

Merits	1. Comparison of numbers related to two corresponding periods is simple to calculate as well as comprehend 2. This can be used in inter firm comparisons of entities belonging to similar industry 3. It brings out the source and deployment of funds at a high level, one can understand and interpret which way the funds have moved 4. It also brings out whether the funds generated out of source of funds are getting utilised or blocked in working capital like debtors , inventories and cash and bank balances

	5.	It can also broadly depict the pattern of source of funds, whether the funds have been internally generated out of profits / reserves or from external sources through infusion of equity or additional debt either through secured or unsecured route
	6.	In broad terms the comparison throws insight in apparent weaknesses in operating cycle, financial liquidity and solvency of the business.
Demerits	1.	The comparison does not highlight interpretation through ratios like current ratio, debt equity ratio etc
	2.	Without the knowledge of internal dynamics of the business, the conclusions may be misleading
	3.	Proper comparison between two or more entities is not possible by this analysis because there is no common base of comparison.

Illustration 1.1: Comparative Balance Sheet

Following are the Balance Sheet of Mayuri Ltd as on 31.3.2012 and 31.3.2013 and interpret the results.

	31.03.2012 Rs crores	31.02.2013 Rs crores
Share capital and liabilities		
Share capital	6393.21	6453.39
Equity share suspense	60.14	-
Equity share warrant	-	1,682.40
Reserves and surplus	57.513.78	73,312.81
Secured loans	9,569.12	6,600.17
Unsecured loans	18.256.61	29.879.51
Current liabilities	16,865.53	21,045.47
Provisions	1,712.87	2,992.62
Deferred tax liability	6,982.02	7,872.54
	1,17,353.28	1,49,838.91
Assets		
Net Fixed Assets	63,660.46	61,883.63
Capital work-in-progress	9,528.13	25,005.84
Investments	16,251.34	22,063.60
Current Assets		
Inventories	10,136.51	12,247.54
Sundry debtors	3,732.42	6,227.58
Cash & bank	1,835.35	4,280.05
Other current assets	3.07	72.54
Loans and advances	12,206.00	18,058.13
	1,17,353.28	1,49,838.91

Solution
Comparative Balance Sheet of Mayuri Ltd   (Rs crores)

	31.03.2012	31.03.2013	Absolute change	% change
Share capital and liabilities				
Share capital	6393.21	6453.39	60.18	0.941
Equity share suspense	60.14	-	(60.14)	(100.00)
Equity share warrant	-	1,682.40	1,682.40	100.00

Reserves and surplus	57.513.78	73,312.81	15,799.03	27.469
Secured loans	9,569.12	6,600.17	(2,968.95)	(31.026)
Unsecured loans	18.256.61	29.879.51	11,622.90	63.664
Current liabilities	16,865.53	21,045.47	4,179.94	24.784
Provisions	1,712.87	2,992.62	1,279.75	74.714
Deferred tax liability	6,982.02	7,872.54	890.52	12.754
Total	1,17,353.28	1,49,838.91	32,485.63	27.682
Assets				
Net Fixed Assets	63,660.46	61,883.63	1,776.83	(2.791)
Capital work-in-progress	9,528.13	25,005.84	15,477.71	162.442
Investments	16,251.34	22,063.60	5,812.26	35.765
Current Assets				
Inventories	10,136.51	12,247.54	2,111.03	20.826
Sundry debtors	3,732.42	6,227.58	2,495.16	66.851
Cash & bank	1,835.35	4,280.05	2,444.70	133.200
Other current assets	3.07	72.54	69.47	2262.866
Loans and advances	12,206.00	18,058.13	5,852.13	47.944
Total	1,17,353.28	1,49,838.91	32,485.63	27.682

Interpretation of the aforesaid comparison is as under:
a) The share capital has increased by Rs.60.18 crores, owing to transfer of equity share suspense account into share capital
b) During the current year equity share warrant of Rs.1,682.40 has been issued
c) Reserves and surplus has shown a significant increase of Rs.15, 799.03 crores (27.469%) in the current year over the previous year.
d) Secured loan has reduced by Rs.2, 968.95 crores over previous year (31.026%)
e) The entity has raised unsecured loans to the tune of Rs.11, 62.90 an increase of 63.664%.
f) Current liabilities and provisions have increased to the tune of 24.784% and 74.714% respectively.
g) Net Fixed Assets of the entity has reduced by 2.791% whereas capital work-in-progress has gone up by Rs. 15,477.71 crores which is evidence to investment by the entity on its upcoming projects which have not been capitalised.
h) On the other hand investments have increased by Rs.5, 812.26 crores, which is an increase of 35.765%.
i) Gross current assets have increased significantly as substantiated by increase in inventories by 20.82%, sundry debtors by 66.851%, cash & bank balances by 133.2 % and loans and advances by 47.944%.

1.3. Common size statements
Common size financial statements are restated financial statement showing percentage of total items with common base for comparison.
The steps followed are as under:

Assets	
	a) Assets side is classified in fixed assets, investments, current assets (CA), fictitious assets showing individually and its total.
	b) Then total assets are taken as common base of 100 and the calculation is made as shown below:
	- Tangible assets / Total assets x 100
	- Investments / Total assets X 100
	- Fictitious assets / Total assets x 100 etc

Liabilities	c) Similarly liabilities side of the Balance Sheet is classified into owners' equity, long term borrowings, current liabilities showing individually and its total. d) The total liabilities are taken as common base of 100 and the calculation is made as shown below: - Owners' equity / Total Liabilities x 100 - Long term borrowings / Total liabilities x 100
Income statement	e) Income statement is classified in sales, cost of goods sold, operating expenses, net profit, interest, tax, earnings after tax etc. Percentage of each element to sales is calculated.

Merits

1. It helps in inter-firm comparison having a common base
2. It shows the changes over the years in relation to total assets, total liabilities etc
3. It helps in vertical analysis of figures
4. It assists in understanding financial strategy of the firms in comparison
5. It shows the relative efficiency of each cost item of two firms

Demerits

1. Does not show changes of each item from period to period
2. The observations are not very useful because there are more definite approaches for the proportion of each item to total
3. If there is no uniform costing system, no similar accounting policy among all the firms of an industry, it is meaningless for studying the comparative position of two entities.

Illustration 1.2: Common size analysis

From the following Balance Sheet , prepare a common size statement:

	31.03.2012 Rs.	31.03.2013 Rs.
Equity share capital (Rs.10 each)	7,00,000	7,50,000
Reserves and surplus	3,00,000	5,00,000
Long term debt	5,00,000	4,50,000
Current liabilities	3,00,000	2,00,000
Total	18,00,000	19,00,000
Tangible assets	12,00,000	11,50,000
Inventories	3,00,000	3,50,000
Trade receivables	2,00,000	2,50,000
Cash & bank	1,00,000	1,50,000
Total	18,00,000	19,00,000

Solution

Common size statement is shown as under:

	On 31.03.2012 % of total	On 31.03.2013 % of total
Assets Tangible assets (Tangible assets / Total assets) x 100	67%	61%

Inventories (Inventories / Total assets) x 100	17%	18%
Trade receivables (Trade receivables / Total assets) x 100	11%	13%
Cash & bank (Cash & bank / Total assets x 100)	5%	8%
	100%	100%
Liabilities Equity share capital (Equity share capital / Total liabilities) x 100	39%	39%
Reserves and surplus (Reserves and surplus / Total liabilities) x 100	17%	26%
Long term debt (Long term debt / Total liabilities) x 100	28%	24%
Current liabilities (Current liabilities / Total liabilities) x 100	16%	11%
	100%	100%

Observations

a) It shows that shareholders' funds of the organisation have improved from 56% (39% + 17%) to 65% (39% + 26%). Conversely, long term debt has shrunk from 28% to 24%. This reflects that the degree of riskiness of the entity's financial solvency have reduced with less dependency on the outside borrowing and more internal generation of funds ploughed back to business (reserves and surplus going up from 17% to 26%).

b) Current Assets as a percentage of total assets have gone up from 33% to 39% whereas current liabilities have gone down from 16% to 11%. This reflects that liquidity position of the entity has improved.

c) Tangible assets as % of total assets have gone down from 67% to 61%. It signifies that the entity believes in more short term measures and need to invest more on long term projects to ensure further growth and long term stability rather than short term profitability.

1.4. Trend Ratios

Trend ratios are calculated in the form of index no. of each financial item in the financial statement of different periods. The method presupposes percentage relation of items with the similar item in the base year. The formula is as under:

$$\text{Trend ratio} = \frac{\text{Value of each item in financial statement of any period}}{\text{Value of same item in financial statement of base period}} \times 100$$

In order to ensure that trend ratios are meaningful following care needs to be taken:
a) There has to be uniform accounting policies followed year on year to make this analysis meaningful
b) Consistency convention is a pre-requisite for this type of analysis
c) Trend percentages need to be calculated only for items having logical relationship with one another
d) Care should be taken to select the base year. This has to be a normal year and be adequately representative of the performance trend
e) Trend percentages should be studied after considering the absolute numbers on which they are based, otherwise they may give misleading and skewed results.
f) The figures of the current year should be adjusted in the light of price level changes as compared to the base year before calculating the trend analysis, otherwise comparison may not be meaningful.

Merits
a) It depicts trend of items with passage of time
b) It shows the manner and rate of improvement or decline of various financial parameters
c) Keeping everything constant , it estimates and predicts the financial parameters of the foreseeable future
d) It also shows horizontal and vertical analysis to reflect behaviour of various financial items with the passage of time.

Demerits
a) Without uniform accounting policies this analysis is meaningless
b) This analysis does not take into account inflation accounting. So in case of inflation figures of base year may be widely differing from the figures of the current year.
c) In today's dynamic business environment where things change very quickly , it would be difficult to use the premise that everything will continue to remain the same going forward in the foreseeable future
d) Trend ratios must be read based on absolute data; otherwise the analysis and conclusion may not be practical in approach.

Illustration 1.3: Trend ratios

Compute the trend ratios from the following data and comment (Rs)

	2010	2011	2012	2013
Cost of material consumed	2,00,000	2,50,000	2,00,000	1,80,000
Labour cost	1,50,000	1,50,000	2,00,000	1,25,000
Other expenses	1,50,000	2,00,000	1,00,000	1,50,000
Cost of sales	5,00,000	6,00,000	5,00,000	4,55,000
Profit	3,00,000	3,00,000	2,50,000	3,45,000
Sales	8,00,000	9,00,000	7,50,000	8,00,000

Solution
Statement of computation of trend ratio (%)

	2010	2011 (2011/2010 x 100)	2012 (2012/2010 x 100)	2013 (2013/2010 x 100)
Cost of material	100	125	100	90

consumed				
Labour cost	100	100	133.3	83.3
Other expenses	100	133.3	66.7	100
Cost of sales	100	120	100	91
Profit	100	100	83.3	115
Sales	100	112.5	93.8	100

Conclusion

From the above numbers, it is evident that the numbers do not show any clear trend except that costs of sales have been showing a downward trend, whereas sales growth remained flat.

Chapter 2. Forecasting techniques

2.1. Introduction

Forecasting is a prediction about a condition or situation at some future time. Business decisions and especially financially related business decisions, depend heavily on forecasts of future events. Decisions related to future investments, borrowing and lending funds depend heavily on forecasts of future business events. Even valuation of enterprise or business verticals or projects also heavily depends on future forecast.

2.2. Need for forecasting techniques

Most enterprises use significant senior management time and sophisticated forecasting tools to map the uncertain future events. Budgeting and forecasting is used to do the following:
   a) Build yardsticks and benchmarks for future performance
   b) Monitor actual performance and compare with budget and forecasts
   c) Handle uncertainty of the future

2.3. Three critical questions to answers

a) estimate the future forecast with accuracy as much as possible
b) the cost benefit trade-off and what efforts need to be put in to generate reasonably accurate forecast
c) Meet the criteria for timeliness. Annual forecast has to be before the commencement of the financial year. Monthly or quarterly forecasts have to be before the commencement of the respective periods.

2.4. Types of forecast

a) Judgement forecast – where forecasts are made based on experience and information available instead of any mathematical and statistical models
b) Time series forecast – where pattern of a time series based on past experience is used to create a model that will predict future movement
c) Casual forecast – based on casual relationship which is expected to be stable over time and casual variables are relatively easy to predict.

2.5. Essential attributes of a good forecast

a) 5 Strong and robust assumptions of the internal factors driving the business and external macro economic factors- like CPI and WPI for forecasting inflation, market size of the product / services
b) Identification of variables which can swing results of forecasts e.g. prediction of sales prices, raw material costs, exchange rates for imports etc.
c) sensitivity analysis, where results of assumptions are adjusted linking possible changes in key variables driving the business

Illustration 2.1: Specimen Profitability forecast

Item	October	November	December	January	February	March	YTD	Remarks
Revenue								
Commission	0	0	0	0	0	0	0	
Trading	0	0	0	0	0	0	0	
Projects	0	0	0	0	0	0	0	
Total revenue	0	0	0	0	0	0	0	
Expenses								
Salaries & wages	0	0	0	0	0	0	0	
Staff welfare expenses	0	0	0	0	0	0	0	
Utilities expense	0	0	0	0	0	0	0	
Rent, rates and taxes	0	0	0	0	0	0	0	
Repairs & maintenance	0	0	0	0	0	0	0	
Tours & travels	0	0	0	0	0	0	0	
Interest pay-out	0	0	0	0	0	0	0	
Other charges	0	0	0	0	0	0	0	
Total expenses	0	0	0	0	0	0	0	
Profit / loss	0	0	0	0	0	0	0	

Financial Analysis for effective Management Decisions

Illustration 2.2: Specimen format of Cash forecast

Cash flow statement

Item	October	November	December	January	February	March	YTD	Remarks
Inflows								
Receipt from customers								
Commission								
Trading								
Project								
Loan received								
Total	0	0	0	0	0	0	0	
Outflows								
Vendor payment								
Salaries & wages								
Staff welfare expenses								
Utilities expense								
Rent, rates and taxes								
Repairs & maintenance								
Tours & travels								
Loan repayment								
Interest pay-out								
Other charges								
Total	0	0	0	0	0	0	0	
Net cash flows								
Add: Opening balance								
Closing balance								

Illustration 2.3: Week-wise rolling cash forecast

CASH FORECAST		ABC Limited							Rs'lakhs
		Jan 2015				Feb 2015			
	Wk 1	Wk2	Wk3	Wk4	Wk 1	Wk2	Wk3	Wk4	
	f'cast	f'cast	f'cast	f'cast	f'cast	f'cast	f'cast	f'cast	
Receipts from Customers	-	67.96	128.64	5.60	12.06	3.56	99.25	35.17	
Customers	-	67.96	14.88	5.60	4.48	3.56	99.25	35.17	
Loan and Advances			1.00						
SAD Refund					7.58				
Cash Sales			112.46						
Security Refund			0.30						
Payments to Vendors	98.22	212.04	21.48	-	67.48	129.33	-	-	
Vendors-RM	86.29	194.04	21.48		67.48	85.73	-	-	
Vendors-Others									
Purchases Charges		18.00				43.60			
LC Margin	11.93								
Cheque issued									
Salary & Allowance	-	-	-	-	14.00	-	-	-	
Salary & Allowances - (Staff)					14.00				

16

Financial Analysis for effective Management Decisions

LTA								
LTC Expenses								
Medical Expenses								
Salary Arrear - (Staff)				7.00				
General Administrative Expense	-	-	0.20	0.20	0.20	0.25	0.20	0.20
Stationary Expenses		-				0.05		
Photocopy Expenses								
Postage and Courier Charges								
Freight	-	-	0.20	0.20	0.20	0.20	0.20	0.20
Transportation General								
Books Newspapers and Periodicals								
Watch and Ward								
Insurance -Assets								
Insurance -Employees								
Insurance-Others								
Meeting Expenses								
Utilities Expense	-	15.00	-	-	1.50	-	-	-
Communication Expenses								
Water tanker Expenses								
Drinking Water								
Electricity Expenses					0.50			
Office Expenses								
Staff Welfare Expenses					0.20			
Generator Fuel Expenses								
Rent Charges					0.80			
Duties and Taxes		15.00						
Repairs & Maintenance	-	-	-	-	-	-	-	-
Repair & Maintenance - Buildings								
Repair & Maintenance-Assets								
Repair & Maintenance-Vehicles								
Repair & Maintenance - Others								
Tours & Travels	-	-	0.50	-	-	0.50	-	-
Local Conveyance								
Tour & Travelling(Domestics)			0.50			0.50		
Tour & Travelling(International)								
Ticket Booking & Cancellation								
Parking Expenses								
Purchase/Custom Duty/Custom Clearing	21.05	-	-	-	-	-	-	-
Custom Duty	21.05							
Cost of Goods Sold								
Custom Clearing								
Demurrage								
D.O Charges								

17

Financial Analysis for effective Management Decisions

Interest Payout - Unsecured/Secured	1.00	-	-	13.85	2.00	-	-	-
Interest - 1	1.00	-		13.85	2.00			
Interest - 2								
Interest - 3								
Interest Paid on Loans								
Other expenses	-	-	1.50	1.50	1.05	1.50	0.50	0.50
Liasioning Expenses					0.50			
Seminar Expenses								
Packing Expenses								
Training Expenses								
Exhibition Expenses								
Business Promotion/Advertisement			1.00			1.00		
Consultancy Charges								
Professional Fees								
Project Expenses			0.50	0.50	0.50	0.50	0.50	0.50
Subscription & MemberShip Fee								
Function Expenses								
Email/Internet/Website Expenses					0.05	.		
Legal Expenses								
Tender Fee								
Bank Charges								
Processing Fees/ Others								
Realised Foreign Exchange Losses								
Unrealised Foreign Exchange Losses								
Miscellaneous Expenses								
Credit Card Exp				1.00				
Other Expenses								
TOTAL PAYMENTS	120.26	227.04	23.68	15.55	86.23	131.58	0.70	0.70
SURPLUS / (DEFICIT)	-120.26	-159.08	104.96	-9.95	-74.17	-128.02	98.55	34.47
OPENING CASH BALANCE	-35.34	-155.60	-314.68	-209.72	-219.67	-293.84	-421.86	-323.31
CLOSING CASH BALANCE	-155.60	-314.68	-209.72	-219.67	-293.84	-421.86	323.31	-288.84

Note: Closing cash balance highlighted in red, indicates negative cash balance. This is physically not possible and more hypothetical to highlight to the management that they need to do something to convert the red into green, in other words organise inflow of cash either through better working capital management or through infusion of cash through equity or borrowings route.
Hence this cash forecast works as a warning signal for the immediate future cash needs of the entity to effectively run the business.

Chapter 3. Ratio Analysis

3.1. Introduction

The major accounting ratios are categorised as under:

- Liquidity ratios
- Capital structure ratios
- Coverage ratios
- Profitability ratios
- Expenses ratios
- Activity ratios
- Asset turnover ratios
- Return on investments
- Shareholders ratios

3.2. Liquidity ratios

Ratio	Rationale
Net working capital: Gross Current assets less Current liabilities	It measures the liquidity of an enterprise
Current ratio: $= \dfrac{\text{Current assets}}{\text{Current liabilities}}$	It reflects the short term liquidity position of the enterprise. In general ratio of 2:1 is considered adequate. If it is lower, then it depicts tightness in liquidity. If it is higher, then there is adequate liquidity, but it may also be possible that funds are tied up in obsolete / slow moving inventories and overdue debts
Liquid ratio / Acid test ratio: $= \dfrac{\text{Quick assets}}{\text{Current liabilities}}$	Quick assets are current assets less inventories, and this ratio is a measure of the liquidity position of the enterprise. In general a ratio of 1: 1 would be considered adequate, as it would signify that the enterprise has enough cash to pay off all its current liabilities

3.3. Capital structure ratios

Ratio	Rationale
Debt equity ratio $= \dfrac{\text{Long term debt}}{\text{Shareholders' equity}}$	This is a very important ratio which depicts the relative proportion of debt and equity in financing the assets of an enterprise. A ratio of 1:1 is considered adequate. If the debt content is higher the enterprise is considered highly geared and if the equity content is higher, then the enterprise is considered low geared. This ratio is also a determinant based on which weighted average cost of capital is calculated. (WACC)

Debt to total capital ratio $=$ $\dfrac{\text{Long term debt}}{\text{Permanent capital}}$ Or	This ratio indicates what proportion of the permanent capital of the enterprise is funded out of long term debt. A ratio of 1:2 is considered adequate
$=$ $\dfrac{\text{Total debt}}{\text{Permanent capital} +}$ Current liabilities Or	It measures the proportion of total assets financed by outside funds. A low ratio is low risk specially for outsiders like creditors
$=$ $\dfrac{\text{Total Shareholders'}}{\text{Total assets}}$ equity	It depicts the proportion of total assets funded by owners' equity.

3.4. Coverage ratios

Ratio	Rationale
Interest coverage $=$ $\dfrac{\text{Earnings before interest and tax}}{\text{Interest}}$	This is a ratio used to ascertain how easily an enterprise can pay its outstanding dues. A ratio of 1:5 is considered satisfactory.
Dividend coverage $=$ $\dfrac{\text{Earnings after tax}}{\text{Preference dividend}}$	This ratio measures the ability of the enterprise to pay dividend on preference shares. A high ratio indicates better ability.
Total coverage $=$ $\dfrac{\text{Earnings before interest and tax}}{\text{Total fixed charges}}$	It shows the overall ability of the enterprise to fulfil the liabilities. A high ratio is better for creditors.

3.5. Profitability ratios

Ratio	Rationale
Gross profit margin $= \dfrac{\text{Gross Profit x 100}}{\text{Sales}}$	This ratio measures the profit in relation to sales. This ratio is measured with the benchmark ratio prevalent in the industry for inter-firm comparison purposes
EBITDA margin Earnings before Interest depreciation, amortisation and $= \dfrac{\text{tax x 100}}{\text{Sales}}$	This is a very critical ratio which is looked at by the outside world including bankers to measure the profitability of the enterprise in the short term and also used as a benchmark for valuation for the medium to long term. This ratio measures the net profit of the enterprise with respect to sale.
Net Profit margin $= \dfrac{\text{Net Profit after interest and tax x 100}}{\text{Sales}}$ Or, $= \dfrac{\text{Net Profit after tax before interest x 100}}{\text{Sales}}$	This ratio measures the net profit of the enterprise with respect to sale. Both these ratios are used to compare with benchmark industry average to evaluate the profitability of the enterprise.

3.6. Expense ratios

Ratio	Rationale
Operating ratio $= \dfrac{\text{Cost of goods sold + other expenses}}{\text{Sales}}$	This ratio is an effective measure to depict the operational efficiency of the business. Lower operating ratio would depict higher profitability and higher operating ratio would signify lower profitability.
Cost of goods sold ratio $= \dfrac{\text{Cost of goods sold}}{\text{Sales}}$	It measures the cost of goods sold per sale.

Specific expenses ratio = $\dfrac{\text{Specific expenses}}{\text{Sales}}$	It measures specific expenses per sale.

3.7. Activity ratios

Ratio	Rationale
Debtors turnover ratio = $\dfrac{\text{Net credit Sales}}{\text{Average net debtors}}$	This reflects how quickly receivables are converted into cash.
Inventory turnover ratio = $\dfrac{\text{Cost of goods sold}}{\text{Average inventories}}$	This reflects how quickly inventories s are sold an converted into cash. This would depend on the nature of industry and can be benchmarked accordingly
Raw material turnover ratio = $\dfrac{\text{Cost of raw material used}}{\text{Average raw material inventory}}$	This reflects how quickly raw material inventories are converted into finished goods. If the ratio is high it would be mean that the enterprise is converting raw material into finished goods very efficiently. If it is other way round, it would mean there are inefficiencies in the production process which needs to be weeded out. The yard stick is the benchmark ratio of the industry in which the enterprise belongs. Same as above
Work in progress turnover ratio = $\dfrac{\text{Cost of goods manufactured}}{\text{Average work in progress inventory}}$	
Creditors turnover ratio = $\dfrac{\text{Net credit purchase}}{\text{Average creditors}}$	This reflects how quickly the enterprise settles its trade payables. Higher the ratio, it would be indication that the enterprise has enough liquidity to pay off its trade payables.

3.8. Asset turnover ratios

Ratio	Rationale
Total Assets turnover ratio $= \dfrac{\text{Net Sales}}{\text{Total assets}}$	It measures the degree of efficiency of an enterprise in utilising its assets during the operations of the enterprise. The higher the ratio, better is the efficiency and effectiveness of the enterprise in managing its assets.
Capital turnover ratio $= \dfrac{\text{Net Sales}}{\text{Capital employed}}$	
Fixed Assets turnover ratio $= \dfrac{\text{Net Sales}}{\text{Fixed assets}}$	
Current Assets turnover ratio $= \dfrac{\text{Net Sales}}{\text{current assets}}$	
Working capital turnover ratio $= \dfrac{\text{Net Sales}}{\text{Net current assets}}$	

3.9. Return on investment ratios

Ratio	Rationale
Return on Assets (ROA) $= \dfrac{(\text{Net Profit after tax}) \times 100}{\text{Total assets}}$ Or, $= \dfrac{(\text{Net Profit after tax} + \text{Interest}) \times 100}{\text{Tangible assets}}$ Or, (Net Profit after tax +	This ratio is a measure of return on the funds invested in the total assets of the enterprise. The higher the ratio, it signifies more efficient use of the total assets.

Interest) x 100 = ------------------------------ Fixed assets **Return on capital employed (ROCE)** (Net Profit after tax) x 100 = ------------------------------ Total capital employed Or, (Net Profit after tax + Interest) x 100 = ------------------------------ Total capital employed Or, (Net Profit after tax + Interest)x 100 = ------------------------------ Total capital employed – intangible assets	This ratio is a measure of return on the funds invested in the capital employed of the enterprise. The higher the ratio, it signifies more efficient use of the total capital employed.
Return on total shareholders' Equity (Net Profit after tax) x 100 = ------------------------------ Total shareholders' equity	This ratio depicts the return on total shareholders' fund deployed in the enterprise. Higher the return, it would signify better return on total shareholders' fund.
Return on total ordinary shareholders' Equity (Net Profit after tax and preference dividend) x 100 = ------------------------------ Ordinary shareholders' equity	This ratio depicts the return on ordinary shareholders' fund deployed in the enterprise. Higher the return, it would signify better return on equity from ordinary shareholders.

3.10. Shareholders' ratios

Ratio	Rationale
Earnings per share (EPS) $= \dfrac{\text{Net Profit of equity holders}}{\text{Number of Ordinary shares}}$	The ratio measures the profit available to the equity holders on a per share basis
Dividend per share (DPS) $= \dfrac{\text{Net Profit after interest and preference dividend paid to ordinary shareholders}}{\text{Number of Ordinary shares outstanding}}$	The ratio measures the profit distributed as dividend to the equity holders on a per share basis
Dividend pay-out ratio (D/P) $= \dfrac{\text{Total dividend to equity holders}}{\text{Total net profit of equity Holders}}$ Or, $= \dfrac{\text{Dividend per ordinary share}}{\text{Earnings per share}}$	This ratio is a measure of percentage share of net profit paid out as dividend to equity shareholders The higher the D/P ratio, more attractive it is for the investor
Earnings yield $= \dfrac{\text{Earnings per share}}{\text{Market value per share}}$	This ratio is a measure of percentage of each rupee invested in the stock that has been earned by the enterprise
Dividend yield $= \dfrac{\text{Dividend per share}}{\text{Market value per share}}$	This ratio is a measure of percentage dividend paid out by the enterprise each year in relation to its share price
Price earnings ratio (P/E) $= \dfrac{\text{Market value per share}}{\text{Earnings per share}}$	This ratio is a measure which signifies the price currently paid by the investor for each rupee of EPS

Earning power	Higher the ratio more expensive is the stock price and more market capitalisation for the owners
= Net profit after tax / Total assets	The ratio is a measure of the earning power of the enterprise as it depicts overall profitability and operational efficiency of an enterprise.

To work out the above ratios, basic numbers are picked up from the financial statements. A specimen format of the financial statements is enumerated below.

Illustration.3.1. Specimen format for computation of financial ratios

	Balance Sheet (specimen format)				Rs Million
Sl no.	Particulars	Note. No.	As at 31.03.16	As at 31.03.15	As at 31.03.14
	EQUITY & LIABILITIES				
1	**Shareholders' funds**				
	(a)Share capital				
	(b)Reserves and surplus				
	(c)Money received against share warrants				
2	**Share application money pending allotment**				
3	**Non-current liabilities**				
	(a) Long term borrowings				
	(b) Deferred tax liabilities (net)				
	(c) Other long term liabilities				
	(d) Long-term provisions				
4	**Current liabilities**				
	(a)Short term borrowings				
	(b) Trade payables				
	(c)Other current liabilities				
	(d) Short term provisions				
	TOTAL				
	ASSETS				
1	**Non-current Assets**				
	(a) Fixed Assets				
	(i) Tangible assets				
	(ii)Intangible assets				
	(iii) Capital work-in-progress				
	(iv) Intangible assets under development				

	(b) Non-current investments				
	(c) Deferred tax assets (net)				
	(d) Long term loans & advances				
	(e) Other non-current assets				
2	Current Assets				
	(a) Current investments				
	(b) Inventories				
	(c)Trade receivables				
	(d) Cash & cash equivalents				
	(e) Short-term loan and advances				
	(f) Other current assets				
	TOTAL				

	Statement of Profit & Loss (specimen format)				**Rs Million**
Sl no.	Particulars	Note no.	As at 31.03.16	As at 31.03.15	As at 31.03.14
I	REVENUE FROM OPERATION				
II	OTHER INCOME				
III	**(TOTAL REVENUE (I + II)**				
IV	EXPENSES:				
	(a) Cost of material consumed				
	(b) Purchase of products for sale				
	(c) Changes in inventories of finished goods, work-in-progress and products for sale				
	(d) Employees cost benefit expenses				
	(e) Finance cost				
	(f) Depreciation and amortisation expenses				
	(g) Product development expenses				
	(h) Other expenses				
	(i) Expenditure transfer to capital and other Account				
	TOTAL EXPENSES				
V	PROFIT BEFORE EXCEPTIONAL AND EXTRA-ORDINARY ITEMS AND TAX (III - IV)				
VI	EXCEPTIONAL ITEMS				
VII	PROFIT BEFORE EXTRAORDINARY ITEMS AND				

	TAX (V-VI)			
VIII	EXTRAORDINARY ITEMS			
IX	PROFIT BEFORE TAX AND CONTINUING			
	OPERATIONS (VII - VIII)			
X	TAX EXPENSES:			
	(a) Current tax			
	(b) Deferred tax			
XI	PROFIT AFTER TAX FOR THE YEAR FROM			
	CONTINUING OPERATION (IX - X)			
XII	Profit / (loss) from discontinuing operations			
XIII	Tax expenses from discontinuing operations			
XIV	Profit / (loss) from discontinuing operations			
	(after tax) (XII-XIII)			
XV	PROFIT/(LOSS) FOR THE PERIOD (XI + XIV)			
	Balance brought forward from previous year			
	Profit available for appropriation:			
	Proposed dividend			
	Transfer to General Reserve			
	Distribution tax			
	Total			
	Balance carried forward			
XVI	Earning per equity share:			
	(1) Basic			
	(2) Diluted			

Notes to Balance Sheet:				Rs Million
Sl no.	Particulars	As at 31.03.16	As at 31.03.15	As at 31.03.14
1	Long term borrowings			
	Secured loans			
	Unsecured loans			
	Total			
2	Tangible assets			
	Gross block			
	Less: Accumulated depreciation			
	Total			

Notes to Statement of Profit & loss				Rs Million
Sl no.	Particulars	As at 31.03.16	As at 31.03.15	As at 31.03.14
1	**Cost of material consumed**			
	Raw material cost			
	Excise			
	Total			
2	**Finance cost**			
	Interest expenses			
	Total			
3	**Depreciation and amortisation expenses**			
	Depreciation			
	Total			

Sl no.	Particulars		As at 31.03.16	As at 31.03.15	As at 31.03.14
	Illustration 3.2: Definitions (Specimen format)				**Rs Million**
1	**Operating Profit**				
	Revenue				
	Less: Raw material cost				
	Excise				
	Other expenses				
	Total				
2	**Gross Profit**				
	Operating profit				
	Less: Interest expenses				
	Total				
3	**Net Profit (Profit After Tax : PAT)**				
	Gross Profit				
	Add: Other income				
	Other non-recurring income				
	Less Depreciation				
	Tax expenses				
	Total				
4	**Profit before tax (PBT)**				
	Net Profit				
	Less: Non-recurring income				
	Add: Tax expenses				
	Total				
5	**Fixed Assets**				
	Net tangible assets				
	Add: Capital work-in-progress				
	Investments				
	Total				
6	**Net Worth**				
	Share capital				
	Reserves & surplus				
	Total				
7	**Capital employed**				
	Total assets				
	Less: Current liabilities				
	Capital employed				

Illustration 3.3: Trend Analysis

Trend Analysis : Balance Sheet (specimen format)					Rs Million
Sl no.	Particulars	As at 31.03.16	As at 31.03.15	As at 31.03.14	Remarks
1	Current Assets				
2	Fixed Assets				
3	Current liabilities				
4	Long term liabilities				

Trend Analysis : Statement of Profit & Loss (specimen format)\					Rs Million
Sl no.	Particulars	As at 31.03.16	As at 31.03.15	As at 31.03.14	Remarks
1	Sales				
2	Raw material cost				
3	Operating profit				
4	Profit before tax (PBT)				
5	Net profit				

Illustration 3.4: Ratio Analysis

Sl no.	Particulars		As at 31.03.16	As at 31.03.15	As at 31.03.14	Rs Million Remarks
Ratio Analysis : (Specimen format)						
1	**Net working capital**					
	(Current Asset - Current liabilities)					
2	**Current ratio**					
	(Current Asset / Current liabilities)					
3	**Quick ratio / Acid test ratio**					
	(Quick Asset / Current liabilities)					
4	**Debt - Equity ratio**					
	(Long term debt / Shareholders' equity)					
5	**Interest coverage ratio**					
	(Operating profit / Interest)					
6	**Operating Profit margin**					
	(Operating profit x 100)/Sales					
7	**Gross Profit margin**					
	(Gross profit x 100)/Sales					
8	**Net Profit margin**					
	(Net profit x 100)/Sales					
9	**Return on Assets**					
	(Operating profit / Average assets)					
10	**Return on investments**					
	(Net profit before tax x 100)/Net worth					
11	**Return on net worth**					
	(Net profit x 100)/Average Net worth					

12	**Return on capital employed**					
	(Net profit after tax x 100)/Total capital employed)					
13	**Cost of goods sold ratio**					
	(Cost of goods sold/Sales)					
14	**Operating ratio**					
	(Cost of goods sold + other expenses /Sales)					
15	**Fixed Assets turnover**					
	(Sales / Fixed assets)					

Case study 3.1. Calculation of major financial ratios and trend analysis

Last three years financial statements of ABC Ltd have been appended herewith.

Balance Sheet of ABC Ltd as at 31.3. 2013   **Rs Million**

Sl no.	Particulars	Note no.	As at 31.03.13	As at 31.03.12	As at 31.03.11
	EQUITY & LIABILITIES				
1	**Shareholders' funds**				
	(a)Share capital		1880.2	1878.8	1879.3
	(b)Reserves and surplus		58282.0	47398.5	39647.8
	(c)Money received against share warrants				
2	**Share application money pending allotment**				
3	**Non-current liabilities**				
	(a) Long term borrowings	1	5669.2	4820.3	3064.1
	(b) Deferred tax liabilities (net)				
	(c) Other long term liabilities				
	(d) Long-term provisions				
4	**Current liabilities**				
	(a)Short term borrowings				
	(b) Trade payables				
	(c)Other current liabilities		25587.3	22453.9	19912.7
	(d) Short term provisions		10918.8	9639.3	6662.7
	TOTAL		102337.5	86190.8	71166.6
	ASSETS				
1	**Non-current Assets**				
	(a) Fixed Assets				
	(i) Tangible assets	2	41582.9	34697.0	33147.2
	(ii)Intangible assets				
	(iii) Capital work-in-progress		21562.1	16028.6	6491.9
	(iv) Intangible assets under development				
	(b) Non-current investments				
	(c) Deferred tax assets (net)				
	(d) Long term loans & advances				
	(e) Other non-current assets				
2	Current Assets				
	(a) Current investments		14756.4	6790.8	8448.1
	(b) Inventories		7789.8	7932.7	7308.6
	(c)Trade receivables		2037.0	3101.7	2892.9
	(d) Cash & cash equivalents		7463.8	9842.4	7434.8
	(e) Short-term loan and advances		7145.5	7797.6	5443.1
	(f) Other current assets				
	TOTAL		102337.5	86190.8	71166.6

Financial Analysis for effective Management Decisions

SI no.	Particulars	Note no.	As at 31.03.13	As at 31.03.12	As at 31.03.11
	Statement of Profit & Loss of ABC Ltd as at 31.3. 2013				**Rs Million**
I	REVENUE FROM OPERATION		80215.9	72299.7	68747.9
II	OTHER INCOME		1361.7	2115.9	1422.4
III	**(TOTAL REVENUE (I + II)**		**81577.6**	**74415.6**	**70170.3**
IV	EXPENSES:				
	(a) Cost of material consumed	1	19862.6	22503.6	28070.4
	(b) Purchase of products for sale				
	(c) Changes in inventories of finished goods, work-in-progress and products for sale				
	(d) Employees cost benefit expenses				
	(e) Finance cost	2	843.0	399.6	738.7
	(f) Depreciation and amortisation expenses	3	3420.9	2941.8	3054.3
	(g) Product development expenses				
	(h) Other expenses		34722.2	31963.3	21463.2
	(i) Expenditure transfer to capital and other account				
	TOTAL EXPENSES		**58848.7**	**57808.3**	**53326.6**
V	PROFIT BEFORE EXCEPTIONAL AND EXTRA-ORDINARY ITEMS AND TAX (III - IV)		22728.9	16607.3	16843.7
VI	EXCEPTIONAL ITEMS		-227.7	-766.4	-2269.5
VII	PROFIT BEFORE EXTRAORDINARY ITEMS AND TAX (V-VI)		22956.6	17373.7	19113.2
VIII	EXTRAORDINARY ITEMS		0	0	0
IX	PROFIT BEFORE TAX AND CONTINUING OPERATIONS (VII - VIII)		22956.6	17373.7	19113.2
X	TAX EXPENSES:				
	(a) Current tax		6889.3	5246.0	4917.0
	(b) Deferred tax				
XI	PROFIT AFTER TAX FOR THE YEAR FROM CONTINUING OPERATION (IX - X)		16067.3	12127.7	14196.2
XII	Profit / (loss) from discontinuing operations				
XIII	Tax expenses from discontinuing operations				
XIV	Profit / (loss) from discontinuing operations (after tax) (XII-XIII)				
XV	PROFIT/(LOSS) FOR THE PERIOD (XI + XIV)				
	Balance brought forward from previous year				
	Profit available for appropriation:		16067.3	12127.7	14196.2
	Proposed dividend		4317.6	3753.3	3750.2
	Transfer to General Reserve				
	Distribution tax				
	Total				
	Balance carried forward		11749.7	8374.4	10446
XVI	Earning per equity share:				
	(1) Basic				
	(2) Diluted				

35

Financial Analysis for effective Management Decisions

Notes to Balance Sheet:

Sl no.	Particulars		As at 31.03.13	As at 31.03.12	As at 31.03.11
1	Long term borrowings				
	Secured loans		5500.0	4500.0	2660.3
	Unsecured loans		169.2	320.3	403.8
	Total		5669.2	4820.3	3064.1
2	Tangible assets				
	Gross block		68262.7	58356.7	54640.7
	Less: Accumulated depreciation		26679.8	23659.7	2493.5
	Total		41582.9	34697	52147.2

Notes to Statement of Profit & loss   **Rs Million**

Sl no.	Particulars		As at 31.03.13	As at 31.03.12	As at 31.03.11
1	**Cost of material consumed**				
	Raw material cost		12046.8	11801.5	18367.2
	Excise		7815.8	10702.1	9703.2
	Total		19862.6	22503.6	28070.4
2	**Finance cost**				
	Interest expenses		843.0	399.6	738.7
	Total		843.0	399.6	738.7
3	**Depreciation and amortisation expenses**				
	Depreciation		3420.9	2941.8	3054.3
	Total		3420.9	2941.8	3054.3

Provide trend analysis and financial ratios based on above information for the last three years.

Financial Analysis for effective Management Decisions

Solution

Working Notes Rs Million

SI no.	Particulars		As at 31.03.13	As at 31.03.12	As at 31.03.11
1	**Operating Profit**				
	Revenue		80215.9	72299.7	68747.9
	Less: Raw material cost		12046.8	11801.5	18367.2
	Excise		7815.8	10702.1	9703.2
	Other expenses		34722.2	31963.3	21463.2
	Total		**25631.1**	**17832.8**	**19214.3**
2	**Gross Profit**				
	Operating profit		25631.1	17832.8	19214.3
	Less: Interest expenses		843.0	399.6	738.7
	Total		24788.1	17433.2	18475.6
3	**Net Profit**				
	Gross Profit		24788.1	17433.2	18475.6
	Add: Other income		1361.7	2115.9	1422.4
	Other non-recurring income		227.7	766.4	2269.5
	Less Deprciation		3420.9	2941.8	3054.3
	Tax expenses		6889.3	5246	4917
	Total		16067.3	12127.7	14196.2
4	**Profit before tax**				
	Net Profit		16067.3	12127.7	14196.2
	Less: Non-recurring income		227.7	766.4	2269.5
	Add: Tax expenses		6889.3	5246	4917
	Total		22728.9	16607.3	16843.7
5	**Fixed Assets**				
	Net tangible assets		41582.9	34697	33147.2
	Add: Capital work-in-progress		21562.1	16028.6	6491.9
	Investments		14756.4	6790.8	8448.1
	Total		77901.4	57516.4	48087.2
6	**Net Worth**				
	Share capital		1880.2	1878.8	1879.3
	Reserves & surplus		58282.0	47398.5	39647.8
	Total		60162.2	49277.3	41527.1
7	**Capital employed**				
	Total assets		102337.5	86190.8	71166.6
	Less: Current liabilities		36506.1	32093.2	26575.4
	Capital employed		65831.4	54097.6	44591.2

Financial Analysis for effective Management Decisions

Trend Analysis : Balance Sheet **Rs Million**

Sl no.	Particulars		As at 31.03.13	As at 31.03.12	As at 31.03.11	Remarks
1	Current Assets		24436.1	28674.4	23079.4	Short term liquidity has improved marginally
2	Fixed Assets		77901.4	57516.4	48087.2	Significant increase in fixed assets, may lead to future profit
3	Current liabilities		36506.1	32093.2	26575.4	Current liabilities going up hence will impact net working capital
4	Long term liabilities		5669.2	4820.3	3064.1	Long term debts have increased significantly

Trend Analysis : Statement of Profit & Loss **Rs Million**

Sl no.	Particulars		As at 31.03.13	As at 31.03.12	As at 31.03.11	Remarks
1	Sales		80215.9	72299.7	68747.9	Sales position has improved
2	Raw material cost		12046.8	11801.5	18367.2	Raw material costs have reduced significantly
3	Operating profit		25631.1	17832.8	19214.3	Operating profit has dipped in 2011-12 but picked up in 2012-13
4	Profit before tax (PBT)		22728.9	16607.3	16843.7	Dipped in 2011-12 but but increased in 2012-13
5	Net profit		16067.3	12127.7	14196.2	Dipped in 2011-12 but but increased in 2012-13

Financial Analysis for effective Management Decisions

Ratio Analysis :   **Rs Million**

Sl no.	Particulars		As at 31.03.13	As at 31.03.12	As at 31.03.11	Remarks
1	**Net working capital** (Current Asset - Current liabilities)		-12070.0	-3418.8	-3496.0	Liquidity position is going from bad to worse
2	**Current ratio** (Current Asset / Current liabilities)		0.67	0.89	0.87	The company does not have enough working capital to pay current debt
3	**Quick ratio / Acid test ratio** (Quick Asset / Current liabilities)		0.46	0.65	0.59	The company does not have enough working capital to pay current debt
4	**Debt - Equity ratio** (Long term debt / Shareholders' equity)		0.094	0.098	0.074	The company has low geared and has potential to borrow more
5	**Interest coverage ratio** (Operating profit / Interest)		30.40	44.63	26.01	This is quite sound, though it has dropped in 2012-13 over 2011-12
6	**Operating Profit margin** (Operating profit x 100)/Sales		31.95%	24.67%	27.95%	It has improved in 2012-13 compared to 2011-12
7	**Gross Profit margin** (Gross profit x 100)/Sales		30.90%	24.11%	26.87%	It has improved in 2012-13 compared to 2011-12
8	**Net Profit margin** (Net profit x 100)/Sales		20.03%	16.77%	20.65%	It has improved in 2012-13 compared to 2011-12
9	**Return on Assets** (Operating profit / Average assets)		27.19%	22.67%	29.18%	It has dropped from 2010-11 but partly gained in 2011-12 but still not satisfactory
10	**Return on investments** (Net profit before tax x 100)/Net worth		37.8%	33.7%	40.6%	It has dropped from 2010-11 but partly gained in 2011-12
11	**Return on net worth** (Net profit x 100)/Average Net worth		29.4%	26.7%	38.9%	Trend not satisfactory
12	**Return on capital employed** (Net profit after tax x 100)/Total capital employed)		24.4%	22.4%	31.8%	Trend not satisfactory
13	**Cost of goods sold ratio** (Cost of goods sold/Sales)		15.0%	16.3%	26.7%	Deteriorating trend is not satisfactory
14	**Operating ratio** (Cost of goods sold + other expenses /Sales)		58.3%	60.5%	57.9%	Trend not satisfactory
15	**Fixed Assets turnover** (Sales / Fixed assets)		1.030	1.257	1.430	Deteriorating trend is not satisfactory

Case study 3.2. Computation of major financial ratios and analysis of trend

Last three years financial statements of XYZ Ltd have been appended herewith.

	Balance Sheet of XYZ Ltd as at 31.3. 2013				Rs Million
Sl no.	Particulars	Note no.	As at 31.03.13	As at 31.03.12	As at 31.03.11
	EQUITY & LIABILITIES				
1	**Shareholders' funds**				
	(a)Share capital		154.7	154.0	154.0
	(b)Reserves and surplus		53998.5	37409.8	24813.3
	(c)Money received against share warrants				
2	**Share application money pending allotment**				
3	**Non-current liabilities**				
	(a) Long term borrowings	1	49626.5	38633.5	35077.2
	(b) Deferred tax liabilities (net)				
	(c) Other long term liabilities				
	(d) Long-term provisions				
4	**Current liabilities**				
	(a)Short term borrowings				
	(b) Trade payables				
	(c)Other current liabilities		31258.3	15335.4	12099.1
	(d) Short term provisions		9858.1	5819.4	3854.8
	TOTAL		144896.1	97352.1	75998.4
	ASSETS				
1	**Non-current Assets**				
	(a) Fixed Assets				
	(i) Tangible assets	2	57459.0	47358.3	41472.8
	(ii)Intangible assets				
	(iii) Capital work-in-progress		23180.1	6604.8	9378.4
	(iv) Intangible assets under development				
	(b) Non-current investments				
	(c) Deferred tax assets (net)				
	(d) Long term loans & advances				
	(e) Other non-current assets				
2	**Current Assets**				
	(a) Current investments		12334.0	10361.9	7098.2
	(b) Inventories		12099.6	9805.6	6424.4
	(c)Trade receivables		3914.6	2873.8	3203.1
	(d) Cash & cash equivalents		3089.6	5779.1	529.7
	(e) Short-term loan and advances		32789.0	14537.2	7859.4
	(f) Other current assets		30.2	31.4	32.4
	TOTAL		144896.1	97352.1	75998.4

* Total assets for 31.3.2010 : Rs.Mil : 57645.5, net worth for 31.3.2010 : Rs. Mil : 18601.1

Financial Analysis for effective Management Decisions

Statement of Profit & Loss of XYZ Ltd as at 31.3. 2013					Rs Million
SI no.	Particulars	Note no.	As at 31.03.13	As at 31.03.12	As at 31.03.11
I	REVENUE FROM OPERATION		76778.3	53681.4	35230.8
II	OTHER INCOME		1994.6	573.1	360.8
III	(TOTAL REVENUE (I + II)		78772.9	54254.5	35591.6
IV	EXPENSES:				
	(a) Cost of material consumed	1	41754.0	24908.9	14652.1
	(b) Purchase of products for sale				
	(c) Changes in inventories of finished goods, work-in-progress and products for sale				
	(d) Employees cost benefit expenses				
	(e) Finance cost	2	2678.9	2430.2	1731.9
	(f) Depreciation and amortisation expenses	3	4330.3	4515.1	3364.7
	(g) Product development expenses				
	(h) Other expenses		8645.7	5813.4	6480.6
	(i) Expenditure transfer to capital and other account				
	TOTAL EXPENSES		57408.9	37667.6	26229.3
V	PROFIT BEFORE EXCEPTIONAL AND EXTRA-ORDINARY ITEMS AND TAX (III - IV)		21364.0	16586.9	9362.3
VI	EXCEPTIONAL ITEMS		1343.2	1559.1	-88.8
VII	PROFIT BEFORE EXTRAORDINARY ITEMS AND TAX (V-VI)		20020.8	15027.8	9451.1
VIII	EXTRAORDINARY ITEMS		0	0	0
IX	PROFIT BEFORE TAX AND CONTINUING OPERATIONS (VII - VIII)		20020.8	15027.8	9451.1
X	TAX EXPENSES:				
	(a) Current tax		4654.0	2655.5	2418.5
	(b) Deferred tax				
XI	PROFIT AFTER TAX FOR THE YEAR FROM CONTINUING OPERATION (IX - X)		15366.8	12372.3	7032.6
XII	Profit / (loss) from discontinuing operations				
XIII	Tax expenses from discontinuing operations				
XIV	Profit / (loss) from discontinuing operations (after tax) (XII-XIII)				
XV	PROFIT/(LOSS) FOR THE PERIOD (XI + XIV)				
	Balance brought forward from previous year				
	Profit available for appropriation:		15366.8	12372.3	7032.6
	Proposed dividend		853.3	620.2	554.3
	Transfer to General Reserve				
	Distribution tax				
	Total				
	Balance carried forward		14513.5	11752.1	6478.3
XVI	Earning per equity share:				
	(1) Basic				
	(2) Diluted				

Financial Analysis for effective Management Decisions

Notes to Balance Sheet:

Sl no.	Particulars		As at 31.03.13	As at 31.03.12	As at 31.03.11
1	Long term borrowings				
	Secured loans		21054.9	17833.9	21156.1
	Unsecured loans		28571.6	20799.6	13921.1
	Total		49626.5	38633.5	35077.2
2	Tangible assets				
	Gross block		73629.0	59189.4	49290.3
	Less: Accumulated depreciation		16170.0	11831.1	7817.5
	Total		57459.0	47358.3	41472.8

Notes to Statement of Profit & loss   **Rs Million**

Sl no.	Particulars		As at 31.03.13	As at 31.03.12	As at 31.03.11
1	**Cost of material consumed**				
	Raw material cost		34194.2	17274.0	10685.0
	Excise		7559.8	7634.9	3967.1
	Total		41754.0	24908.9	14652.1
2	**Finance cost**				
	Interest expenses		2678.9	2430.2	1731.9
	Total		2678.9	2430.2	1731.9
3	**Depreciation and amortisation expenses**				
	Depreciation		4330.3	4515.1	3364.7
	Total		4330.3	4515.1	3364.7

Provide trend analysis and major financial ratios for the last three years.

Solution

Working Notes				Rs Million
Sl no.	Particulars	As at 31.03.13	As at 31.03.12	As at 31.03.11
1	**Operating Profit**			
	Revenue	76778.3	53681.4	35230.8
	Less: Raw material cost	34194.2	17274	10685
	Excise	7559.8	7634.9	3967.1
	Other expenses	8645.7	5813.4	6480.6
	Total	**26378.6**	**22959.1**	**14098.1**
2	**Gross Profit**			
	Operating profit	26378.6	22959.1	14098.1
	Less: Interest expenses	2678.9	2430.2	1731.9
	Total	23699.7	20528.9	12366.2
3	**Net Profit**			
	Gross Profit	23699.7	20528.9	12366.2
	Add: Other income	1994.6	573.1	360.8
	Other non-recurring income	-1343.2	-1559.1	88.8
	Less Deprciation	4330.3	4515.1	3364.7
	Tax expenses	4654	2655.5	2418.5
	Total	15366.8	12372.3	7032.6
4	**Profit before tax**			
	Net Profit	15366.8	12372.3	7032.6
	Less: Non-recurring income	-1343.2	-1559.1	88.8
	Add: Tax expenses	4654	2655.5	2418.5
	Total	21364.0	16586.9	9362.3
5	**Fixed Assets**			
	Net tangible assets	57459	47358.3	41472.8
	Add: Capital work-in-progress	23180.1	6604.8	9378.4
	Investments	12334	10361.9	7098.2
	Total	92973.1	64325	57949.4
6	**Net Worth**			
	Share capital	154.7	154	154
	Reserves & surplus	53998.5	37409.8	24813.3
	Total	54153.2	37563.8	24967.3
7	**Capital employed**			
	Total assets	144896.1	97352.1	75998.4
	Less: Current liabilities	41116.4	21154.8	15953.9
	Capital employed	103779.7	76197.3	60044.5

Financial Analysis for effective Management Decisions

Trend Analysis : Balance Sheet   **Rs Million**

Sl no.	Particulars		As at 31.03.13	As at 31.03.12	As at 31.03.11	Remarks
1	Current Assets		51892.8	32995.7	18016.6	Short term liquidity has improved Significantly
2	Fixed Assets		92973.1	64325	57949.4	Significant increase in fixed assets, may lead to future profit
3	Current liabilities		41116.4	21154.8	15953.9	Current liabilities have increased significantly in line with current assets
4	Long term liabilities		49626.5	38633.5	35077.2	Long term debts have increased owing to more investment

Trend Analysis : Statement of Profit & Loss   **Rs Million**

Sl no.	Particulars		As at 31.03.13	As at 31.03.12	As at 31.03.11	Remarks
1	Sales		76778.3	53681.4	35230.8	Sales position has improved significantly
2	Raw material cost		34194.2	17274	10685	Raw material costs have increased three times
3	Operating profit		26378.6	22959.1	14098.1	Operating profit has significantly picked up in 2012-13
4	Profit before tax (PBT)		21364.0	16586.9	9362.3	PBT has increased significantly
5	Net profit		15366.8	12372.3	7032.6	Net profit has improved significantly and doubled in three years

Financial Analysis for effective Management Decisions

Ratio Analysis :   **Rs Million**

Sl no.	Particulars		As at 31.03.13	As at 31.03.12	As at 31.03.11	Remarks
1	Net working capital (Current Asset - Current liabilities)		10776.4	11840.9	2062.7	Liquidity position has improved significantly
2	Current ratio (Current Asset / Current liabilities)		1.26	1.56	1.13	The company has enough working capital to pay current debt
3	Quick ratio / Acid test ratio (Quick Asset / Current liabilities)		0.97	1.10	0.73	The company has enough working capital to pay current debt
4	Debt - Equity ratio (Long term debt / Shareholders' equity)		0.916	1.028	1.405	The company's gearing ratio has improved from high gearing to low gearing
5	Interest coverage ratio (Operating profit / Interest)		9.85	9.45	8.14	This is not quite sound and needs to improve
6	Operating Profit margin (Operating profit x 100)/Sales		34.36%	42.77%	40.02%	It has deteriorated in 2012-13 compared to 2011-12
7	Gross Profit margin (Gross profit x 100)/Sales		30.87%	38.24%	35.10%	It has deteriorated in 2012-13 compared to 2011-12
8	Net Profit margin (Net profit x 100)/Sales		20.01%	23.05%	19.96%	It has improved in 2012-13 compared to 2011-12
9	Return on Assets (Operating profit / Average assets)		21.78%	26.49%	21.10%	It has dropped from 2010-11 but partly gained in 2011-12 but still not satisfactory
10	Return on investments (Net profit before tax x 100)/Net worth		39.5%	44.2%	37.5%	ROI trend is on a upward trend and appears impressive
11	Return on net worth (Net profit x 100)/Average Net worth		33.5%	39.6%	32.4%	Trend significantly improved
12	Return on capital employed (Net profit after tax x 100)/Total capital employed)		14.8%	16.2%	11.7%	Trend not satisfactory and needs to improve
13	Cost of goods sold ratio (Cost of goods sold/Sales)		44.5%	32.2%	30.3%	Deteriorating trend is not satisfactory
14	Operating ratio (Cost of goods sold + other expenses /Sales)		55.8%	43.0%	48.7%	Trend not satisfactory
15	Fixed Assets turnover (Sales / Fixed assets)		0.826	0.835	0.608	Improving trend is satisfactory

Case study 3.3: Calculation of financial ratios

Financial performance summary of Company A is provided as under: (Rs lakhs)

SR.NO.	SUBJECT	2012-13	2011-12	2010-11	2009-10	2008-09
1	Share Capital	39.90	39.90	39.90	39.90	39.90
2	Reserves	317.98	306.91	296.31	291.72	258.09
3	Accumulated losses if any	-	-	-	-	-
4	Net Worth	357.88	346.81	336.21	331.62	297.99
5	Term Loans	240.15	12.19	26.87	44.24	34.36
6	Deferred Payment Liabilities	-	-	-	-	-
7	Working Capital Borrowings	-	-	-	-	6.08
8	Capital employed	598.03	359.00	363.08	375.86	338.43
9	Gross Block	179.26	193.68	121.49	76.89	72.01
10	Depreciation	15.96	27.42	27.50	13.63	15.36
11	Net Block	163.30	166.26	93.99	63.26	56.65
12	Investments	434.47	354.47	254.47	208.47	63.22
13	Other non-current assets	-	-	-	-	-
14	Current Assets	1,289.31	364.88	887.49	776.19	946.33
15	Current Liability (Inc W.C Loan)	1,289.05	526.61	872.86	672.06	727.77
16	Net working capital	0.26	-161.73	14.63	104.13	218.56
17	Capital employed	598.03	359.00	363.09	375.86	338.43
18	Income	1,447.44	1,430.89	1,327.38	1,396.46	1,208.75
19	Expenses	1,416.45	1,388.22	1,276.87	1,346.02	868.80
20	Operating Profit (EBIDTA)	30.99	42.67	50.51	50.44	339.95
21	Depreciation	15.96	27.42	27.51	13.63	15.35
22	EBIT	15.03	15.25	23.00	36.81	324.60
23	Tax	4.62	4.69	7.11	-	118.64
24	Net Profit (PAT)	10.41	10.56	15.89	36.81	205.96

Please calculate the following financial ratios and carry out an interpretation of the same:
a) Debt equity ratio
b) Current ratio
c) EBITDA as a % of sales
d) PAT as a % of sales
e) Capital turnover ratio
f) Return on capital employed
g) Return on Equity

Financial Analysis for effective Management Decisions

Solution

Based on the financial summary provided in the question the financial ratios have been worked out which is enumerated in the table as under:

Financial Performance Summary   Rs Lakhs

SR.NO.	SUBJECT	2012-13	2011-12	2010-11	2009-10	2008-09
1	Capital	39.90	39.90	39.90	39.90	39.90
2	Reserves	317.98	306.91	296.31	291.72	258.09
3	Accumulated losses if any	-	-	-	-	-
4	Net Worth	357.88	346.81	336.21	331.62	297.99
5	Term Loans	240.15	12.19	26.87	44.24	34.36
6	Deferred Payment Liabilities	-	-	-	-	-
7	Working Capital Borrowings	-	-	-	-	6.08
8	Capital employed	598.03	359.00	363.08	375.86	338.43
9	Gross Block	179.26	193.68	121.49	76.89	72.01
10	Depreciation	15.96	27.42	27.50	13.63	15.36
11	Net Block	163.30	166.26	93.99	63.26	56.65
12	Investments	434.47	354.47	254.47	208.47	63.22
13	Other non-current assets	-	-	-	-	-
14	Cutrrent Assets	1,289.31	364.88	887.49	776.19	946.33
15	Current Liability (Inc W.C Loan)	1,289.05	526.61	872.86	672.06	727.77
16	Net working capital	0.26	-161.73	14.63	104.13	218.56
17	Capital employed	598.03	359.00	363.09	375.86	338.43
18	Debt equity ratio	0.67	0.04	0.08	0.13	0.12
19	Current Ratio	1.00	0.69	1.02	1.15	1.30
20	Income	1,447.44	1,430.89	1,327.38	1,396.46	1,208.75
21	Expenses	1,416.45	1,388.22	1,276.87	1,346.02	868.80
22	Operating Profit (PBIDT)	30.99	42.67	50.51	50.44	339.95
23	EBITDA / Sales %	2.1%	3.0%	3.8%	3.6%	28.1%
24	Depreciation	15.96	27.42	27.51	13.63	15.35
25	EBIT	15.03	15.25	23.00	36.81	324.60
26	Tax	4.62	4.69	7.11	-	118.64
27	Net Profit (PAT)	10.41	10.56	15.89	36.81	205.96
28	Net Profit /Sales %	0.7%	0.7%	1.2%	2.6%	17.0%
29	Cash Accrual (NP+ DEP)	26.37	37.98	43.40	50.44	221.31
30	Capital turnover ratio	2.42	3.99	3.66	3.72	3.57
31	Return on capital employed %	2.5%	4.2%	6.3%	9.8%	95.9%
32	Return on net worth %	4.2%	4.4%	6.8%	11.1%	108.9%

The financial analysis of the above ratios is highlighted in the form of charts and interpretations have been provided below each of these charts in the form of a report.

Table 1: Sources of funds

Balance Sheet summary

SUBJECT	2012-13	2011-12	2010-11	2009-10	2008-09
Capital	39.90	39.90	39.90	39.90	39.90
Reserves	317.98	306.91	296.31	291.72	258.09
Accumulated losses if any	-	-	-	-	-
Net Worth	357.88	346.81	336.21	331.62	297.99
Term Loans	240.15	12.19	26.87	44.24	34.36
Deferred Payment Liabilities	-	-	-	-	-
Working Capital Borrowings	-	-	-	-	6.08
Capital employed	598.03	359.00	363.08	375.86	338.43
Debt equity ratio	0.67	0.04	0.08	0.13	0.12

The chart shows that company A had minimal debt till 2011-12. Thereafter in 2012-13 the term loan has gone up showing a skewed debt equity ratio (percentage of debt to equity). This indicates that the company is slowly going ahead and depending on debt. May be its internal cash generation is not as good as it was earlier.

The trend related to application of funds in table 2 will help understand the situation better.

Table 2: Application of funds

Balance Sheet summary

SUBJECT	2012-13	2011-12	2010-11	2009-10	2008-09
Net Block	163.30	166.26	93.99	63.26	56.65
Investments	434.47	354.47	254.47	208.47	63.22
Other non-current assets	-	-	-	-	-
Current Assets	1,289.31	364.88	887.49	776.19	946.33
Current Liability (Inc WC Loan)	1,289.05	526.61	872.85	672.06	727.77
Net working capital	0.26	-161.73	14.63	104.13	218.56
Capital employed	598.03	359.00	363.09	375.86	338.43

As expected the situation shows that net working capital has become negative in 2011-12, which shows that the company is going through acute shortage of working capital. Though the situation has slightly revived in 2012-13, still it is quite alarming that the company is running short of liquidity.

Table 3: Income trend

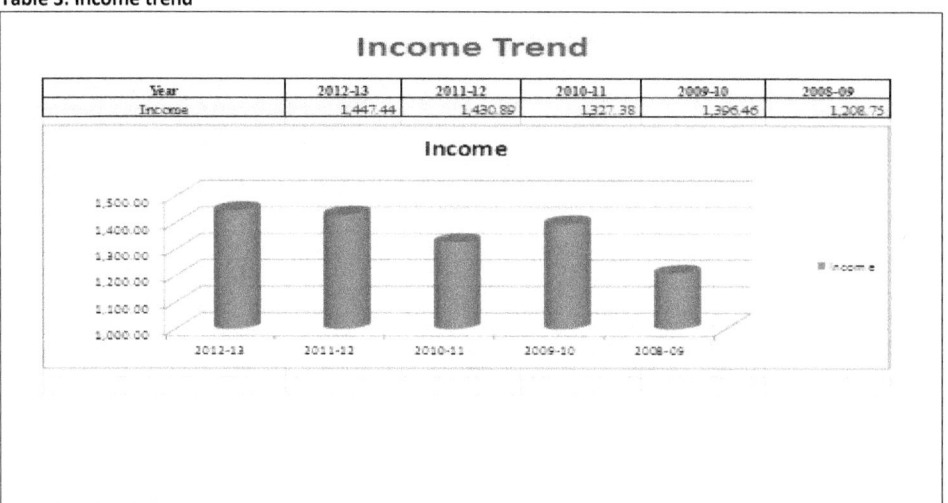

Income Trend

Year	2012-13	2011-12	2010-11	2009-10	2008-09
Income	1,447.44	1,430.89	1,327.38	1,396.46	1,208.75

The income trend according to table 3 shows an upward trend though there has been a dip in 2010-11

Table 4: EBITDA trend

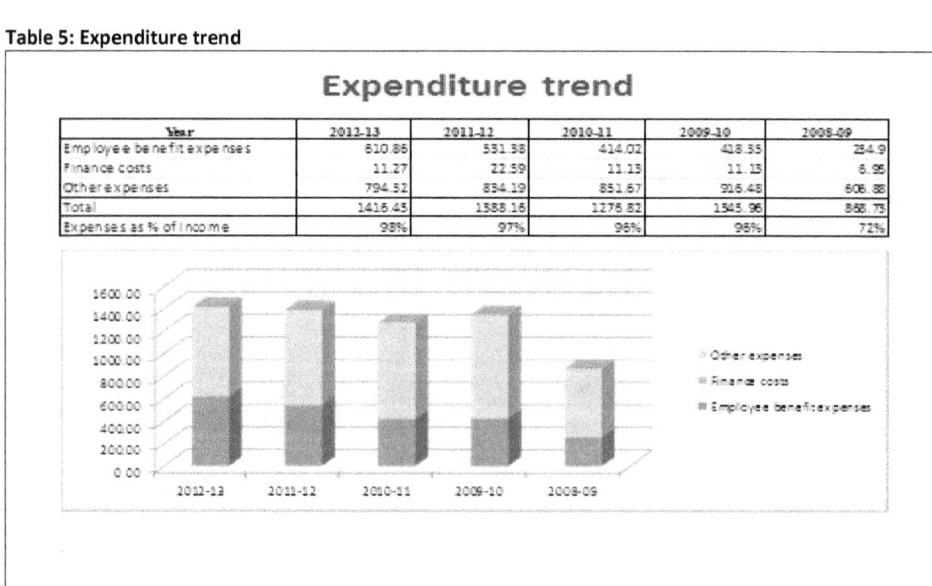

EBITDA Trend

Rs lakhs

Year	2012-13	2011-12	2010-11	2009-10	2008-09
Income	1,447.44	1,430.89	1,327.38	1,396.46	1,208.75
Expenses	1,416.45	1,388.22	1,276.87	1,346.02	868.80
Operating Profit (PBIDT)	30.99	42.67	50.51	50.44	339.95
EBITDA / Sales %	2.1%	3.0%	3.8%	3.6%	28.1%

Table 4 states that, owing to increase in expenditure trend more than revenue trend the EBITDA level has started to drop significantly reflecting eroding profitability.

Table 5: Expenditure trend

Expenditure trend

Year	2012-13	2011-12	2010-11	2009-10	2008-09
Employee benefit expenses	610.86	531.38	414.02	418.35	254.9
Finance costs	11.27	22.59	11.13	11.13	6.95
Other expenses	794.32	834.19	851.67	916.48	606.88
Total	1416.45	1388.16	1276.82	1345.96	868.73
Expenses as % of Income	98%	97%	96%	96%	72%

Table 5 corroborates the fact that expenditure specially other expenses and employee benefit expenses have significantly increased.

The above tables 3, 4 and 5 show that the profitability of Company A has reduced significantly leading to huge cash crunch.

Table 6: Net cash accrual

Year	2012-13	2011-12	2010-11	2009-10	2008-09
Cash Accrual (NP+DEP)	26.37	37.98	43.40	50.44	221.31

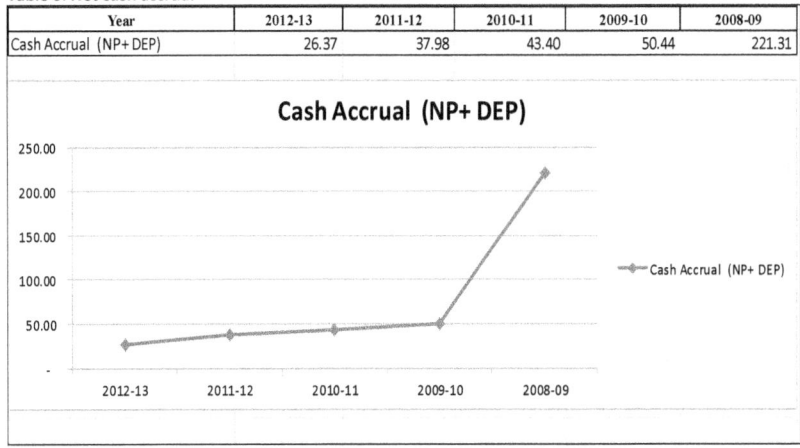

The table above shows net cash accrual, which is the sum of Profit after tax plus depreciation, going down regularly resulting in the cash crunch. The net cash accrual position confirms the cash crunch as depicted by declining working capital trend highlighted in table 2 above.

Table 7: Shareholders return

Year	2012-13	2011-12	2010-11	2009-10	2008-09
Return on capital employed %	2.5%	4.2%	6.3%	9.8%	95.9%
Return on net worth %	2.9%	3.0%	4.7%	11.1%	69.1%

At the same time Return on capital employed (EBIT / Capital Employed %) has been dropping from 2008-09 onwards till 2012-13, which reveals that along with liquidity crunch, profitability has also eroded over the years.

Financial Analysis for effective Management Decisions

Case study 3.4. Calculation of financial ratios
Comparative financial results of ABC Ltd are shown as under:

Comparative Balance Sheet　　　　　　　　　　　　　　　　　Rs lakhs

SR.NO.	Particulars	2012-13	2011-12	2010-11	2009-10	2008-09
1	Capital	539.90	539.90	539.90	539.90	539.90
2	Reserves	304.44	306.91	296.31	291.72	258.09
3	Accumulated losses if any	-	-	-	-	-
4	Net Worth	844.34	846.81	836.21	831.62	797.99
5	Term Loans	640.15	512.19	226.87	144.24	34.36
6	Deferred Payment Liabilities	-	-	-	-	-
7	Working Capital Borrowings	-	-	-	-	6.08
8	Capital employed	1,484.49	1,359.00	1,063.08	975.86	838.43
9	Gross Block	679.26	693.68	621.49	576.89	572.01
10	Depreciation	29.50	27.42	27.50	13.63	15.36
11	Net Block	649.76	666.26	593.99	563.26	556.65
12	Investments	434.47	354.47	254.47	208.47	63.22
13	Other non-current assets	-	-	-	-	-
14	Current Assets	1,689.31	864.88	887.49	876.19	946.33
15	Current Liability (Inc W.C Loan)	1,289.05	526.61	672.87	672.06	727.77
16	Net working capital	400.26	338.27	214.62	204.13	218.56
17	Capital employed	1,484.49	1,359.00	1,063.08	975.86	838.43

Comparative Statement of Profit & Loss　　　　　　　　　　　Rs lakhs

1	Income	6,447.44	4,830.89	4,327.38	3,396.46	2,408.75
2	Employee benefit expenses	2610.86	2531.38	2414.02	2418.35	1654.9
3	Finance costs	111.27	122.59	111.13	111.13	106.95
4	Other expenses	2994.32	1634.25	1351.72	516.54	401.90
5	Expenses					2,163.75

		5,716.45	4,288.22	3,876.87	3,046.02	
6	Operating Profit (EBIDTA)	730.99	542.67	450.51	350.44	245.00
7	Depreciation	15.96	27.42	27.51	13.63	15.35
8	EBIT	715.03	515.25	423.00	336.81	229.65
9	Tax	235.96	170.03	139.59	111.15	75.78
10	Net Profit (PAT)	479.07	345.22	283.41	225.66	153.87

Please calculate the following ratios and provide your analysis of the same:

a) Profitability ratios
b) Expense ratios
c) Liquidity ratios
d) Turnover ratios
e) Solvency ratios
f) Return on investment

Solution
   a) Profitability ratios

SR.NO.	Particulars	2012-13	2011-12	2010-11	2009-10	2008-09
1	EBITDA / Income %	11.3%	11.2%	10.4%	10.3%	10.2%
2	EBIT / Income %	11.1%	10.7%	9.8%	9.9%	9.5%
3	PAT / Income %	7.4%	7.1%	6.5%	6.6%	6.4%

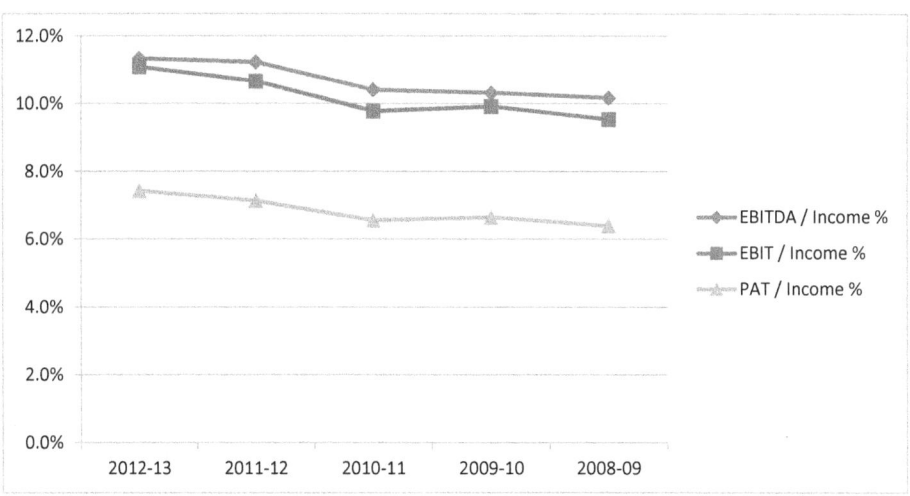

Profitability ratios as above show a clear trend of improvement showing that the profitability position of the company is quite healthy and look promising going forward.

b) Expense ratios

SR.NO.	Particulars	2012-13	2011-12	2010-11	2009-10	2008-09
1	Total expense / Income %	88.7%	88.8%	89.6%	89.7%	89.8%
2	Other expense / Income %	46.4%	33.8%	31.2%	15.2%	16.7%
3	Employee cost / Income %	40.5%	52.4%	55.8%	71.2%	68.7%

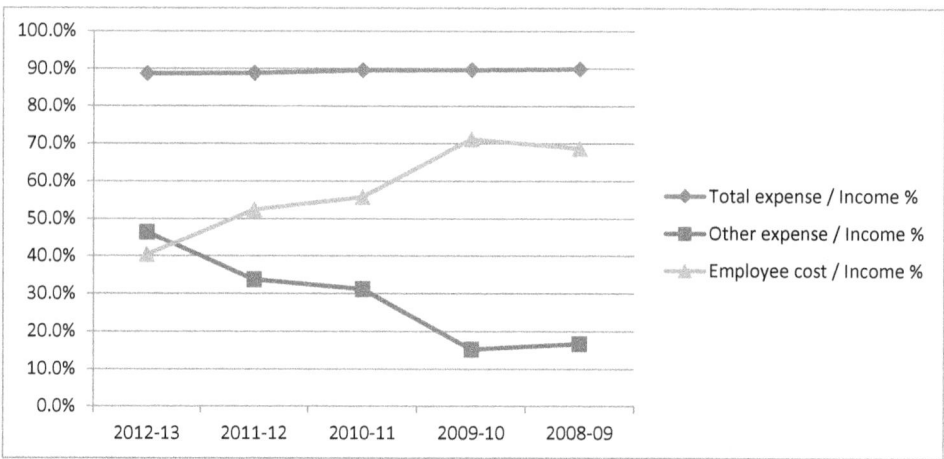

The above ratios show that there has been a reduction of employee cost to income ratio. However, other expenses to income trend shows a significant increase. However, overall expenses to income ratio remains in reigned in showing proper expenditure control.

c) Liquidity ratio

SR.NO.	Particulars	2012-13	2011-12	2010-11	2009-10	2008-09
1	Current ratio	1.31	1.64	1.32	1.30	1.30

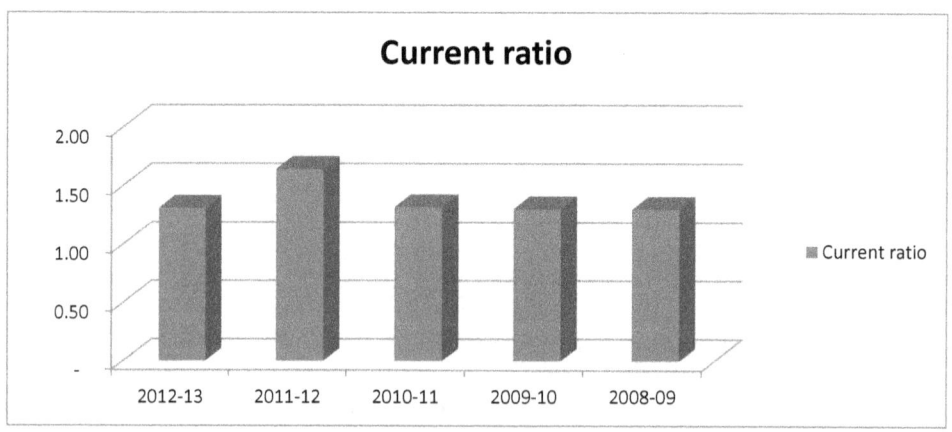

Current ratio has been dropping below zero, showing effective working capital management. However, there remains a risk of working capital tightness in the foreseeable if not managed properly.

d) Turnover ratios

SR.NO.	Particulars	2012-13	2011-12	2010-11	2009-10	2008-09
1	Total assets turnover ratio	2.32	2.56	2.49	2.06	1.54
2	Capital turnover ratio	4.34	3.55	4.07	3.48	2.87
3	Fixed Assets turnover ratio	9.92	7.25	7.29	6.03	4.33
4	Current Asset turnover ratio	3.82	5.59	4.88	3.88	2.55
5	Working capital turnover ratio	16.11	14.28	20.16	16.64	11.02

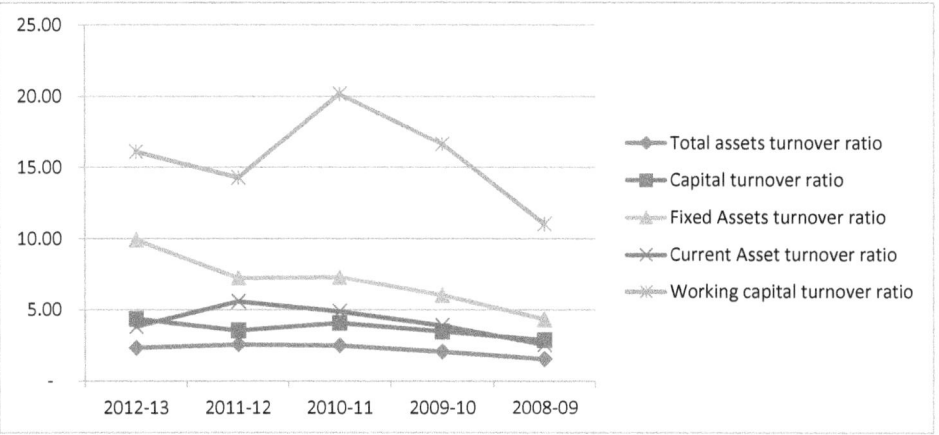

On an overall basis turnover ratios have shown an increasing trend, depicting effective utilisation of the assets of the enterprise.

e) Solvency ratios

SR.NO.	Particulars	2012-13	2011-12	2010-11	2009-10	2008-09
1	Debt equity ratio	0.76	0.60	0.27	0.17	0.04
2	Total debt to total assets	0.34	0.30	0.18	0.12	0.03
3	Shareholders' funds / total assets	0.45	0.50	0.65	0.70	0.75

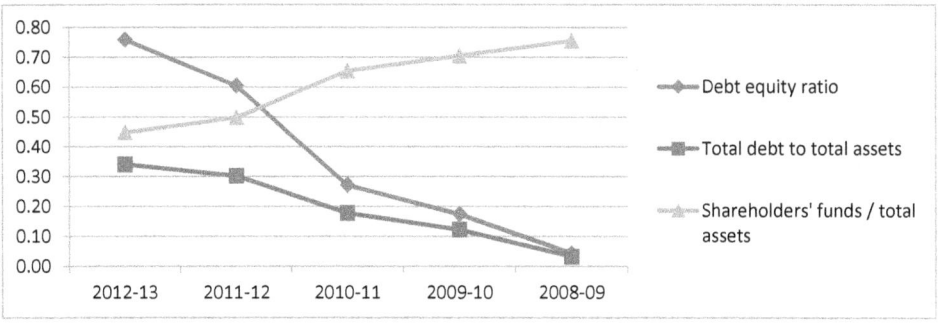

The various trends shown in the above ratios depict that debt to equity ratio have been increasing, which signify that the enterprise has started going for increasing debt vis-à-vis equity.

f) Return on investment

SR.NO.	Particulars	2012-13	2011-12	2010-11	2009-10	2008-09
1	Return on assets (ROA)	25.4%	20.3%	22.2%	19.1%	14.6%
2	Return on capital employed (ROCE)	48.2%	37.9%	39.8%	34.5%	27.4%
3	Return on Equity (ROE)	56.7%	40.8%	33.9%	27.1%	19.3%

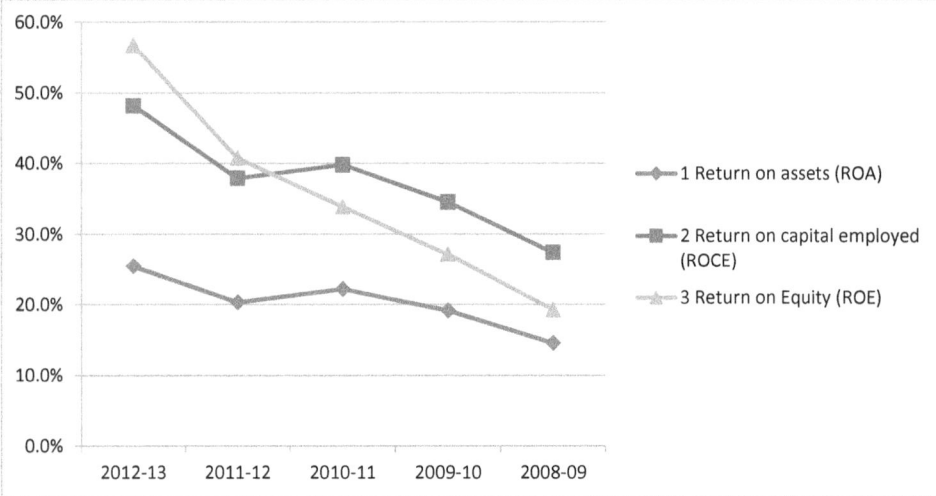

The return on investment has been showing positive trend, which shows that the enterprise has high profitability with growth and there is enough room for ploughing back these profits in the enterprise for generating future growth potential. Overall the enterprise shows quite a healthy returns with profitability and would always be the target for investment for the investor, if its shares are traded in stock exchange.

Case study 3.5. Asset turnover ratios

An analyst is comparing the non-current asset turnover ratios of two listed enterprises A Ltd and B Ltd engaged in similar businesses. The non-current asset turnover ratio of A Ltd is almost 50% higher than that of B Ltd. The analyst concludes that A Ltd having higher asset turnover ratio is utilising the non-current assets far more effectively. Please give your reasons why this conclusion may not be valid.

Solution

The observation of the analyst may be incorret based on the following reasons:

a) B Ltd having lower non-current asset turnover ratio, may have a policy of revaluing non-current assets, in which case the revalued assets will be much higher than the carrying value of the non-current assets. Hence comparing two enterprises A Ltd valuing non-current assets in cost model and B Ltd in revaluation model, may lead to incongruous conclusions.

b) It may also be possible that the A Ltd has non-current assets which have been commissioned much earlier compared to that of B Ltd. Accordingly, the carrying value of the non-current assets in A Ltd are considerably lesser than B Ltd. Hence this can also result in an anomaly where the conclusion derived from apparent results may not be correct.

Case study 3.6. Computation of financial ratios and writing a report on performance.
Alpha Ltd operates a number of retail outlets across India. In recent years the company has found it necessary to provide credit facilities to its customers with the objective of achieving growth in revenue. As a result of this the liability of the bankers of this enterprise has increased substantially. The financial statements of the last three years are appended below.

Sl no.	Balance Sheet of Vespa Ltd as at 31.3. 2013	Note No.	As at 31.03.11	As at 31.03.12	Rs Million As at 31.03.13
	EQUITY & LIABILITIES				
1	**Shareholders' funds**				
	(a)Share capital		90.0	90.0	90.0
	(b)Reserves and surplus		252.0	262.0	262.0
	(c)Money received against share warrants				
2	**Share application money pending allotment**				
3	**Non-current liabilities**				
	(a) Long term borrowings				
	(b) Deferred tax liabilities (net)				
	(c) Other long term liabilities				
	(d) Long-term provisions				
4	**Current liabilities**				
	(a)Short term borrowings		200.0	200.0	320.0
	(b) Trade payables				
	(c)Other current liabilities	1	640.0	840.0	928.0
	(d) Short term provisions				
	TOTAL		1182.0	1392.0	1600.0
	ASSETS				
1	**Non-current Assets**				
	(a) Fixed Assets				
	(i) Tangible assets		278.0	290.0	332.0
	(ii)Intangible assets				
	(iii) Capital work-in-progress				
	(iv) Intangible assets under development				
	(b) Non-current investments				
	(c) Deferred tax assets (net)				
	(d) Long term loans & advances				
	(e) Other non-current assets				
2	Current Assets				
	(a) Current investments				
	(b) Inventories		400.0	540.0	620.0
	(c)Trade receivables		492.0	550.0	633.0
	(d) Cash & cash equivalents		12.0	12	15.0

	(e) Short-term loan and advances				
	(f) Other current assets				
	TOTAL		1182.0	1392.0	1600.0

Notes to Balance Sheet:					
Sl no.	Particulars		As at	As at	As at
			31.03.13	31.03.12	31.03.11
1	Other current liabilities				
	Payable		300.0	300.0	310.0
	Taxation		20.0	20.0	8.0
	Overdraft		320.0	520.0	610.0
	Total		640.0	840.0	928.0

	Statement of Profit & Loss of Vespa Ltd as at 31.3. 2013				**Rs Million**
Sl no.	Particulars	Note No.	As at 31.03.11	As at 31.03.12	As at 31.03.13
I	REVENUE FROM OPERATION		1850.0	2200.0	2500.0
II	OTHER INCOME		0	0	0
III	**(TOTAL REVENUE (I + II)**		**1850.0**	**2200.0**	**2500.0**
IV	EXPENSES:				
	(a) Cost of material consumed				
	(b) Purchase of products for sale				
	(c) Changes in inventories of finished goods,				
	work-in-progress and products for sale				
	(d) Employees cost benefit expenses				
	(e) Finance cost	1	-20.0	0.0	20.0
	(f) Depreciation and amortisation expenses				
	(g) Product development expenses				
	(h) Other expenses	2	1800.0	2140.0	2450.0
	(i) Expenditure transfer to capital and other				
	Account				
	TOTAL EXPENSES		**1780.0**	**2140.0**	**2470.0**
V	PROFIT BEFORE EXCEPTIONAL AND EXTRA-		70.0	60.0	30.0
	ORDINARY ITEMS AND TAX (III - IV)				
VI	EXCEPTIONAL ITEMS		0.00	0.00	0.00
VII	PROFIT BEFORE				

	EXTRAORDINARY ITEMS AND TAX (V-VI)		70.00	60.00	30.00
VIII	EXTRAORDINARY ITEMS		0.00	0.00	0.00
IX	PROFIT BEFORE TAX AND CONTINUING OPERATIONS (VII - VIII)		70.00	60.00	30.00
X	TAX EXPENSES:				
	(a) Current tax		23.00	20.00	10.00
	(b) Deferred tax				
XI	PROFIT AFTER TAX FOR THE YEAR FROM CONTINUING OPERATION (IX - X)		47.00	40.00	20.00
XII	Profit / (loss) from discontinuing operations				
XIII	Tax expenses from discontinuing operations				
XIV	Profit / (loss) from discontinuing operations (after tax) (XII-XIII)				
XV	PROFIT/(LOSS) FOR THE PERIOD (XI + XIV)				
	Balance brought forward from previous year				
	Profit available for appropriation:		47.00	40.00	20.00
	Proposed dividend		30.00	30.00	20.00
	Transfer to General Reserve				
	Distribution tax				
	Total				
	Balance carried forward		17.0	10.0	0.0
XVI	Earning per equity share:				
	(1) Basic				
	(2) Diluted				

Notes to Statement of Profit & loss					Rs Million
Sl no.	Particulars		As at 31.03.11	As at 31.03.12	As at 31.03.13
1	**Finance cost**				
	Interest from credit sales		45.0	60.0	90.0
	Interest payable		-25.0	-60.0	-110.0
	Total		20.0	0.0	-20.0
2	**Other expenses**				
	Cost of sales		1250.0	1500.0	1750.0
	Operating cost		550.0	640.0	700.0

	Total		1800.0	2140.0	2450.0

Other information					Rs. Million
Sl no.	Particulars		As at 31.03.11	As at 31.03.12	As at 31.03.13
1	Level of credit sales		375.0	263.0	213.0
2	Depreciation		70.0	60.0	55.0

The loans are secured by a floating charge over the assets of Alpha. They are due for repayment on 31st March 2013.

The bank overdraft is unsecured. The bank has set a limit of Rs.630 million on the overdraft. Owing to the steady increase in bank overdraft the company has sent a request to the bankers to increase the limit. The request was received by the bank on 15th May 2013, two weeks after the financial statements for the year ended 31st March 2013 were published.

Required:

Write a report to the regional manager of the bank analysing the financial performance and position of the enterprise for the period covered by the financial statements.

Solution

The report to regional manager would be as under:

To: The Regional Manager
From: Management Accountant
Dated: 17.12.2013
Sub: Financial performance of Alpha Ltd

Executive Summary

As requested I have carried out a financial analysis of the financial statements of Alpha Ltd for the last three years in order to identify reasons for increase in overdraft facilities for the entity. My observations are as under:

1. **Revenue**
   Revenue of the entity has improved by around 19% in 2011-12 over 2010-11 and by around 13.6% in 2012-13 over 2011-12. (Table 2)
2. **Profitability**
   Net profit of the entity has dropped significantly by 14.9% in 2011-12 over 2010-11 and by 50% in 2012-13 over 2011-12. (Table 2). The reason for this drop has been explained by drop in profit margins - gross margin of 30% in 2012-13, getting reduced to operating margin of only 2% in 2012-13 – the reason for this drop being attributable to interest charges of 28% on sales during this period. Interest charges have increased by 140% in 2011-12 and 83.3% in 2012-13 (Table 2).
   This had an overall impact on Return on Capital Employed which dropped from 13.74% in 2011 to 5.68% in 2013.(Table 4).
   The decline in profitability of Alpha Ltd has led to significant decline of the cash position of the entity.

Financial Analysis for effective Management Decisions

3. **Capital structure**

The gearing ratio of the entity showed a marked increase from 0.5848 in 2010-11 to 0.9091 in 2012-13. This has resulted in the increase in interest charges as highlighted above. This has also led to significant deterioration in interest cover from 2.0 in 2010-11 to 0.45 in 2012-13. (Table 3).

4. **Liquidity**

The current ratio of the entity has been hovering around 1.08 to 1.02 in the last three years. This has been further compounded by weak acid test ratio of 0.60 to 0.52. This clearly shows that the entity is currently going through a severe liquidity crunch. (Table 3)

5. **Conclusion**

The entity's performance has significantly deteriorated over the last three years despite a healthy increase in revenue. Accordingly, it may not be appropriate to go for an expansion of overdraft facility currently. Instead a strategy of going for long term sources of financing at a comparatively lower rate of interest may be much more sound at this stage of the enterprise. Hence proposed increase of overdraft limit needs to be carefully considered.

Thanks & Regards,

Management Accountant

Table 1 - Trend Analysis : Balance Sheet   **Rs Million**

Sl no.	Particulars		As at 31.03.11	As at 31.03.12	As at 31.03.13	Remarks
1	Current Assets		904.0	1102.0	1268.0	Current assets have increased by 22% in 2011-12 and 15% in 2012-13
	% increase over previous year			21.9%	15.1%	
2	Fixed Assets		278.0	290.0	332.0	Showed increasing trend in fixed assets, marginal investments made in 2012-13
	% increase over previous year			4.3%	14.5%	
3	Current liabilities		840.0	1040.0	1248.0	Current liabilities have increased by 24% in 2011-12 and 20% in 2012-13,
	% increase over previous year			23.8%	20.0%	

Table 2 - Trend Analysis : Statement of Profit & Loss　　　　　　　　**Rs Million**

Sl no.	Particulars		As at 31.03.11	As at 31.03.12	As at 31.03.13	Remarks
1	Revenue % increase over previous year		1850	2200 18.9%	2500 13.6%	Sales position has improved by around 19% in 2011-12, and by 13.6% in 2012-13
2	Cost of sales % increase over previous year		1250	1500 20.0%	1750 16.7%	Cost of sales have increased by 20% in 2011-12 and 16.7% in 2012-13
3	Operating profit % increase over previous year		600	700 16.7%	750 7.1%	Operating profit has shown increasing trend over two years
4	Interest % increase over previous year		25.0	60.0 140.0%	110.0 83.3%	Interest payable has increased by 140% in 2011-12 and 83.3% in 2012-13
5	Net profit % increase/decrease over previous year		47.0	40.0 -14.9%	20.0 -50.0%	Net profit has dropped significantly in 2012-13 By 50%

Table 3 - Ratio Analysis : Liquidity and solvency ratios

Sl no.	Particulars		As at 31.03.11	As at 31.03.12	As at 31.03.13	Remarks
1	Net working capital (Current Asset - Current liabilities)		64.0	62.0	20.0	Liquidity position has reduced over 2011-12 and 2012-13
2	Current ratio (Current Asset / Current liabilities)		1.08	1.06	1.02	Liquidity position has remained unsatisfactory
3	Quick ratio / Acid test		0.60	0.54	0.52	Liquidity position has

	ratio (Quick Asset / Current liabilities)				remained unsatisfactory
4	**Debt - Equity ratio** (Debt / Shareholders' equity)	0.5848	0.5682	0.9091	The company's gearing ratio has shown an increasing trend and is currently at 0.91. This has resulted in high interest charges
5	**Interest coverage ratio** (Operating profit / Interest)	2.00	1.00	0.45	This ratio has significantly dropped from 2010-11 showing exposure on debt servicing

	Table 4: Profitability and turnover ratios				
Sl no.	Particulars	As at 31.03.11	As at 31.03.12	As at 31.03.13	Remarks
1	**Margin ratios**				
1.1.	**Gross Profit margin** (Operating profit x 100)/Sales	32.43%	31.82%	30.00%	Operating margin trend has dropped marginally
1.2.	**Interest expenses / sales %**	29.73%	29.09%	28.00%	This ratio has dropped marginally
1.3.	**Operating profit / sales %** (gross profit x 100)/Sales	2.70%	2.73%	2.00%	Gross margin ratio has dropped compared to 2011-12 but not satisfactory
1.4	**Net Profit margin** (Net profit x 100)/Sales	2.54%	1.82%	0.80%	This shows a deteriorating trend and net margin has significantly dropped over the years
2	**Turnover ratios**				
2.1.	**Fixed Assets turnover** (Sales / Fixed assets)	6.655	7.586	7.530	Shows marginal improvement
2.2.	**Working capital turnover** (Sales / Net current assets)	28.91	35.48	125.00	Showed an upward trend over 2010-11 and 2011-12
2.3.	**Assets turnover ratio** (Sales / total assets)	1.57	1.58	1.56	Remained at same levels
3	**Return on assets (ROA)** (Net profit margin x Assets turnover ratio)	3.98%	2.87%	1.25%	Showed significant drop over 2010-11 and 2011-12 and is not satisfactory
4	**Equity multiplier** (Sales / Net worth)	5.409	6.250	7.102	Showed reasonable improvement over 2010-11 but still lot of room for improvement
5	**Return on Equity (ROE)** (ROA X Equity multiplier)	21.51%	17.96%	8.88%	Showed significant drop over 2010-11 and 2011-12 and is not satisfactory

6	**Return on capital employed** (Net profit after tax x 100) /Total capital employed)		13.74%	11.36%	5.68%	Trend not satisfactory and has dropped significantly

Working Notes

Particulars					Rs Million
Sl no.	Particulars		As at 31.03.11	As at 31.03.12	As at 31.03.13
1	**Gross Profit**				
	Revenue		1850.0	2200.0	2500.0
	Less: Cost of sales		1250.0	1500.0	1750.0
	Total		**600.0**	**700.0**	**750.0**
	Gross Profit margin on revenue		**32.4%**	**31.8%**	**30.0%**
2	**Operating profit**				
	Gross profit		600.0	700.0	750.0
	Less: Operating cost		550.0	640.0	700.0
	Total		**50.0**	**60.0**	**50.0**
	Operating profit margin on revenue		**2.7%**	**2.7%**	**2.0%**
3	**Net Profit**				
	Gross Profit		50.0	60.0	50.0
	Add: Other income		0	0	0
	Other non-recurring income		0.0	0.0	0.0
	Less Interest		-20.0	0.0	20.0
	Tax expenses		23	20	10
	Total		**47.0**	**40.0**	**20.0**
	Net Profit to Revenue %		**2.5%**	**1.8%**	**0.8%**
4	**Fixed Assets**				
	Net tangible assets		278.0	290.0	332.0
	Add: Capital work-in-progress				
	Investments				
	Total		**278.0**	**290.0**	**332.0**
	Fixed Asset turnover ratio		6.65	7.59	7.53
5	**Net Worth**				
	Share capital		90.0	90.0	90.0
	Reserves & surplus		252.0	262.0	262.0
	Total		**342.0**	**352.0**	**352.0**
6	**Capital employed**				
	Total assets		1182.0	1392.0	1600.0

	Less: Current liabilities		840.0	1040.0	1248.0
	Capital employed		342.0	352.0	352.0

Case study 3.7. Computation of financial ratios

The following are the financial statements of Scala Ltd.

Balance Sheet of Scala Ltd as at 31.3. 2013   **Rs Million**

Sl no.	Particulars	Note no.	As at 31.03.13	As at 31.03.12
	EQUITY & LIABILITIES			
1	Shareholders' funds			
	(a)Share capital	1	120.0	120.0
	(b)Reserves and surplus	2	116.0	118.0
	(c)Money received against share warrants			
2	Share application money pending allotment			
3	Non-current liabilities			
	(a) Long term borrowings		80.0	80.0
	(b) Deferred tax liabilities (net)			
	(c) Other long term liabilities			
	(d) Long-term provisions			
4	Current liabilities			
	(a)Short term borrowings			
	(b) Trade payables		72	110
	(c)Other current liabilities			
	(d) Short term provisions (tax)		20	20
	TOTAL		408.0	448.0
	ASSETS			
1	Non-current Assets			
	(a) Fixed Assets			
	(i) Tangible assets		260.0	278.0
	(ii)Intangible assets			
	(iii) Capital work-in-progress			
	(iv) Intangible assets under development			
	(b) Non-current investments			
	(c) Deferred tax assets (net)			
	(d) Long term loans & advances			
	(e) Other non-current assets			
2	Current Assets			
	(a) Current investments			
	(b) Inventories		84.0	74.0
	(c)Trade receivables		58.0	46.0
	(d) Cash & cash equivalents		6.0	50
	(e) Short-term loan and advances			
	(f) Other current assets			
	TOTAL		408.0	448.0

Notes to Balance Sheet:

Sl no.	Particulars		As at 31.03.13	As at 31.03.12
1	Share capital			
	Ordinary share capital of Re.1 each		70	70
	8% Preference share capital		50	50
			120	120
2	Reserves and surplus			
	Securities premium		34.0	34.0
	Revaluation reserve		20.0	0.0
	Profit & loss account		62.0	84.0
	Total		116.0	118.0

Statement of Profit & Loss of Scala Ltd as at 31.3. 2013   **Rs Million**

Sl no.	Particulars	Note no.	As at 31.03.13	As at 31.03.12
I	REVENUE FROM OPERATION		418.0	392.0
II	OTHER INCOME		0	0
III	**(TOTAL REVENUE (I + II)**		**418.0**	**392.0**
IV	EXPENSES:			
	(a) Cost of material consumed	1	314.0	302.0
	(b) Purchase of products for sale			
	(c) Changes in inventories of finished goods, work-in-progress and products for sale			
	(d) Employees cost benefit expenses			
	(e) Finance cost		4.0	4.0
	(f) Depreciation and amortisation expenses		18.0	18.0
	(g) Product development expenses			
	(h) Other expenses		28.0	22.0
	(i) Expenditure transfer to capital and other Account			
	TOTAL EXPENSES		**364.0**	**346.0**
V	PROFIT BEFORE EXCEPTIONAL AND EXTRA-ORDINARY ITEMS AND TAX (III - IV)		54.0	46.0
VI	EXCEPTIONAL ITEMS		0.00	0.00
VII	PROFIT BEFORE EXTRAORDINARY ITEMS AND TAX (V-VI)		54.00	46.00
VIII	EXTRAORDINARY ITEMS		0.00	0.00
IX	PROFIT BEFORE TAX AND CONTINUING OPERATIONS (VII - VIII)		54.00	46.00
X	TAX EXPENSES:			
	(a) Current tax		20.00	20.00

	(b) Deferred tax		
XI	PROFIT AFTER TAX FOR THE YEAR FROM CONTINUING OPERATION (IX - X)	34.00	26.00
XII	Profit / (loss) from discontinuing operations		
XIII	Tax expenses from discontinuing operations		
XIV	Profit / (loss) from discontinuing operations (after tax) (XII-XIII)		
XV	PROFIT/(LOSS) FOR THE PERIOD (XI + XIV)		
	Balance brought forward from previous year		
	Profit available for appropriation:	34.00	26.00
	Proposed dividend –Equity	12.00	10.00
	- preference	4.00	4.00
	Transfer to General Reserve		
	Distribution tax		
	Total		
	Balance carried forward	18.0	12.0
XVI	Earning per equity share:		
	(1) Basic		
	(2) Diluted		

Notes to Statement of Profit & loss   **Rs Million**

Sl no.	Particulars		As at 31.03.13	As at 31.03.12
1	**Cost of material consumed**			
	Opening inventory		74.0	58.0
	Purchases		324.0	318.0
			398.0	376.0
	Less: Closing inventory		84.0	74.0
	Total		314.0	302.0

Calculate and comment on the following ratios for Scala Ltd:
1) ROCE
2) All liquidity and solvency ratios
3) All profitability and turnover ratios
4) Equity gearing
5) Total gearing
6) Interest coverage
7) Dividend coverage
8) EPS
9) PE if market value of ordinary shares is Rs.2.40.

Solution

Ratio Analysis : Liquidity and solvency ratios					
Sl no	Particulars		As at 31.03.13	As at 31.03.12	Remarks

1	Net working capital (Rs million) (Current Asset - Current liabilities)		56.0	40.0	Liquidity position has increased over 2012-13 over 2011-12
2	Current ratio (Current Asset / Current liabilities)		1.61	1.31	Liquidity position has improved but still unsatisfactory
3	Quick ratio / Acid test ratio (Quick Asset / Current liabilities)		0.70	0.74	Liquidity position has remained unsatisfactory
4	Total gearing ratio (Debt / Shareholders' funds)		0.411	0.409	The company's gearing ratio has been constant and low, the company can borrow more
5	Equity gearing ratio (Debt / Shareholders' equity)		0.699	0.691	Equity gearing has been constant and is low geared by less than 100
6	Interest coverage ratio (Operating profit / Interest)		14.50	12.50	This ratio has improved over 2011-12 and shows satisfactory position on debt servicing
7	Dividend coverage ratio (Operating profit / dividend)		2.13	1.86	This ratio has improved over 2011-12
8	Cost of goods sold ratio (Cost of goods sold/Sales)		0.75	0.77	Deteriorating trend is not satisfactory
9	Operating ratio (Cost of goods sold + other expenses /Sales)		0.82	0.83	Trend not satisfactory

Ratio analysis - Profitability and turnover ratios					
SI no.	Particulars		As at 31.03.13	As at 31.03.12	Remarks
1	Margin ratios				
1.1.	Gross Profit margin (Gross profit x 100)/Sales		24.88%	22.96%	Gross margin trend has increased marginally
1.2.	Interest expenses / sales %		0.96%	1.02%	This ratio has dropped marginally
1.3.	Operating profit / sales % (operating profit x 100)/Sales		13.88%	12.76%	Operating margin ratio has increased compared to 2011-12 but not satisfactory
1.4	Net Profit margin (Net profit x 100)/Sales		8.13%	6.63%	This has increasing trend and net margin has improved over the years
2	Turnover ratios				
2.1.	Debtors turnover ratio (Sales / Receivables)		7.207	8.522	Shows deteriorating trend where receivables are turned over less
2.2.	Days sales outstanding (DSO) (Receivables / Sales per day)		50.65	42.83	Corroborated by increase in DSO
2.3.	Inventory turnover ratio (Cost of goods sold / Inventories)		3.74	4.08	Shows deteriorating trend where inventories are

					turned over have reduced
2.4	**Inventories days sales (IDS)** (Inventories / Cost of goods sold per day)		97.64	89.44	Corroborated by increase in IDS
2.5	**Creditors turnover ratio** (Cost of goods sold + other expenses) / creditors)		4.8	2.9	Creditors management has improved
2.6.	**Creditors days outstanding** (Creditors / Cost of goods sold per day)		76.84	123.92	Creditors payout has improved
2.7.	**Working capital turnover** (Sales / Net current assets)		7.46	9.80	Showed an downward trend over 2011-12
2.8.	**Fixed Assets turnover** (Sales / Fixed assets)		1.608	1.410	Trend improved marginally but needs to improve further
2.9.	**Assets turnover ratio** (Sales / total assets)		1.02	0.88	Improved over previous year
3	**Return on assets (ROA)** (Net profit margin x Assets turnover ratio)		8.33%	5.80%	Showed significant improvement over 2011-12 but is not satisfactory
4	**Equity multiplier** (Sales / Net worth)		1.771	1.647	Showed reasonable improvement over 2011-12 but still lot of room for improvement
5	**Return on Equity (ROE)** (ROA X Equity multiplier)		14.76%	9.56%	Showed significant improvement over 2011-12 but needs to improve
6	**Return on capital employed** (Net profit after tax x 100)/Total capital employed)		18.35%	15.72%	Trend not satisfactory and has dropped significantly
7	**Earnings per share (EPS)** (Net profit after tax - preference dividend) / no. of shares)		Rs. 21.4	Rs.15.7	Showed significant improvement
8	**Price earnings ratio** (Market price/ EPS)		11.21		Quite high which indicates the market has confidence in the performance of the company

Working Notes   **Rs Million**

Sl no.	Particulars		As at 31.03.13	As at 31.03.12
1	**Gross Profit**			
	Revenue		418.0	392.0
	Less: Cost of sales		314.0	302.0
	Total		**104.0**	**90.0**
	Gross Profit margin on revenue		**24.9%**	**23.0%**
2	**Operating profit**			
	Gross Profit		104.0	90.0

	Less: Depreciation	18.0	18.0
	Other expenses	28.0	22.0
	Operating profit	58.0	50.0
	Operating Profit margin on revenue	**13.9%**	**12.8%**
3	**Total Assets**		
	Net tangible assets	260.0	278.0
	Add: Net Current Assets	56.0	40.0
	Total	**316.0**	**318.0**
	Asset turnover ratio	**1.32**	**1.23**
4	**Net Worth**		
	Share capital	120.0	120.0
	Reserves & surplus	116.0	118.0
	Total	**236.0**	**238.0**
	Return on equity	**12.7%**	**9.2%**
5	**Capital employed**		
	Total assets	408.0	448.0
	Less: Current liabilities	92.0	130.0
	Capital employed	**316.0**	**318.0**
	Return on capital employed	**18.4%**	**15.7%**

Chapter 4. Return on Investment

4.1. Introduction

Short term and long term profitability of shareholders' investments in an entity is evaluated through Return on Equity (ROE) and growth in investment. Growth in earnings also is determined by growth in investment and the profitability of that investment. For forecasting profitability of an entity we need understand both profitability and growth and the factors which drive them. The analysis of drivers of ROE is often called Profitability Analysis and the analysis of drivers of growth is called growth analysis. In this chapter we are going to cover ROE and Profitability Analysis. Growth Analysis will be covered in the next chapter.

As we have seen in our earlier chapters, reformulation of financial statements is the corner stone on which the edifice of profitability analysis and growth analysis rests.

4.2. Analysis of profitability

Profitability analysis determines the state of viability of the firm as of today. In its practical approach it carries out the following:
   a) Calculate the ROE of the enterprise based on current performance
   b) Identify the value drivers which would build up to the current ROE.
   c) Based on these drivers, assess the forecast and predict the future ROE, which in turn talks about the overall growth of the enterprise.

Because of these attributes, profitability analysis becomes an effective tool to carry out:
   a) Management planning as to how to survive and grow with the current businesses
   b) Strategy analysis as to retain, grow or dispose of verticals which are not profitable
   c) Decision analysis related to future of the business based on business vision, mission and strategic intent
   d) Enterprise valuation, which is always required for future growth through inorganic route

4.3. Return on Equity (ROE)

As we have seen in our earlier chapters Return on Equity (ROE) is calculated as under:

$$\text{Return on Equity (ROE)} = \frac{\text{Comprehensive Income}}{\text{Average Shareholders' Equity (SE)}}$$

Return on Equity is cascaded into three levels of drivers. These are:
   a) Level 1 identifies the effect of financing and operating liability leverage;
   b) Level 2 identifies effect of profit margins and asset turnovers on operative profitability, and
   c) Level 3 identifies the drivers of profit margins, asset turnovers and the borrowing cost.

Before we get into this drill down, let us understand the nomenclatures:

Financial statements line items		Ratios used for drill down	
Earnings	= Comprehensive income	ROE	= Return on Equity
SE	= Shareholders' equity	RNOA	= Return on net operating assets
OI	= Operating Income	ROOA	= Return on operating assets
NOA	= Net Operating Assets	NBC	= Net borrowing cost
NFE	= Net Financial expenses	OLLEV	= Operating liability leverage
NFO	= Net Financial obligations	OLSPREAD	= Operating liability leverage spread
		FLEV	= Financial leverage

71

	SPREAD = Operating spread PM = Operating profit margin ATO = Asset turnover

4.3.1. Level I Drill down

This is determined by Operating profitability, financial leverage and the Operating spread.

Operating profitability is defined by the definition of ROE which as mentioned above is

$$\text{Return on Equity (ROE)} = \frac{\text{Comprehensive Income}}{\text{Average Shareholders' Equity (SE)}}$$

Comprehensive income is the numerator of ROE and aggregates operating income (OI) and net financial expense (NFE) as depicted in a reformulated income statement. Shareholders' Equity (SE) in the denominator is net operating assets (NOA) less net financial obligations (NFO). Hence ROE is broken down to the following:

$$\text{Return on Equity (ROE)} = \frac{\text{OI - NFE}}{\text{NOA - NFE}}$$

Operating Income (OI) is calculated by the net operating assets (NOA) and the operating profitability measure, Return on net operating assets (RNOA) expressed in percentage terms.
The net financial expense (NFE) on the other hand is calculated by the net financial obligations (NFO) and the rate at which the NFE is incurred is the net borrowing cost (NBC) expressed in percentage terms. Accordingly, the ROE is expressed as under:

$$\text{Return on Equity (ROE)} = \frac{\text{NOA}}{\text{SE}} \times \text{RNOA} - \frac{\text{NFO}}{\text{SE}} \times \text{NBC}$$

Where, RNOA = Operating Income (OI) / Net Operating Assets (NOA) and
NBC = Net financial expenses (NFE) / Net Financial Obligation (NFO)

The ratio above is further rearranged as under:

$$\text{Return on Equity (ROE)} = \text{RNOA} + \frac{\text{NFO}}{\text{SE}} \times (\text{RNOA} - \text{NBC})$$
$$= \text{RNOA} + (\text{Financial leverage x operating spread})$$
$$= \text{RNOA} + (\text{FLEV X SPREAD})$$

Hence first level drivers of ROE are:

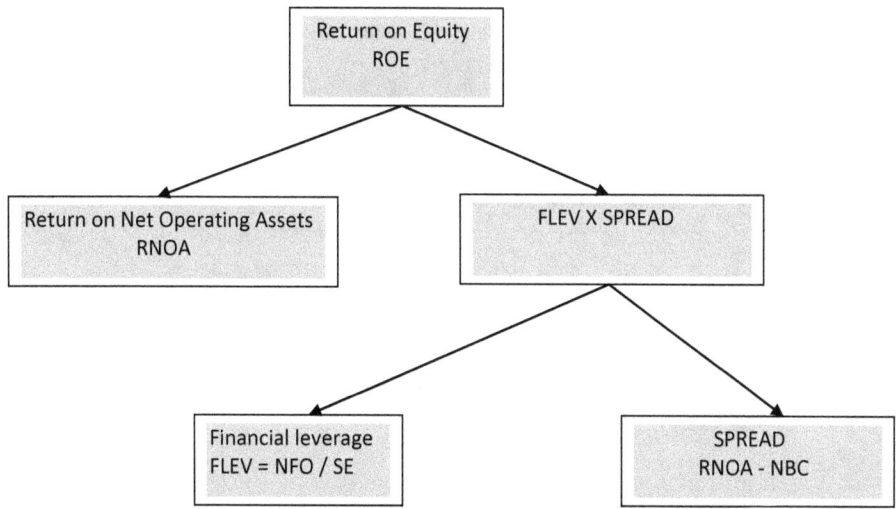

4.3.2. Financial leverage

Financial leverage is the degree to which net operating assets are financed by borrowing with net financial obligations (NFO) or by equity. The measure FLEV = NFO / SE captures financial leverage. To the extent that net operating assets are financed by net financial obligations rather than equity, the return on equity is affected. A typical FLEV is around 0.4, but there would considerable variation between industries and enterprises at large.

4.3.3. Operating spread

Operating Spread is the difference between the return on net operating assets and the net borrowing cost and represented as:

SPREAD = Return on Net Operating Assets (RNOA) – Net Borrowing Cost (NBC)

This formula says that the ROE is levered up over the return from operations if the enterprise has financial leverage and the return from operations is greater than the borrowing cost. The enterprise earns more on its equity if the net operating assets are financed by net debt, provided those assets earn more than the cost of debt.

4.4.4. Net Borrowing cost

The net borrowing cost (NBC) is a weighted average of the cost for the different sources of net financing. It can be calculated as under:

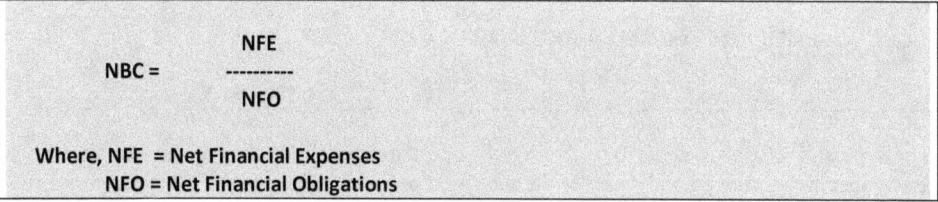

$$NBC = \frac{NFE}{NFO}$$

Where, NFE = Net Financial Expenses
NFO = Net Financial Obligations

The drivers of Net Borrowing cost are:

$$NBC = \frac{FO}{NFO} \times \frac{\text{After tax interest on financial obligations (FO)}}{FO}$$

Minus

$$\frac{FO}{NFO} \times \frac{\text{After tax interest on financial assets (FA)}}{FA}$$

Minus

$$\frac{FA}{NFO} \times \frac{\text{Unrealised gains on financial assets (FA)}}{FA}$$

Plus

$$\frac{\text{Preference shares}}{NFO} \times \frac{\text{Preference dividend}}{\text{Preference shares}}$$

Where,
FO   = Financial obligations
NFO = Net Financial Obligations
FA   = Financial Assets

Hence from the above, the drivers of Net Borrowing Cost (NBC) are:
a) After tax interest on Financial obligations
b) After tax interest on financial assets
c) Unrealised gains on financial assets
d) Preference dividend

4.4.5. Operating liability leverage

Similar to financial leverage, just as financial liabilities can lever up the ROE, so can operating liabilities lever up the return on net operating assets. Operating liabilities are obligations incurred in the course of operations and are distinct from financial obligations incurred to finance the operations. The operating liability leverage is expressed as under:

$$\text{Operating liabilities leverage (OLLEV)} = \frac{OI}{NOA}$$

The typical OLLEV is about 0.4. We know, operating liabilities reduce the net operating assets that are employed and so lever the return on net operating assets. To the extent a firm can get credit in its operations with no explicit interest, it reduces its investment in net operating assets and levers its RNOA. On the other hand vendors who provide credit without interest also charge higher prices for the goods and services they supply than would be the case if the firm paid cash. Hence, operating leverage, like financial leverage, can be unfavourable as well as favourable.

To conclude, ROE is affected by both financial leverage and operating liability leverage. Without either type of leverage, ROE would be equal to ROOA, the rate of return on operating assets. Operating liability leverage levers RNOA over ROOA and financial leverage levers ROE over RNOA.

Hence, ROE = ROOA + (RNOA – ROOA) + (ROE – RNOA)

Hence, in overall profitability analysis the ratios stack up as under:

	Year 1	Year 2	Year 3	Year 4	Year 5
Sales Revenue (Rs Million)					
Profitability:					
EBITDA / Sales %					
Net profit margin %					
Asset turnover					
Return on Equity %					
Return on Net Operating Assets %					
Financial leverage					
Operating Spread					
Net borrowing cost %					
Operating Liability Leverage					

4.4.6. Second level drill down: Drivers of Operating Profitability

We have seen above

ROE = RNOA + (FLEV X SPREAD), which is
ROE = RNOA + (FLEV X (RNOA – NBC)
ROE = (PM X ATO) + (FLEV X (RNOA – NBC))

The two drivers of RNOA are:

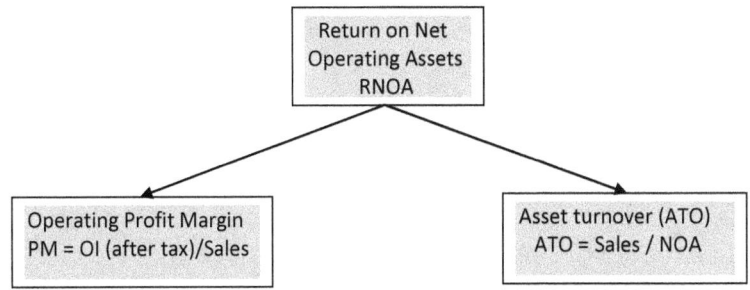

75

Operating Profit Margin depicts profitability of the entity towards each rupee of sales.

Asset Turnover ratio depicts the sales revenue per rupee of net operating assets. It measures the ability of the NOA to generate sales and to what degree. For example if ATO is say 4.0, it signifies that the entity is using 25 paise of net operating assets to generate a rupee of sales.

The decomposition of operating profitability is known as the **DuPont financial model**. It states that profitability in operations arises from two sources, namely,

a) Operating income as a percentage of sales, which means higher the earning per rupee of sales, it will push up the RNOA and

b) Turnover of Net operating assets to sales, which means higher the turnover of net operating assets, higher would be the sales as well as RNOA as a resultant.

This signifies that an enterprise can optimise Return on Net Operating Assets (RNOA) by increasing profit margins as well as by levering up margins by using operating assets and operating liabilities more efficiently to generate sales.

4.4.7. Third level drill down: Drivers of ROE

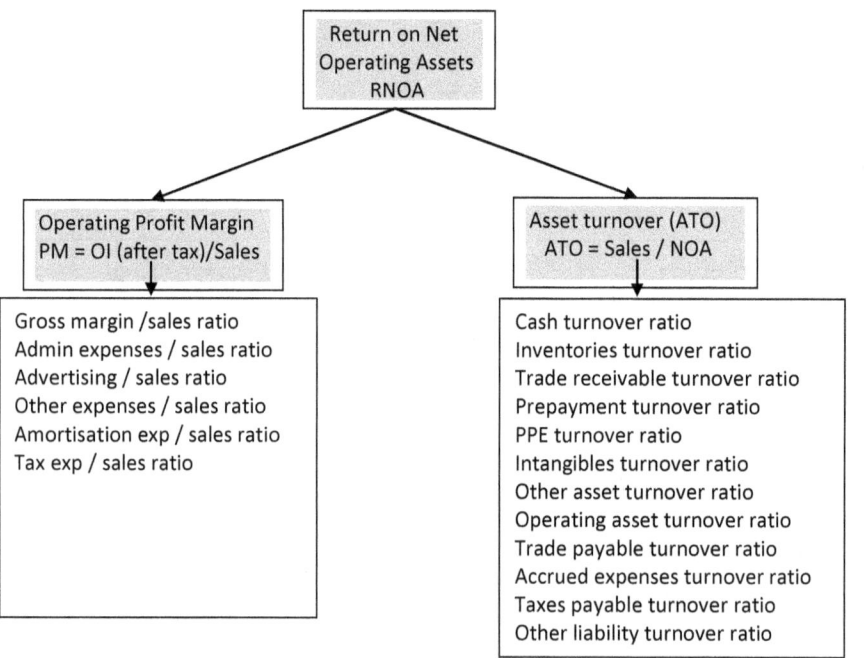

4.4.8. Operating Profit margin drivers

Items	Ratios
Gross margin /sales ratio	$= \dfrac{\text{Gross margin}}{\text{Sales}}$
Admin expenses / sales ratio	Administration expenses

	$= \dfrac{\text{-----------------------------------}}{\text{Sales}}$
Advertising / sales ratio	$= \dfrac{\text{Advertising expenses}}{\text{Sales}}$
Other expenses / sales ratio	$= \dfrac{\text{Other expenses}}{\text{Sales}}$
Amortisation exp / sales ratio	$= \dfrac{\text{Amortisation expenses}}{\text{Sales}}$
Tax exp / sales ratio	$= \dfrac{\text{Tax expenses}}{\text{Sales}}$
Net margin / sales ratio (resultant of all of above)	$= \dfrac{\text{Net margin}}{\text{Sales}}$

4.4.9. Turnover drivers

Items	Ratios
Cash turnover ratio	$= \dfrac{\text{Sales}}{\text{Cash}}$
Inventories turnover ratio	$= \dfrac{\text{Cost of goods sold}}{\text{Inventory}}$
Inventories days sales (IDS)	$= \dfrac{365}{\text{Inventory turnover}}$
Trade receivable turnover ratio	$= \dfrac{\text{Sales}}{\text{Trade Receivable}}$
Days sales Outstanding (DSO)	$= \dfrac{365}{\text{Trade receivable turnover}}$

Trade payable turnover ratio	$$= \frac{\text{Purchases}}{\text{Trade Payable}}$$ $$= \frac{365}{\text{Trade payable turnover}}$$
PPE turnover ratio	$$= \frac{\text{Sales}}{\text{Property, Plant \& Equipment}}$$
Intangibles turnover ratio	$$= \frac{\text{Sales}}{\text{Intangible properties}}$$
Prepayment turnover ratio	$$= \frac{\text{Sales}}{\text{Prepayments}}$$
Accrued expenses turnover ratio	$$= \frac{\text{Cost of goods sold}}{\text{Accrued expenses}}$$
Other liabilities turnover ratio	$$= \frac{\text{Cost of goods sold}}{\text{Other liabilities}}$$
Tax payable turnover ratio	$$= \frac{\text{Sales}}{\text{Tax payable}}$$

4.10. DuPont Analysis

In line with the above analysis and as discussed above, students would also like to go through the DuPont Financial Analysis. Similar to above, in this metrix, the following metrix would be considered:

4.10.1. Return on Assets (ROA)

This is expressed as under:

$$\text{ROA} = \frac{\text{Net Income}}{\text{Total Assets}} \times 100$$

This ratio is then broken into:

> **ROA = Net profit margin x Asset turnover ratio**
>
> $$= \frac{\text{Net profit margin}}{\text{Sales}} \times \frac{\text{Sales}}{\text{Total Assets}}$$

From the above it is evident that the drivers of ROA are:
a) Profit margin and
b) Asset turnover ratio

These ratios can be further cascaded down to elements in both the streams under profit margin as well as turnover ratios similar to the ratios highlighted in 4.3.3. above.

4.10.2. Return on Equity (ROE)

This is expressed as under:

> $$\text{ROE} = \frac{\text{Net Income}}{\text{Owners' equity}} \times 100$$

This ratio is then broken into:

> **ROE = Net Income x Asset turnover ratio**
>
> $$= \frac{\text{Net Income}}{\text{Sales}} \times \frac{\text{Sales}}{\text{Owners' Equity}}$$

From the above it is evident that the drivers of ROA are:
a) Profit margin and
b) Asset turnover ratio

Case study.4.1. DuPont Financial Analysis

Calculate ratios in line with DuPont analysis based on the following numbers: (Rs lakhs)

Item	2012	2011	2010	2009
Net Income	6068	6945	5157	3566

Revenue	26273	25070	20847	16202
Assets	31471	28880	23735	17504
Owners' equity	23377	19295	16872	12140

Also provide your observations on the health of the enterprise based on the analysis.

Solution

The ratios based on DuPont analysis are as under:

Item	2012	2011	2010	2009	Remarks
Net Income	6068	6945	5157	3566	
Revenue	26273	25070	20847	16202	
Assets	31471	28880	23735	17504	
Owners' equity	23377	19295	16872	12140	
Ratios					
Profit margin (net income / sales %)	23.1%	27.7%	24.7%	22.0%	Profitability is dropping in 2012
Asset turnover ratio (Assets / Sales)	0.835	0.868	0.878	0.926	Similarly there appears to be lower efficiency in utilisation of assets
Return on assets % Profit margin x asset turnover	19.3%	24%	21.7%	20.4%	Has resulted in drop in Return on Assets
Equity multiplier (Sales/Equity)	1.35	1.50	1.41	1.44	Decrease in leverage in 2012
Return on Equity % (ROA X Equity multiplier)	26.0	36.0	30.6	29.4	There is sharp decline in ROE in 2012, lowest in the last four years.

On an overall analysis it shows that there is a significant negative trend on profitability margin as well as return on assets and return on equity in 2012 and this is wake-up call of the management of the enterprise to take note of this, analyse the reasons of this decline and take remedial measures .

Case study.4.2. DuPont Analysis

Using the Balance Sheet and Statement of Profit & loss of LMN Ltd please carry out a DuPont Analysis for three years and provide your interpretations.

SI no.	Balance Sheet of LMN Ltd as at 31.3. 2013				Rs Million
	Particulars	Note No.	As at 31.03.13	As at 31.03.12	As at 31.03.11
	EQUITY & LIABILITIES				
1	Shareholders' funds				
	(a)Share capital		636.0	318.0	318.0
	(b)Reserves and surplus		11551.1	10298.97	8069.33
	(c)Money received against share warrants				
2	Share application money pending allotment				

3	Non-current liabilities				
	(a) Long term borrowings	1	4785.7	6642.9	9598.3
	(b) Deferred tax liabilities (net)				
	(c) Other long term liabilities				
	(d) Long-term provisions				
4	Current liabilities				
	(a)Short term borrowings				
	(b) Trade payables				
	(c)Other current liabilities		4374.2	4438.04	4042.8
	(d) Short term provisions		7540.26	6096.85	4936.49
	TOTAL		28887.2	27794.7	26964.9
	ASSETS				
1	Non-current Assets				
	(a) Fixed Assets				
	(i) Tangible assets	2	13082.0	13428.3	13713.6
	(ii)Intangible assets				
	(iii) Capital work-in-progress		19.5	134.08	329.02
	(iv) Intangible assets under development				
	(b) Non-current investments				
	(c) Deferred tax assets (net)				
	(d) Long term loans & advances				
	(e) Other non-current assets				
2	Current Assets				
	(a) Current investments		585.6	607.38	613.9
	(b) Inventories		591.87	482.5	293.59
	(c)Trade receivables		926.2	807.7	933.52
	(d) Cash & cash equivalents		946.3	1280.66	745.5
	(e) Short-term loan and advances		12625.6	11021.89	9980.44
	(f) Other current assets		110.08	32.21	355.41
	TOTAL		28887.21	27794.7	26964.9

Notes to Balance Sheet:					
Sl no.	Particulars		As at 31.03.13	As at 31.03.12	As at 31.03.11
1	Long term borrowings				
	Secured loans		0.0	2000.0	9598.29
	Unsecured loans		4785.71	4642.86	0
	Total		4785.7	6642.9	9598.3
2	Tangible assets				
	Gross block		18864.1	18465.34	17917.84
	Less: Accumulated depreciation		5782.0	5037.03	4204.29
	Total		13082.0	13428.31	13713.6

	Statement of Profit & Loss of LMN Ltd as at 31.3. 2013				Rs Million
Sl no.	Particulars	Note No.	As at 31.03.13	As at 31.03.12	As at 31.03.11
I	REVENUE FROM OPERATION		9772.79	9801.22	5889.49
II	OTHER INCOME		452.01	556.07	338.74
III	**(TOTAL REVENUE (I + II)**		**10224.8**	**10357.29**	**6228.2**
IV	EXPENSES:				
	(a) Cost of material consumed	1	957.1	324.92	297.7
	(b) Purchase of products for sale				
	(c) Changes in inventories of finished goods, work-in-progress and products for sale				
	(d) Employees cost benefit expenses				
	(e) Finance cost	2	583.5	718.7	745.0
	(f) Depreciation and amortisation expenses	3	777.8	955.37	1293.2
	(g) Product development expenses				
	(h) Other expenses		4107.7	3882.86	2622.84
	(i) Expenditure transfer to capital and other Account				
	TOTAL EXPENSES		**6426.1**	**5881.82**	**4958.7**
V	PROFIT BEFORE EXCEPTIONAL AND EXTRA-		3798.7	4475.47	1269.53
	ORDINARY ITEMS AND TAX (III - IV)				
VI	EXCEPTIONAL ITEMS		125.0	68.8	-296.1
VII	PROFIT BEFORE EXTRAORDINARY ITEMS				
	TAX (V-VI)		3673.66	4406.64	1565.59
VIII	EXTRAORDINARY ITEMS		0	0	0
IX	PROFIT BEFORE TAX AND CONTINUING				
	OPERATIONS (VII - VIII)		3673.66	4406.64	1565.59
X	TAX EXPENSES:				
	(a) Current tax		1336.0	1444.6	590.7
	(b) Deferred tax				
XI	PROFIT AFTER TAX FOR THE YEAR FROM				
	CONTINUING OPERATION (IX - X)		2337.67	2962.0	974.85
XII	Profit / (loss) from discontinuing operations				
XIII	Tax expenses from discontinuing				

	operations				
XI V	Profit / (loss) from discontinuing operations (after tax) (XII-XIII)				
XV	PROFIT/(LOSS) FOR THE PERIOD (XI + XIV)				
	Balance brought forward from previous year				
	Profit available for appropriation:		2337.67	2962.0	974.85
	Proposed dividend		636.0	318.0	318.0
	Transfer to General Reserve				
	Distribution tax				
	Total				
	Balance carried forward		1701.7	2644	656.8
XV I	Earning per equity share:				
	(1) Basic				
	(2) Diluted				

Notes to Statement of Profit & loss					Rs Million
Sl no.	Particulars		As at 31.03.13	As at 31.03.12	As at 31.03.11
1	**Cost of material consumed**				
	Raw material cost		917.77	315.6	296.9
	Excise		39.33	9.34	0.78
	Total		957.1	324.92	297.7
2	**Finance cost**				
	Interest expenses		583.5	718.67	744.96
	Total		583.5	718.7	745.0
3	**Depreciation and amortisation expenses**				
	Depreciation		777.8	955.37	1293.2
	Total		777.8	955.37	1293.2
4	**Exceptional items**				
	Other non-recurring income		125.0	68.83	-296.06
	Total		125.0	68.8	-296.1

Solution

Working Notes					Rs Million
Sl no.	Particulars		As at 31.03.13	As at 31.03.12	As at 31.03.11
1	**Operating Profit**				
	Revenue		9772.79	9801.22	5889.49

	Less: Raw material cost	917.77	315.58	296.92
	Excise	39.33	9.34	0.78
	Other expenses	4107.7	3882.86	2622.84
	Total	**4707.99**	**5593.44**	**2968.95**
2	**Gross Profit**			
	Operating profit	4707.99	5593.44	2968.95
	Less: Interest expenses	583.5	718.7	745.0
	Total	4124.5	4874.8	2224.0
3	**Net Profit**			
	Gross Profit	4124.5	4874.8	2224.0
	Add: Other income	452.01	556.07	338.74
	Other non-recurring income	-125.0	-68.8	296.1
	Less Depreciation	777.8	955.37	1293.2
	Tax expenses	1335.99	1444.64	590.74
	Total	2337.7	2962.0	974.8
4	**Fixed Assets**			
	Net tangible assets	13082.04	13428.31	13713.55
	Add: Capital work-in-progress	19.5	134.08	329.02
	Investments	585.59	607.38	613.9
	Total	13687.13	14169.77	14656.47
5	**Net Worth**			
	Share capital	636	318	318
	Reserves & surplus	11551.1	10299.0	8069.3
	Total	12187.1	10616.97	8387.33

Statement of DuPont Analysis

Sl no.	Particulars	As at 31.03.13	As at 31.03.12	As at 31.03.11	Remarks
1	**Margin ratios**				
1.1	**Operating Profit margin**				
	(Operating profit x100)/Sales	48.17%	57.07%	50.41%	Operating margin trend has dropped marginally
1.2	**Interest expenses / sales %**	5.97%	7.33%	12.65%	This ratio has dropped sharply owing sales going up and interest remaining at same levels

1.3.	Gross margin / sales % (gross profit x 100)/Sales	42.20%	49.74%	37.76%	Gross margin ratio has dropped compared to 2011-12.
1.4	Net Profit margin				
	(Net profit x 100)/Sales	23.92%	30.22%	16.55%	Shows an upward trend compared 2010-11 but dropped from previous year
2	Turnover ratios				
2.1.	Fixed Assets turnover				
	(Sales / Fixed assets)	0.714	0.692	0.402	Shows marginal improvement
2.2.	Working capital turnover				
	(Sales / Net current assets)	3.08	3.21	1.98	Showed an upward trend over 2010-11 but has reduced from 2011-12
2.3.	Assets turnover ratio				
	(Sales / total assets)	0.34	0.35	0.22	Shows reasonable improvement
3	Return on assets (ROA)				
	(Net profit margin x Assets turnover ratio)	8.09%	10.66%	3.62%	Showed reasonable improvement over 2010-11 but still lot of room for improvement
4	Equity multiplier				
	(Sales / Net worth)	0.802	0.923	0.702	Showed reasonable improvement over 2010-11 but still lot of room
5	Return on Equity (ROE) (ROA X Equity multiplier)	6.49%	9.84%	2.54%	Showed reasonable improvement over 2010-11 but still lot of room for improvement

Case study.4.3. DuPont Analysis

Using the Balance Sheet and Statement of Profit & loss of DEF Ltd please carry out a DuPont Analysis for three years and provide your interpretations.

Sl no.	Balance Sheet of DEF Ltd as at 31.3. 2013				Rs Million
	Particulars	Note No.	As at 31.03.13	As at 31.03.12	As at 31.03.11
	EQUITY & LIABILITIES				
1	**Shareholders' funds**				
	(a)Share capital		4225.3	4225.3	4225.3
	(b)Reserves and surplus		139350.5	114256.6	72045.3
	(c)Money received against share warrants				
2	**Share application money pending allotment**				
3	**Non-current liabilities**				
	(a) Long term borrowings	1	86.9	3.9	3.9
	(b) Deferred tax liabilities (net)				
	(c) Other long term liabilities				
	(d) Long-term provisions				
4	**Current liabilities**				
	(a)Short term borrowings				
	(b) Trade payables				
	(c)Other current liabilities		13742.0	12377.8	9478.0
	(d) Short term provisions		1981.3	1235.8	1849.5
	TOTAL		159386.0	132099.4	87602.0
	ASSETS				
1	**Non-current Assets**				
	(a) Fixed Assets				
	(i) Tangible assets	2	41049.2	36372.8	22356.0
	(ii)Intangible assets				
	(iii) Capital work-in-progress		11083.9	5253.4	6349.9
	(iv) Intangible assets under development				
	(b) Non-current investments				
	(c) Deferred tax assets (net)				
	(d) Long term loans & advances				
	(e) Other non-current assets				
2	Current Assets				
	(a) Current investments		69288.7	63324.5	44033
	(b) Inventories		5456.6	5181.0	4992.8
	(c)Trade receivables		1649.4	4436.6	5566.2
	(d) Cash & cash equivalents		27191.5	13627.8	1197.0
	(e) Short-term loan and advances		3666.7	3903.3	3107.1
	(f) Other current assets		0	0	0
	TOTAL		159386	132099.4	87602.0

Notes to Balance Sheet:				
Sl no.	Particulars	As at 31.03.12	As at 31.03.12	As at 31.03.11
1	Long term borrowings			
	Secured loans	83.0	0.0	0
	Unsecured loans	3.9	3.9	3.9
	Total	86.9	3.9	3.9
2	Tangible assets			
	Gross block	58555.1	51219.2	34997.9
	Less: Accumulated depreciation	17505.9	14846.4	12641.9
	Total	41049.2	36372.8	22356.0

	Statement of Profit & Loss of DEF Ltd as at 31.3. 2013				Rs Million
Sl no.	Particulars	Note No.	As at 31.03.13	As at 31.03.12	As at 31.03.11
I	REVENUE FROM OPERATION		56885.1	78954.7	85474.2
II	OTHER INCOME		8320.3	5316.5	1139.5
III	**(TOTAL REVENUE (I + II)**		**65205.4**	**84271.2**	**86613.7**
IV	EXPENSES:				
	(a) Cost of material consumed	1	11055.4	13752.6	9448.5
	(b) Purchase of products for sale				
	(c) Changes in inventories of finished goods,				
	work-in-progress and products for sale				
	(d) Employees cost benefit expenses				
	(e) Finance cost	2	218.8	230.5	284.4
	(f) Depreciation and amortisation expenses	3	2852.7	2205.1	1560.8
	(g) Product development expenses				
	(h) Other expenses		18488.1	11222.3	11779.1
	(i) Expenditure transfer to capital and Other account				
	TOTAL EXPENSES		**32615.0**	**27410.5**	**23072.8**
V	PROFIT BEFORE EXCEPTIONAL AND EXTRA-		32590.4	56860.7	63540.9
	ORDINARY ITEMS AND TAX (III - IV)				
VI	EXCEPTIONAL ITEMS		-1316.2	-3804.9	-1247.6
VII	PROFIT BEFORE EXTRAORDINARY ITEMS AND				
	TAX (V-VI)		33906.6	60665.6	64788.5
VIII	EXTRAORDINARY ITEMS		0	0	0

IX	PROFIT BEFORE TAX AND CONTINUING				
	OPERATIONS (VII - VIII)		33906.6	60665.6	64788.5
X	TAX EXPENSES:				
	(a) Current tax		6630.5	16689.6	20365.3
	(b) Deferred tax				
XI	PROFIT AFTER TAX FOR THE YEAR FROM				
	CONTINUING OPERATION (IX - X)		27276.1	43976	44423.2
XII	Profit / (loss) from discontinuing operations				
XIII	Tax expenses from discontinuing operations				
XIV	Profit / (loss) from discontinuing operations				
	(after tax) (XII-XIII)				
XV	PROFIT/(LOSS) FOR THE PERIOD (XI + XIV)				
	Balance brought forward from previous year				
	Profit available for appropriation:		27276.1	43976.0	44423.2
	Proposed dividend		1690.1	2112.6	2112.6
	Transfer to General Reserve				
	Distribution tax				
	Total				
	Balance carried forward		25586.0	41863.4	42310.6
XVI	Earning per equity share:				
	(1) Basic				
	(2) Diluted				

Notes to Statement of Profit & loss					Rs Million
Sl no.	Particulars		As at 31.03.13	As at 31.03.12	As at 31.03.11
1	**Cost of material consumed**				
	Raw material cost		6525.8	5338.2	2718.2
	Excise		4529.6	8414.4	6730.3
	Total		11055.4	13752.6	9448.5
2	**Finance cost**				
	Interest expenses		218.8	230.5	284.4
	Total		218.8	230.5	284.4
3	**Depreciation and amortisation expenses**				
	Depreciation		2852.7	2205.1	1560.8

	Total		2852.7	2205.1	1560.8
4	**Exceptional items**				
	Other non-recurring income		1316.2	3804.9	1247.6
	Total		1316.2	3804.9	1247.6

Solution

Working Notes					**Rs Million**
Sl no.	Particulars		As at 31.03.13	As at 31.03.12	As at 31.03.11
1	**Operating Profit**				
	Revenue		56885.1	78954.7	85474.2
	Less: Raw material cost		6525.8	5338.2	2718.2
	Excise		4529.6	8414.4	6730.3
	Other expenses		18488.1	11222.3	11779.1
	Total		**27341.6**	**53979.8**	**64246.6**
2	**Gross Profit**				
	Operating profit		27341.6	53979.8	64246.6
	Less: Interest expenses		218.8	230.5	284.4
	Total		27122.8	53749.3	63962.2
3	**Net Profit**				
	Gross Profit		27122.8	53749.3	63962.2
	Add: Other income		8320.3	5316.5	1139.5
	Other non-recurring income		1316.2	3804.9	1247.6
	Less Depreciation		2852.7	2205.1	1560.8
	Tax expenses		6630.5	16689.6	20365.3
	Total		27276.1	43976.0	44423.2
4	**Fixed Assets**				
	Net tangible assets		41049.2	36372.8	22356
	Add: Capital work-in-progress		11083.9	5253.4	6349.9
	Investments		69288.7	63324.5	44033
	Total		121421.8	104950.7	72738.9
5	**Net Worth**				
	Share capital		4225.3	4225.3	4225.3
	Reserves & surplus		139350.5	114256.6	72045.3
	Total		143575.8	118481.9	76270.6

	DuPont Analysis						
Sl no.	Particulars			As at 31.03.1	As at 31.03.12	As at 31.03.11	Remarks

			3			
1	**Margin ratios**					
1.1.	**Operating Profit margin**					
	(Operating profit x 100)/Sales		48.06%	68.37%	75.16%	Operating margin trend has dropped significantly
1.2.	**Interest expenses / sales %**		0.38%	0.29%	0.33%	Remained more or less constant across three years
1.3.	**Gross margin / sales %** (gross profit x 100)/Sales		47.68%	68.08%	74.83%	Gross margin ratio has dropped significantly compare to 2010-11 and 2011-12
1.4	**Net Profit margin** (Net profit x 100)/Sales		47.95%	55.70%	51.97%	Shows an upward trend compared 2010-11 but dropped from previous year
2	**Turnover ratios**					
2.1.	**Fixed Assets turnover** (Sales / Fixed assets)		0.468	0.752	1.175	Shows major decline in the turnover of assets to turnover
2.2.	**Working capital turnover** (Sales / Net current assets)		2.56	5.83	24.18	Shows major decline in the turnover of assets to turnover
2.3.	**Assets turnover ratio** (Sales / total assets)		0.36	0.60	0.98	Shows major decline in the turnover of assets to turnover
3	**Return on assets (ROA)** (Net profit margin x Assets turnover ratio)		17.11%	33.29%	50.71%	Showed significant deterioration over 2010-11 and 2011-12
4	**Equity multiplier** (Sales / Net worth)		0.396	0.666	1.121	Showed significant deterioration over 2010-11 and 2011-12
5	**Return on Equity (ROE)** (ROA X Equity multiplier)		6.78%	22.18%	56.83%	Showed significant deterioration over 2010-11 and 2011-12

Chapter 5. Analysis of changes in income

5.1. Introduction

In general concept of income is defined by different terms like profit, net profit or net income.

In the words of Harry Norris, income is generally conceived to be residue which emerges out of matching expired cost against revenue. Here the definition is given from the standpoint of Income Statement or Statement of Profit and Loss. As per this definition, income is the excess of revenue over expired cost, which signifies benefit of expenses incurred already exhausted.

According to Morton Backer, income is defined as aggregate of value received in exchange of goods and services of an enterprise that results in augmentation of enterprise assets. Here the definition is from the standpoint of Balance Sheet of an enterprise. As per this definition the net income is substantiated by net increase in net assets of the enterprise during an accounting period. The categories of concept of income are enumerated below.

Accounting concept of income	Income is defined as the excess of total revenue earned over expired cost. Here, total revenue includes the revenue earned from operating activities and gains from other incidental activities of the enterprise. Expired cost consists of expenses incurred for generating revenue for the business and losses from other incidental activities of the enterprise. The equation is as under: Accounting Income (I)=Revenue earned from operating activities (R) + Other incidental gains (G) – (Expenses (E) + Other incidental losses (L). Or, $I = (R + G)-(E+L)$ Hence, from the standpoint of accounting concept, income is the excess of revenue earned from operating activities and gains from other incidental activities less the expenses incurred for generating revenue and losses from other incidental activities of the enterprise.
Economic concept of income	From the economic standpoint, income is defined as the maximum amount which a firm can distribute to its owners during a period. As per economic concept, income refers to the net increase in capital of the enterprise during a period. The net increase in capital is the difference between closing capital and opening capital of the enterprise for a period after adjustment of capital consumed and fresh capital introduced during that period. The equation is as under: Economic Income (E) = Consumption of capital during the period (Cc + Capital at the end of the period (C1) – Capital at the beginning of the period (C0) – Fresh capital introduced during the period (Ci) Or, $E = Cc + (C1 – C0) – Ci$ Hence, from the standpoint of economic concept, income is the difference between the capital employed in an enterprise at two points of time. For ascertainment of economic income, opening and closing capital are to be taken at their fair market value and not at historical cost.

In addition to above there are two approaches which are commonly followed for measurement of income. These are:

Transaction approach of income measurement	Revenue earned from operating activities (R) + Other revenue gains (G) – (Expenses (E)+ Other revenue losses (L). Or, I = (R + G)-(E+L)
Balance Sheet approach of Income measurement	Income (I) = Net Assets at the end of the period (NA1) – Net Assets at the beginning of the period (NA0) + Withdrawal of capital during the period (W) – Fresh capital introduced during the period (F) Or, I = NA1 – NA0 + W – F In this approach, the emphasis is on principles of capital maintenance and income is recognised when capital increases.

5.2. Analysis of income

Basic approach in analysis of income is shown in the table below:

	Particulars	Amount
	Net sales	X
Less:	Factory cost of goods sold	X
	Gross Income / Gross Margin / Gross Profit (GP)	X
Less:	Operating expenses	X
	Operating Income	X
Add:	Non-operating incomes and gains	X
Less:	Non-operating expenses and losses	X
	Earnings/Profit before Interest, Depreciation, Amortisation and Tax (EBITDA/PBDIT)	X
Less:	Depreciation	X
	Earnings/Profit before interest and tax (EBIT/PBIT)	X
Less:	Borrowing cost	X
	Earnings before tax (EBT/PBT)	X
Less:	Income tax	X
	Earnings/Profit after tax (EAT / PAT)	X
Less:	Preference Dividend	X
	Earnings / Profit available to equity shareholders (A)	X
	Number of equity shares (B)	X
	Earnings per share (A/B = C)	X

5.3. The factors responsible for changes in income are:

Increase in income / profit	Decrease in income / profit
Increase in sales volume	Decrease in sales volume
Increase in unit selling price	Decrease in unit selling price
Decrease in unit cost price	Increase in unit cost price

5.4. Techniques in income analysis
Techniques applied in analysis of income are appended in the specimen formats below:

5.4.1. Technique for analysis of change in sales

	Amount Rs.
a) Change in sales due to change in quantity (Change in quantity x base year's unit selling price)	x

	Amount Rs.
b) Change in sales due to change in price (Change in unit selling price x base year's quantity)	x
c) Change in sales due to change in quantity and price taken together (Changes in unit selling price x changes in quantity)	x
Total increase in sales	x

5.4.2. Technique for analysis of change in cost

	Amount Rs.
a) Increase in cost due to change in quantity (Change in quantity x base year's unit cost price)	X
b) Increase in cost due to change in cost price (Change in unit cost price x base year's quantity)	X
c) Increase in cost due to increase in quantity and price taken together (Changes in unit cost price x changes in quantity)	x
Total increase in cost	X

5.4.3. Technique for analysis of change in income / profit

	Amount Rs.
Changes in profit due to changes in sales:	
a) Increase in profit due to change in quantity (Change in quantity x base year's unit selling price)	X
b) Decrease in profit due to change in unit selling price (Change in unit selling price x base year's quantity)	X
c) Decrease in profit due to change in quantity and price (Changes in unit selling price x changes in quantity)	x
Total increase in sales(A)	X

	Amount Rs.
Changes in profit due to changes in cost:	
a) Decrease in profit due to change in quantity (Change in quantity x base year's unit cost price	X
b) Decrease in profit due to change in unit cost price (Change in unit cost price x base year's quantity	X
c) Decrease in profit due to change in quantity and price (Changes in unit cost price x changes in quantity)	x
Total increase in cost(B)	X
Total increase in profit (A-B)	X

Case study 5.1.

The comparative information for two years relating to ABC Ltd is as follows:

Year	2011 Amount Rs.	2012 Amount Rs.
Sales (A)	12,00,000	14,62,500
Units sold (B)	4,000	4,500
Sales invoice per unit (A/B)	300	325

Account for the change in sales due to:
   a) Change in quantity
   b) Change in price
   c) Change in quantity and price taken together

Solution

Year	2011 Amount Rs.	2012 Amount Rs.	Changes Rs.
Sales	12,00,000	14,62,500	+262,500
Units sold	4,000	4,500	+500
Sales invoice per unit	300	325	+25

Statement showing account for changes in sales

	Amount Rs.
d) Change in sales due to change in quantity (Change in quantity x base year's unit selling price = (4500 – 4000) x Rs.300	1,50,000
e) Change in sales due to change in price (Change in unit selling price x base year's quantity = (Rs.325 – Rs.300) x 4000	1,00,000
f) Change in sales due to change in quantity and price taken together (Changes in unit selling price x changes in quantity) = (Rs.325 – Rs.300) x (4500 – 4000)	12,500
Total increase in sales	2,62,500

Note: Here, the base year is 2011

Case study 5.2.

Following figures have been extracted from the records of XYZ Ltd is as follows:

Year	2011 Amount Rs.	2012 Amount Rs.
Sales	5,00,000	8,40,000
Units sold	10,000	14,000

Account for the change in sales value due to:
   a) Change in sales quantity
   b) Change in selling price
   c) Change in quantity and price taken together

Solution

Year	2011 Amount Rs.	2012 Amount Rs.	Changes Rs.
Sales (A)	5,00,000	8,40,000	+3,40,000
Units sold (B)	10,000	14,000	+4,000
Sales invoice per unit (A/B)	50	60	+10

Statement showing account for changes in sales

	Amount Rs.
a) Change in sales due to change in quantity (Change in quantity x base year's unit selling price = (14,000 – 10,000) x Rs.50	2,00,000
b) Change in sales due to change in price (Change in unit selling price x base year's quantity = (Rs.60 – Rs.50) x 10,000	1,00,000
c) Change in sales due to change in quantity and price taken together (Changes in unit selling price x changes in quantity) = (Rs.60 – Rs.50) x (14,000 – 10,000)	40,000
Total increase in sales	3,40,000

Note: Here, the base year is 2011

Case study 5.3.
Following figures have been extracted from the records of KBC Ltd is as follows:

Year	2011 Amount Rs.	2012 Amount Rs.
Sales	4,00,000	5,25,000
Units sold	10,000	15,000

Account for the change in sales value due to:
a) Change in sales quantity
b) Change in selling price
c) Change in quantity and price taken together

Solution

Year	2011 Amount Rs.	2012 Amount Rs.	Changes Rs.
Sales (A)	4,00,000	5,25,000	+1,25,000
Units sold (B)	10,000	15,000	+5,000
Sales invoice per unit (A/B)	40	35	-5

Statement showing account for changes in sales

	Amount Rs.
a) Increase in sales due to change in quantity (Change in quantity x base year's unit selling price = (15,000 – 10,000) x Rs.40	2,00,000
b) Decrease in sales due to change in price (Change in unit selling price x base year's quantity = (Rs.35 – Rs.40) x 10,000	(50,000)
c) Decrease in sales due to change in quantity and price taken together (Changes in unit selling price x changes in quantity) = (Rs.35 – Rs.40) x (15,000 – 10,000)	(25,000)
Total increase in sales	1,25,000

Note: Here, the base year is 2011

Case study 5.4.

Following figures have been extracted from the records of KYC Ltd is as follows:

Year	2011 Amount Rs.	2012 Amount Rs.
Cost of goods sold	4,00,000	7,50,000
Units sold	20,000	30,000

Account for the change in cost of goods sold due to:
a) Change in sales quantity
b) Change in cost price
c) Change in quantity and price taken together

Solution

Year	2011 Amount Rs.	2012 Amount Rs.	Changes Rs.
Cost of goods sold	4,00,000	7,50,000	+3,50,000
Units sold	20,000	30,000	+10,000
Sales invoice per unit	20	25	+5

Statement showing account for changes in cost of goods sold

	Amount Rs.
d) Increase in cost due to change in quantity (Change in quantity x base year's unit cost price = (30,000 – 20,000) x Rs.20	2,00,000
e) Increase in cost due to change in cost price (Change in unit cost price x base year's quantity = (Rs.25 – Rs.20) x 20,000	1,00,000
f) Increase in cost due to increase in quantity and price taken together (Changes in unit cost price x changes in quantity) = (Rs.25 – Rs.20) x (30,000 – 20,000)	50,000
Total increase in cost	3,50,000

Note: Here, the base year is 2011

Case study 5.5.
Following figures have been extracted from the records of Zee Ltd is as follows:

Year	2011 Amount Rs.	2012 Amount Rs.
Cost of goods sold	3,60,000	5,60,000
Units sold	12,000	20,000

Account for the change in cost due to:
a) Change in sales quantity
b) Change in cost price
c) Change in quantity and price taken together

Solution

Year	2011 Amount Rs.	2012 Amount Rs.	Changes Rs.
Cost of goods sold	3,60,000	5,60,000	+2,00,000
Units sold	12,000	20,000	+8,000
Sales invoice per unit	30	28	-2

Statement showing account for changes in cost of goods sold

	Amount Rs.
a) Increase in cost due to change in quantity (Change in quantity x base year's unit cost price = (20,000 – 12,000) x Rs.30	2,40,000
b) Decrease in cost due to change in cost price (Change in unit cost price x base year's quantity = (Rs.28 – Rs.30) x 12,000	(24,000)
c) Decrease in cost due to change in quantity and price taken together (Changes in unit cost price x changes in quantity) = (Rs.28 – Rs.30) x (20,000 – 12,000)	(16,000)
Total increase in cost	2,00,000

Note: Here, the base year is 2011

Case study 5.6.
Following figures have been extracted from the records of Klick Ltd is as follows:

Year	2011 Amount Rs.	2012 Amount Rs.
Sales	6,00,000	8,40,000
Cost of goods sold	4,00,000	6,30,000
Units sold	20,000	30,000

Account for the change in profit due to:
a) Change in sales quantity
b) Change in cost price

c) Change in selling price

Solution

Year	2011 Amount Rs.	2012 Amount Rs.	Changes Rs.
Sales (a)	6,00,000	8,40,000	+2,40,000
Cost of goods sold (b)	4,00,000	6,30,000	+2,30,000
Gross Profit (a – b)	200,000	2,10,000	+10,000
Units sold (c)	20,000	30,000	+10,000
Selling price per unit (a/c)	30	28	-2
Cost price per unit (b/c)	20	21	+1

Statement showing account for changes in profit

	Amount Rs.
Changes in profit due to changes in sales:	
d) Increase in profit due to change in quantity (Change in quantity x base year's unit selling price = (30,000 – 20,000) x Rs.30	3,00,000
e) Decrease in profit due to change in unit selling price (Change in unit selling price x base year's quantity = (Rs.28 – Rs.30) x 20,000	(40,000)
f) Decrease in profit due to change in quantity and price (Changes in unit selling price x changes in quantity) = (Rs.28 – Rs.30) x (30,000 – 20,000)	(20,000)
Total increase in sales(A)	2,40,000

	Amount Rs.
Changes in profit due to changes in cost:	
d) Decrease in profit due to change in quantity (Change in quantity x base year's unit cost price = (30,000 – 20,000) x Rs.20	(2,00,000)
e) Decrease in profit due to change in unit cost price (Change in unit cost price x base year's quantity = (Rs.21 – Rs.20) x 20,000	(20,000)
f) Decrease in profit due to change in quantity and price (Changes in unit cost price x changes in quantity) = (Rs.21 – Rs.20) x (30,000 – 20,000)	(10,000)
Total increase in cost(B)	(2,30,000)
Total increase in profit (A-B)	10,000

Note: Here, the base year is 2011

Case study 5.7.

Following figures have been extracted from the records of Blip Ltd is as follows:

Year	2011 Amount Rs.	2012 Amount Rs.
Sales	5,00,000	7,20,000
Cost of goods sold	4,00,000	6,00,000
Gross Profit	1,00,000	1,20,000

It is learnt that sales volume for the year 2012 has increased by 20% over the year 2011. Account for changes in gross profit in the year 2012.

Solution
Let the number of units sold in 2011 be 100.
Then, the number of units sold in 2012 = 100 +20% of 100 = 120

Year	2011 Amount Rs.	2012 Amount Rs.	Changes Rs.
Sales (a)	5,00,000	7,20,000	+2,20,000
Cost of goods sold (b)	4,00,000	6,00,000	+2,00,000
Gross Profit (a – b)	1,00,000	1,20,000	+20,000
Units sold (c)	100	120	+20
Selling price per unit (a/c)	5,000	6,000	+1,000
Cost price per unit (b/c)	4,000	5,000	+1,000

Statement showing account for changes in profit

	Amount Rs.
Changes in profit due to changes in sales:	
a) Increase in profit due to change in quantity (Change in quantity x base year's unit selling price = (120 – 100) x Rs.5000	1,00,000
b) Increase in profit due to change in unit selling price (Change in unit selling price x base year's quantity = (Rs.6000 – 5000) x 100	1,00,000
c) Increase in profit due to change in quantity and price (Changes in unit selling price x changes in quantity) = (Rs.6000 – Rs.5000) x (120 – 100)	20,000
Total increase in sales(A)	2,20,000

	Amount Rs.
Changes in profit due to changes in cost:	
a) Decrease in profit due to change in quantity (Change in quantity x base year's unit cost price = (120 – 100) x Rs.4,000	(80,000)
b) Decrease in profit due to change in unit cost price (Change in unit cost price x base year's quantity = (Rs.5000 – Rs.4000) x 100	(1,00,000)
c) Decrease in profit due to change in quantity and price (Changes in unit cost price x changes in quantity) = (Rs.5000 – Rs.4000) x (120 – 100)	(20,000)
Total increase in cost(B)	(2,00,000)
Total increase in profit (A-B)	20,000

Note: Here, the base year is 2011

Case study 5.8.

Following figures have been extracted from the records of D Ltd is as follows:

Year	2011 Amount Rs.	2012 Amount Rs.
Sales	5,00,000	6,32,500
Cost of goods sold		
Materials	2,50,000	3,30,000
Labour	1,50,000	1,65,000
Variable overheads	30,000	35,200
Fixed Expenses	50,000	60,000
Net Profit	20,000	42,300

It is learnt that sales volume for the year 2012 has increased by 10% over the year 2011. Moreover cost of materials, labour and overhead have gone up by 10% each. Account for changes in net profit in the year 2012.

Solution

Let the number of units sold in 2011 be 100.

Then, the number of units sold in 2012 = 100 +10% of 100 = 110

Year	2011 Amount Rs.	2012 Amount Rs.	Changes Rs.
Sales (a)	5,00,000	6,32,500	+1,32,500
Material cost (b)	2,50,000	3,30,000	+80,000
Labour cost (c)	1,50,000	1,65,000	+15,000
Variable overhead (d)	30,000	35,200	+5,200
Gross Profit (a – b-c-d)=(e)	70,000	1,02,300	+32,300
Fixed Expenses (f)	50,000	60,000	+10,000
Net Profit(e-f)=(g)	20,000	42,300	+22,300
Units sold (h)	100	110	+10
Selling price per unit (a/h)= (i)	5,000	5,750	+750
Material Cost per unit (b/h)= (j)	2,500	3,000	+500
Labour cost per unit (c/h) = (k)	1,500	1,500	0
Variable Overhead cost per unit (d/h) = (l)	300	320	+20

Statement showing account for changes in profit

	Amount Rs.
Changes in profit due to changes in sales:	
d) Increase in profit due to change in quantity (Change in quantity x base year's unit selling price = (110 – 100) x Rs.5000	50,000
e) Increase in profit due to change in unit selling price (Change in unit selling price x base year's quantity = (Rs.5750 – 5000) x 100	75,000
f) Increase in profit due to change in quantity and price (Changes in unit selling price x changes in quantity) = (Rs.5750 – Rs.5000) x (110 – 100)	7,500
Total increase in sales(A)	1,32,500

Changes in profit due to changes in material cost:	
d) Decrease in profit due to change in quantity (Change in quantity x base year's unit cost price = (110 – 100) x Rs.2,500	(25,000)
e) Decrease in profit due to change in unit cost price (Change in unit cost price x base year's quantity = (Rs.3000 – Rs.2500) x 100	(50,000)
f) Decrease in profit due to change in quantity and price (Changes in unit cost price x changes in quantity) = (Rs.3000 – Rs.2500) x (110 – 100)	(5,000)
Total increase in material cost(B)	(80,000)

Changes in profit due to changes in labour cost:	
a) Decrease in profit due to change in quantity (Change in quantity x base year's unit cost price = (110 – 100) x Rs.1,500	(15,000)
b) Decrease in profit due to change in unit cost price (Change in unit cost price x base year's quantity = (Rs.1500 – Rs.1500) x 100	0
c) Decrease in profit due to change in quantity and price (Changes in unit cost price x changes in quantity) = (Rs.1500 – Rs.1500) x (110 – 100)	0
Total increase in labour cost(C)	(15,000)

Changes in profit due to changes in variable overhead cost:	
a) Decrease in profit due to change in quantity (Change in quantity x base year's unit cost price = (110 – 100) x Rs.300	(3,000)
b) Decrease in profit due to change in unit cost price (Change in unit cost price x base year's quantity = (Rs.320 – Rs.300) x 100	(2,000)
c) Decrease in profit due to change in quantity and price (Changes in unit cost price x changes in quantity) = (Rs.320 – Rs.300) x (110 – 100)	(200)
Total increase in variable overhead cost(D)	(5,200)
Net increase in Gross Profit ((A-B-C-D) =E)	32,300
Change in profit owing to change in fixed expenses (60000 – 50000) (F)	(10,000)
Net increase in Net Profit ((E – F)=G)	22,300

Note: Here, the base year is 2011

101

Chapter 6. Distress Analysis

6.1. Meaning

Corporate distress stands for a particular situation in a firm when it is unable to meet its debt. In other words when the value of the total assets of a company is insufficient to discharge its total external liabilities, the said company can be said to be a "distress company".

6.2. Factors contributing to distress analysis

Corporate distress may be the result of any of the following factors:

A.Internal factors	a) Unfavourable liquidity position b) Obsolete production process c) Obsolete product leading to zero market penetration d) Incompetent administrative set-up e) Prohibitive material cost f) Poor production capacity utilisation g) Poor labour productivity h) High labour turnover i) Improper sales strategy j) Defective pricing policy k) Poor supply chain infrastructure l) Lack of quality leadership m) Improper inventory management n) Improper receivables management
B.External factors	a) Non-availability of raw materials b) Shortage of power c) Shortage of water and other utilities d) Imposition of Government price control e) Prohibitive legislation owing to environmental and ecological issues f) Economic unrest g) Political unrest h) High foreign currency fluctuation in case of export houses i) High cost of imported raw materials in cases of currency fluctuations j) Unfavourable import and export policies k) High cost of funds l) Hyper inflation m) Unfavourable taxation policy of the Government n) Natural disaster o) War

All the above reasons may be attributable to lead a corporate distress to potential bankruptcy or insolvency.

6.3. Indicators of corporate distress

It needs to be understood that bankruptcy of an enterprise does not happen in a day. An enterprise goes bankrupt gradually, and in regular day to day operation, certain manifestations and signs will come up which would lead to financial distress and possible bankruptcy.

Following are a list of indicators which manifest financial distress of an enterprise:

Areas	Description
Operating activities	Low production capacity utilisation

	High rate of rejection of output
	Low input output ratio
	High operating cost compared to competition
	High level of obsolescence of machines and manufactured products
	Delay in payment of wages
	High labour turnover
	Declining sales volume
	Accumulation finished goods in the warehouses
	Failure of distribution network
	Defective marketing strategy
Financing activities	Rapidly increasing debts
	Major shortfall of revenues vis-à-vis expenses
	Non-payment of statutory liabilities
	High interest charges to be paid month on month
	Continuous default on interest and repayment of debt
	Non-payment of salaries for multiple months
	Deteriorating liquidity position of the enterprise
	Paying a debt by taking another debt
	Increase in foreign currency debt owing to fluctuation in exchange rate
Financial statements	Delay in year-end closure
	Non-submission of financial information to bankers
	Window dressing in balance sheet
	Utilisation of loans received for long term for short term purposes
	Frequent changes in accounting policies to cook up profit
	Delay in conducting audit
Other factors	Frequent change in leadership
	Non-committal approach of promoters
	Fall in market value of shares

6.4. Distress prediction

Distress prediction is a very essential tool in the field of finance to assess the future probable financial condition of a corporate entity, in order that any impending financial crisis that may crop up in the near future may be detected in advance and actions taken to avert the same.

6.5. Models used for corporate distress prediction

There are various models used for distress prediction used by the corporates, to assess the sustenance and survival of an enterprise in the long run. The types of models are as under:
a) Univariate model   : In this model, a single variable is used for corporate distress prediction
b) Multivariate model: In this model, a number of variables are used for corporate distress prediction.

William H Beaver's study of Univariate Analysis of corporate distress prediction	He used two stages of examination, namely, a) A comparison of mean values of financial ratios taken into consideration of two types of enterprises b) Examination of predictive power of financial ratio with the help of Dichotomous Classification test. The steps are as under:

	1) Select at random two types of firms .i.e. failed firms and non-failed firms 2) A single uniform ratio (e.g. current ratio, debt-equity ratio, or operating cost to sales ratio) is calculated 3) Firms are arranged in descending order of the value of ratio as calculated in (2) above 4) A simple average of two consecutive ratios at every stage as arranged in (3) above is calculated (called the cut-off point) 5) Now the ratio of every firm as calculated in (2) above is compared with (4) above at every stage. For example, in case of total debts to total assets ratio, if the actual ratio of a firm is lower than the respective cut-off point, the condition of the firm is predicted as non-failed firm. Conversely, if the actual ratio is higher than the respective cut-off point, the condition is predicted as a failed firm. Similarly in the case of current ratio, if the actual ratio of a firm is higher than the respective cut-off point, the condition of the firm is predicted as non-failed firm. Conversely, if the actual ratio is lower than the respective cut-off point, the condition is predicted as a failed firm. 6) If any deviation of such prediction from the actual position of the firm is observed, then such deviation is counted as an error. 7) Determine the optimum cut-off point where the number of total errors is minimum 8) Determine the percentage of error included in total prediction
Edward I Altman's study of Multivariate Analysis	A multivariate model was discovered on the basis of Multiple Discriminant Analysis (MDA). Out of the 22 accounting ratios he selected 5 of them to measure: a) Liquidity position of the firms b) Reinvestment of earnings of the firms c) Profitability of the firms d) Financial leverage of the firms e) Sales generating ability of firm's assets. Based on this , he came up with an equation as under: $Z = 1.2X1 + 1.4X2 + 3.3X3 + 0.6X4 + 1.0 X5$ Where, Z = Overall index of multiple index function and the five variables are: X1 = Working capital to total assets (a liquidity measure) X2= Retained earnings to total assets (a measure of reinvestment of earnings) X3 = EBIT to total assets (a profitability measure) X4 = Market value of equity & preference to book value of total Debt (a measure of leverage)

X5 = Sales to total assets (a measure of sales-generating ability of the firms' assets.

If the calculated value of Z score is lower than 1.81, it is predicted that the enterprise is a failed or bankrupt entity.

If the calculated value of Z score is higher than 2.99, it is predicted that the enterprise is a non-failed or non-bankrupt entity.

If the Z score falls between 1.81 and 2.99, which is referred to as the grey area, it is predicted that the enterprise consists of both bankrupt and non-bankrupt elements and therefore requires further investigation to determine its solvency status.

Case study 6.1.

From the information given below relating to Spurious Ltd, calculate Altman's Z score and comment:

Working capital / total assets = 25%
Retained earnings / total assets = 30%
Earnings before interest and taxes / total assets = 15%
Market value of equity / book value of total debt = 150%
Sales / Total assets = 2%

Solution
As per Altman's Model (1968) of Corporate Distress Prediction
Z = 1.2X1 + 1.4 X2 + 3.3 X3 + 0.6 X4 +1.0X5
Here the five variables are as under:

Working capital / total assets = 25%	= X1
Retained earnings / total assets = 30%	= X2
Earnings before interest and taxes / total assets = 15%	= X3
Market value of equity / book value of total debt = 150%	= X4
Sales / Total assets = 2%	= X5

Transposing the values in the formula:
$Z = (1.2 \times 25\%) + (1.4 \times 30\%) +(3.3 \times 15\%) + (0.6 \times 150\%) + (1.0 \times 2\%)$
$Z = 0.30 + 0.42 + 0.495 + 0.90 + 0.02$
$Z = 2.135$

Conclusion:
The calculated value of Z score lies between 1.81 and 2.99, which is marked as Grey Area. It is predicted that the company consists of both bankrupt and non-bankrupt elements (i.e. combination of failed and non-failed elements) and therefore, requires further investigation to determine its status of solvency.

Case study 6.2.

From the information given below relating to Glorious Ltd, calculate Altman's Z score and comment:

Working capital / total assets = 45%
Retained earnings / total assets = 25%
Earnings before interest and taxes / total assets = 30%
Market value of equity / book value of total debt = 250%
Sales / Total assets = 3 times

Solution

As per Altman's Model (1968) of Corporate Distress Prediction

Z = 1.2X1 + 1.4 X2 + 3.3 X3 + 0.6 X4 +1.0X5

Here the five variables are as under:

Working capital / total assets = 45%	= X1
Retained earnings / total assets = 25%	= X2
Earnings before interest and taxes / total assets = 30%	= X3
Market value of equity / book value of total debt = 250%	= X4
Sales / Total assets = 3 times	= X5

Transposing the values in the formula:

$Z = (1.2 \times 45\%) + (1.4 \times 25\%) + (3.3 \times 30\%) + (0.6 \times 250\%) + (1.0 \times 3)$

$Z = 0.54 + 0.35 + 0.99 + 1.50 + 3$

$Z = 6.38$

Conclusion:

The calculated value of Z score lies much higher than 2.99. It is predicted with assurance that the company is a non-bankrupt and non-failed company.

Case study 6.3.

From the information given below relating to Perilous Ltd, calculate Altman's Z score and comment:

Working capital / total assets = 25%

Retained earnings / total assets = 5%

Earnings before interest and taxes / total assets = 10%

Market value of equity / book value of total debt = 50%

Sales / Total assets = 1.5 times

Solution

As per Altman's Model (1968) of Corporate Distress Prediction

Z = 1.2X1 + 1.4 X2 + 3.3 X3 + 0.6 X4 +1.0X5

Here the five variables are as under:

Working capital / total assets = 25%	= X1
Retained earnings / total assets = 5%	= X2
Earnings before interest and taxes / total assets = 10%	= X3
Market value of equity / book value of total debt = 30%	= X4
Sales / Total assets = 0.75 times	= X5

Tranposing the values in the formula:

$Z = (1.2 \times 25\%) + (1.4 \times 5\%) + (3.3 \times 10\%) + (0.6 \times 30\%) + (1.0 \times 1.5)$

$Z = 0.30 + 0.07 + 0.33 + 0.18 + 0.75$

$Z = 1.68$

Conclusion:

The calculated value of Z score lies much lower than 1.81. It can be predicted that the company is a bankrupt and failed company.

Case study 6.4.

From the information given below relating to Calculus Ltd, calculate Altman's Z score and comment after calculating the following ratios:

Working capital / total assets

Retained earnings / total assets

Earnings before interest and taxes / total assets

Market value of equity / book value of total debt

Sales / Total assets

Balance Sheet of Calculus Ltd as on 31.3.2013

SR.NO.	Particulars	Amount Rs lakhs
1	Capital 3,99,000 shares of Rs.10 each	39.90
2	Reserves	317.98
3	Accumulated losses if any	-
4	Net Worth	357.88
5	Term Loans	240.15
6	Deferred Payment Liabilities	-
7	Working Capital Borrowings	-
8	Capital employed	598.03
9	Gross Block	179.26
10	Depreciation	15.96
11	Net Block	163.30
12	Investments	434.47
13	Other non-current assets	-
14	Current Assets	1,289.31
15	Current Liability	1,289.05
16	Net working capital	0.26
17	Capital employed	598.03

Market value of the shares is Rs.15

Statement of Profit & Loss of Calculus Ltd as on 31.3.2013

Particulars	Amount Rs lakhs
Income	1447.44
Expenses	1416.45
Operating Profit (PBIDT)	30.99
Depreciation	15.96
EBIT	15.03
Tax	4.62
Net Profit (PAT)	10.41

Solution

Calculation of the following ratios:

Ratios	Results	
Working capital / total assets	0.26/1887.08 = 0.000138	X1
Retained earnings / total assets	10.41 / 1887.08 = 0.00055	X2
Earnings before interest and taxes / total assets	15.03 / 1887.08 = 0.00796	X3
Market value of equity / book value of total debt	(Rs.15 x 399000) / 240.15 = 59.85 / 240.15 = 0.2492	X4
Sales / Total assets	1447.44 / 1887.08 = 0.7670	X5

As per Altman's Model (1968) of Corporate Distress Prediction

$Z = 1.2X1 + 1.4 X2 + 3.3 X3 + 0.6 X4 + 1.0X5$

Transposing the variables into the formula, we can see the following:

$Z = (1.2 \times 0.000138) + (1.4 \times 0.00055) + (3.3 \times 0.00796) + (0.6 \times 0.2492) + (1.0 \times 0.7670)$

= 0.0001656+0.00077+0.0263+0.1495+0.767

= 0.9438

The calculated value of Z score lies much lower than 1.81. It can be predicted that the company is a bankrupt and failed company.

Case study 6.5.

From the information provided relating to a company, calculate Altman's Z score and comment on the financial condition of the company:

Particulars	Rs
Equity share capital of Rs.10 each fully paid up	2,00,000
12% preference share capital of Rs.100 each	1,00,000
Fixed Assets	3,00,000
Current Assets	2,00,000
Fictitious assets	25,000
Current liabilities	1,00,000
10% debentures	2,00,000
General reserve	75,000
Profit & Loss A/c (Cr)	50,000
Sales	10,00,000
Earnings before tax	1,30,000
Interest on debentures	20,000
Market value of each equity share	15
Market value of each preference share	150

Solution

Working Notes

1. Calculation of working capital:
   Current Assets – Current Liabilities
   Rs.2, 00, 000 – Rs. 1, 00,000 = 1, 00,000

2. Calculation of Total Assets:
   Total assets = Fixed Assets + Current Assets
   $$= Rs.3, 00,000 + Rs.2, 00,000$$
   $$= Rs.5, 00,000$$

3. Calculation of retained earnings:
   =Retained earnings = Reserves & surplus – Miscellaneous expenditure
   =General reserve + Profit & Loss (cr) – Fictitious assets
   =Rs.75000 + 50,000 – 25,000
   =Rs.1, 00,000

4. Calculation of Earnings before Interest & Tax (EBIT)
   EBIT = EBT + Interest on debentures
   $$= Rs.1, 30,000 + Rs.20, 000$$
   $$= Rs.1, 50,000$$

5. Calculation of Market value of Equity & Preference shares
   = Market value of equity shares + Market value of preference shares
   = (20,000 shares x Rs.15) + (1000 shares x Rs.150)
   = Rs.3, 00, 000 + Rs.1, 50,000
   = Rs.4, 50,000

6. Calculation of book value of total debts
   Book value of total debts
   = Long term debts + current liabilities
   = 10% debentures + Current liabilities
   =Rs.2, 00,000 + Rs.1, 00,000
   = Rs.3, 00,000

Ratios	Results	
Working capital / total assets (1 / 2)	1,00,000/5,00,000 = 0.20	X1
Retained earnings / total assets (3 / 2)	1,00,000 / 5,00,000 = 0.20	X2
Earnings before interest and taxes / total assets (4 / 2)	1,50,000 / 5,00,000 = 0.30	X3
Market value of equity / book value of total debt (5 /6)	4,50,000 / 3,00,000 = 1.50	X4
Sales / Total assets (Sales / 6)	10,00,000 / 5,00,000 = 2.0	X5

As per Altman's Model (1968) of Corporate Distress Prediction
Z = 1.2X1 + 1.4 X2 + 3.3 X3 + 0.6 X4 +1.0X5

Transposing the variables into the formula, we can see the following:
Z = (1.2 X 0.20) + (1.4 X 0.20) + (3.3 X 0.30) + (0.6 X 1.5) + (1.0 x 2.0)
   = 0.24+0.28+0.99+0.90+2.0

= 4.41

The calculated value of Z score lies much higher than 2.99. It can be strongly predicted that the company is a non-bankrupt and non-failed company.

Case study 6.6.

Balance Sheet of Quatro Ltd as on 31st March 2012

Liabilities		Amount Rs in crores	Assets	Amount Rs in crores
Equity shares		20.80	Fixed Assets	105.60
Long term liabilities		104.00	Current Assets	57.60
Current liabilities		78.40	Profit & Loss A/c	40.00
	Total	203.20		203.20
			Total	

Additional information:
1. Depreciation written off Rs.8 crores
2. Preliminary expenses written off Rs.1.60 crores
3. Net loss Rs.25.60 crores

Ascertain the stage of sickness.

Solution

The Corporate Distress Prediction prescribed by the NCAER study talks about following three parameters predicting the stage of corporate sickness:
1. Cash profit position (a profitability measure)
2. Net working capital position (a liquidity measure)
3. Net worth position (a solvency measure)

In the instant case, the above parameters are calculated as under:

$$\textbf{1. Cash profit} = \text{Net Profit} + \frac{\text{Non-cash expenses}}{\text{Losses debited to Profit \& Loss A/c}} - \frac{\text{Non-cash incomes}}{\text{Gains credited to Profit \& Loss A/c}}$$

Transposing the values

= Net Profit + Depreciation written off + Preliminary expenses written off

= (Rs.25.60 crores) + (Rs.8 crores) + (Rs.1.60 crores)

= **(Rs.16 crores)**

2. Net working capital = Current Assets – Current liabilities

= (Rs.57.60 crores – Rs.78.40 crores)

= **(Rs.20.80 crores)**

3. Net worth = Share capital + Reserves & surplus – Miscellaneous Expenditure – Profit & Loss A/c

In the current case, net worth = equity share capital – Profit & Loss A/c (Dr)

= (Rs.20.80 crores – Rs.40.00 crores)

= **(Rs.19.20 crores)**

Conclusion:

According to NCAER Research Study, out of above mentioned three parameters, if any one of the parameters becomes negative in case of an enterprise, it can be predicted that the enterprise has a tendency towards sickness. In the present case, all the three parameters as calculated in 1, 2 and 3 above, are negative in value. Hence, it can be strongly predicted that the company has become a sick company and the stage of sickness is "fully sick". Accordingly, immediate revival measures are required to revive the enterprise.

Case study 6.7.

The following information is revealed from the Balance Sheet of Queen Ltd as on 31st March 2013:

Equity shares	: Rs.22.90 crores
Reserve & surplus	: Rs.10.30 crores
Long term liabilities	: Rs.95.60 crores
Current liabilities	: Rs.77.60 crores
Fixed Assets	: Rs.108.90 crores
Current Assets	: Rs. 49.80 crores
Profit & Loss (Dr)	: Rs. 47.70 crores
Depreciation written off	: Rs.8.60 crores
Preliminary expenses written off	: Rs.2.80 crores
Net loss	: (Rs.23.70 crores)

Ascertain the stage of sickness.

Solution

The Corporate Distress Prediction prescribed by the NCAER study talks about following three parameters predicting the stage of corporate sickness:

1. Cash profit position (a profitability measure)
2. Net working capital position (a liquidity measure)
3. Net worth position (a solvency measure)

In the instant case, the above parameters are calculated as under:

$$\text{1. Cash profit} = \text{Net Profit} + \frac{\text{Non-cash expenses}}{\text{Losses debited to Profit \& Loss A/c}} - \frac{\text{Non-cash incomes}}{\text{Gains credited to Profit \& Loss A/c}}$$

Transposing the values

= Net Profit + Depreciation written off + Preliminary expenses written off

= (Rs.23.70 crores) + (Rs.8.60 crores) + (Rs.2.80 crores)

= **(Rs.12.30 crores)**

2. Net working capital = Current Assets – Current liabilities

= (Rs.49.80 crores – Rs.77.60 crores)

= **(Rs.27.80 crores)**

3. Net worth = Share capital + Reserves & surplus – Miscellaneous Expenditure – Profit & Loss A/c

In the current case, net worth = equity share capital – Profit & Loss A/c (Dr)

= (Rs.22.90 crores +Rs.10.30 crores – Rs.47.70 crores)

= **(Rs.14.50 crores)**

Conclusion:

According to NCAER Research Study, out of above mentioned three parameters, if any one of the parameters becomes negative in case of an enterprise, it can be predicted that the enterprise has a tendency towards sickness. In the present case, all the three parameters as calculated in 1, 2 and 3 above, are negative in value. Hence, it can be strongly predicted that the company has become a sick company and the stage of sickness is "fully sick". Accordingly, immediate revival measures are required to revive the enterprise.

Chapter 7: Management Reporting

7.1. Report summary

Reporting is an important part of any accounting software. A user shall have access to some pre-defined reports (MIS, Management reports, etc.) and he can also create his customized reports. Users can create customized reports at any level, i.e., ledger, groups, transactions, party, period, etc.

7.2. Financial Reporting

Reporting formats shall be provided of following pre-defined reports and MIS:

a) Draft Tax Audit Reports and Annexures
b) Draft GST audit Report
c) Management report (as listed below)
d) Purchase Register
e) Customer ageing report
f) Vendor ageing report
g) Sales Register
h) Profitability Analysis by product, by channel, by location and by business vertical,
i) Ratio Analysis
j) Balance Sheet (Vertical and Horizontal)
k) Projected Balance sheet
l) Profit & Loss Account (Vertical and Horizontal)
m) Comparative monthly / Quarterly Profit and Loss and Balance Sheet
n) Trial Balance
o) Comparative Ratio Analysis
p) Cash flow summary – both direct and indirect
q) Schedule of Gross block, depreciation calculation and net block
r) Schedule of depreciation calculation by asset class –under Income Tax Act
s) Exception Reports (Negative balances, opposite balances, etc.)
t) Statutory Reports (PF Forms, GST Forms, etc.)
u) Overdue payments
v) Tax computation summary
w) Deferred tax asset / liability computation
x) Bank Reconciliation Statement
y) Other Reconciliation Statements
z) Taxes payment register
aa) Open purchase order report
bb) Open Sales order report

7.3. Financial Reporting

7.3.1. Balance Sheet: (Schedule III – Part I)

Specimen Balance Sheet format as detailed in Schedule III – Part I is reproduced below.

Name of Company............
Balance Sheet as at...........

Particulars	Note no.	Figures as at the end of current reporting period	Figures as at the end of previous reporting period
1	2	3	4
I. Equity and Liabilities			
(1)Shareholders' funds			
a) Share capital			
b) Reserve and surplus			
c) Money received against share warrants			
(2)Share application money pending allotment			
(3)Non-current liabilities			
a) Long term borrowings			
b) Deferred tax liabilities (net)			
c) Other long term liabilities and			
d) Long term provisions and			
(4)Current liabilities which covers			
a) Short term borrowings			
b) Trade payables			
c) Other current liabilities			
d) Short term provisions			
TOTAL			
II. Assets			
Non-current assets			
(I)(a) Fixed Assets			
(i) Tangible assets,			
(ii) Intangible assets,			
(iii) capital work-in-progress			
(iv)Intangibles under development			
(b) Non-current investments			
(c) Deferred tax assets (net)			
(d) Long term loans and advances and			
(e) other non-current assets and			
(2)Current assets			
(a) Current investments			
(b) Inventories			
(c) Trade receivables			
(d) Cash and cash equivalents			

(e) Short term loans and advances and			
(f) Other current assets			
TOTAL			

The format above is followed by General Instructions for preparation of Balance Sheet in Schedule III, which is summarised as under:

1.An asset shall be classified as current when it satisfies any of the following criteria:
   a) It is expected to be realized in, or is intended for sale of consumption in the company's normal operating cycle;
   b) It is held primarily for the purpose of being traded;
   c) It is expected to be realized within twelve months after the reporting date ; or
   d) It is cash or cash equivalent unless it is restricted from being exchanged or used to settle a liability for at least twelve months after the reporting date.
   All other assets shall be classified as non-current.

2. An operating cycle is the time between the acquisition of assets for processing and their realization in cash or cash equivalents. Where the normal operating cycle cannot be identified. It is assumed to have a duration of 12 months.

3. A liability shall be classified as current when it satisfies any of the following criteria
   (a) It is expected to be settled in the company's normal operating cycle
   (b) It is held primarily for the purpose of being traded
   (c) it is due to be settled within twelve months after the reporting date or
   (d) The company does not have an unconditional right to defer settlement of the liability for at least 12 months after the reporting date. The terms of a liability , that could , at the option of counter-party result in its settlement by the issue of equity instruments do not affect its classification
   All other liabilities shall be classified as non-current.

4. A receivable shall be classified as a "trade receivable" if it is in respect of the amount due on account of goods sold or services rendered in the normal course of business

5. A payable shall be classified as a "trade payable" If it is in respect of the amount due on account of goods purchased or services received in the normal course of business.
6. A company shall disclose the following in the notes to accounts

7.3.2. Statement of profit & loss: (Schedule III – Part II)

Specimen format of Statement of Profit & Loss as detailed in Schedule III – Part II is reproduced below.

Name of Company............
Profit & Loss statement for the year ended ....

S/No	Particulars	Note no.	Figures as at the end of current reporting period	Figures as at the end of previous reporting period
1	2	3		
I	REVENUE FROM OPERATION			
II	OTHER INCOME			
III	**(TOTAL REVENUE (I + II)**			
IV	EXPENSES:			
	(a) Cost of material consumed			
	(b) Purchase of stock-in-trade			
	(c) Changes in inventories of finished goods,			
	work-in-progress and stock-in-trade			
	(d) Employees benefit expenses			
	(e) Finance cost			
	(f) Depreciation and amortisation expenses			
	(h) Other expenses			
	TOTAL EXPENSES			
V	PROFIT BEFORE EXCEPTIONAL AND EXTRA-			
	ORDINARY ITEMS AND TAX (III - IV)			
VI	EXCEPTIONAL ITEMS			
VII	PROFIT BEFORE EXTRAORDINARY ITEMS AND			
	TAX (V-VI)			
VIII	EXTRAORDINARY ITEMS			
IX	PROFIT BEFORE TAX (VII - VIII)			
X	TAX EXPENSES:			
	(a) Current tax			
	(b) Deferred tax			
XI	PROFIT/(LOSS) FOR THE PERIOD FROM			
	CONTINUING OPERATIONS (IX - X)			
XII	Profit / (loss) from discontinuing operations			
XIII	Tax expenses from discontinuing operations			
XIV	Profit / (loss) from discontinuing operations			
	(after tax) (XII-XIII)			
XV	PROFIT/(LOSS) FOR THE PERIOD (XI + XIV)			

XVI	Earning per equity share:			
	(1) Basic			
	(2) Diluted			

The format above is followed by General Instructions for preparation of Statement of Profit & Loss in Schedule III. These are summarised as under:

1. The provisions of this Part shall apply to the Income and expenditure account referred to in sub-section (2) of Section 210 of the Act, in like manner as they apply to a statement of profit and loss.

2. Revenue from operations

(A) In respect of a company other than a finance company revenue from operations shall disclose separately in the notes revenue from

      (a) Sale of products ;

      (b) Sale of services ;

      (c) Other operating revenues ;

      (d) Less: excise duty

(B) In respect of a finance company, revenue from operations shall include revenue from:

      (a)Interest

      (b)Other financial services

Revenue from each of the above heads shall be disclosed separately by way of Notes to Accounts to the extent applicable.

7.3.3. Amendments to schedule III of the Companies Act 2013 incorporating financial reporting requirements under Indian Accounting Standards (Ind AS)

Central Government has made the following amendments to schedule III of the said Act as under:-

1. In Schedule III, before the heading General instructions for preparation of Balance Sheet and Statements of Profit and Loss of a Company the following shall be inserted:

Division I

Financial Statements for a company whose Financial Statements are required to comply with the Companies (Accounting Standards) Rules, 2006.

2. In Schedule III, the following shall be inserted after the end of para 4 under the heading General instructions for the preparation of consolidated financial statements:

Division II

Financial Statements for a company whose financial statements are drawn up in compliance of Companies (Indian Accounting Standards) Rules, 2015 and as amended from time to time.

GENERAL INSTRUCTIONS FOR PREPARATION OF FINANCIAL STATEMENTS OF A COMPANY required to comply with Ind AS.

7.3.3.1. PART I –BALANCE SHEET

Name of the Company.........................

Balance Sheet as at ....

(Rupees in............)

		Particulars	Note no.	Figures as at the end of current reporting period	Figures as at the end of the previous reporting period

	1	2	3	4
	ASSETS			
(1)	**Non-current assets**			
	(a) Property, Plant and Equipment			
	(b) Capital work-in-progress			
	(c) Investment Property			
	(d) Goodwill			
	(e) Other Intangible assets			
	(f) Intangible assets under development			
	(g) Biological Assets other than bearer plants			
	(h) Financial Assets			
	(i) Investments			
	(ii) Trade receivables			
	(iii) Loans			
	(iv) Others (to be specified)			
	(i) Deferred tax assets (net)			
	(j) Other non-current assets			
(2)	**Current assets**			
	(a) Inventories			
	(b) Financial Assets			
	(i) Investments			
	(ii) Trade receivables			
	(iii) Cash and cash equivalents			
	(iv) Bank balances other than (iii) above			
	(v) Loans			
	(vi) Others (to be specified)			
	(c) Current Tax Assets (Net)			
	(d) Other current assets			
	Total assets			
	Equity and Liabilities			
	Equity			
	(a) Equity Share capital			
	(b) Other Equity			
	LIABILITIES			
(1)	**Non-current liabilities**			
	(a) Financial Liabilities			
	(i) Borrowings			
	(ii) Trade payables			
	(iii) Other financial liabilities (other than those specified in (b) below, to be specified)			
	(b) Provisions			
	(c) Deferred tax liabilities (Net)			
	(d) Other non-current liabilities			
(2)	**Current liabilities**			
	(a) Financial Liabilities			

(i) Borrowings (ii) Trade payables (iii) Other financial liabilities (other than those specified in (c) below)			
(b) Other current liabilities (c) Provisions (d) Current Tax Liabilities (Net) **Total equity and liabilities**			

See accompanying notes to the financial statements

7.3.3.2. STATEMENT OF CHANGES IN EQUITY

Name of the Company.........................
Statement of Changes in Equity for the period ended ....
(Rupees in..................)

a) Equity share capital

Balance at the beginning of the reporting period	Changes in equity share capital during the year	Balance at the end of the reporting period

b. Other Equity

	Share application money pending allotment	Equity component of compound financial instruments	Reserves & surplus- Capital Reserve	Reserves & surplus- Securities premium reserve	Reserves & surplus- Other reserves (specify nature)	Reserves & surplus- Retained earnings	Other comprehensive Income- Debt instruments through Other Comprehensive Income	Other comprehensive Income- Equity instruments through Other Comprehensive Income	Other comprehensive Income- Effective portion of Cash Flow Hedges	Other comprehensive Income- Revaluation Surplus	Other comprehensive Income- Exchange differences on translating the financial statements of a foreign operation	Other comprehensive Income- Other items of other comprehensive income (specify nature)	Money received against share warrants	TOTAL
Balance at the beginning of the reporting period														
Changes in accounting policy/prior period errors														
Restated balance at the beginning of the reporting period														
Total Comprehensive Income for the year														
Dividends														
Transfer to retained earnings														
Any other change (to be specified)														
Balance at the end of the reporting period														

Note: Remeasurment of net defined benefit plans, fair value changes relating to own credit risk and share of Other Comprehensive Income in Associates and Joint Ventures shall be recognised as a part of retained earnings with separate disclosure of such items along with the relevant amounts in the Notes.

Notes
GENERAL INSTRUCTIONS FOR PREPARATION OF BALANCE SHEET
1. An entity shall classify an asset as current when:
   (a) it expects to realise the asset, or intends to sell or consume it, in its normal operating cycle;
   (b) it holds the asset primarily for the purpose of trading;
   (c) it expects to realise the asset within twelve months after the reporting period; or
   (d) the asset is cash or a cash equivalent unless the asset is restricted from being exchanged or used to settle a liability for at least twelve months after the reporting period.

An entity shall classify all other assets as non-current.

2. The operating cycle of an entity is the time between the acquisition of assets for processing and their realisation in cash or cash equivalents. When the entity's normal operating cycle is not clearly identifiable, it is assumed to be twelve months.

3. An entity shall classify a liability as current when:
   (a) it expects to settle the liability in its normal operating cycle;
   (b) it holds the liability primarily for the purpose of trading;
   (c) the liability is due to be settled within twelve months after the reporting period; or
   (d) it does not have an unconditional right to defer settlement of the liability for at least twelve months after the reporting period. Terms of a liability that could, at the option of the counterparty, result in its settlement by the issue of equity instruments do not affect its classification.

An entity shall classify all other liabilities as non-current.

4. A receivable shall be classified as a 'trade receivable' if it is in respect of the amount due on account of goods sold or services rendered in the normal course of business.

5. A payable shall be classified as a 'trade payable' if it is in respect of the amount due on account of goods purchased or services received in the normal course of business.

7.3.3.3. PART II – STATEMENT OF PROFIT AND LOSS

Name of the Company..........................
Statement of Profit and Loss for the period ended ....
(Rupees in............)

S/No	Particulars	Note no.	Figures for the current reporting period	Figures for the previous reporting period
1	2	3		
I	Revenue from Operations			
II	Other Income			
III	**Total Income** **(I + II)**			
IV	EXPENSES:			
	Cost of material consumed			
	Purchases of stock-in-trade			
	Changes in inventories of finished goods, stock-in-trade and work-in-progress			
	Employees benefit expenses			
	Finance cost			
	Depreciation and amortisation			

	expenses			
	Other expenses			
	Total expenses (IV)			
V	Profit/(loss) before exceptional items and tax (I- IV)			
VI	Exceptional items			
VII	Profit/(loss) before tax (V-VI)			
VIII	Tax expenses:			
	(a) Current tax			
	(b) Deferred tax			
IX	Profit (Loss) for the period from continuing operations (VII-VIII)			
X	Profit / (loss) from discontinued operations			
XI	Tax expenses from discontinued operations			
XII	Profit / (loss) from discontinued operations (X-XI)			
XIII	Profit/(loss) for the period (IX+XII)			
XIV	Other Comprehensive Income A (i) Items that will not be reclassified to profit or loss (ii) Income tax relating to items that will not be reclassified to profit or loss B (i) Items that will be reclassified to profit or loss (ii) Income tax relating to items that will be reclassified to profit or loss			
XV	Total Comprehensive Income for the period (XIII+XIV)(Comprising Profit (Loss) and Other Comprehensive Income for the period)			
XVI	Earning per equity share (for continuing operations): (1) Basic (2) Diluted			
XVII	Earning per equity share (for discontinued operations): (1) Basic (2) Diluted			
XVIII	Earnings per equity share(for discontinued & continuing operations) (1) Basic (2) Diluted			

See accompanying notes to the financial statements

7.3.4. Preparation of consolidated Financial Statements

According to Schedule III, where a company is required to prepare Consolidated Financial Statements i.e. consolidated balance sheet and consolidated statement of profit and loss, the company shall *mutatis mutandis* follow the requirements of this Schedule as applicable to a company in the preparation of balance sheet and statement of profit & loss. In addition, the consolidated financial statements shall disclose the information as per the requirements specified in the applicable Accounting Standards including the following:

(i)   Profit & Loss attributable to "minority interest" and to owners of the parent in the statement of profit & loss shall be presented as allocation for the period.

(ii)   "Minority interests" in the balance sheet within equity shall be presented separately from the equity of the owners of the parent.

In the consolidated financial statements, the following shall be disclosed by way of additional information:

	Net Assets, i.e. total assets minus total liabilities		Share in profit or loss	
Name of the entity in the	As % of consolidated net assets	Amount	As % of consolidated profit or loss	Amount
(1)	(2)	(3)	(4)	(5)
Parent Subsidiaries Indian 1. 2. 3.				
	Net Assets, i.e. total assets minus total liabilities		Share in profit or loss	
Name of the entity in the	As % of consolidated net assets	Amount	As % of consolidated profit or loss	Amount
(1)	(2)	(3)	(4)	(5)
Foreign 1. 2. 3.				
Minority Interests in all subsidiaries				

Associates (Investment as per the equity method) Indian 1. 2. 3. Foreign 1. 2. 3.				
Joint Ventures (as per proportionate consolidation / investment as per the equity method) Indian 1. 2. 3. Foreign 1. 2. 3.				
TOTAL				

All subsidiaries, associates and joint ventures (whether Indian or foreign) will be covered under consolidated financial statements.

All entity shall disclose the list of subsidiaries or associates or joint ventures which have not been consolidated in the consolidated financial statements along with the reasons of not consolidating.

It needs to be clarified that, the requirement of attaching the Balance Sheet, Profit & Loss account, report of Board of Directors, Auditors Report, statement of the Holding Company's interest in the subsidiary and other reports as was required under section 212 of the Companies Act 1956 has been dispensed with.

7.3.5. Amendments to schedule III of the Companies Act 2013 incorporating financial reporting requirements under Indian Accounting Standards (Ind AS)

PART III- GENERAL INSTRUCTIONS FOR THE PREPARATION OF CONSOLIDATED FINANCIAL STATEMENTS
1. Where a company is required to prepare Consolidated Financial Statements, i.e., consolidated balance sheet, consolidated statement of changes in equity and consolidated statement of profit and loss, the company shall *mutatis mutandis* follow the requirements of this Schedule as applicable to a company in the preparation of balance sheet, statement of changes in equity and statement of profit and loss. In addition, the consolidated financial statements shall disclose the information as per the requirements specified in the applicable

Indian Accounting Standards notified under the Companies (Indian Accounting Standards) Rules 2015, including the following:

(i) Profit or loss attributable to 'non-controlling interest' and to 'owners of the parent' in the statement of profit and loss shall be presented as allocation for the period. Further, 'total comprehensive income' for the period attributable to 'non-controlling interest' and to 'owners of the parent' shall be presented in the statement of profit and loss as allocation for the period. The aforesaid disclosures for 'total comprehensive income' shall also be made in the statement of changes in equity. In addition to the disclosure requirements in the Indian Accounting Standards, the aforesaid disclosures shall also be made in respect of 'other comprehensive income'.

(ii) 'Non-controlling interests' in the Balance Sheet and in the Statement of Changes in Equity, within equity, shall be presented separately from the equity of the 'owners of the parent'.

(iii) Investments accounted for using the equity method.

Name of the entity in the group	Net Assets, i.e. total assets minus total liabilities		Share in profit or loss		Share in other comprehensive income		Share in total comprehensive income	
	As % of consolidated net assets	Amount	As % of consolidated profit or loss	Amount	As % of consolidated other comprehensive income	Amount	As % of total comprehensive income	Amount
Parent Subsidiaries Indian 1. 2. 3. Foreign 1. 2. 3.								
Non-controlling Interests in all subsidiaries								
Associates (Investment as per the equity method) Indian 1. 2. 3. Foreign 1. 2. 3.								
Joint Ventures (as per proportionate consolidation / investment as per the equity method) Indian 1. 2. 3. Foreign 1. 2. 3.								
TOTAL								

All subsidiaries, associates and joint ventures (whether Indian or foreign) will be covered under consolidated financial statements.

An entity shall disclose the list of subsidiaries or associates or joint ventures which have not been consolidated in the consolidated financial statements along with the reasons of not consolidating.

7.4. Management reporting
7.4.1. An overview
Management Reporting would comprise hierarchical business MIS as under:
  a) Financial Dash Board
  b) Sales Summary
  c) Processes
  d) Employees

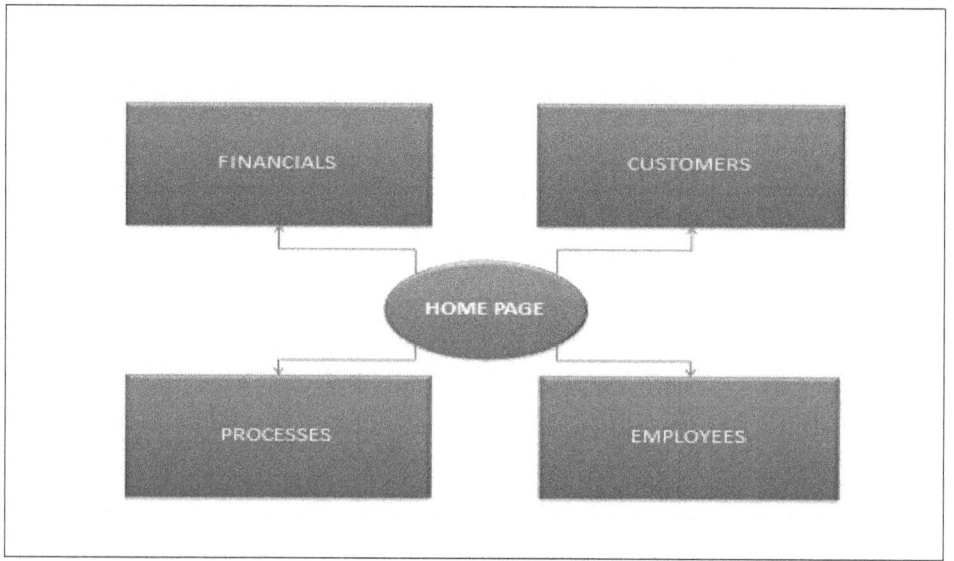

7.4.2. Financial Dash Board
  a) Key Financials
  b) Profitability Analysis
  c) Solvency Analysis
  d) Liquidity Analysis
  e) Return on Investment

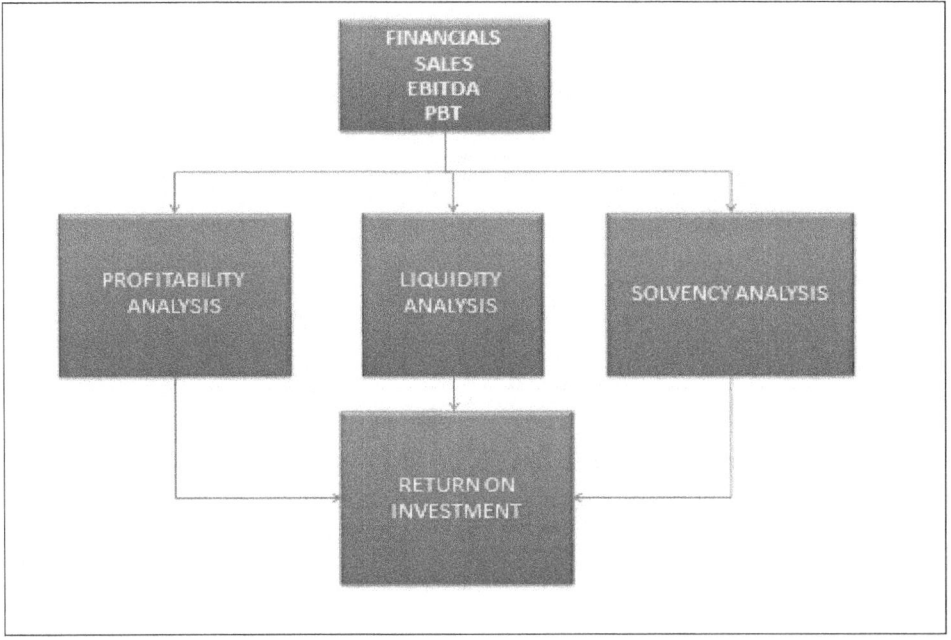

7.4.3. Cost trend
   a) Costs by functional cost centres
   b) Product cost trend
   c) Cost by facilities
   d) Cost by job / activity
   e) Variances with budget and previous year

7.4.4. Profitability Analysis
   a) Product profitability analysis
   b) Customer profitability analysis
   c) Market segment wise profitability analysis
   d) Distribution Channel wise profitability analysis

7.5. Financial Dash Board
7.5.1. Profitability Analysis

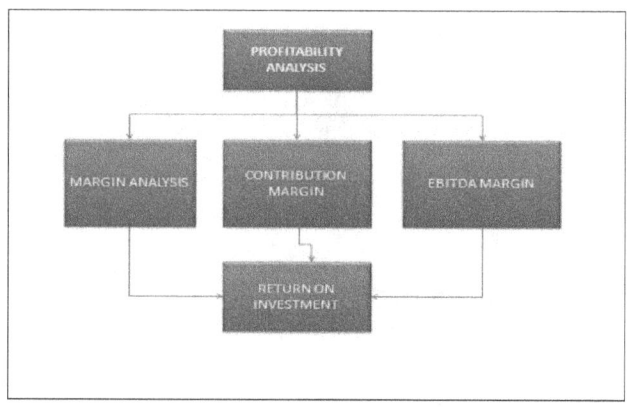

Year	2014-15	%	2015-16	%	YTD July 2016	%
Sales	13,637.2		15,264.0		3,576.7	
Other income	96.3		65.8		18.6	
Sales and other income	13,733.5		15329.83		3595.34	
Raw material consumed / Traded goods	3,980.7	29.0%	4,590.4	29.9%	1,172.6	32.6%
Purchase of carpets	2,226.6	16.2%	1,800.2	11.7%	354.0	9.8%
Materials purchased for resale	159.1	1.2%	34.6	0.2%	11.9	0.3%
Changes in inventories	(648.3)	-4.7%	(536.7)	-3.5%	(381.3)	-10.6%
Manufacturing and other direct expenses	4,078.3	29.7%	4,870.5	31.8%	1,341.9	37.3%
Contribution	3937.1	28.7%	4570.9	29.8%	1096.2	30.5%
Employee benefit expenses	582.6	4.2%	723.1	4.7%	321.8	9.0%
Other Expenses (Admin and selling)	1,409.7	10.3%	1,581.1	10.3%	494.7	13.8%
CSR Expenses	11.5	0.1%	16.5	0.1%	5.5	0.2%
Other Expenses	2003.9	14.6%	2320.7	15.1%	822.0	22.9%
Operating Profit (EBIDTA)	1933.2	14.1%	2250.2	14.7%	274.3	7.6%
EBITDA / Sales %	14.1%		14.7%		7.6%	
Depreciation	171.1	1.2%	226.4	1.5%	80.0	2.2%
EBIT	1762.2	12.8%	2023.82	13.2%	194.25	5.4%
EBIT / Sales %	12.8%		13.2%		5.4%	
Finance cost	550.7	4.0%	518.1	3.4%	221.1	6.2%
Prior period charges	-		-		-	
PBT	1211.4	8.8%	1505.8	9.8%	-26.9	-0.7%
Tax	326.7	2.4%	435.1	2.8%	-	0.0%
Net Profit (PAT)	884.8	6.4%	1070.7	7.0%	-26.9	-0.7%
Net Profit /Sales %	6.4%		7.0%		-0.7%	
Cash Accrual (NP+DEP)	1055.8		1297.1		53.1	

7.5.2. Month-wise key financials

Year	2014-15	2015-16	Apr-16	May-16	Jun-16	Jul-16	YTD July 2016
Sales and other income	13,733	15,330	814	887	1,007	887	3,595
Raw material consumed / Traded goods	3,981	4,590	255	359	319	240	1,173
Purchase of carpets	2,227	1,800	96	100	78	80	354
Materials purchased for resale	159	35	0	7	1	4	12
Changes in inventory	-648	-537	81	-379	68	-152	-381
Manufacturing and direct expenses	4,078	4,870	236	352	368	385	1,342
Employee benefit expenses	583	723	75	79	78	90	322
Other expenses	1,410	1,581	91	127	134	142	495
CSR Expenses	12	17	0	0	5	1	6
Expenses	11,800	13,080	836	643	1,051	791	3,321
EBITDA	1,933	2,250	-21	244	-44	96	274
EBITDA / Sales %	14.1%	14.7%	-2.6%	27.5%	-4.4%	10.8%	7.6%
Depreciation	171	226	20	20	20	20	80
EBIT	1,762	2,024	-41	224	-64	76	194
Finance charges	551	518	57	51	54	60	221
PBT	1,211	1,506	-98	173	-119	16	-27
Tax	327	435	0	45	-45.0	0.0	0
PAT	885	1,071	-98	128	-73	16	-27

7.5.3. Margin Analysis

Year	2014-15	2015-16	YTD May 2016	YTD June 2016	YTD July 2016
EBITDA as a % of Sales & other income	14.1%	14.7%	13.1%	6.6%	7.6%
EBIT as % of Sales & other income	12.8%	13.2%	10.7%	4.4%	5.4%
PBT as % of Sales & other income	8.8%	9.8%	4.4%	-1.6%	-0.7%
PAT as % of Sales & other income	6.4%	7.0%	1.8%	-1.8%	-0.7%

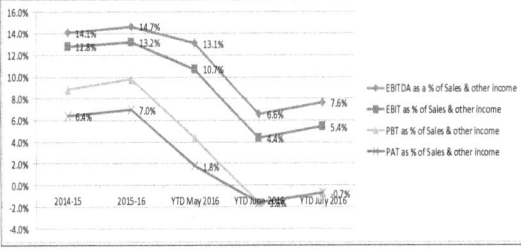

Financial Analysis for effective Management Decisions

7.5.4. Revenue trend

Year	2014-15	2015-16	YTD June 2016	YTD July 2016
Revenue	13637	15264	2699	3577
Break-even sales	9508	10280	2859	3683

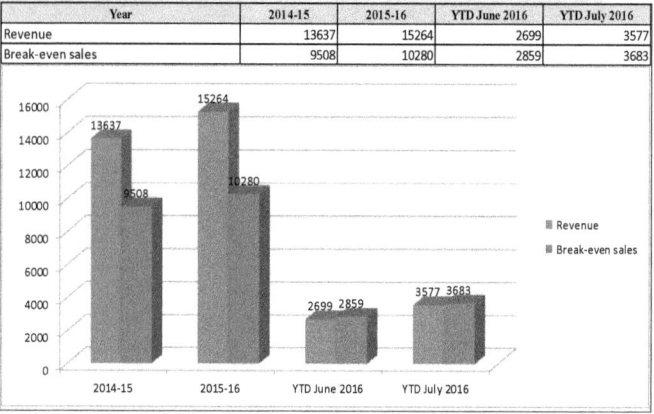

7.5.5. Expenditure trend

Year	2014-15	2015-16	Apr-16	May-16	Jun-16	Jul-16
Raw material / traded products	3981	4590	255	359	319	240
Purchase of goods	2227	1800	96	100	78	80
Materials purchased for resale	159	35	0	7	1	4
Changes in inventory	-648	-537	81	-379	68	-152
Manufacturing and direct expenses	4078	4870	236	352	368	385
Employee benefit expenses	583	723	75	79	78	90
Other expenses	1410	1581	91	127	134	142
CSR Expenses	12	17	0	0	5	1
Depreciation	171	226	20	20	20	20
Finance charges	551	518	57	51	54	60
Total	12522	13824	912	714	1124	871

7.5.6. Expenditure trend as a percentage of sales

Year	2014-15	2015-16	Apr-16	May-16	Jun-16	Jul-16
Raw material / traded products	29.0%	29.9%	31.3%	40.4%	31.7%	27.1%
Purchase of goods	16.2%	11.7%	11.8%	11.2%	7.8%	9.0%
Materials purchased for resale	1.2%	0.2%	0.0%	0.8%	0.1%	0.4%
Changes in inventory	-4.7%	-3.5%	10.0%	-42.7%	6.8%	-17.1%
Manufacturing and direct expenses	29.7%	31.8%	29.0%	39.6%	36.6%	43.5%
Employee benefit expenses	4.2%	4.7%	9.2%	8.9%	7.7%	10.2%
Other expenses	10.3%	10.3%	11.2%	14.3%	13.3%	16.1%
CSR Expenses	0.1%	0.1%	0.0%	0.0%	0.4%	0.1%
Depreciation	1.2%	1.5%	2.5%	2.3%	2.0%	2.3%
Finance charges	4.0%	3.4%	7.0%	5.7%	5.3%	6.8%
Expenses as % of Revenue	91.2%	90.2%	112.0%	80.5%	111.7%	98.2%

7.5.7. EBITDA Trend

Year	2014-15	2015-16	YTD May 2016	YTD June 2016	YTD July 2016
Sales and other income	13,733	15,330	1,702	2,708	3,595
Expenses	11,800	13,080	1,479	2,530	3,321
Operating Profit (EBIDTA)	1,933	2,250	223	178	274
EBITDA / Sales %	14.1%	14.7%	13.1%	6.6%	7.6%

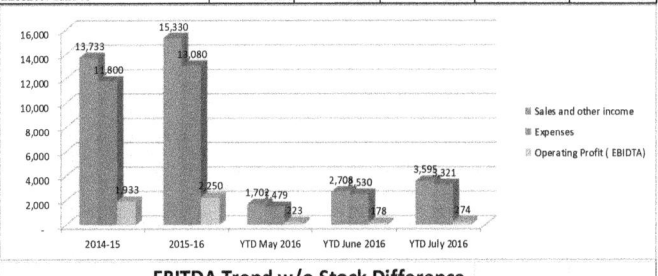

Year	2014-15	2015-16	YTD May 2016	YTD June 2016	YTD July 2016
Income	13,733	15,330	1,702	2,708	3,595
Expenses	12,449	13,616	1,777	2,760	3,702
Operating Profit (EBIDTA)	1,285	1,713	-75	-51	-107
EBITDA / Sales %	9.4%	11.2%	-4.4%	-1.9%	-3.0%

129

7.5.8. Contribution Analysis

Year	2014-15	2015-16	YTD June 2016	YTD July 2016
Sales and other income	13,733	15,330	2,708	3,595
Total	13,733	15,330	2,708	3,595
Raw material / traded products	3,981	4,590	933	1,173
Purchase of carpets	2,227	1,800	274	354
Materials purchased for resale	159	35	8	12
Manufacturing and direct expenses	4,078	4,870	956	1,342
Changes in inventory	-648	-537	-230	-381
Variable cost total	9,796	10,759	1,942	2,499
Contribution	3,937	4,571	767	1,096
Contribution / revenue %	28.7%	29.8%	28.3%	30.5%
Employee benefit expenses	583	723	231	322
Other expenses	1,410	1,581	352	495
CSR Expenses	12	17	5	6
Depreciation	171	226	60	80
Finance charges	551	518	161	221
Fixed cost total	2,726	3,065	809	1,123
Fixed Expenses as % of revenue	19.8%	20.0%	29.9%	31.2%
PBT	1,211	1,506	-43	-27
PBT as % of revenue	8.8%	9.8%	-1.6%	-0.7%
Break even sales	9,508	10,280	2,859	3,683

7.5.9. Solvency analysis

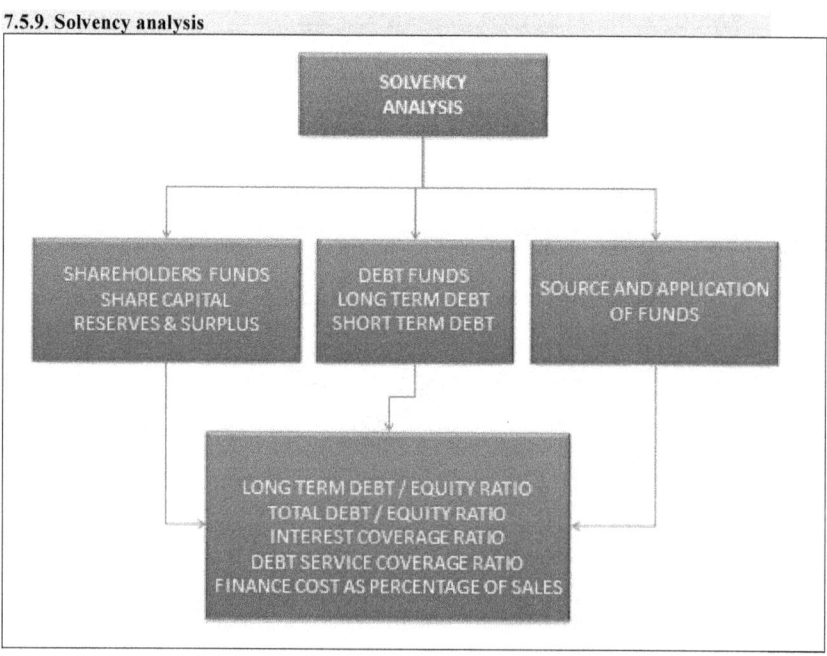

7.5.9.1. Source and Application of funds

Capital Employed - Source   Rs lakhs

Year	2013-14	2014-15	2015-16	YTD Jun 2016	YTD July 2016
Shareholders funds	2930	3806	4876	4833	4849
Long term borrowings	212	94	173	159	159
Deferred tax Liabilities	0	5	40	40	40
Other long term liabilities	57	57	10	10	10
Long term provisions	21	29	38	38	38
Short term borrowings	3513	4231	6086	6331	6332
Capital employed	6733	8222	11222	11411	11427

Capital Employed - Application   Rs lakhs

Year	2013-14	2014-15	2015-16	YTD Jun 2016	YTD July 2016
Net tangible assets	1,036	1,347	3,291	3,329	3,381
Intangible assets	42	28	9	10	10
Capital work-in-progress	25	625	190	255	364
Deferred tax assets	1	0	0	0	0
Non-current investments	86	91	81	81	81
Long term loans and advance	32	93	41	136	71
Net current assets	5,511	6,037	7,610	7,600	7,520
Capital employed	6,733	8,222	11,222	11,411	11,427

7.5.9.2. Debt equity ratio

Year	2011-12	2012-13	2013-14	2014-15	2015-16	YTD June 2016	YTD June 2016
Debt equity ratio	0.11	0.13	0.07	0.02	0.04	0.03	0.03
Debt Equity Ratio (including short term)	1.72	1.79	1.27	1.14	1.28	1.34	1.34

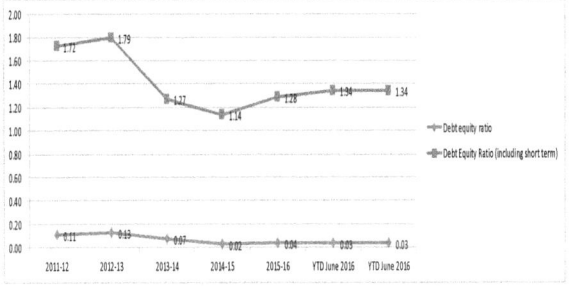

7.5.9.3. Financial Cost trend

Year	2013-14	2014-15	2015-16	YTD July 2016
Interest cost	384	551	518	221
Interest cost as % of revenue	3.2%	4.0%	3.4%	6.2%
Interest coverage ratio	3.26	3.20	3.91	0.88

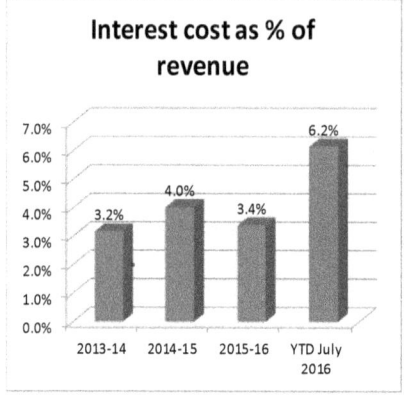

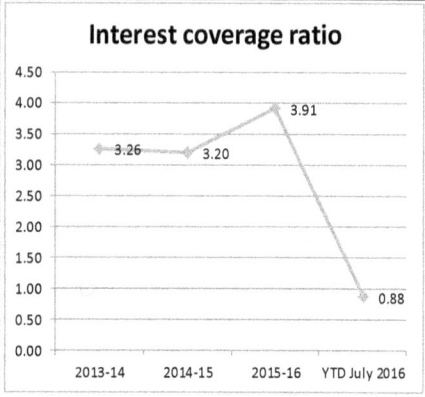

7.5.10. Liquidity Analysis

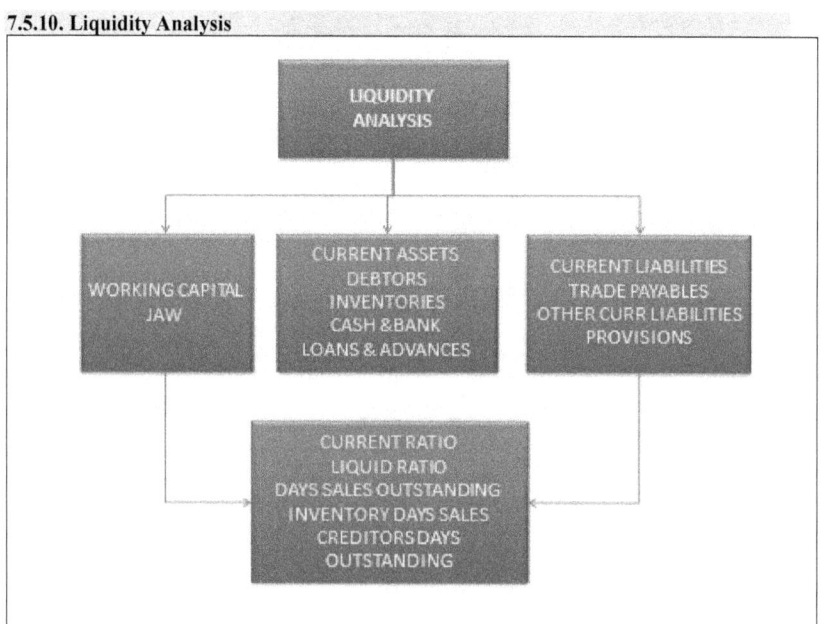

Financial Analysis for effective Management Decisions

7.5.10.1. Working capital jaw

Year	2013-14	2014-15	2015-16	YTD Jun 2015	YTD July 2015
Gross current assets	7,785	9,126	10,920	10,985	11,101
Current liabilities & provisions	2,274	3,089	3,310	3,385	3,582
Working capital	5,511	6,037	7,610	7,600	7,520

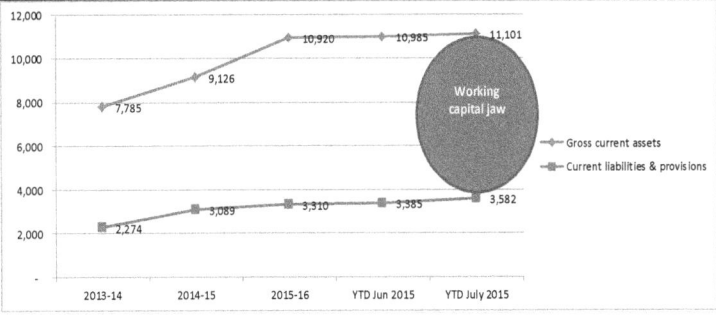

7.5.10.2. Current Assets trend

Year	2013-14	2014-15	2015-16	YTD June 2016	YTD July 2016
Current Investments	88	70	115	115	115
Inventories	2,814	4,761	5,544	5,793	5,897
Sundry debtors	3,461	3,088	4,214	3,868	3,893
Cash & bank balances	65	54	35	53	40
Loans & Advances	1,357	1,153	1,013	1,156	1,157
Gross current assets	7,785	9,126	10,920	10,985	11,101

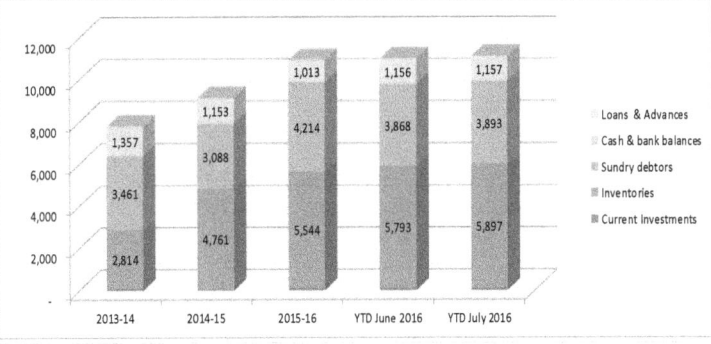

Financial Analysis for effective Management Decisions

7.5.10.3. Current Liabilities trend

Year	2013-14	2014-15	2015-16	YTD June 2016	YTD July 2016
Trade payable	1,714	2,527	2,558	2,749	2,907
Other current liabilities	534	556	746	629	668
Provisions	26	6	6	6	6
Current Liabilities	2,274	3,089	3,310	3,385	3,582

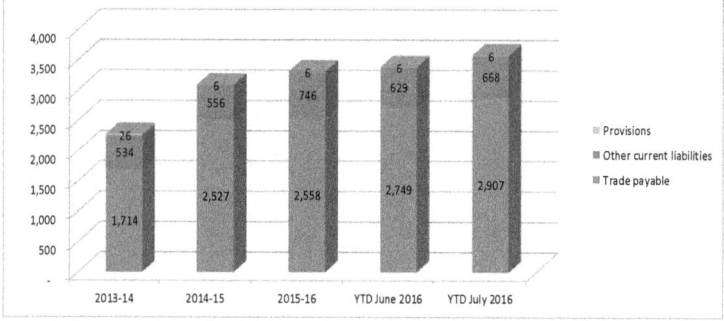

7.5.10.4. Current Ratio

Year	2013-14	2014-15	2015-16	YTD Jun 2016	YTD July 2016
Current ratio	3.4	3.0	3.3	3.2	3.1
Liquid ratio	2.2	1.4	1.3	1.5	1.5

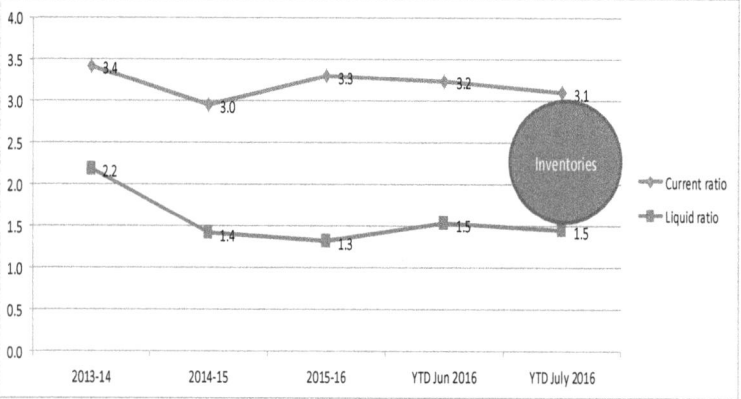

7.5.10.5. Inventory trend

Year	2013-14	2014-15	2015-16	YTD June 2016	YTD July 2016
Raw material and components	1909	3208	3454	3473	3425
Work-in-progress	298	367	606	816	905
Finished goods - traded goods	141	220	273	351	345
Finished goods	466	966	1211	1153	1222
Total inventories	2814	4761	5544	5793	5897

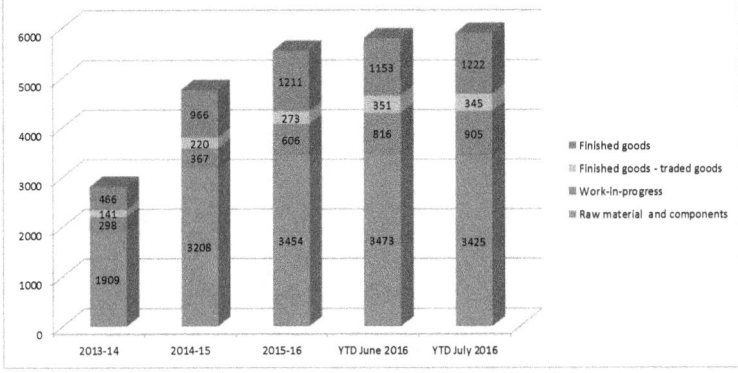

7.5.10.6. Days Sales Outstanding (DSO)

Year	2013-14	2014-15	2015-16	YTD June 2016	YTD July 2016
Days Sales Outstanding (DSO)	104.06	82.06	100.33	128.52	129.93

Days Sales Outstanding (DSO)

Financial Analysis for effective Management Decisions

7.5.10.7. Inventories Days Sales (IDS)

Year	2013-14	2014-15	2015-16	YTD June 2016	YTD July 2016
Total inventory	114.76	177.38	188.07	268.53	283.14
Raw material and components	195.38	294.11	274.61	335.21	350.52
Work-in-progress	20.58	23.43	37.56	74.52	93.81
Finished goods - traded goods	33.06	36.10	55.40	114.99	116.84
Finished goods	32.35	36.00	41.08	53.47	58.68

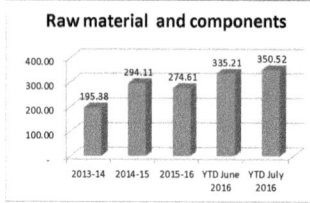

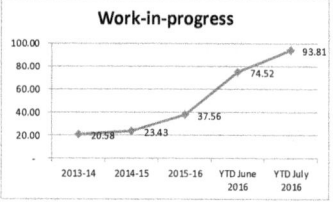

7.5.10.8. Creditors Days Outstanding (CDO)

Year	2013-14	2014-15	2015-16	YTD June 2016	YTD July 2016
Creditors days outstanding	77.06	95.53	92.37	120.41	129.42

Creditors days outstanding

7.5.11. Cash flow summary

Year	2013-14	2014-15	2015-16	YTD July 2016
Sources of Funds				
Increase in Shareholders funds	341.72	875.86	1,070.04	-26.86
Long term borrowings	78.17	-118.15	79.00	-14.60
Deferred tax Liabilities	-	4.90	34.82	-0.00
Other long term liabilities	57.49	-	-47.98	-0.00
Long term provisions	9.16	8.12	9.67	-
Short term borrowings	673.39	718.20	1,854.44	246.62
Opening Balance - Cash in hand	93.72	65.41	54.26	34.64
Total Available Funds	1,253.65	1,554.35	3,054.27	239.80
Utilization of Funds				
Net fixed assets	-38.08	311.35	1,943.54	90.33
Intangible assets	-8.34	-13.62	-19.39	0.94
Capital work-in-progress	53.25	600.37	-435.34	174.23
Deferred tax assets	-0.82	-1.19	-	-
Non-current investments	5.72	4.50	-9.55	-
Long term loans and advances	-2.87	60.77	-52.22	30.49
Current investments	1.50	-17.54	45.00	-
Inventories	265.82	1,946.92	782.87	352.77
Debtors	1,205.39	-373.75	1,126.01	-320.85
Other current assets Loans & Advances	622.51	-203.54	-139.80	143.63
Current assets	2,095.22	1,352.09	1,814.08	175.55
Trade payables	995.49	812.82	30.82	349.73
Other current liabilities	-55.16	21.54	190.26	-78.04
Provisions	-45.92	-20.19	0.43	-
Current liabilities & provisions	894.41	814.17	221.51	271.68
Net current assets	1,200.81	537.93	1,592.56	-96.13
Total Utilization of Funds	1,209.67	1,500.09	3,019.62	199.86
Closing cash balance	43.98	54.25	34.65	39.94
Reconcilition of cash surplus / deficit				
Opening balance	93.72	65.41	54.26	34.64
Closing balance	43.98	54.26	34.64	39.94
(Surplus) / deficit	49.74	11.14	19.62	-5.30

137

7.5.12. Return on Investment

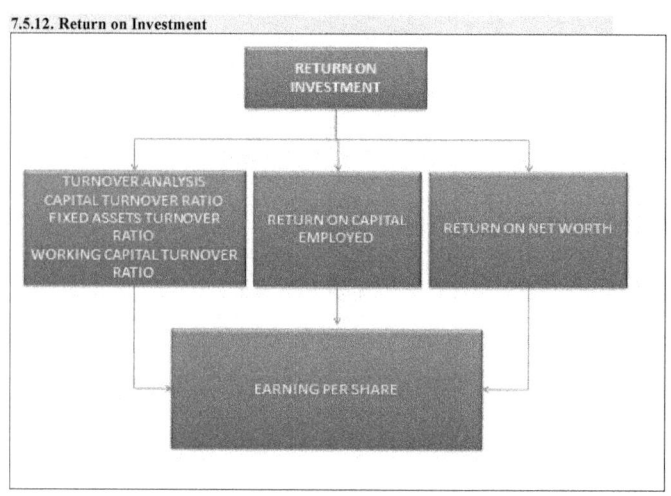

7.5.12.1. Return on capital employed and capital turnover ratio

Year	2011-12	2012-13	2013-14	2014-15	2015-16	YTD July 2016
EBIT / Sales %	9.3%	8.7%	10.3%	12.8%	13.2%	5.4%
Capital turnover ratio	1.50	1.56	1.80	1.67	1.37	0.94
Return on capital employed %	13.9%	13.5%	18.6%	21.4%	18.0%	5.1%

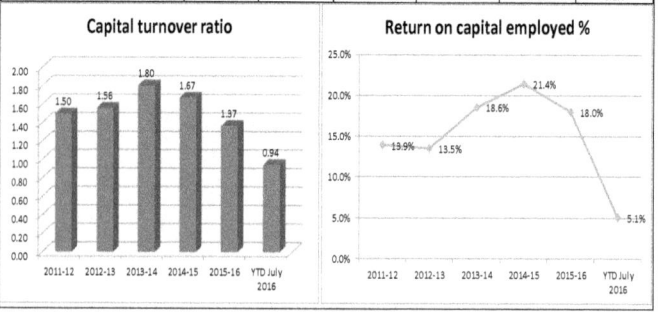

138

Financial Analysis for effective Management Decisions

7.5.12.2. Shareholders Return

Year	2011-12	2012-13	2013-14	2014-15	2015-16	YTD July 2016
Return on net worth %	15.0%	14.9%	21.6%	23.2%	22.0%	-1.7%

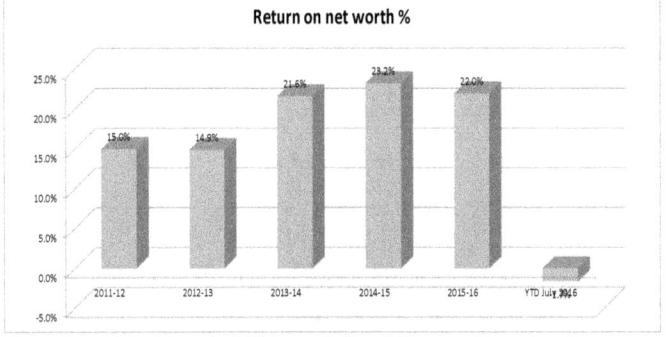

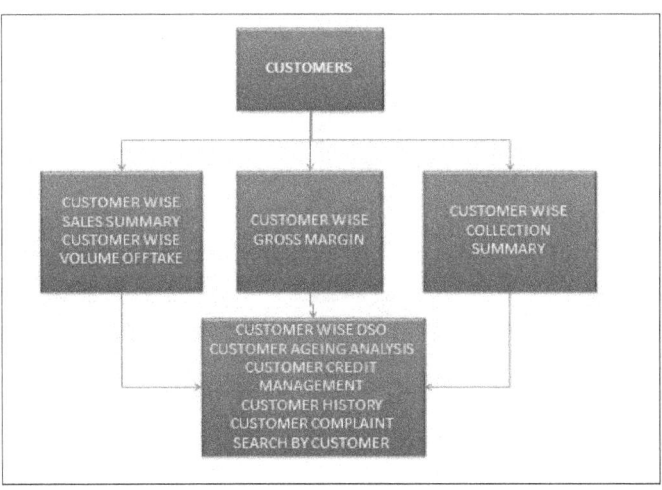

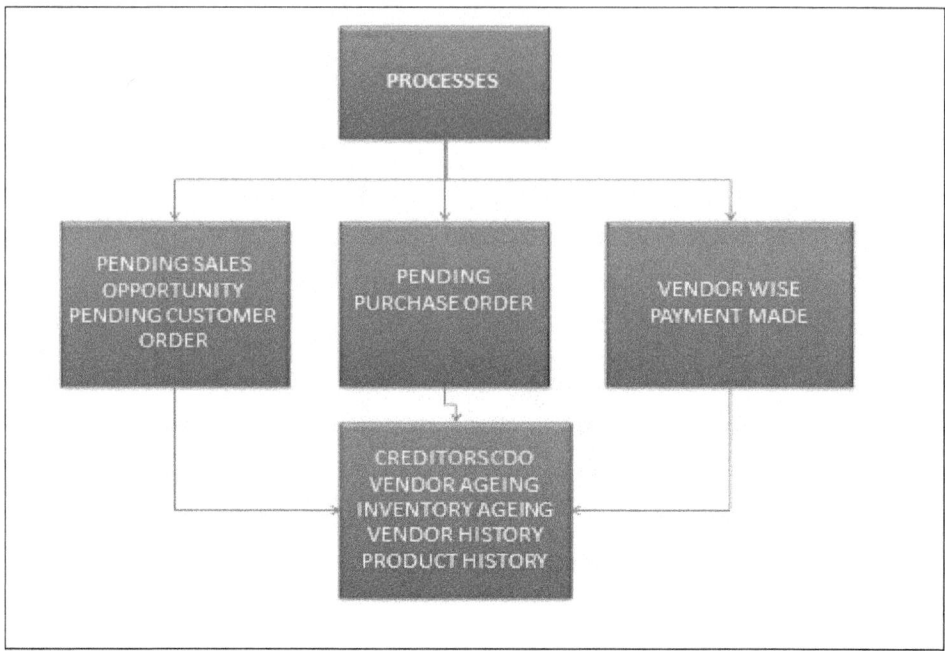

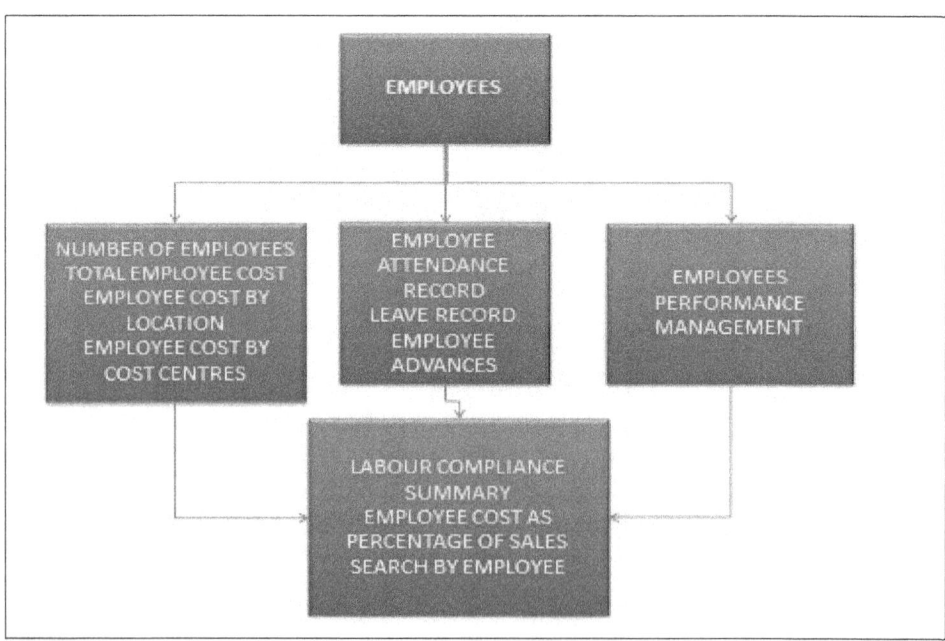

Case Study 7.1. A heavy engineering company manufacturing earth mover

Financial Summary   (Rs. in lakh)

SR.NO.	SUBJECT	2014-15	2013-14	2012-13	2011-12	2010-11
1	Capital	600.00	600.00	600.00	600.00	600.00
2	Reserves	(124.04)	(166.15)	(199.18)	(240.79)	(574.33)
3	Share application pending allotment	-	-	-	-	-
4	Net Worth	475.96	433.85	400.82	359.21	25.67
5	Long term borrowings	772.48	763.66	718.03	846.03	679.17
6	Deferred tax Liabilities	-	-	-	-	-
7	Long term provisions	0.00	0.00	-	-	-
8	Short term borrowings	165.98	156.11	160.58	113.33	90.45
9	Capital employed	1,414.42	1,353.62	1,279.43	1,318.57	795.29
10	Net Block	127.17	120.99	123.84	128.44	139.25
11	Non-current investments	-	-	13.00	13.03	13.03
12	Other non-current assets	487.14	44.31	263.50	202.32	35.84
13	Long term loans and advance	29.89	17.84	28.29	7.74	21.13
14	Inventories	724.31	536.87	123.00	86.29	79.29
15	Sundry debtors	1,344.80	1,265.19	1,616.82	1,126.99	1,194.86
16	Cash & bank balances	8.02	136.92	88.77	307.51	241.59
17	Other current assets, Loans & advances	123.49	188.11	124.63	142.92	106.29
18	Current Assets	2,200.62	2,127.09	1,953.22	1,663.71	1,622.03
19	Current Liability	1,412.76	939.61	1,082.94	678.50	1,035.99
20	Provisions	17.64	17.00	19.48	18.17	-
21	Current Liability & provisions	1,430.40	956.61	1,102.42	696.67	1,035.99
22	Net working capital	770.22	1,170.48	850.80	967.04	586.04
23	Pre-operative expenses					
24	Capital employed	1,414.42	1,353.62	1,279.43	1,318.57	795.29
25	Debt equity ratio	1.62	1.76	1.79	2.36	26.46
26	Current Ratio	1.54	2.22	1.77	2.39	1.57
27	Liquid ratio	1.03	1.66	1.66	2.26	1.49
28	Sales	2,013.63	1,428.11	2,043.80	2,011.24	1,838.53
29	Other income	31.52	17.30	12.86	35.30	18.82
30	Income	2,045.15	1,445.41	2,056.66	2,046.54	1,857.35
31	Raw material consumed / Traded goods	1,647.10	1,321.34	1,639.76	1,584.38	1,413.67
32	Changes in inventory	(187.43)	(413.87)	(36.71)	(7.01)	25.79
33	Personnel expenses	130.64	145.89	117.51	90.02	79.83
34	Other expenses	347.33	291.63	235.66	268.13	196.08
35	Expenses	1,937.64	1,344.99	1,956.22	1,935.52	1,715.37
36	Operating Profit (PBIDT)	107.51	100.42	100.44	111.02	141.98
37	EBITDA / Sales %	5.3%	6.9%	4.9%	5.4%	7.6%
38	Depreciation	13.38	18.45	18.80	18.02	17.28
39	EBIT	94.13	81.97	81.64	93.00	124.70
40	EBIT / Sales %	4.6%	5.7%	4.0%	4.5%	6.7%
41	Finance cost	34.38	31.89	20.55	35.90	19.63
42	PBT	59.75	50.08	61.09	57.10	105.07
43	Extra-ordinary item	-	-	-	310.14	
44	Tax	17.64	17.05	19.48	33.70	44.33
45	Net Profit (PAT)	42.11	33.03	41.61	333.54	60.74
46	Net Profit /Sales %	2.1%	2.3%	2.0%	1.1%	3.3%
47	Cash Accrual (NP+ DEP)	55.49	51.48	60.41	351.56	78.02
48	Fixed Assets turnover ratio	3.17	7.89	4.80	5.82	8.88
49	Working capital turnover ratio	2.66	1.23	2.42	2.12	3.17
48	Capital turnover ratio	1.45	1.07	1.61	1.55	2.34
49	Return on capital employed %	6.7%	6.1%	6.4%	7.1%	15.7%
50	Return on net worth %	8.8%	7.6%	10.4%	6.5%	236.6%

Financial Analysis for effective Management Decisions

Month-wise profitability summary

Year	2014-15	2013-14	2012-13	2011-12	2010-11
Sales and other income	2,045.15	1,445.41	2,056.66	2,046.54	1,857.35
Raw material consumed / Traded goods	1,647.10	1,321.34	1,639.76	1,584.38	1,413.67
Changes in inventory	(187.43)	(413.87)	(36.71)	(7.01)	25.79
Personnel expenses	130.64	145.89	117.51	90.02	79.83
Other expenses	347.33	291.63	235.66	268.13	196.08
Expenses	1,937.64	1,344.99	1,956.22	1,935.52	1,715.37
EBITDA	107.51	100.42	100.44	111.02	141.98
EBITDA / Sales %	5.3%	6.9%	4.9%	5.4%	7.6%
Depreciation	13.38	18.45	18.80	18.02	17.28
EBIT	94.13	81.97	81.64	93.00	124.70
Finance charges	34.38	31.89	20.55	35.90	19.63
PBT	59.75	50.08	61.09	57.10	105.07
Extra-ordinary item	0	0	0	310.14	0
Tax	17.64	17.05	19.48	33.70	44.33
PAT	42.11	33.03	41.61	333.54	60.74

Margin Analysis

Year	2014-15	2013-14	2012-13	2011-12	2010-11
EBITDA as a % of Revenue	5.3%	6.9%	4.9%	5.4%	7.6%
EBIT as % of Revenue	4.6%	5.7%	4.0%	4.5%	6.7%
PAT as % of Revenue	2.1%	2.3%	2.0%	1.1%	3.3%

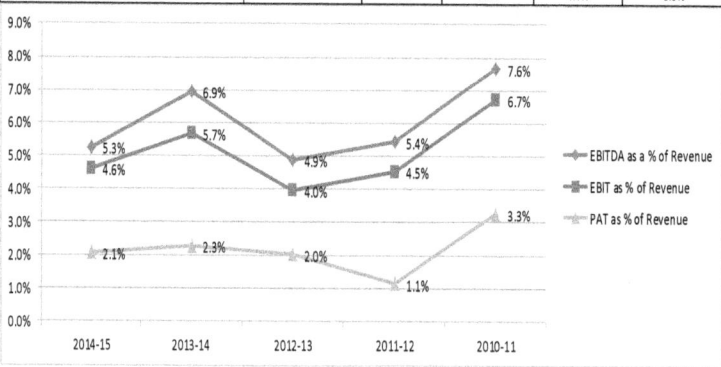

Financial Analysis for effective Management Decisions

Revenue trend

Year	2014-15	2013-14	2012-13	2011-12	2010-11
Revenue	2014	1428	2044	2011	1839
Break-even sales	1836	1311	1780	1797	1390

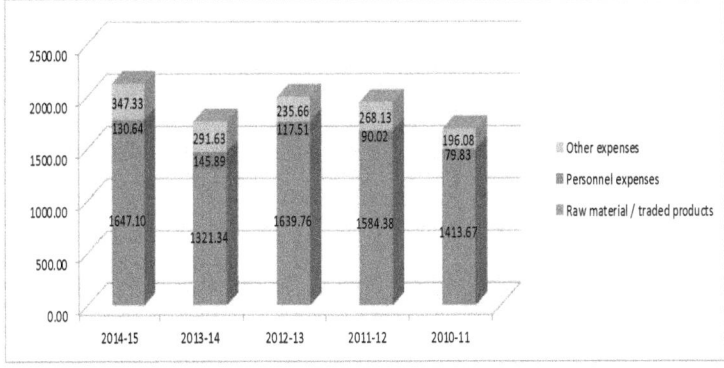

Expenditure trend

Year	2014-15	2013-14	2012-13	2011-12	2010-11
Raw material / traded products	1647.10	1321.34	1639.76	1584.38	1413.67
Personnel expenses	130.64	145.89	117.51	90.02	79.83
Other expenses	347.33	291.63	235.66	268.13	196.08
Total	2125.07	1758.86	1992.93	1942.53	1689.58

Financial Analysis for effective Management Decisions

Expenditure as percentage on sales

Year	2014-15	2013-14	2012-13	2011-12	2010-11
Raw material as % of Revenue	80.5%	91.4%	79.7%	77.4%	76.1%
Personnel expenses as % of Revenue	6.4%	10.1%	5.7%	4.4%	4.3%
Other expenses /Revenue %	17.0%	20.2%	11.5%	13.1%	10.6%
Expenses as % of Revenue	94.7%	121.7%	96.9%	94.9%	91.0%

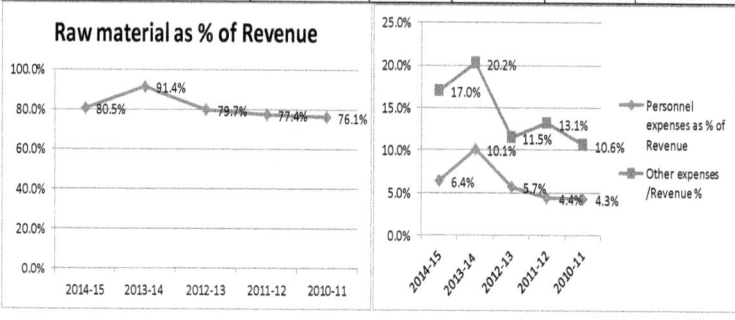

EBITDA Trend

Year	2013-14	2012-13	2011-12	2011-12	2010-11
Income	2,045	1,445	2,057	2,047	1,857
Expenses	1,938	1,345	1,956	1,936	1,715
Operating Profit (EBIDTA)	108	100	100	111	142
EBITDA / Sales %	5.3%	6.9%	4.9%	5.4%	7.6%

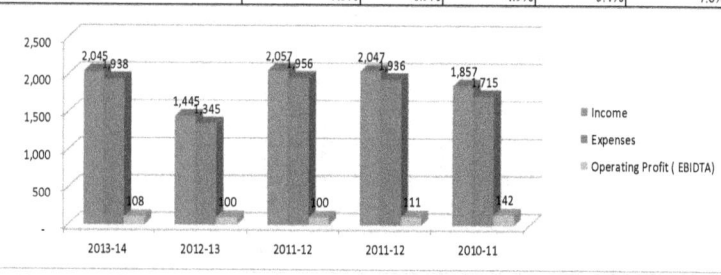

Without stock difference

Year	2013-14	2012-13	2011-12	2011-12	2010-11
Income	2,045	1,445	2,057	2,047	1,857
Expenses	2,125	1,759	1,993	1,943	1,690
Operating Profit (EBIDTA)	-80	-313	64	104	168
EBITDA / Sales %	-3.9%	-21.7%	3.1%	5.1%	9.0%

Financial Analysis for effective Management Decisions

Contribution Analysis

Year	2014-15	2013-14	2012-13	2011-12	2010-11
Revenue	2,045	1,445	2,057	2,047	1,857
Total	2,045	1,445	2,057	2,047	1,857
Raw material	1,647	1,321	1,640	1,584	1,414
Stock difference	-187	-414	-37	-7	26
Variable cost total	1,460	907	1,603	1,577	1,439
Contribution	585	538	454	469	418
Contribution / revenue %	28.6%	37.2%	22.1%	22.9%	22.5%
Personnel expenses	131	146	118	90	80
Other expenses	347	292	236	268	196
Depreciation	13	18	19	18	17
Finance charges	34	32	21	36	20
Fixed cost total	526	488	393	412	313
Fixed Expenses as % of revenue	25.7%	33.8%	19.1%	20.1%	16.8%
PBT	60	50	61	57	105
PBT as % of revenue	2.9%	3.5%	3.0%	2.8%	5.7%
Break even sales	1,836	1,311	1,780	1,797	1,390

Source and Application of funds

Capital Employed - Source   Rs lakhs

Year	2014-15	2013-14	2012-13	2011-12	2010-11
Share capital	600.00	600.00	600.00	600.00	600.00
Reserves and surplus	(124.04)	(166.15)	(199.18)	(240.79)	(574.33)
Shareholders funds	475.96	433.85	400.82	359.21	25.67
Long term borrowings	772.48	763.66	718.03	846.03	679.17
Short term borrowings	165.98	156.11	160.58	113.33	90.45
Capital employed	1,414.42	1,353.62	1,279.43	1,318.57	795.29

Capital Employed - Application

Year	2014-15	2013-14	2012-13	2011-12	2010-11
Net block (including capital WIP)	127.17	120.99	123.84	128.44	139.25
Other non-current assets	487.14	44.31	263.50	202.32	35.84
Long term loans and advances	29.89	17.84	28.29	7.74	21.13
Non-current investments	-	-	13.00	13.03	13.03
Net current assets	770.22	1,170.48	850.80	967.04	586.04
Capital employed	1,414.42	1,353.62	1,279.43	1,318.57	795.29

Debt Equity ratio

Year	2014-15	2013-14	2012-13	2011-12
Debt equity ratio	1.62	1.76	1.79	2.36

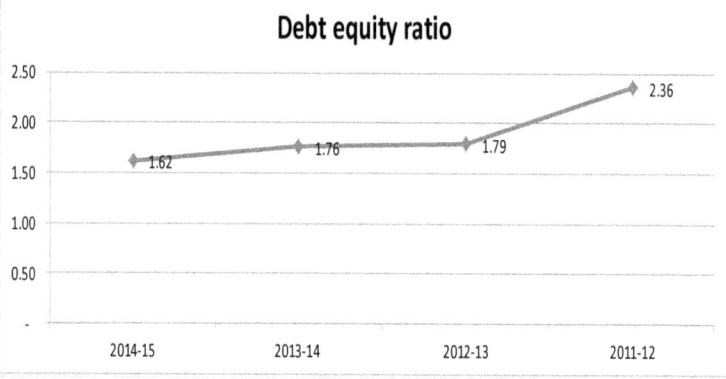

Working capital trend

Year	2014-15	2013-14	2012-13	2011-12	2010-11
Gross current assets	2,200.62	2,127.09	1,953.22	1,663.71	1,622.03
Current liabilities & provisions	1,430.40	956.61	1,102.42	696.67	1,035.99
Working capital	**770.22**	**1,170.48**	**850.80**	**967.04**	**586.04**

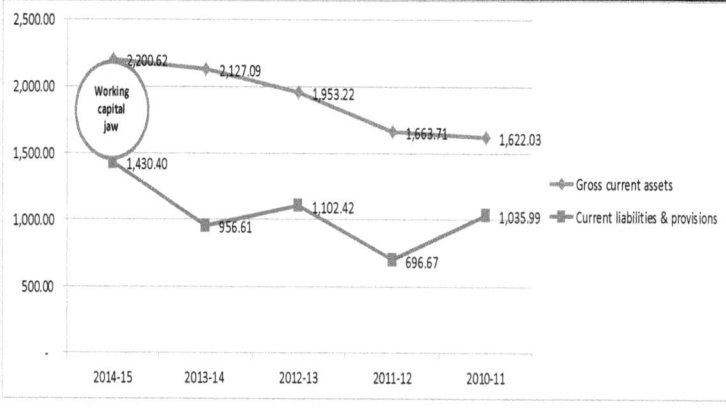

Financial Analysis for effective Management Decisions

Current Assets and Current Liabilities

Gross Current Assets

Rs lakhs

Year	2014-15	2013-14	2012-13	2011-12	2010-11
Inventories	724.31	536.87	123.00	86.29	79.29
Sundry debtors	1,344.80	1,265.19	1,616.82	1,126.99	1,194.86
Cash & bank balances	8.02	136.92	88.77	307.51	241.59
Loans & Advances	123.49	188.11	124.63	142.92	106.29
Gross current assets	2,200.62	2,127.09	1,953.22	1,663.71	1,622.03

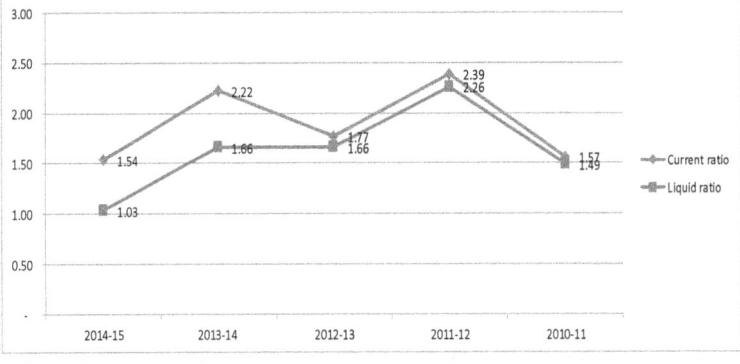

Current liabilities

Year	2014-15	2013-14	2012-13	2011-12	2010-11
Current liabilities	1,412.76	939.61	1,082.94	678.50	1,035.99
Provisions	17.64	17.00	19.48	18.17	-
Total	1,430.40	956.61	1,102.42	696.67	1,035.99

Current ratio and liquid ratio

Year	2014-15	2013-14	2012-13	2011-12	2010-11
Current ratio	1.54	2.22	1.77	2.39	1.57
Liquid ratio	1.03	1.66	1.66	2.26	1.49

Financial Analysis for effective Management Decisions

Days Sales Outstanding (DSO)

Year	2014-15	2013-14	2012-13	2011-12	2010-11
Days Sales Outstanding (DSO)	236.72	315.11	283.01	198.25	231.59

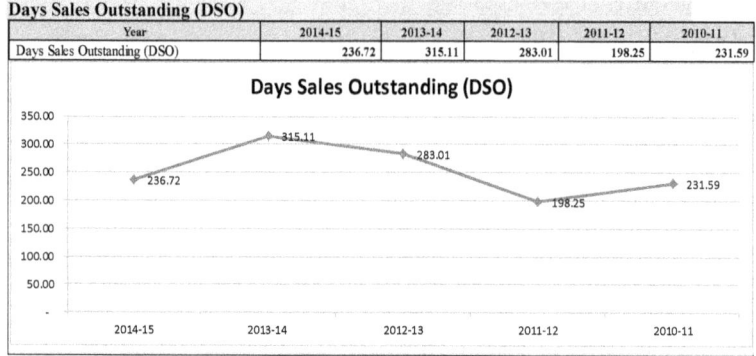

Inventory Days Sales (IDS)

Year	2014-15	2013-14	2012-13	2011-12	2010-11
Inventory days sales (IDS)	158.31	146.27	27.00	19.61	20.19

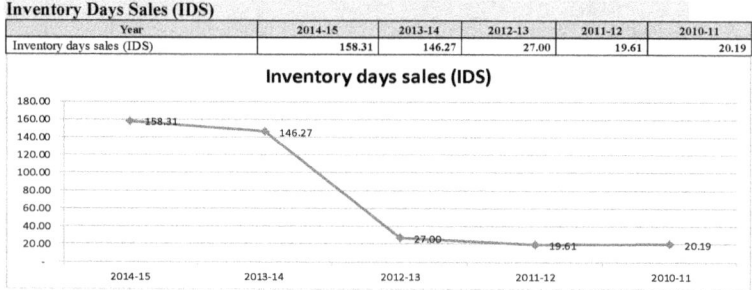

Creditors Days Outstanding (CDO)

Year	2014-15	2013-14	2012-13	2011-12	2010-11
Creditors days outstanding	265.76	256.05	202.88	129.58	217.42

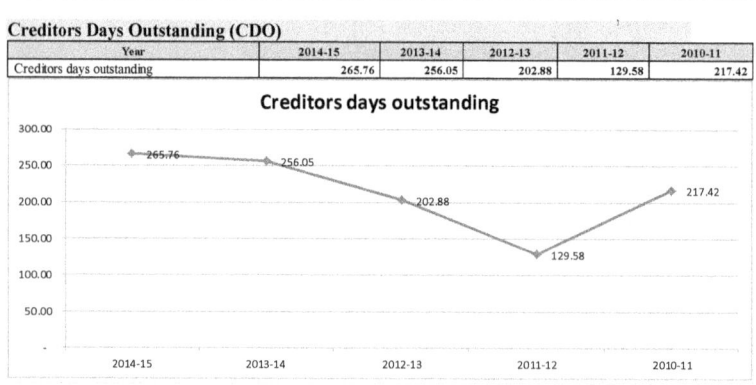

Financial Analysis for effective Management Decisions

Return on Capital Employed

Year	2014-15	2013-14	2012-13	2011-12	2010-11
EBIT / Sales %	4.6%	5.7%	4.0%	4.5%	6.7%
Capital turnover ratio	1.45	1.07	1.61	1.55	2.34
Return on capital employed %	6.7%	6.1%	6.4%	7.1%	15.7%

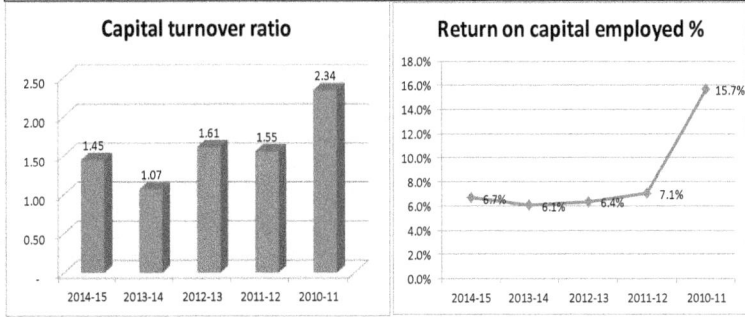

Total Shareholders Return

Year	2014-15	2013-14	2012-13	2011-12
Return on net worth %	8.8%	7.6%	10.4%	6.5%

Return on net worth %

149

7.6. Cost centre trend

Cost centre:		Cost centre report					Rs lakhs
Previous Year (value)		Particulars	Current Year		Variance	
Month	YTD		Month	YTD	Month	YTD
		Salaries and wages				
		Staff welfare expenses				
		Power & fuel				
		Rent				
		Rates and taxes				
		Repairs and maintenance - buildings				
		Repairs and maintenance - Plant				
		Repairs and maintenance - vehicle				
		Repairs and maitenance - general				
		Internet charges				
		Telephone charges				
		Travelling expenses				
		Conveyance charges				
		Insurance charges				
		Security charges				
		Printing and stationery				
		Books and Periodicals				
		Fees and subscription				
		Miscellaneous expenses				
		Total				

Cost centre:		Cost centre report						Rs lakhs
Previous Year (value)		Particulars	CY- Budget		CY - Actual		Variance	
Month	YTD		Month	YTD	Month	YTD	Month	YTD
		Salaries and wages						
		Staff welfare expenses						
		Power & fuel						
		Rent						
		Rates and taxes						
		Repairs and maintenance - buildings						
		Repairs and maintenance - Plant						
		Repairs and maintenance - vehicle						
		Repairs and maitenance - general						
		Internet charges						
		Telephone charges						
		Travelling expenses						
		Conveyance charges						
		Insurance charges						
		Security charges						
		Printing and stationery						
		Books and Periodicals						
		Fees and subscription						
		Miscellaneous expenses						
		Total						

Financial Analysis for effective Management Decisions

Cost centre:				Cost centre report															Rs lakhs
Previous Years (value)		Particulars	CY-BUD	CY-ACT	VARN+/-					CURRENT YEAR									
2014-15	2015-16		YTD	YTD	YTD	APR	MAY	JUNE	JULY	AUG	SEPT	OCT	NOV	DEC	JAN	FEB	MAR
		Salaries and wages															
		Staff welfare expenses															
		Power & fuel															
		Rent															
		Rates and taxes															
		Repairs and maintenance - buildings															
		Repairs and maintenance - Plant															
		Repairs and maintenance - vehicle															
		Repairs and maintenance - general															
		Internet charges															
		Telephone charges															
		Travelling expenses															
		Conveyance charges															
		Insurance charges															
		Security charges															
		Printing and stationery															
		Books and Periodicals															
		Fees and subscription															
		Miscellaneous expenses															
		Total															

7.7. Profitability Analysis

			Productwise Profitability Summary (Rs lakhs)										
SKU - L/ft/kit													Month / YTD
Previous Year total			Particulars		PRODUCT A			PRODUCT B			TOTAL		
Volume	Value	Per unit			Volume	Value	Per unit	Volume	Value	Per unit	Volume	Value	Per unit
			Sales										
			Sales revenue										
			Less: Discount										
			Net sales	A									
			Variable cost										
			Material consumed/traded products										
			Stock variance										
			Direct manufacturing cost										
			Freight outward / distribution cost										
			Total variable cost	B									
			Contribution	(A-B)= C									
			Contribution / Unit										
			Fixed cost										
			Employee benefit expenses										
			Administration expenses										
			Selling expenses										
			Total fixed cost	D									
			EBITDA Margin	(C-D)=E									
			Depreciation	F									
			EBIT	(E-F)=G									
			EBIT Margin										
			Interest	H									
			PBT	(E-F-G)=H									

151

Financial Analysis for effective Management Decisions

Profitability Analysis

PROFIT & LOSS ACCOUNT FOR THE YEAR ENDED 20XX

Rs lakhs

SL NO.	PARTICULARS	SCHEXX.NO	Location 1	Location 2	Location 3	Location 4	Location 5	TOTAL Current Year	TOTAL Previous Year
1	Sales for the year								
	Less: Excise duty								
	: Stock Transfer								
	Net Sales								
2	Cost of Sales								
	Opening Stock								
	Add: Purchases								
	Less: Excise duty								
	: Stock Transfer								
	: Cash Discount/Rebate								
	Net Purchase								
	Less: Closing Stock								
3	Manufacturing Expenses	1							
4	Gross Profit								
5	Add: Other Income	11							
6	EXPENDITURE	1							
	Administrative Expenses								
	Selling Expenses								
	Establishment Expenses								
	Total								
7	Earning Before Interest, Depreciation & Taxes								
	Financial Expenses								
	Depreciation								
	Total								
8	Net Profit for the year (before tax)								
9	Less: Firm Tax								
10	Net Profit for the year (After tax)								

Channel-wise Profitability Summary (Rs lakhs)

Month / YTD

Previous Year total			Particulars		CHANNEL A			CHANNEL B			TOTAL		
Volume	Value	Per unit			Volume	Value	Per unit	Volume	Value	Per unit	Volume	Value	Per unit
			Sales										
			Sales revenue										
			Less: Discount										
			Net sales	A									
			Variable cost										
			Material consumed/traded products										
			Stock variance										
			Direct manufacturing cost										
			Freight outward / distribution cost										
			Total variable cost	B									
			Contribution	(A-B)= C									
			Contribution / Unit										
			Fixed cost										
			Employee benefit expenses										
			Administration expenses										
			Selling expenses										
			Total fixed cost	D									
			EBITDA Margin	(C-D)=E									
			Depreciation	F									
			EBIT	(E-F)=G									
			EBIT Margin										
			Interest	H									
			PBT	(E-F-G)+H									

Financial Analysis for effective Management Decisions

Customer-wise Profitability Summary (Rs lakhs)

Month / YTD

Previous Year total			Particulars		CUSTOMER A			CUSTOMER B			TOTAL		
Volume	Value	Per unit			Volume	Value	Per unit	Volume	Value	Per unit	Volume	Value	Per unit
			Sales										
			Sales revenue										
			Less: Discount										
			Net sales	A									
			Variable cost										
			Material consumed/traded products										
			Stock variance										
			Direct manufacturing cost										
			Freight outward / distribution cost										
			Total variable cost	B									
			Contribution	(A-B)=C									
			Contribution / Unit										
			Fixed cost										
			Employee benefit expenses										
			Administration expenses										
			Selling expenses										
			Total fixed cost	D									
			EBITDA Margin	(C-D)=E									
			Depreciation	F									
			EBIT	(E-F)=G									
			EBIT Margin										
			Interest	H									
			PBT	(E-F-G)=H									

Project-wise Profitability Summary (Rs lakhs)

Month / YTD

Previous Year total			Particulars		PROJECT A			PROJECT B			TOTAL		
Volume	Value	Per unit			Volume	Value	Per unit	Volume	Value	Per unit	Volume	Value	Per unit
			Sales										
			Sales revenue										
			Less: Discount										
			Net sales	A									
			Variable cost										
			Material consumed/traded products										
			Stock variance										
			Direct manufacturing cost										
			Freight outward / distribution cost										
			Total variable cost	B									
			Contribution	(A-B)=C									
			Contribution / Unit										
			Fixed cost										
			Employee benefit expenses										
			Administration expenses										
			Selling expenses										
			Total fixed cost	D									
			EBITDA Margin	(C-D)=E									
			Depreciation	F									
			EBIT	(E-F)=G									
			EBIT Margin										
			Interest	H									
			PBT	(E-F-G)=H									

Financial Analysis for effective Management Decisions

Product A			Product-wise Profitability Analysis (Rs / lakhs)								Month / YTD
Previous Year (value)			Particulars	BUDGET			ACTUAL			VARIANCE % +/-	
Volume	Value	Per unit		Volume	Value	Per unit	Volume	Value	Per unit	Volume	Value
			Sales								
			Sales revenue								
			Less: Discount								
			Net sales A								
			Variable cost								
			Material consumed/traded products								
			Stock variance								
			Direct manufacturing cost								
			Freight outward / distribution cost								
			Total variable cost B								
			Contribution (A-B)= C								
			Contribution / Unit								
			Fixed cost								
			Employee benefit expenses								
			Administration expenses								
			Selling expenses								
			Total fixed cost D								
			EBITDA Margin (C-D)=E								
			Depreciation F								
			EBIT (E-F)=G								
			EBIT Margin								
			Interest H								
			PBT (E-F-G)=H								

Product B			Product-wise Profitability Analysis (Rs / lakhs)								Month / YTD
Previous Year (value)			Particulars	BUDGET			ACTUAL			VARIANCE % +/-	
Volume	Value	Per unit		Volume	Value	Per unit	Volume	Value	Per unit	Volume	Value
			Sales								
			Sales revenue								
			Less: Discount								
			Net sales A								
			Variable cost								
			Material consumed/traded products								
			Stock variance								
			Direct manufacturing cost								
			Freight outward / distribution cost								
			Total variable cost B								
			Contribution (A-B)= C								
			Contribution / Unit								
			Fixed cost								
			Employee benefit expenses								
			Administration expenses								
			Selling expenses								
			Total fixed cost D								
			EBITDA Margin (C-D)=E								
			Depreciation F								
			EBIT (E-F)=G								
			EBIT Margin								
			Interest H								
			PBT (E-F-G)=H								

Financial Analysis for effective Management Decisions

SBU - I/II/III			SBU-wise Profitability Analysis (Rs / lakhs)								Month / YTD
Previous Year (value)			Particulars	BUDGET			ACTUAL			VARIANCE % +/-	
Volume	Value	Per unit		Volume	Value	Per unit	Volume	Value	Per unit	Volume	Value
			Sales								
			Sales revenue								
			Less: Discount								
			Net sales A								
			Variable cost								
			Material consumed/traded products								
			Stock variance								
			Direct manufacturing cost								
			Freight outward / distribution cost								
			Total variable cost B								
			Contribution (A-B)= C								
			Contribution / Unit								
			Fixed cost								
			Employee benefit expenses								
			Administration expenses								
			Selling expenses								
			Total fixed cost D								
			EBITDA Margin (C-D)=E								
			Depreciation F								
			EBIT (E-F)=G								
			EBIT Margin								
			Interest H								
			PBT (E-F-G)=H								

LEGAL ENTITY:			Profitability Analysis (Rs / lakhs)								Month / YTD
Previous Year (value)			Particulars	BUDGET			ACTUAL			VARIANCE % +/-	
Volume	Value	Per unit		Volume	Value	Per unit	Volume	Value	Per unit	Volume	Value
			Sales								
			Sales revenue								
			Less: Discount								
			Net sales A								
			Variable cost								
			Material consumed/traded products								
			Stock variance								
			Direct manufacturing cost								
			Freight outward / distribution cost								
			Total variable cost B								
			Contribution (A-B)= C								
			Contribution / Unit								
			Fixed cost								
			Employee benefit expenses								
			Administration expenses								
			Selling expenses								
			Total fixed cost D								
			EBITDA Margin (C-D)=E								
			Depreciation F								
			EBIT (E-F)=G								
			EBIT Margin								
			Interest H								
			PBT (E-F-G)=H								

Financial Analysis for effective Management Decisions

Product		Particulars		CY-BUD	CY-ACT	VAR(+/-)	CURRENT YEAR											Rs lakhs
Previous Years (value)				YTD	YTD	YTD	APR	MAY	JUNE	JULY	AUG	SEPT	OCT	NOV	DEC	JAN	FEB	MAR
2014-15	2015-16																	
		Sales																
		Sales revenue																
		Less Discount																
		Net sales	A															
		Variable cost																
		Material consumed/traded products																
		Stock variance																
		Direct manufacturing cost																
		Freight outward / distribution cost																
		Total variable cost	B															
		Contribution	(A-B)=C															
		Contribution / Unit																
		Fixed cost																
		Employee benefit expenses																
		Administration expenses																
		Selling expenses																
		Total fixed cost	D															
		EBITDA Margin	(C-D)=E															
		Depreciation	F															
		EBIT	(E-F)=G															
		EBIT Margin	H															
		Interest																
		PBT	(H-I)=J															

SKU		Particulars		CY-BUD	CY-ACT	VAR(+/-)	CURRENT YEAR											Rs lakhs
Previous Years (value)				YTD	YTD	YTD	APR	MAY	JUNE	JULY	AUG	SEPT	OCT	NOV	DEC	JAN	FEB	MAR
2014-15	2015-16																	
		Sales																
		Sales revenue																
		Less Discount																
		Net sales	A															
		Variable cost																
		Material consumed/traded products																
		Stock variance																
		Direct manufacturing cost																
		Freight outward / distribution cost																
		Total variable cost	B															
		Contribution	(A-B)=C															
		Contribution / Unit																
		Fixed cost																
		Employee benefit expenses																
		Administration expenses																
		Selling expenses																
		Total fixed cost	D															
		EBITDA Margin	(C-D)=E															
		Depreciation	F															
		EBIT	(E-F)=G															
		EBIT Margin	H															
		Interest																
		PBT	(H-I)=J															

Financial Analysis for effective Management Decisions

Legal entity		Particulars		Profitability Analysis															Rs lakhs
Previous Years (value)				CY-BUD	CY-ACT	VARN+/-	CURRENT YEAR												
2014-15	2015-16			YTD	YTD	YTD	APR	MAY	JUNE	JULY	AUG	SEPT	OCT	NOV	DEC	JAN	FEB	MAR
		Sales																
		Sales revenue																
		Less: Discount																
		Net sales	A															
		Variable cost																
		Material consumed/traded products																
		Stock variance																
		Direct manufacturing cost																
		Freight outward / distribution cost																
		Total variable cost	B															
		Contribution	(A-B)=C															
		Contribution / Unit																
		Fixed cost																
		Employee benefit expenses																
		Administration expenses																
		Selling expenses																
		Total fixed cost	D															
		EBITDA Margin	(C-D)=E															
		Depreciation	F															
		EBIT	(E-F)=G															
		EBIT Margin	H															
		Interest																
		PBT	(H-I)=															

7.8. Financial and Non-financial tracker

7.8.1. Financial tracker

Profitability Analysis

PROFITABILITY ANALYSIS	2014-15	2015-16	YTD	Month
Sales				
Other income				
Income				
Raw material consumed				
Purchase of traded products / services				
Materials purchased for resale				
Changes in inventory				
Manufacturing and other direct expenses				
Employee benefit expenses				
Other expenses (Admin and selling)				
CSR Expenses				
Expenses				
Operating Profit (EBIDTA)				
EBITDA / Sales %				
Depreciation				
EBIT				
EBIT / Sales %				
Finance cost				
Prior period charges				
PBT				
Tax				
Net Profit (PAT)				
Net Profit /Sales %				
Cash Accrual (NP+ DEP)				
Earnings per share - basic and diluted				

Solvency Analysis

SOLVENCY ANALYSIS	2014-15	2015-16	YTD	Month
Capital employed				
Capital				
Reserves				
Share application pending allotment				
Net Worth				
Long term borrowings				
Deferred tax Liabilities				
Other long term liabilities				
Long term provisions				
Short term borrowings				
Capital employed				
Opening WDV				
Add: Capex				
Closing WDV				
Less: Depreciation				
Net Block				
Intangible assets				
Capital work-in-progress				
Deferred tax assets				
Non-current investments				
Long term loans and advance				
Current Assets				
Current Liability & provisions				
Net working capital				
Pre-operative expenses				
Capital employed				
Long term debt to Total Equity				
Total debt to total equity				
Capital turnover ratio				
Fixed Assets turnover ratio				
Working capital turnover ratio				
Return on capital employed %				
Return on net worth %				

Liquidity Analysis

LIQUIDITY ANALYSIS	2014-15	2015-16	YTD	Month
Current investments				
Raw material and components				
Work-in-progress (unfinished goods)				
Finished goods - traded goods				
- Finished goods				
Inventories				
Sundry debtors				
Cash & bank balances				
Other current assets, Loans & advances				
Current Assets				
Trade payables				
Other current liabilities				
Provisions				
Current Liability & provisions				
Net working capital				
Current Ratio				
Liquid ratio				
DSO				
IDS				
CDO				

7.8.2. Non-financial tracker

7.8.2.1. Sales

SALES	2014-15	2015-16	YTD	Month
Product / service attributes				
Product wise price trend				
Service wise price trend				
Customer wise price trend				
Product availability to product sales				
Product wise profitbility analysis				
Service wise profitability analysis				
Customer wise profitability analysis				
Customer preference trend				
Revenue growth strategy				
Expand revenue opportunities				
Customers acquired in last twelve months				
Customers retained in last twelve months				
Conversion of targets to customers pattern				
Customer ageing analysis				
Enhance customer value				
customer service turnaround time				
Effectively handle customer communication				
Redressal of customer complaints				
Reduction of customer waiting time				
Carry out customer survey				
% Recall after delivery				
% of achieved deliveries to planned				
% of products released on due date				
Deliveries on time as ordered				
Deliveries on time to new markets				
EVA by customer				
% of free replacement to sales				
% sales returns to total sales				
Percentage of on time delivery				
Sales opportunity pending sales order				
Sales order pending sales invoice				
Efficient after sales service				
Frequency of customers violating credit limit				

7.8.2.2. Purchases

PURCHASES	2014-15	2015-16	YTD	Month
Vendor evaluation history				
% Conformity in product specifications				
% General quality of products				
Documented quality system				
% Short delivery period to standard delivery period				
% On time delivery to total delivery				
% defectives to actual purchases				
Frequency of rectification or repair period				
Availability of Technical documentation				
Percentage of waste reduction				
Competitive prices trend				
Frequency of by-passing L1 quotation				
Minimum purchasing quantity				
Computation of Economic Ordering Quantity				
Written order and delivery acknowledgement				
Supplementary PO to total PO - %, Nos and Value				
Foreclosed PO to total PO - % Nos and Value				
Communication cost per vendor				
Terms of payment				
Frequency of vendors paid later than credit period				
Turn around time on reconciliation of creditors statement of account				
Pending Purchase Requisition and date				
Pending Purchase Order and date				
Pending Goods receipt note on materials received				
Pending vendor invoices on goods received				
Pending payments on vendor invoice				
Percentage free replacement by vendor				
Percentage recall of product by vendor				
Percentage rectification and return of product				
Percentage price amendment to price of products				
Pending service orders , performance not completed				
Pending service bills not paid				

7.8.2.3. Materials

MATERIALS	2014-15	2015-16	YTD	Month
Maximum level				
Minimum level				
Re-order level				
Danger level				
Inventory ageing analysis				
ABC Analysis of top twenty inventory items				
Finished goods - made to order				
Finished goods - made to stock				
No. of BOMs created				
No.of variants of BOMs created				
Batch no and manufacturing date by product				
Material availability by storage locations				
Material sent out on job work not returned				
Obsolete materials as % of total materials				
Defective materials as % of total materials				
Availability of negative balances of materials				
Report on material stock and consumption				
Frequency of physical verification of materials				
Valuation of raw materials				
Valuation of work-in-progress				
Valuation of finished goods				
Quality parameters of in-process materials				
Quality parameters of finished goods				
Input output analysis				
Inventory turnover ratio				
Yield variance Year on Year				
Value variance Year on Year				
Consumption variance Year on Year				
Material rate variance Year on Year				

7.8.2.4. Manpower

EMPLOYEES	2014-15	2015-16	YTD	Month
Turnover per employee				
Gross Margin per employee				
Number of repeat calls				
Number of trained people in bar-coding				
Number of training hours delivered				
Staff feedback sessions per month				
Survey response from customers				
Surveyed satisfaction of IT staff				
Waiting time for a call-back				
Workstation hours				
Worst case responses				
No of People trained				
No of seminars delivered				
Number of hours billed				
Help desk hours				
Hours of education				
Hours of skills training				
Lost staff hours				
Number of projects held up owing to employees				
Frequency of absenteeism				
Frequency of Employee performance management				
Average age of employees				
Pattern of number of years of service - employeewise				
Average employee retention period				
% staff welfare to employee cost				
% recruitment cost to total sales				
% of incentive to total sales				
% employee cost to total sales				

7.8.2.5. Other Expenses

EXPENSES	2014-15	2015-16	YTD	Month
% direct expense to total expense				
% material consumed to total expense				
% direct manufacturing expense to total expense				
% wages to direct manufacturing expenses				
% employee cost to total sales				
% administration cost to total sales				
% selling & distribution cost to total sales				
% foreign travel cost to total sales				
% domestic travel cost to total sales				
% commission paid to total sales				
% spend on digital marketing to total sales				
% spend on exhibition to total sales				
% spend on marketing to total sales				
% spend on repairs & maintenance to sales				
% spend on insurance to total sales				
% spend on security establishment to total sales				
% spend on power & fuel to total sales				
% spend on freight outward to total sales				
% spend on loading / unloading to total sales				
% spend on discount and schemes to total sales				
% spend on exports sales to total sales				
% spend on R&D to total sales				
% interest cost to total sales				
Interest coverage ratio				
Debt service coverage ratio				
% depreciation on total sales				
% demurrage on total sales				
No of own vehicles and cost per vehicle				
No of hired vehicles and cost per vehicle				
% hired transport cost to total delivery cost				
% transport cost to total sales				
% stock write-off to total sales				
% bad / doubtful debts to total sales				

7.8.3. Cost of production

Name of the Manufacturer:
Address of the Manufacturer:
Registration No of Manufacturer:
Description of product captively consumed:
Excise Tariff Heading:
Statement of Cost of Production of _____ manufactured / to be manufactured during the period _____

S/L No		Qty	
Q1	Quantity Produced (Unit of Measure)		
Q2	Quantity Despatched (Unit of Measure)		
	Particulars	**Total cost Rs**	**Cost/unit Rs**
1.	Material Consumed		
2.	Direct Wages and Salaries		
3.	Direct Expenses		
4.	Works Overheads		
5.	Quality Control Cost		
6.	Research & Development Cost		
7.	Administrative Overheads (relating to production activity)		
8.	Total (1 to 7)		
9.	Add : Opening stock of Work - in –Progress		
10.	Less : Closing stock of Work -in- Progress		
11.	Total (8+9-10)		
12.	Less : Credit for Recoveries/Scrap/By-Products / misc income		
13.	Packing cost		
14.	Cost of production (11 - 12 + 13)		
15.	Add: Inputs received free of cost		
16.	Add: Amortised cost of Moulds, Tools, Dies & Patterns etc received free of cost		
17.	Cost of Production for goods produced for captive consumption (14 + 15 + 16)		
18.	Add : Opening stock of finished goods		
19.	Less : Closing stock of finished goods		
20.	Cost of production for goods despatched (17 + 18 - 19)		

7.8.4. Operating costs

Name of the Manufacturer:
Address of the Manufacturer:

Statement of Operating costs of own fleet for the period ....

S/L No		
A	**QUANTITATIVE INFORMATION**	
A1	Number of Vehicles	
A2	Number of trips	
A3	Goods transported - inward (UM)	
A4	Goods transported – outward (UM)	
A5	Goods transported – inward – Km	
A6	Goods transported – outward – Km	
A7	Total Goods transported inward – basis of apportionment (Specify)	
A8	Total Goods transported outward – basis of apportionment (Specify)	
A9	**Total (A7+A8)**	
B	**COST INFORMATION**	
	Cost of operation	
	Variable cost	
B1	Salaries & Wages of Drivers, Cleaners and others	
B2	Fuel & Lubricants	
B3	Consumables	
B4	Amortized cost of Tyre, Tube & Battery	
B5	Spares	
B6	Repair & Maintenance	
B7	Other Variable Cost (specify)	
B8	**Total Variable Cost (B1 to B7)**	
	Fixed Cost	
B9	Insurance	
B10	Licence Fee, Permit Fee and Taxes	
B11	Depreciation	
B12	Other Fixed Costs (Specify)	
B13	**Total Fixed Cost (B9 to B12)**	
B14	**Total Operating Cost (B8+B13)**	
C	**APPORTIONMENT** (Basis to be specified) - usage	
C1	Inward Transport Cost (B14 *A7/ A9)	
C2	Outward Transport Cost (B14 *A8/A9)	
C3	Transit insurance for inward movement	
C4	Transit insurance for outward movement	
C5	Total transportation cost for inward movement (C1+C3)	
C6	Total transportation cost for outward movement (C2+C4)	

Note:
1. Cost of Battery, and Tyres and Tubes shall to be amortised over its useful life.
2. Asset Register shall be maintained for determination of depreciation and amortization cost.
3. Separate Cost Sheet shall be prepared for different types of vehicles.

Statement of Hired Outward Transportation Cost for the period ending.......

A	Quantitative Information	
A1	Quantity of goods transported – outward (UM)	
B	COST INFORMATION	(Rs)
B1	Hired Transport Charges	
B2	Transit Insurance	
B3	Other (specify)	
B4	Total Transportation cost (B1 to B3)	

7.8.5. Working Capital statement

UNIT WISE WORKING CAPITAL STATEMENT

SI.No.	PARTICULARS	Schedule NO.	Location 1	Location 2	Location 3	Location 4	Location 5	AMOUNT (Rs.) Current Year	AMOUNT (Rs.) Previous Year
A	CURRENT ASSETS :								
1	Stocks (At cost or market value whichever is lower)								
2	Sundry Debtors	2							
3	Cash and Bank Balances:	3							
	i) Cash in hand								
	ii) Balances with Banks								
4	LOANS & ADVANCES								
	i) Security Deposites	4							
	ii) Advances to staff & others	5							
	iii) Earnest Money Deposits	6							
5	Advance To Suppliers	7							
6	Accured Interest on FDR								
7	Vat (Modvat)/Sales tax Refundable								
8	Goods in transit								
9	Excise duty (Modvat)/PLA								
10	Service Tax (Modvat)								
12	Excise duty Refundable (DGFT)								
			-	-	-	-	-	-	-
B	Less: CURRENT LIABILTIES AND PROVISIONS								
1	Sundry Creditors	8							
2	Advance against sales of goods	9							
3	Tax Deducted at Sources								
4	Sales tax Local/Central/WCT								
5	Service Tax \ Excise duty\SWACHH BHARAT CESS								
6	Security Deposit against 'C' Forms								
7	Dealer Deposit (Our Sub Dealers)								
8	EXPENSES PAYABLE	10							
	i) Salary & Wages Payable								
	ii) Others Expenses								
			-	-	-	-	-	-	-
	Net Current Assets (A-B)		-	-	-	-	-	-	-

7.8.6. Capacity utilisation analysis:

Capacity Utilization Analysis along with estimated impact on costs and profitability (Product-wise, Product Group-wise and Unit-wise)
- Under-utilization of Capacities
- Idle Capacities
- Non-Productive Assets
- Trend Analysis
- opportunity Analysis
- Outsourcing/Sub-Contracting Vs. Internal Capacities
- Plant Break-down hours with impact on productivity, costs and profitability
- Scope of Expansion and likely cost-benefit analysis

7.8.7. Productivity analysis:

Productivity Analysis along with estimated impact on costs and profitability (Product-wise, Product Group-wise and Unit-wise)
- Production/Operations/Process Cycle Time and Productivity
- Input-Output Analysis compared with Budgets or Standards or Industry Norms
- Conversion Efficiency Analysis
- Cost of wastages in operations

7.8.8. Utilities / energy efficiency analysis:

Utilities/Energy Efficiency Analysis (Utility-wise, Unit-wise, Product-wise, and Product Group-wise)
- Utility Productivity compared with Budgets or Standards or Industry Norms
- Input-Output Efficiency – impact on costs and profitability
- Energy Conversion Ratio highlighting wastage & inefficiency
- Energy Consumption Ratio for each product/operation and each product/ activity group compared with Budgets or Standards or Industry Norms

7.8.9. Cost and Contribution analysis:

Key-Expense Ratios vs. Cost of Production / Cost of Sales
- Abnormal & Non-Recurring Costs – impact on profitability
- Key Costs Trend Analysis indicating estimated impact on future profitability
- Cost-effectiveness Analysis: Cost of

Operation/Process vs. Benefits
- Cost of Management vs. Net Turnover or Gross Margin or Net Margin
- Cost Variance Analysis vs. Standards or Budgets – impact on profitability
- Volume Variance Analysis vs. Standards or Budgets – impact on profitability
- Marginal Cost and Contribution Analysis for each product/activity, each product/activity group, each market segment, each customer segment, etc.
- Service Department-wise cost trends (element-wise)

7.8.10. Product / service profitability:

Product/Service Profitability (for key products/services only)
- Product,
- Turnover, % to Total,
- Capital Employed, % to Total CE,
- Gross Margin, % to Total,
- GM/Turnover,
- GM/CE,
- Net Margin, % to Total,
- NM/Turnover,
- NM/CE,

7.8.11. Market / customer profitability:

Market/Customer Profitability – similar analysis as above
- Market Distribution – Indigenous vs. Overseas broken into smaller geographical divisions/segments
- Customer Distribution – in order of percentage share in each product/ activity and in each product/activity group
- Indicate cost of servicing each market/customer and its efficiency in terms of business, contributions, gross/net margins, scope of sustainability, etc.
- Indicate cost of each supply chain vs. benefits
- Indicate impact of FTAs and Dumping on each product, product-group or each market/customer.

7.8.12. Working capital analysis:

Movement of Debtors vs. Credit Sales
- Days Debtors Analysis – impact on cash flow and profitability
- Overseas Debtors – impact of likely FE Variations

- Movement of Creditors vs. Credit Purchases
- Days Creditors Analysis – impact on supplies and product-line
- Inventory Turnover
- Cash Flow Turnover – impact on profitability

7.8.13. Inventory analysis:

Inventory Analysis - Basis of valuation & Consistency
- Turnover efficiency: Cost of Goods Sold/Average Inventory
- Return on Inventory: GM/Average Inventory, NM/Average Inventory
- Slow-moving or dead inventory
- ABC analysis; Period holding analysis
- Policy for Insurance Spares; Inventory Holding due to changes in technology, changes in production process, obsolescence, etc.

7.8.14. Manpower Analysis

Manpower Analysis (Function-wise, Unit-wise, Product-wise, and Product Group-wise)
- Manpower Productivity vs. Returns compared with Budgets or Standards or Industry Norms
- Manpower Pyramid – Ratio of Top Management to Middle Management to Officers to Workmen to Contract Labour
- Idle Man-hours to Total Man-hours with reason-wise analysis and impact on productivity, costs and profitability
- Manpower Absenteeism Vs. Total paid Man-days
- Cost of Manpower Pyramid Analysis – broken into broad categories (including contract labour)
- Cost of Training to Total Employee Cost

Chapter 8: Financial Modelling

8.1. Financial Modelling - concepts and application

8.1.1. Definition of Financial modelling
Financial modelling is the art and science of building a financial model, or the process of using a financial model for financial decision making and analysis. A model usually represents an ongoing or a project that requires investment. Financial models are not limited to profit making entities. Non-profits, governments, personal finances – all can be represented by financial models.

8.1.2. Uses of financial modelling
Financial modelling is applied broadly in the following areas:
a) Assists in decision making and business modelling of enterprises and evaluate the viability of projects
b) Carry out historical analysis of a company's performance
c) Do projections of its financial performance into the future
d) It is a pre-requisite for investment banking, equity research and commercial banking as project appraisal and risk evaluation using different scenarios may be calculated
e) Project finance related to a new entity, a vertical, a unit or a region
f) Carry out complex transactions like mergers and acquisitions
g) Creation of alternatives and sensitivities to evaluate and compare the base case scenarios for financial analysts as well as non-finance persons for assessment of projects and investment opportunities.
h) Commercial banks use financial modelling to check credit worthiness of applicants for disbursement of loans
i) Private equity firms use financial modelling to evaluate investments in PE alternatives and calculation of return based on exit strategies
j) Finally financial modelling assists in optimising economic value added and total shareholder returns

8.2. Types and categories of financial models

8.2.1. The types of financial models are as under:

Macroeconomic financial models	These models are developed by Government departments, NGOs, or economic consulting firms and used to forecast macro-economic growth of the country. The areas that are generally delved into though these models are foreign exchange rates and impact of its changes, interest rates, gross national product (GNP), gross domestic product (GDP) growth, inflation rates, disposable income etc
Industry financial models	The industry models are macro-economic models which forecast key financial indicators of respective industries, growth sectors and these are helpful for research analysts and industry associations
Corporate financial models	These are entity related models, which address the operations and financial performance of the corporates including business and strategy plans linked to vision , mission and strategic intent of these corporates

8.2.2. The categories of financial models are briefly explained as under:

Deterministic financial models	These are financial models where a set of financial variables are entered as input data into the program to generate a series of mathematical calculations and comes up with results e.g.Net Present Value, Internal Rate of Return calculations, business valuation , calculation of cost of equity based on Capital Asset Pricing Model , calculation of business plan and financial projections etc.
Simulation based financial models	In these financial models a range of input variables are used to generate and compute mathematical results through number of iterations. These are applied using statistical tools like mean, standard deviation, co-efficient of variation, regression analysis, time series etc. These scenarios are used where risk and uncertainty need to be mapped, and the financial analyst can use these as tools to measure risk and uncertainties using higher level of granularity.
Specialised financial models	These models are narrower in scope and are used for specific needs of the business, like customer profitability analysis, project finance, marginal contribution analysis, make or buy decisions, service related cost modules like health care and hospitality industries, activity based cost management models etc.

8.3. Possible applications of financial models

Some applications of financial models are highlighted below along with possible areas from which inputs are extracted:

Financial model – possible applications	Input received from
Financial performance – dash board	Financial statements
Business plan projections	Financial statements for existing data, assumptions on future growth and inflation factor
Project finance	Inputs around cost of debt and equity based on internal and external variables, like beta factor, industry risk premium, inflation factor, industry growth factor etc.
Credit analysis	Internal inputs from organisation
Portfolio management	External data from stock exchange, money markets etc
Enterprise risk management	Internal and external inputs and variables
Valuation of business	Financial statements, mathematical formula like, NPV, IRR, terminal values, growth factors etc

8.4. Users of financial models

The users and their respective uses of financial models show how critical these are in overall business environment. These are briefly summarised as under:

Users	Applications

Top management for decision support	Financial performance highlights
	Business Plan and financial projections
	Business Analysis
	Sensitivity on critical variables – value drivers
	Cash forecast
	Loan and repayment schedules
	Financial evaluation of projects including project financing
	   - Expansion projects
	   - Investment in new projects
	   - Merger & Acquisitions
	Financing models using
	   - Restructuring of existing loans
	   - Right issue
	   - IPO
	   - Private placement of shares, debentures, convertible debentures and their returns
	   - Equity injections
	   - Discontinuance of unprofitable verticals/ business/units
	   - Impairment of tangible and intangible assets or group of assets
	   - Fair value of investments
	   - Impairment of investments
	   - Derivatives and forward contracts
	   - Interest swaps and currency swaps etc.

Bank and financial institutions	Financial performance summary of the last three to five years Possible business and profitability trends Serviceability of business to service debts Rate of return of the business
Investment bankers and fund managers	Identify potential investment opportunities Identify unprofitable investments which needs to be disposed off Risk management analysis
Equity investors	Analysis of business performance Assessment of future business potential Analysis of entry and exit strategy Valuation of business Estimation of terminal value Estimation of NPV Estimation of project IRR and equity IRR

IPO, offer for sale, Listing requirements, right issues etc.	Objective of the proposed activity and its impact
	Determination of offer price and its justification for:
	   - Underwriters
	   - Pre – IPO investors
	   - Private placements
	   - IPO / right issue investors

Rating agencies	Analysis of company's credit worthiness Analysis of company's ability to pay its debt Issuing instrument ratings

	Issuing entity's ratings

Case study 8.1

Financial performance summary of Enterprise A Ltd is provided as under: (Rs lakhs)

SR.NO.	SUBJECT	2012-13	2011-12	2010-11	2009-10	2008-09
1	Share Capital	39.90	39.90	39.90	39.90	39.90
2	Reserves	317.98	306.91	296.31	291.72	258.09
3	Accumulated losses if any	-	-	-	-	-
4	Net Worth	357.88	346.81	336.21	331.62	297.99
5	Term Loans	240.15	12.19	26.87	44.24	34.36
6	Deferred Payment Liabilities	-	-	-	-	-
7	Working Capital Borrowings	-	-	-	-	6.08
8	Capital employed	598.03	359.00	363.08	375.86	338.43
9	Gross Block	179.26	193.68	121.49	76.89	72.01
10	Depreciation	15.96	27.42	27.50	13.63	15.36
11	Net Block	163.30	166.26	93.99	63.26	56.65
12	Investments	434.47	354.47	254.47	208.47	63.22
13	Other non-current assets	-	-	-	-	-
14	Current Assets	1,289.31	364.88	887.49	776.19	946.33
15	Current Liability (Inc W.C Loan)	1,289.05	526.61	872.86	672.06	727.77
16	Net working capital	0.26	-161.73	14.63	104.13	218.56
17	Capital employed	598.03	359.00	363.09	375.86	338.43
18	Income	1,447.44	1,430.89	1,327.38	1,396.46	1,208.75
19	Expenses	1,416.45	1,388.22	1,276.87	1,346.02	868.80
20	Operating Profit (EBIDTA)	30.99	42.67	50.51	50.44	339.95
21	Depreciation	15.96	27.42	27.51	13.63	15.35
22	EBIT	15.03	15.25	23.00	36.81	324.60
23	Tax	4.62	4.69	7.11	-	118.64
24	Net Profit (PAT)	10.41	10.56	15.89	36.81	205.96

The above comparative financials show five years trends which are used as basic raw material for financial modelling for analysis and company valuation.

8.5. Steps followed in financial modelling process

The steps followed in financial model process are developed as under:

Step 1	Gather historical financial statements and analyse it
Step 2	Compute ratios from historical financial statements to develop some of the assumptions about revenue, expenses split into fixed and variable depending on the nature and working capital
Step 3	Discuss assumptions and parameters with all the relevant departments / verticals of the organisation to ensure accuracy and validity as well as consensus

Step 4	Develop revenue parameters based on installed capacity, build-up of volumes over the years – both in terms of goods and services and prices, including growth assumptions. expenses, working capital and capital expenditures by working through value drivers
Step 5	Develop constituents of expenses and inflation for future years
Step 6	Develop working capital based on value drivers based on parameters related to inventories, receivables, payables etc.
Step 7	Develop capex outflows build up including calculation of depreciation for respective components of capex, like buildings, plant & machinery, equipments etc.
Step 8	Calculate source of funds and spread between debt and equity
Step 9	Calculate the projected income statement, projected balance sheet and projected cash flow statement
Step 10	Calculate interest on term loans and working capital based on repayment schedule of the loan
Step 11	Calculate Weighted Average Cost of Capital by valuing cost of equity and cost of debt
Step 12	Calculate terminal value based on free cash flow of the last year of the projected cash flow
Step 13	Develop valuation of the business on base case using NPV, work out sensitivities of critical alternatives and highlight assumptions
Step 14	Calculate return on investment of the cash flows in the form of Project IRR and Equity IRR
Step 15	Tie up cash generation as per projected Balance Sheet with the cumulative free cash flows to ensure that the financial modelling has been done accurately without any apparent calculation errors

8.6. Specific elements for financial models related to Balance Sheet and Profit & Loss
Specific elements that need to be looked into while carrying out financial modelling for Balance Sheet and Profit & Loss items are listed as under:

A. Balance Sheet items

i)Tangible Assets	a) each class of assets should show - opening balance - additions / deletions - depreciation - impairment if any - closing balance

	b) assets under finance lease linked to deferred income c) divide additions into: - sustainability capital expenditure - new projects (CWIP) - capacity expansion (CWIP) - interest capitalisation - forex impact on capitalisation if any d) in case of projects / capacity expansion - identify cost of project - link increase in capacity with incremental production and revenue - sources of finance linked to capacity expansion / new project split into debt and equity e) Calculate intangible assets e.g. acquired brand, goodwill etc. f)Impact on cash flow g) Tax benefits on capital expenditure
ii)Working capital	a)Analyse historical financial statements b)Calculate Debtors holding – days sales outstanding (DSO) – (last years'(trade receivables x 365) / turnover) c) Calculate Inventories holding – inventory days sales (IDS) – (last years'(inventories x 365) / cost of goods sold) d)Calculate creditors holding – (last years' (trade payables x 365)/cost of goods sold) e)Use these turnover ratios to project the elements of working capital holding for the projection years f)Calculate cash flow impact by working out changes in working capital
iii)(Shareholders' funds: Share capital – statement of changes in equity	a) show for share capital - opening balance - new shares issued - other adjustments e.g. buy back of shares - closing balance b) reserves and surplus - opening balance - transfers from statement of Profit & Loss to the extent of Profit for the period - transfers to other reserves - payout of dividend - creation of revaluation reserves and transfer to retained earnings on disposal of tangible assets which have been revalued - closing balance
iv)Loan funds	a)Long term borrowings - opening balance - new loans sanctioned and debt draw down - repayment of loans as per repayment schedule - calculation of interest and charge to statement of Profit & Loss - aggregate all long term borrowings - calculate summary of maturity - closing balance - calculate debt equity ratio b)Short term borrowings - opening balance - new loans sanctioned in line with working capital requirement

	- repayment of loans as per repayment schedule - calculation of interest and charge to statement of Profit & Loss - aggregate all short term borrowings - closing balance c)cash flow impact
v)Weighted average cost of capital (WACC)	a)Calculate cost of equity - Use Capital Asset Pricing Model to calculate cost of equity - Collect risk free rate - Collect industry beta factor - Calculate risk premium based on industry risk rate b)Calculate cost of debt - using interest rate - use tax rate - calculate net of tax of cost of debt c)Calculate debt equity ratio d)Calculate weighted average cost of capital (WACC) based on debt equity ratio

B. Statement of Profit & Loss

i)Revenue	a)Manufacturing companies - installed capacity - link capacity utilisation % with revenue - plan new capacity / enhancement based on new projects - calculate total market based on market research - determine market share in each product category by territory - calculate prices as per market price trend - develop revenue projections based on future trend - Use value drivers like distribution channel, sales force, availability of delivery vans (for FMCG products), number of distributors, number of retail outlets, availability of cold chain for dairy products and ice creams, availability of storage facilities across length and breadth of the country or abroad -analysis of tax both VAT/ State and central tax b)Finance companies - assets and liabilities - use deposit growth and loan to deposit ratio - investments e.g. capital expenditure and increases in loan
ii)Other income	a)estimate sale of scrap / sludge sales b)calculate income linked to short term investments c)cash surplus linked to projections d)calculate income on average deposit rates
iii) Cost of materials consumed	a)calculate a production vs distribution analysis based on revenue forecast b)calculate value of production c)calculate raw material consumption d)calculate other input costs like freight inward, loading and unloading expenses etc. d)adjust opening and closing stock values e)arrive at cost of materials consumed
iv)Variable and fixed costs	a)estimate variable costs linked to production b)estimate fixed costs irrespective of production

	c) calculate impact of variable and fixed cost on capacity expansion
	d)identify variable cost value drivers
	e)identify fixed cost value drivers
	f)use macro-economic growth factors to project growth for the future
v)Taxation matters	a)Calculate unabsorbed business losses
	b)Calculate unabsorbed depreciation
	c)Calculation difference between book depreciation and tax depreciation
	d)Calculate current tax provision
	e)Calculate deferred tax assets and liabilities and link to probability of future economic return specially for deferred tax assets
	f)Calculate MAT liability if applicable

C. Cash flow statement

i)Cash flow statement	a) Analyse cash flows from operating activities
	b)Analyse cash flows from investing activities
	c)Analyse cash flows from financing activities
	d)link cash flow statement for the period with opening balance and tie up with closing balance

8.7. Input variables for financial modelling

The principal input variables for financial modelling are:
   a) Installed capacity
   b) Actual production volume including plant down time
   c) PVD analysis
   d) Sales volume
   e) Distribution channels – specially for FMCG products
   f) Storage and warehousing facilities
   g) Logistics variable including number of delivery vehicles
   h) Selling price
   i) Key variable cost elements
   j) Key fixed cost elements
   k) LIBOR / MIBOR rate to be assumed
   l) Forex rates if plant/ equipments are to be imported
   m) Working capital parameters like DSO, IDS and creditors turnover etc.
   n) Debt equity ratio
   o) Weighted average cost of capital
   p) Terminal value calculations while valuation is business is carried out

8.8. Outputs expected out of financial modelling

The outputs generally expected out of a financial model would be as under:
a) executive summary highlighting the results of evaluation
b) statement of profit and loss for the projected period
c) Balance Sheet for the projected period
d) Cash flow statement for the projected period
e) Statement of equity
f) Critical financial ratios:
   - EBITDA / Sales %
   - Debt service coverage ratio

- PAT / Sales %
- Debt equity ratio
- Current ratio
- Liquid ratio
- Capital turnover ratio
- Return on Net assets (RONA)
- Return on Equity (ROE)

g) Company free cash flow both for each year as well as cumulative
h) Payback period
i) NPV and
j) Project IRR and Equity IRR
k) Valuation of business
l) Sensitivity analysis based on critical value drivers

8.9. Net Present Value (NPV) & Internal Rate of Return (IRR)

8.9.1. Distinction between NPV and IRR

The distinction between Net Present Value (NPV) and Internal Rate of Return (IRR) is as under:

Net Present Value	Internal Rate of Return
• Net Present Value is the present value of future cash inflows less cash outflows discounted at weighted average cost of capital. • If the financial value is positive then it is assumed that the project is going to generate incremental cash flows greater than weighted average borrowing cost of the organisation or the project under consideration. • Conversely if the value is negative then it is presumed that cost of borrowing exceeds the return from the project and hence the project is not viable. • In net present value cash flows are assumed to be re-invested at rates pertaining to weighted average cost of capital	• Internal Rate of Return (IRR) is a rate of return where the present value of cash inflows equates the present value of cash outflows for a specific project. • If the internal rate of return is lower than the weighted average cost of capital, then the project is not viable. • Conversely if the internal rate of return is higher than the weighted average cost of capital then the project is considered viable. • Accordingly, in case of Internal Rate of Return (IRR) re-investment is assumed at IRR rates.

Case study 8.2. Calculation of NPV and Project IRR

Enterprise B Ltd is a tea packaging company which is looking for financial investor and the promoters want to divest to the tune of 30% of their stake in the business. The relevant details are as under:

YEAR --------------------		2012-13
Installed capacity	Kgs / p.m.	2500000
Current utilisation	Kgs / p.m.	1200000
Capacity utilisation %		48%
Revenue Rate per kg (Rs)	8.0	
Expenditure per kg (Rs)	7.0	
Surplus per kg (Rs)	1.0	
Surplus per kg p.a. (Rs)		

Capacity utilisation will increase by 10% every year and optimal capacity expected to 85%.
Rental income is Rs.18 lakhs per month and is expected to grow by 5%.
Statement of Profit and Loss and Balance Sheet for the year 2012-13 is as under:

Statement of Profit & Loss   (Rs lakhs)

YEAR --------------------		2012-13
Revenue		226.0
Expenses		221.6
Misc. Expenses written off		
Total		221.6
EBITDA		4.3
EBITDA / Sales %		2%
Depreciation		0.00
PBIT		4.35
Interest		0.00
PBT		4.35
Tax 33%		1.44
PAT		2.91

Balance Sheet   (Rs lakhs)

YEAR --------------------		2012-13
Share capital		1247.0
Add: Profit / Loss		2.9
Shareholders' funds		1249.9
Debt funds		
Long term loan		1693.6
Less repayment		0.0
Net		1693.6

Financial Analysis for effective Management Decisions

Short term borrowings	456.6
Creditors	128.6
Total	3528.6
Gross Block	3183.6
Depreciation	0.0
Net block	3183.6
Investments	126.4
Inventories	19.7
Debtors	102.5
Other current assets	34.6
Cash	27.2
Cash generation	0.0
Total	3528.6

Gross block consists of Land Rs.3183.6 lakhs and buildings Rs.1500 lakhs having a useful life of 25 years. Borrowing cost is 13%, risk free rate is 8.5%, beta factor for the industry is 1.1 and risk premium is 5.5%. Tax rate as given in the financials to be taken at 33%. Assume growth rate of 5%.

Calculate the following:
a) Projected Profit & loss up to 2020-21
b) Projected Balance Sheet up to 2020-21
c) Projected Cash flow statement up to 20-21
d) NPV and Project IRR of the project.

Solution
Schedule 1: Financial parameters
These parameters have been worked out per month based on numbers provided.

Financial parameters										
YEAR ------------------		2012-13	2013-14	2014-15	2015-16	2016-17	2017-18	2018-19	2019-20	2020-21
Installed capacity	Kgs / p.m.	2500000	2500000	2500000	2500000	2500000	2500000	2500000	2500000	2500000
Current utilisation	Kgs / p.m.	1200000	1320000	1452000	1597200	1756920	1932612	2125873.2	2125873.2	2125873.2
Capacity utilisation %		48%	53%	58%	64%	70%	77%	85%	85%	85%
Revenue Rate per kg (Rs)	8.0		1,05,60,000	1,16,16,000	1,27,77,600	1,40,55,360	1,54,60,896	1,70,06,986	1,70,06,986	1,70,06,986
Expenditure per kg (Rs)	7.0		92,40,000	1,01,64,000	1,11,80,400	1,22,98,440	1,35,28,284	1,48,81,112	1,48,81,112	1,48,81,112
Surplus per kg (Rs)	1.0		13,20,000	14,52,000	15,97,200	17,56,920	19,32,612	21,25,873	21,25,873	21,25,873
Surplus per kg p.a. (Rs)			1,58,40,000	1,74,24,000	1,91,66,400	2,10,83,040	2,31,91,344	2,55,10,478	2,55,10,478	2,55,10,478

Schedule 2: Revenue projections
Based on above parameters revenue projections have been carried out per annum.

Rs lakhs

YEAR ------------------		2012-13	2013-14	2014-15	2015-16	2016-17	2017-18	2018-19	2019-20	2020-21
Rental Income	A		18.0	18.9	19.8	20.8	21.9	23.0	24.1	25.3
			216.0	226.8	238.1	250.0	262.5	275.7	289.5	303.9
Revenue from Packing	B		1,267.2	1,393.9	1,533.3	1,686.6	1,855.3	2,040.8	2,040.8	2,040.8
Total Revenue	A+B		1,483.2	1,620.7	1,771.5	1,936.7	2,117.9	2,316.5	2,330.3	2,344.8

Financial Analysis for effective Management Decisions

Schedule 3: Statement of Projected Profit & Loss (Rs lakhs)

YEAR -------------------	2012-13	2013-14	2014-15	2015-16	2016-17	2017-18	2018-19	2019-20	2020-21
Revenue	226.0	1483.2	1620.7	1771.5	1996.7	2117.9	2316.5	2330.3	2344.8
Expenses	221.6	1108.8	1219.7	1341.6	1475.8	1623.4	1785.7	1785.7	1785.7
Misc.Expenses written off		33.6							
Total	221.6	1142.4	1219.7	1341.6	1475.8	1623.4	1785.7	1785.7	1785.7
EBITDA	4.3	340.8	401.0	429.8	460.9	494.5	530.8	544.6	559.0
EBITDA / Sales %	2%	23%	25%	24%	24%	23%	23%	23%	24%
Depreciation	0.00	60.00	60.00	60.00	60.00	60.00	60.00	60.00	60.00
PBIT	4.35	280.78	341.04	369.81	400.88	434.47	470.79	484.57	499.04
Interest	0.00	231.84	216.69	196.74	170.98	137.73	95.17	41.30	7.91
PBT	4.35	48.94	124.36	173.07	229.91	296.74	375.62	443.27	491.13
Tax 33%	1.44	16.15	41.04	57.11	75.87	97.92	123.95	146.28	162.07
PAT	2.91	32.79	83.32	115.96	154.04	198.82	251.67	296.99	329.06

The projected profit & loss provides a fair reflection of earnings potential of the business in future years.

Schedule 4: Working capital summary (Rs lakhs)

YEAR -------------------	2012-13	2013-14	2014-15	2015-16	2016-17	2017-18	2018-19	2019-20	2020-21
Debtors	102.54	370.8	270.1	295.2	322.8	358.0	386.1	388.4	390.4
Inventories	19.71	92.4	101.6	111.8	123.0	135.3	148.8	148.8	148.8
Other current assets	34.56	0.0	0.0	0.0	0.0	0.0	0.0	0.0	0.0
Cash & bank	27.24	20.0	20.0	20.0	20.0	20.0	20.0	20.0	20.0
Gross Current Assets	184.05	483.2	391.8	427.0	465.8	508.3	554.9	557.2	559.6
Creditors	128.6	184.8	203.3	223.6	246.0	270.6	297.6	297.6	297.6
Net working capital	55.4	298.4	188.5	203.4	219.8	237.7	257.3	259.6	262.0
Working capital change	55.4	-243.0	109.9	-15.0	-16.4	-17.9	-19.6	-2.3	-2.4

Working capital projections have been considered based on assumptions of debtors as number of months sales, inventories as month of cost of goods sold and creditors as number of months on cost of goods sold.

Schedule 5: Balance Sheet (Rs lakhs)

YEAR -------------------	2012-13	2013-14	2014-15	2015-16	2016-17	2017-18	2018-19	2019-20	2020-21
Share capital	1247.0	1249.9	1282.7	1366.0	1481.9	1636.0	1834.8	2086.5	2383.5
Add: Profit / Loss	2.9	32.8	83.3	116.0	154.0	198.8	251.7	297.0	329.1
Shareholders funds	1249.9	1282.7	1366.0	1481.9	1636.0	1834.8	2086.5	2383.5	2712.5
Debt funds									
Long term loan	1693.6	1693.6	1597.6	1471.6	1309.6	1099.6	829.6	475.6	80.6
Less repayment	0.0	96.0	126.0	162.0	210.0	270.0	354.0	395.0	80.5
Net	1693.6	1597.6	1471.6	1309.6	1099.6	829.6	475.6	80.6	0.0
Short term borrowings	456.6	668.2	540.9	541.9	554.3	583.3	645.3	685.6	379.4
Creditors	128.6	184.8	203.3	223.6	246.0	270.6	297.6	297.6	297.6
Total	3528.6	3733.2	3581.7	3557.0	3535.8	3518.3	3504.9	3447.2	3389.6
Gross Block	3183.6	3183.6	3123.6	3069.6	3003.6	2943.6	2883.6	2823.6	2763.6
Depreciation	0.0	60.0	60.0	60.0	60.0	60.0	60.0	60.0	60.0
Net block	3183.6	3123.6	3069.57	3003.57	2943.58	2883.58	2823.58	2763.59	2703.59
Investments	126.4	126.4	126.4	126.4	126.4	126.4	126.4	126.4	126.4
Inventories	19.7	92.4	101.6	111.8	123.0	135.3	148.8	148.8	148.8
Debtors	102.5	370.8	270.1	295.2	322.8	358.0	386.1	388.4	390.8
Other current assets	34.6	0.0	0	0	0	0	0	0	0
Cash	27.2	20.0	20.0	20.0	20.0	20.0	20.0	20.0	20.0
Cash generation	0.0		0	0	0	0	0	0	0
Total	3528.6	3733.2	3581.7	3557.0	3535.8	3518.3	3504.9	3447.2	3389.6

Schedule 6: Depreciation summary   **Rs lakhs**

YEAR -----------------	2012-13	2013-14	2014-15	2015-16	2016-17	2017-18	2018-19	2019-20	2020-21
Gross Book Value	3183.6	3183.6	3123.6	3063.6	3003.6	2943.6	2883.6	2823.6	2763.6
Add: Capex	0.0	0.0	0.0	0.0	0.0	0.0	0.0	0.0	0.0
TOTAL	3183.6	3183.6	3123.6	3063.6	3003.6	2943.6	2883.6	2823.6	2763.6
Less: Land	1683.6	1683.6	1683.6	1683.6	1683.6	1683.6	1683.6	1683.6	1683.6
Depreciable asset	1500.0	1500.0	1440.0	1380.0	1320.0	1260.0	1200.0	1140.0	1080.0
Opening net book value		3183.6	3123.6	3063.6	3003.6	2943.6	2883.6	2823.6	2763.6
Less: Depreciation									
Depreciable asset		60.0	60.0	60.0	60.0	60.0	60.0	60.0	60.0
Total	0.0	60.0	60.0	60.0	60.0	60.0	60.0	60.0	60.0
Net book value	3183.6	3123.6	3063.6	3003.6	2943.6	2883.6	2823.6	2763.6	2703.6

Depreciation has been calculated based on useful life of depreciable assets. One could take depreciation rates as well.

Schedule 7: Calculation of Weighted Average Capital Cost (WACC)

Cost of equity	%	Rs lakhs	Rs lakhs
CAPM = Rf + Beta (Rp)			
=0.085 + 1.1*0.055	14.55%	1,247.0	181.4
Debt (1-33%)	8.71%	1,693.6	147.5
		2,940.5	328.9
WACC	11.19%		

*Rf = Risk free rate as given in the problem
 Beta = as given in the problem
 Rp = Risk premium as given in the problem
 Debt taken at 13% net of tax as given

Weighted average cost of capital has been calculated based on debt and equity spread given in the Balance Sheet. Cost of debt and equity has been calculated as above.

Schedule 8: Calculation of terminal value   **(Rs lakhs)**

Cash flow for 2020-21		394.6
Growth rate assumed	5%	
Terminal value =		6696.5
(FCF of 2020-21 *1.05)/(WACC-0.05))		

Terminal value has been calculated as follows:
  a) Free Cash flow for 2020-21 has been considered
  b) Free cash flow has been divided by the weighted average cost of capital (WACC)
  c) Growth rate has been assumed at 5%.
  d) The formula for terminal value calculations are:
      FCF of 2020 x 1.05 / WACC – 0.05

184

Financial Analysis for effective Management Decisions

Schedule 9: Cash flow summary   Rs lakhs

YEAR ------------------	2012-13	2013-14	2014-15	2015-16	2016-17	2017-18	2018-19	2019-20	2020-21	Terminal value
NOPAT	2.9	324.6	360.0	371.7	385.0	396.5	406.8	398.3	397.0	
Equity	1247.0	0.0	0.0	0.0	0.0	0.0	0.0	0.0	0.0	
Capex	-3183.6	0.0	0.0	0.0	0.0	0.0	0.0	0.0	0.0	
Investment	-126.4									
Working capital change	-55.4	-243.0	109.9	-15.0	-16.4	-17.9	-19.6	-2.3	-2.4	
Free cash flow	-2115.5	81.6	469.9	357.7	368.7	378.6	387.2	396.0	394.6	6696.5
Cumulative free cash flow	-2115.5	-2033.9	-1564.0	-1206.2	-837.6	-458.9	-71.7	324.3	718.9	

NOPAT is Net operating profit after tax, which has been taken from the Statement of Profit & loss. Cumulative free cash flow depicts that year 2019-20 the pay back of the investment has commenced with generation of positive cash flows. Based on these free cash flows, NPV and Project IRR would work out as under:

Schedule 10: Calculation of NPV and IRR

WACC			11.19%
		NPV	₹ 2,171
	Project	IRR	23.6%

Conclusion: Based on the above financial modelling, NPV has been calculated at by discounting future cash flows at a WACC of 11.19% and worked out to Rs.2171 lakhs.
Similarly the Project IRR has also worked out to a healthy 23.6%. This signifies that the investment is quite lucrative and prospective financial investor can proceed to look at this option positively.

Case study 8.3. Calculation of NPV and Project IRR

D Ltd is a setting up a project in Nimrana, Haryana to manufacture products to be used for Solar power a project cost of Rs. 2635.78 lakhs. Means of financing would be Rs.400 lakhs from equity brought in the entrepreneurs and Rs.1000 lakhs as term loan at 13.5% repayable at Rs. 50 lakhs in year 1 and at Rs.135 lakhs for year 2 to year 7 and balance in year 8. Rest of the funding would be through unsecured loan at 13.5% to the extent of 75% of working capital estimates.

The installed capacity of products manufactured and sold would be:

S.No.	Product Mix	Installed Capacity	Unit Sale Price	Income P.A. At Installed Capacity (100% CU)
		(Nos /Annum)	(Rs)	(Rs. Lakh)
1.	Charge controllers	78000	800	624.00
2.	Solar Inverters	3300	250000	8250.00
	Total			8874.00

Capacity utilisation percent would be as under:

Years	Yr1	Yr 2	Yr 3	Yr 4	Yr 5	Yr 6	Yr 7	Yr 8	Yr 9
Capacity utilisation %	50%	60%	70%	75%	80%	80%	80%	85%	85%

Cost of material consumption would be:

185

Financial Analysis for effective Management Decisions

Material	Rate Rs
Charge controllers	592.0
Solar Inverters	185000.0

Other expenses are as under:

Expenses	Parameters
Salaries & wages (at full capacity)	Rs.387.30 lakhs
Utilities cost (at full capacity)	Rs.60.88 lakhs
Factory overhead	3% of turnover
Selling expenses	3% of turnover
Admin expenses	2% of turnover
Depreciation on SLM basis	Rs.218.96 lakhs
Taxation	33%

Working capital estimates are as under:

Particulars	Parameters
Raw material holding	One month on raw material consumed
Goods in process	Half month on cost of production
Finished goods	One month on cost of sales
Utilities	One month expense
Factory overheads	One month expense
Selling & admin expense	One month expense
Credit sales	Two months
Creditors on purchase of raw materials	Paid in cash

Other parameters also provided:

Particulars	Parameters
Risk free rate	8.5%
Beta factor	1.1
Risk premium	5.5%

Calculate the following (ignore inflation):
  a) Weighted average cost of capital
  b) Statement of profit & loss for nine years
  c) Balance Sheet projections for nine years
  d) Cash flow statement for nine years
  e) Terminal value
  f) NPV
  g) Project IRR

Solution

a) **Weighted average cost of capital**

Cost of equity	%	Rs lakhs	Rs lakhs
CAPM = Rf + Beta (Rp)			
=0.085 + 1.1*0.055	14.55%	1,000.0	145.5
Debt (1-33%)	9.05%	1,000.0	90.5
		2,000.0	236.0
WACC	11.80%		

Working Notes:

WN1 Calculation of Revenue

S.No.	Product Mix	Installed Capacity	Unit Sale Price	Income P.A. At Installed Capacity (100% CU)
		(Nos /Annum)	(Rs)	(Rs. Lakh)
1.	Charge controllers	78000	800	624.00
2.	Solar Inverters	3300	250000	8250.00
	Total			8874.00

WN2 Calculation of raw material cost

S.No.	Product Mix	Installed Capacity	Unit Sale Price	Income P.A. At Installed Capacity (100% CU)
		(Nos /Annum)	(Rs)	(Rs. Lakh)
1.	Charge controllers	78000	592	461.76
2.	Solar Inverters	3300	185000	6105.00
	Total			6566.76

Financial Analysis for effective Management Decisions

WN3A working capital statement — Rs lakhs

Sl.No	Particulars	Period (Month)	2014-15	2015-16	2016-17	2017-18	2018-19	2019-20	2020-21	2021-22	2022-23
1	Raw Material (Mfg)	1	273.62	328.34	383.06	410.42	437.78	437.78	437.78	465.15	465.15
	Raw Material (Trade)										
2	Utilities	1	2.54	3.04	3.55	3.81	4.06	4.06	4.06	4.06	4.06
3	Wages & Salaries	1	16.14	19.37	22.59	24.21	25.82	25.82	25.82	27.43	27.43
4	Factory Overheads	1	18.49	22.19	25.88	27.73	29.58	29.58	29.58	31.43	31.43
5	Selling Expenses	1	11.09	13.31	15.53	16.64	17.75	17.75	17.75	18.86	18.86
6	Goods in process	1/2	151.72	182.06	212.40	227.57	242.74	242.74	242.74	257.78	257.78
7	Stock of Finish Goods	1	321.93	386.30	450.68	482.87	515.05	515.05	515.05	546.99	546.99
8	Credit Sales	2	759.50	887.40	1,035.30	1,109.25	1,183.20	1,183.20	1,183.20	1,257.15	1,257.15
9	Total		1,438.51	1,726.20	2,013.88	2,157.72	2,301.57	2,301.57	2,301.57	2,445.28	2,445.28
10	Bank Limits										
10.1	Non Fund Based for 1 cycles										
	FLC LIMIT										
10.2	Fund Based										
	Bank Finance Available										
	@ of 75% of Item 1,6,7,8		1,115.08	1,358.08	1,561.08	1,474.68	1,184.08	1,184.08	1,184.08	1,295.29	1,295.29

WN3B working capital summary — Rs lakhs

Particulars		2014-15	2015-16	2016-17	2017-18	2018-19	2019-20	2020-21	2021-22	2022-23
Raw material		273.62	328.34	383.06	410.42	437.78	437.78	437.78	465.15	465.15
Goods in process		151.72	182.06	212.40	227.57	242.74	242.74	242.74	257.78	257.78
Finished goods		321.93	386.30	450.68	482.87	515.05	515.05	515.05	546.99	546.99
Total Inventories		747.27	896.70	1,046.14	1,120.86	1,195.57	1,195.57	1,195.57	1,269.91	1,269.91
Trade receivables		759.50	887.40	1,035.30	1,109.25	1,183.20	1,183.20	1,183.20	1,257.15	1,257.15
Loans & advances										
Cash & bank										
Gross current Assets		1,486.77	1,784.10	2,081.44	2,230.11	2,378.77	2,378.77	2,378.77	2,527.06	2,527.06
Trade payables		48.25	57.91	67.56	72.38	77.21	77.21	77.21	81.78	81.78
Net working capital		1,438.51	1,726.20	2,013.88	2,157.72	2,301.57	2,301.57	2,301.57	2,445.28	2,445.28
Net working capital change		-1,438.51	-287.68	-287.68	-143.84	-143.84	-	-	-143.72	-

Financial Analysis for effective Management Decisions

b) Statement of Profit & Loss   Rs
   lakhs

	Particulars	2014-15	2015-16	2016-17	2017-18	2018-19	2019-20	2020-21	2021-22	2022-23
	CAPACITY UTILISATION IN %	50%	60%	70%	75%	80%	80%	80%	85%	85%
A1	INCOME (MFG)	4437.00	5324.40	6211.80	6655.50	7099.20	7099.20	7099.20	7542.90	7542.90
A2	INCOME (TRADE)									
A	TOTAL INCOME	4437.00	5324.40	6211.80	6655.50	7099.20	7099.20	7099.20	7542.90	7542.90
A2										
B.	COST OF PRODUCTION									
i	RAW MATERIAL COST-MFG	3283.38	3940.06	4596.73	4925.07	5253.41	5253.41	5253.41	5581.75	5581.75
	Raw material cost / Income %	74%	74%	74%	74%	74%	74%	74%	74%	74%
ii	WAGES & SALARIES	193.65	232.38	271.11	290.48	309.84	309.84	309.84	329.21	329.21
iii	OVERHEAD/RM EXPENCES 3 %	133.11	159.73	186.35	199.67	212.98	212.98	212.98	226.29	226.29
iv	UTILITY EXP (Power/Fuel)	30.44	36.53	42.62	45.66	48.70	48.70	48.70	48.70	48.70
C	COST OF PRODT(Bi-Biv)	3641.32	4369.44	5097.55	5461.61	5825.67	5825.67	5825.67	6186.68	6186.68
D	SELLING & ADMN. EXPENSES									
i	SELLING EXPENCES 3%	133.11	159.73	186.35	199.67	212.98	212.98	212.98	226.29	226.29
ii	ADMINISTRATIVE EXPENSES 2%	88.74	106.49	124.24	133.11	141.98	141.98	141.98	150.86	150.86
E	COST OF SALES (C+D)	3863.17	4635.66	5408.14	5794.39	6180.63	6180.63	6180.63	6563.83	6563.83
F	PBD&I (A-E)	573.83	688.74	803.66	861.12	918.57	918.57	918.57	979.07	979.07
	EBITDA / INCOME %	13%	13%	13%	13%	13%	13%	13%	13%	13%
G	DEPRECIATION	218.96	218.96	218.96	218.96	218.96	218.96	218.96	218.96	218.96
H	PROFIT AFTER DEP'N (F-G)	354.87	469.78	584.70	642.15	699.61	699.61	699.61	760.11	760.11
I	FINANCIAL COST									
i	TERM LOAN INTT(Rs 6 Cr @13.5%)	135.00	128.25	110.03	91.80	73.58	55.35	37.13	18.90	0.00
ii	WORKING CAP. INTEREST	264.53	286.51	297.98	284.09	257.31	205.83	159.85	108.58	12.46
J	OP. PROFITS BEFORE TAX(H-I)	-44.66	55.03	176.69	266.26	368.73	438.43	502.64	632.63	747.65
K	LESS TAXATION	0.00	18.16	58.31	87.87	121.68	144.68	165.87	208.77	246.73
L	PROFIT AFTER TAX (J-J)	-44.66	36.87	118.38	178.40	247.05	293.75	336.77	423.86	500.93
M	PROPOSED DIVIDEND	0.00	0.00	0.00	0.00	0.00	0.00	0.00	0.00	0.00
N	DIVIDEND TAX @ 10%	0.00	0.00	0.00	0.00	0.00	0.00	0.00	0.00	0.00
O	RETAINED PROFIT	-44.66	36.87	118.38	178.40	247.05	293.75	336.77	423.86	500.93
P	ADD:DEPN	218.96	218.96	218.96	218.96	218.96	218.96	218.96	218.96	218.96
Q	NET CASH ACCRUAL	174.30	255.83	337.34	397.36	466.01	512.71	555.73	642.82	719.89

189

Financial Analysis for effective Management Decisions

c) Balance Sheet projections
Rs lakhs

YEAR ----------------			2014-15	2015-16	2016-17	2017-18	2018-19	2019-20	2020-21	2021-22	2022-23
Share capital			1000.00	955.34	992.20	1110.59	1288.98	1536.03	1829.78	2166.55	2590.41
Add: Profit / Loss			-44.66	36.87	118.38	178.40	247.05	293.75	336.77	423.86	500.93
Shareholders funds			955.34	992.20	1110.59	1288.98	1536.03	1829.78	2166.55	2590.41	3091.34
Debt funds											
Long term loan			1000.00	950.00	815.00	680.00	545.00	410.00	275.00	140.00	0.00
Less repayment			50.00	135.00	135.00	135.00	135.00	135.00	135.00	140.00	0.00
Net			950.00	815.00	680.00	545.00	410.00	275.00	140.00	0.00	0.00
Short term borrowings			1115.08	1338.08	1561.08	1474.68	1184.08	1184.08	1184.08	804.29	92.29
Short term borrowings(shortfall)			844.42	784.20	646.20	629.70	721.90	340.60	0.00	0.00	0.00
Creditors			48.25	57.91	67.56	72.38	77.21	77.21	77.21	81.78	81.78
Total			3913.09	3987.39	4065.42	4010.74	3929.22	3706.67	3567.83	3476.48	3265.41
Gross Block			2635.78	2416.82	2197.86	1978.90	1759.94	1540.98	1322.02	1103.05	884.09
Depreciation			218.96	218.96	218.96	218.96	218.96	218.96	218.96	218.96	218.96
Net block			2416.82	2197.86	1978.90	1759.94	1540.98	1322.02	1103.05	884.09	665.13
Investments											
Inventories			747.27	896.70	1046.14	1120.86	1195.57	1195.57	1195.57	1269.91	1269.91
Trade receivables			739.50	887.40	1035.30	1109.25	1183.20	1183.20	1183.20	1257.15	1257.15
Short term & loans & advances			0.00	0.00	0.00	0.00	0.00	0.00	0.00	0.00	0.00
Cash			9.51	5.43	5.09	20.70	9.50	5.88	86.00	65.33	73.22
Total			3913.10	3987.39	4065.42	4010.74	3929.25	3706.67	3567.83	3476.48	3265.41

d) Cash flow projections
Rs lakhs

YEAR -------------------			2014-15	2015-16	2016-17	2017-18	2018-19	2019-20	2020-21	2021-22	2022-23	Terminal value
NOPAT			354.87	451.62	526.39	554.29	577.93	554.93	593.74	551.34	513.39	
Depreciation			218.96	218.96	218.96	218.96	218.96	218.96	218.96	218.96	218.96	
Equity			1000.00									
Investment												
Capex			-2635.78									
Working capital change			-1438.51	-287.68	-287.68	-143.84	-143.84	0.00	0.00	-143.72	0.00	
Free cash flow			-2500.46	382.90	457.67	629.41	653.05	773.89	752.70	626.59	732.35	6207.65
Cumulative free cash flow			-2500.46	-2117.56	-1659.90	-1030.49	-377.44	396.45	1149.15	1775.74	2508.09	

e) Calculation of terminal value

Cash flow for 2022-23		732.35
Growth rate assumed	nil	
Terminal value =		6207.65
(FCF of 2022-23)/(WACC)		

f) Calculation of NPV and IRR

WACC			11.80%
		NPV	₹ 2,836
Project		IRR	27.0%

Case study 8.4. Calculation of NPV and sensitivity analysis through financial modelling

From the following details relating to a project analyse the sensitivity of the project to changes in initial project cost, annual cash inflow and cost of capital:

Initial project cost (Rs)	1,20, 000
Annual cash inflow (Rs)	45,000
Project life (years)	4
Weighted average cost of capital	10%

Use financial modelling to determine which of the three factors, the project is most sensitive?
(Use annuity factors: 10% - 3.169, 11% - 3.109)

Solution

Calculation of NPV on base case   Rs.

Present Value of annual cash inflow (Rs.45000 x 3.169)	(A)	1,42,605
Less: Initial project cost	(B)	1,20,000
Net Present Value (NPV)	((A-B)= C)	22,605

Sensitivity 1: If initial project cost varied by 10%

Present Value of annual cash inflow (Rs.45000 x 3.169)	(A)	1,42,605
Less: Initial project cost (Rs.120000 x 1.10)	(B)	1,32,000
Net Present Value (NPV)	((A-B)= C)	10,605
Change in NPV (22,605-10,605)/22,605 X 100		53.08%

Sensitivity 2: If annual cash flow varied by 10%

Present Value of annual cash inflow (Rs.40500 x 3.169)	(A)	1,28,345
Less: Initial project cost	(B)	1,20,000
Net Present Value (NPV)	((A-B)= C)	8,345
Change in NPV (22605 - 8345/22,605 X 100)		63.08%

Sensitivity 3: If cost of capital varied adversely by 10%

Present Value of annual cash inflow (Rs.45000 x 3.109)	(A)	1,39,905
Less: Initial project cost	(B)	1,20,000
Net Present Value (NPV)	((A-B)= C)	19,905
Change in NPV (22605 - 199055/22,605 X 100)		11.94%

Conclusion: Project is most sensitive to sensitivity 2 i.e. annual cash flow.

Case study 8.5. NPV

Emmie Ltd has a machine having an additional life of 5 years, which costs Rs.1,00,000 and which has a book value of Rs.25,000. A new machine costing Rs.2,20,000 is available. Though its capacity is the same as that of the old machine, it will mean a saving in variable cost to the extent of Rs.70000 p.a. The life of the machine would be five years at the end of which it will have a scrap value of Rs.40, 000. The rate of income tax is 60%, and Emmie Ltd does not make an investment, if it yields less than 12%. The old machine if sold will fetch Rs.10,000.

Advise Emmie Ltd whether the old machine should be replaced or not.

Note:

P.V. of Re.1 receivable annually for 5 years at 12%   =3.605
P.V. of Re.1 receivable at the end of 5 years at 12%   =0.567
P.V. of Re.1 receivable at the end of 1 year at 12%   =0.893.

(ICMA – RTP 2013)

Solution

1.Statement of Annual Cash Flow:

	Rs.	Rs.
Cash inflow		70,000
Less: Depreciation on new machine (220000 - 40000)/5	36,000	
Less: Depreciation on old machine (25000/5)	5,000	31,000
Net Profit		39,000
Less: Tax @ 60%		23,400
Net inflow after tax		15,600
Add: Depreciation		31,000
Annual cash inflow		46,600

2.Statement of Net Present Value:

		Rs.	Rs.
P.V. of cash inflow for five years		46,600 x 3605	1,67,993
P.V. of scrap value at the end of five years		40,000 x 0.567	22,680
P.V. of total cash inflow	(A)		1,90,673
Less: P.V. of cash outflow (220,000 – 10,000)	(B)		2,10,000
Net Present Value	(A – B)		(19,327)

Conclusion: Since the Net Present Value is negative it is not viable to instal the new machine. Accordingly the old machine should be continued and not replaced.

Case study 8.6: Project IRR and Equity IRR

ABC Ltd, an infrastructure company is evaluating a proposal to build, operate and transfer a section of 35 kilometers of road at a project cost of Rs.200 crores to be financed as under:

Equity share capital Rs.50 crores, loans at the rate of interest of 15% p.a. from financial institutions Rs.150 crores. The project after completion will be opened to traffic and a toll will be collected for a period of 15 years from the vehicles using the road. The company is also required to maintain the road during the above 15 years and after the completion of that period, it will be handed over to the Highway authorities at zero value.

It is estimated that the toll revenue will be Rs.50 crores per annum and the annual toll collection expenses including maintenance of the roads will amount to 5% of the project cost. The company considers to write off the total cost of the project in 15 years on a straight line basis. For corporate income tax purposes the company is allowed to take depreciation @ 10% on WDV basis. The financial institutions are agreeable for the repayment of the loan in 15 equal annual instalments – consisting of principal and interest.

Calculate Project IRR and Equity IRR. Ignore corporate taxation.

Explain the difference between Project IRR and Equity IRR.

Solution

1. **Statement of computation of Project IRR**
     The equation is as under:
     COO = Cash outflow at time zero
     CFi = Net cash flow at different points of time
     N = Life of the project and
     R = Rate of discount (IRR)
     Applying the variables in the formula in the financial model
     COO = Rs.200 crores

CFi = Rs.40 crores p.a. for 15 years (Toll revenue Rs.50 crores – toll collection expense Rs.10 Crores = Rs.40 crores p.a. for 15 years)

Therefore,

Rs.200 crores = Rs.40 crores / $(1+r)^{15}$

2. **The value of the IRR of the project:**

First an approximation is made on the basis of cash flow data. This is done with reference to the payback period.

The payback period in the instant case is = Rs.200 crores / Rs.40 crores = 5 years.

From the Present value annuity table the range is 5.092 (18%) and 4.876 (19%). Hence it may be concluded that project IRR would range between 18% and 19%.

The estimate of IRR of cash inflow for the project for both these rates are:

At 18% = Rs.40 crores x 5.092

      = Rs.203.68 crores

At 19% = Rs.40 crores x 4.876

      = Rs.195.04 crores

Using interpolation method the exact Project IRR would be as under:

IRR = 18% + ((Rs.203.68 crores – Rs.200 crores)/(Rs.203.68 crores – Rs.195.04 crores))x 1%

    = 18% + (Rs.3.68 crores / Rs.8.64 crores) x 1%

    = 18% + 0.426%

    = **18.43%**

3. **Statement of computation of Equity IRR**

Cash flow at zero date from equity   Cash inflow available for equity shareholders

$$\text{Shareholders} = \frac{\text{Cash inflow available for equity shareholders}}{(1+r)n}$$

Where, r = Equity IRR

     n = life of the project

Applying the variables in the formula in the financial model

Cash inflow available for equity shareholders = Rs.50 crores

Cash inflow for equity shareholders Rs.14.35 crores (Rs.40 crores – Rs.25.65* crores equated yearly instalment on loan from financial institution as per working below)

*Equated annual instalment : (principal + interest) on loan:

Amount of loan	= Rs.150 crores
Rate of interest	= 15% p.a.
No.of years	= 15
Cumulative discount	= 5.847
Equated instalment	= Rs.150 crores / 5.847
	= Rs.25.65 crores

4. **The value of the equity IRR of the project:**

First an approximation is made on the basis of cash flow data. This is done with reference to the payback period.

The payback period in the instant case is = Rs.50 crores / Rs.14.35 crores = 3.484 years.

From the Present value annuity table the range is between 25% (3.859) and 30% (3.268).

The estimate of IRR of cash inflow for the project for both these rates are:

At 25% = Rs.14.35 crores x 3.859

      = Rs.55.3766 crores

At 30% = Rs.14.35 crores x 3.268

      = Rs.46.896 crores

Using interpolation method the exact equity IRR would be as under:

IRR =25% + ((Rs.55.377 crores – Rs.50 crores)/(Rs.55.377 crores – Rs.46.896 crores))x 5%

= 25% + (Rs.5.377 crores / Rs.8.4806 crores) x 5%

    = 25% + 3.17%

    = 28.17%

5. **Difference between Project IRR and Equity IRR**

   From the above the project IRR is 18.4% whereas equity IRR is 28.17%. The reason for this is that ABC Ltd is earning 18.4% whereas the loan from financial institution is being paid only 15%. Hence this difference between the rate of return and cost of funds of 3.4% has pushed up the equity IRR which is calculated as under:

   3.4% x (Rs.150 crores / Rs.50 crores) = 10.2% is added to the project IRR of 18.4% and hence explains the equity IRR of 28%.

Chapter 9: Business Valuation and Fair Value

9.1. Business Valuation

A business valuation is an examination conducted towards rendering an estimate or opinion as to the fair market value of a business interest at a given point in time. It is more an art than science, and a properly conducted valuation is nothing but an informed opinion based on fact together with best judgement. According to Damodaran "valuation is not an objective exercise, and any preconceptions and biases that an analyst brings to the process will find their way into value".

It is to be understood that business valuation is no precise science. There is no legal framework which drives or dictates how valuation should be performed. Since this is an informed opinion, valuation is generally stated as a range of values.

9.2. Purpose of business valuation

According to the Statement for Valuation Services issued by the AICPA, USA, purposes of valuation have been classified into four categories. These are:

Purpose of valuation	Illustrations
1. Valuation for transactions	Business Purchase Business Sale M & A Reverse merger Recapitalisation Restructuring Leverage Buy Out Management by Objective Management buy-in Buy sell agreement IPO ESOPs Buy back of shares Project planning etc.
2. Valuation of court cases	Bankruptcy Contractual disputes Ownership disputes Dissenting and oppressive shareholder cases Divorce cases Intellectual property disputes etc
3. Valuation of compliances	Fair value accounting issues
4. Valuation for planning	Estate planning Personal financial planning M & A planning Strategic planning

9.3. Stakeholders to business valuation

The stakeholders to business valuation are:

> ➤ Shareholders
> ➤ The company itself
> ➤ Financial experts
> ➤ The buyers of property and business
> ➤ Banks and others
> ➤ Mutual funds and hedge funds
> ➤ Insurance companies
> ➤ Governments
> ➤ Economy at large

9.4. Uncertainties in business valuation

We are aware the uncertainties are an integral part of the valuation process. We have to always bear in mind that, in valuing a business, we are valuing a going concern, the portrayal of which evolves out of its legacy – the past, the present and possible evolution into the future based on its current performance and vision, mission and strategic intent for the future. Sources of uncertainties are:

a) Uncertainties in estimation of inputs – some of which relate to the future
b) Uncertainties related to business enterprise in question
c) Uncertainties in the perception of the industry in which the business enterprise has to perform
d) Uncertainties related to macro economy in which the enterprise has to function

The general approach followed to sand paper the uncertainties are:

a) Application of better valuation models, which can factor in uncertainties
b) Application of ranges in valuation rather than using snapshot numbers
c) Use of probabilistic estimates to factor the risks and rewards
d) Consider a disclaimer on inputs provided or use of parameters provided by others, say for example, using the growth rate – more a passing the buck approach

9.5. What is fair value?

In accordance with Indian Accounting Standards, *Ind AS 113, Fair value measurement* is defined as under:

the price that would be received to sell an asset or paid to transfer a liability in an orderly transaction between market participants at the measurement date.

9.5.1. Fair value measurement of Asset and liability

When measuring fair value for an asset or a liability, an entity shall take into account the characteristics of the asset or liability if market participants would take those characteristics into account when pricing the asset or liability at the measurement date. Such characteristics include, for example, the following:

(a) the condition and location of the asset; and
(b) restrictions, if any, on the sale or use of the asset.

The asset or liability measured at fair value might be either of the following:
(a) a stand-alone asset or liability (e.g. a financial instrument or a non-financial asset); or
(b) a group of assets, a group of liabilities or a group of assets and liabilities (e.g. a cash-generating unit or a business).

9.5.2. Transaction

A fair value measurement assumes that the asset or liability is exchanged in an orderly transaction between market participants to sell the asset or transfer the liability at the measurement date under current market conditions.

A fair value measurement assumes that the transaction to sell the asset or transfer the liability takes place either:
(a) in the *principal market* for the asset or liability; or
(b) in the absence of a principal market, in the *most advantageous market* for the asset or liability.

9.5.3. Market participants

An entity shall measure the fair value of an asset or a liability using the assumptions that market participants would use when pricing the asset or liability, assuming that market participants act in their economic best interest.
The entity shall identify characteristics that distinguish market participants generally, considering factors specific to all the following:
(a) the asset or liability;
(b) the principal (or most advantageous) market for the asset or liability; and
(c) market participants with whom the entity would enter into a transaction in that market.

9.5.4. The price

a) *Price*	a) Fair value is the *price* that would be received to sell an asset or paid to transfer a liability in an orderly transaction in the principal (or most advantageous) market at the measurement date under current market conditions (i.e. an exit price) regardless of whether that price is directly observable or estimated using another valuation technique.
b) *Transaction costs*	The price in the principal (or most advantageous) market used to measure the fair value of the asset or liability shall not be adjusted for *transaction costs.* Transaction costs shall be accounted for in accordance with other Ind ASs. Transaction costs are not a characteristic of an asset or a liability; rather, they are specific to a transaction and will differ depending on how an entity enters into a transaction for the asset or liability.
c) *Transport costs*	Transaction costs do not include *transport costs.* If location is a characteristic of the asset (as might be the case, for example, for a commodity), the price in the principal (or most advantageous) market shall be adjusted for the costs, if any, that would be incurred to transport the asset from its current location to that market.

9.5.5. Application to non-financial assets

A fair value measurement of a non-financial asset takes into account a market participant's ability to generate economic benefits by using the asset in its *highest and best use* or by selling it to another market participant that would use the asset in its highest and best use.

The highest and best use of a non-financial asset takes into account the use of the asset that is physically possible, legally permissible and financially feasible, as follows:

(a) A use that is physically possible takes into account the physical characteristics of the asset that market participants would take into account when pricing the asset (e.g. the location or size of a property).

(b) A use that is legally permissible takes into account any legal restrictions on the use of the asset that market participants would take into account when pricing the asset (e.g. the zoning regulations applicable to a property).

(c) A use that is financially feasible takes into account whether a use of the asset that is physically possible and legally permissible generates adequate income or cash flows (taking into account the costs of converting the asset to that use) to produce an investment return that market participants would require from an investment in that asset put to that use.

9.5.6. Application to liabilities and an entity's own equity instruments - General Principles

A fair value measurement assumes that a financial or non-financial liability or an entity's own equity instrument (e.g. equity interests issued as consideration in a business combination) is transferred to a market participant at the measurement date. The transfer of a liability or an entity's own equity instrument assumes the following:

(a) A liability would remain outstanding and the market participant transferee would be required to fulfil the obligation. The liability would not be settled with the counterparty or otherwise extinguished on the measurement date.

(b) An entity's own equity instrument would remain outstanding and the market participant transferee would take on the rights and responsibilities associated with the instrument. The instrument would not be cancelled or otherwise extinguished on the measurement date.

9.5.7. *Liabilities and equity instruments held by other parties as assets*

When a quoted price for the transfer of an identical or a similar liability or entity's own equity instrument is not available and the identical item is held by another party as an asset, an entity shall measure the fair value of the liability or equity instrument from the perspective of a market participant that holds the identical item as an asset at the measurement date. In such cases fair value will be measured as under:

(a) using the quoted price in an *active market* for the identical item held by another party as an asset, if that price is available.

(b) if that price is not available, using other observable inputs, such as the quoted price in a market that is not active for the identical item held by another party as an asset.

(c) if the observable prices in (a) and (b) are not available, using another valuation technique, such as:

(i) an *income approach* (e.g. a present value technique that takes into account the future cash flows that a market participant would expect to receive from holding the liability or equity instrument as an asset,

(ii) a *market approach* (e.g. using quoted prices for similar liabilities or equity instruments held by other parties as assets;

9.5.8. *Liabilities and equity instruments not held by other parties as assets*
When a quoted price for the transfer of an identical or a similar liability or entity's own equity instrument is not available and the identical item is not held by another party as an asset, an entity shall measure the fair value of the liability or equity instrument using a valuation technique from the perspective of a market participant that owes the liability or has issued the claim on equity.

9.5.9. Non-performance risk
The fair value of a liability reflects the effect of *non-performance risk.* Non-performance risk includes, but may not be limited to, an entity's own credit risk (as defined in Ind AS 107, *Financial Instruments: Disclosures).* Non-performance risk is assumed to be the same before and after the transfer of the liability.

9.5.10. Restriction preventing the transfer of a liability or an entity's own equity instrument
When measuring the fair value of a liability or an entity's own equity instrument, an entity shall not include a separate input or an adjustment to other *inputs* relating to the existence of a restriction that prevents the transfer of the item. The effect of a restriction that prevents the transfer of a liability or an entity's own equity instrument is either implicitly or explicitly included in the other inputs to the fair value measurement.

9.5.11. Financial liability with a demand feature
The fair value of a financial liability with a demand feature (eg a demand deposit) is not less than the amount payable on demand, discounted from the first date that the amount could be required to be paid.

9.5.12. Application to financial assets and financial liabilities with offsetting positions in market risks or counterparty credit risk
a) An entity that holds a group of financial assets and financial liabilities is exposed to market risks (as defined in Ind AS 107) and to the credit risk (as defined in Ind AS 107) of each of the counterparties.
b) If the entity manages that group of financial assets and financial liabilities on the basis of its net exposure to either market risks or credit risk, the entity is permitted to apply an exception to this Ind AS for measuring fair value.
c) That exception permits an entity to measure the fair value of a group of financial assets and financial liabilities on the basis of the price that would be received to sell a net long position (i.e. an asset) for a particular risk exposure or paid to transfer a net short position (i.e. a liability) for a particular risk exposure in an orderly transaction between market participants at the measurement date under current market conditions.
d) Accordingly, an entity shall measure the fair value of the group of financial assets and financial liabilities consistently with how market participants would price the net risk exposure at the measurement date.

9.5.13. Fair value at initial recognition
a) When an asset is acquired or a liability is assumed in an exchange transaction for that asset or liability, the transaction price is the price paid to acquire the asset or received to assume the liability (an *entry price).* In contrast, the fair value of the asset or liability is the price that would be received to sell the asset or paid to transfer the liability (an exit price).
b) Entities do not necessarily sell assets at the prices paid to acquire them. Similarly, entities do not necessarily transfer liabilities at the prices received to assume them.

c)In many cases the transaction price will equal the fair value (e.g. that might be the case when on the transaction date the transaction to buy an asset takes place in the market in which the asset would be sold).

9.5.14. Valuation techniques

An entity shall use valuation techniques that are appropriate in the circumstances and for which sufficient data are available to measure fair value, maximising the use of relevant observable inputs and minimising the use of unobservable inputs.

Three widely used valuation techniques are the *market approach*, the *cost approach* and the *income approach*. These are summarised below.

Valuation techniques	Description
Market approach	a)The market approach uses prices and other relevant information generated by market transactions involving identical or comparable (i.e. similar) assets, liabilities or a group of assets and liabilities, such as a business.(Para B5) b)Valuation techniques consistent with the market approach often use market multiples derived from a set of comparables. c)Multiples might be in ranges with a different multiple for each comparable. The selection of the appropriate multiple within the range requires judgement, considering qualitative and quantitative factors specific to the measurement.(Para B6) c) Valuation techniques consistent with the market approach include matrix pricing. Matrix pricing is a mathematical technique used principally to value some types of financial instruments, such as debt securities, without relying exclusively on quoted prices for the specific securities, but rather relying on the securities' relationship to other benchmark quoted securities.(Para B7)
Cost approach	The cost approach reflects the amount that would be required currently to replace the service capacity of an asset (often referred to as current replacement cost).
Income approach	The income approach converts future amounts (e.g. cash flows or income and expenses) to a single current (i.e. discounted) amount. When the income approach is used, the fair value measurement reflects current market expectations about those future amounts. Valuation techniques include, for example, the following: (a) present value techniques; (b) option pricing models, such as the Black-Scholes-Merton formula or a binomial model (i.e. a lattice model), that incorporate present value techniques and reflect both the time value and the intrinsic value of an option; and (c) the multi-period excess earnings method, which is used to measure the fair value of some intangible assets.

Valuation techniques used to measure fair value shall be applied consistently. However, a change in a valuation technique or its application (e.g. a change in its weightage when multiple valuation techniques are used or a change in an adjustment applied to a valuation technique) is appropriate if the change results in a measurement that is equally or more representative of fair value in the circumstances. That might be the case if, for example, any of the following events take place:

      (a) new markets develop;
      (b) new information becomes available;
      (c) information previously used is no longer available;
      (d) valuation techniques improve; or
      (e) market conditions change.

9.5.15. Present value techniques

i) Present value (i.e. an application of the income approach) is a tool used to link future amounts (e.g.cash flows or values) to a present amount using a discount rate. A fair value measurement of an asset or a liability using a present value technique captures all the following elements from the perspective of market participants at the measurement date:

(a) an estimate of future cash flows for the asset or liability being measured.

(b) expectations about possible variations in the amount and timing of the cash flows representing the uncertainty inherent in the cash flows.

(c) the time value of money, represented by the rate on risk-free monetary assets that have maturity dates or durations that coincide with the period covered by the cash flows and pose neither uncertainty in timing nor risk of default to the holder (i.e. a risk-free interest rate).

(d) the price for bearing the uncertainty inherent in the cash flows (i.e. a *risk premium*).

(e) other factors that market participants would take into account in the circumstances.

(f) for a liability, the non-performance risk relating to that liability, including the entity's (i.e. the obligor's) own credit risk.

ii) Also, all the following general principles govern the application of any present value technique used to measure fair value:

(a) Cash flows and discount rates should reflect assumptions that market participants would use when pricing the asset or liability.

(b) Cash flows and discount rates should take into account only the factors attributable to the asset or liability being measured.

(c) To avoid double-counting or omitting the effects of risk factors, discount rates should reflect assumptions that are consistent with those inherent in the cash flows.

For example, a discount rate that reflects the uncertainty in expectations about future defaults is appropriate if using contractual cash flows of a loan (i.e. a discount rate adjustment technique).

That same rate should not be used if using expected (i.e. probability-weighted) cash flows (i.e. an expected present value technique) because the expected cash flows already reflect Assumptions about the uncertainty in future defaults; instead, a discount rate that is commensurate with the risk inherent in the expected cash flows should be used.

(d) Assumptions about cash flows and discount rates should be internally consistent. For example, nominal cash flows, which include the effect of inflation, should be discounted at a rate that includes the effect of inflation. The nominal risk-free interest rate includes the effect of inflation.

Real cash flows, which exclude the effect of inflation, should be discounted at a rate that excludes the effect of inflation. Similarly, after-tax cash flows should be discounted using an after-tax discount rate.

Pre-tax cash flows should be discounted at a rate consistent with those cash flows.

(e) Discount rates should be consistent with the underlying economic factors of the currency in which the cash flows are denominated.

9.5.16. Inputs to valuation techniques

i) Valuation techniques used to measure fair value shall maximise the use of relevant observable inputs and minimise the use of unobservable inputs.

ii) To increase consistency and comparability in fair value measurements and related disclosures, this Ind AS establishes a fair value hierarchy that categorises into three levels, the inputs to valuation techniques used to measure fair value. The fair value hierarchy gives the highest priority to quoted prices (unadjusted) in active markets for identical assets or liabilities (Level 1 inputs) and the lowest priority to unobservable inputs (*Level 3 inputs*).

iii)Level 1

Level 1 inputs are quoted prices (unadjusted) in active markets for identical assets or liabilities that the entity can access at the measurement date. A quoted price in an active market provides the most reliable evidence of fair value and shall be used without adjustment to measure fair value whenever available. The emphasis within Level 1 is on determining both of the following:

(a) the principal market for the asset or liability or, in the absence of a principal market, the most advantageous market for the asset or liability; and
(b) whether the entity can enter into a transaction for the asset or liability at the price in that market at the measurement date.

iv) Level 2

Level 2 inputs are inputs other than quoted prices included within Level 1 that are observable for the asset or liability, either directly or indirectly. If the asset or liability has a specified (contractual) term, a Level 2 input must be observable for substantially the full term of the asset or liability. Level 2 inputs include the following:

(a) quoted prices for similar assets or liabilities in active markets.
(b) quoted prices for identical or similar assets or liabilities in markets that are not active.
(c) inputs other than quoted prices that are observable for the asset or liability, for example:
   (i) interest rates and yield curves observable at commonly quote intervals;
   (ii) implied volatilities; and
   (iii) credit spreads.
(d) *market-corroborated inputs.*

Adjustments to Level 2 inputs will vary depending on factors specific to the asset or liability. Those factors include the following:

(a) the condition or location of the asset;
(b) the extent to which inputs relate to items that are comparable to the asset or liability (including those factors described in paragraph 39); and
(c) the volume or level of activity in the markets within which the inputs are observed.

v)Level 3

Level 3 inputs are unobservable inputs for the asset or liability.

Unobservable inputs shall be used to measure fair value to the extent that relevant observable inputs are not available, thereby allowing for situations in which there is little, if any, market activity for the asset or liability at the measurement date. However, the fair value measurement objective remains the same, i.e. an exit price at the measurement date from the perspective of a market participant that holds the asset or owes the liability. Therefore, unobservable inputs shall reflect the assumptions that market participants would use when pricing the asset or liability, including assumptions about risk.

9.5.17. Disclosure

An entity shall disclose information that helps users of its financial statements assess both of the following:

(a) for assets and liabilities that are measured at fair value on a recurring or non-recurring basis in the balance sheet after initial recognition, the valuation techniques and inputs used to develop those measurements.

(b) for recurring fair value measurements using significant unobservable inputs (Level 3), the effect of the measurements on profit or loss or other comprehensive income for the period.

To achieve the above an entity shall consider all the following:

(a) the level of detail necessary to satisfy the disclosure requirements;

(b) how much emphasis to place on each of the various requirements;

(c) how much aggregation or disaggregation to undertake; and

(d) whether users of financial statements need additional information to evaluate the quantitative information disclosed.

If the disclosures provided in accordance with this Ind AS and other Ind ASs are insufficient to meet the objectives above, an entity shall disclose additional information necessary to meet those objectives.

Also to achieve the above the objective an entity shall disclose, at a minimum, the following information for each class of assets and liabilities measured at fair value (including measurements based on fair value within the scope of this Ind AS) in the balance sheet after initial recognition:

    (a) for recurring and non-recurring fair value measurements, the fair value measurement at the end of the reporting period, and for non-recurring fair value measurements, the reasons for the measurement.

    Recurring fair value measurements of assets or liabilities are those that other Ind ASs require or permit in the balance sheet at the end of each reporting period.

    Non-recurring fair value measurements of assets or liabilities are those that other Ind ASs require or permit in the balance sheet in particular circumstances (eg when an entity measures an asset held for sale at fair value less costs to sell in accordance with Ind AS 105, *Non-current Assets Held for Sale and Discontinued Operations,* because the asset's fair value less costs to sell is lower than its carrying amount).

    (b) for recurring and non-recurring fair value measurements, the level of the fair value hierarchy within which the fair value measurements are categorised in their entirety (Level 1, 2 or 3).

    (c) for assets and liabilities held at the end of the reporting period that are measured at fair value on a recurring basis, the amounts of any transfers between Level 1 and Level 2 of the fair value hierarchy, the reasons for those transfers and the entity's policy for determining when transfers between levels are deemed to have occurred Transfers into each level shall be disclosed and discussed separately from transfers out of each level.

    (d) for recurring and non-recurring fair value measurements categorised within Level 2 and Level 3 of the fair value hierarchy, a description of the valuation technique(s) and the inputs used in the fair value measurement. If there has been a change in valuation technique (e.g. changing from a market approach to an income approach or the use of an additional valuation technique), the entity shall disclose that change and the reason(s) for making it.

    (e) for recurring fair value measurements categorised within Level 3 of the fair value hierarchy, a reconciliation from the opening balances to the closing balances, disclosing separately changes during the period attributable to the following:

(i) total gains or losses for the period recognised in profit or loss, and the line item(s) in profit or loss in which those gains or losses are recognised.

(ii) total gains or losses for the period recognised in other comprehensive income, and the line item(s) in other comprehensive income in which those gains or losses are recognised.

(iii) purchases, sales, issues and settlements (each of those types of changes disclosed separately).

(iv) the amounts of any transfers into or out of Level 3 of the fair value hierarchy, the reasons for those transfers and the entity's policy for determining when transfers between levels are deemed to have occurred (see paragraph 95). Transfers into Level 3 shall be disclosed and discussed separately from transfers out of Level 3.

(f) for recurring fair value measurements categorised within Level 3 of the fair value hierarchy, the amount of the total gains or losses for the period in (e)(i) included in profit or loss that is attributable to the change in unrealised gains or losses relating to those assets and liabilities held at the end of the reporting period, and the line item(s) in profit or loss in which those unrealised gains or losses are recognised.

(g) for recurring and non-recurring fair value measurements categorised within Level 3 of the fair value hierarchy, a description of the valuation processes used by the entity (including, for example, how an entity decides its valuation policies and procedures and analyses changes in fair value measurements from period to period).

(h) for recurring fair value measurements categorised within Level 3 of the fair value hierarchy:

(i) for all such measurements, a narrative description of the sensitivity of the fair value measurement to changes in unobservable inputs if a change in those inputs to a different amount might result in a significantly higher or lower fair value measurement.

(ii) for financial assets and financial liabilities, if changing one or more of the unobservable inputs to reflect reasonably possible alternative assumptions would change fair value significantly, an entity shall state that fact and disclose the effect of those changes. The entity shall disclose how the effect of a change to reflect a reasonably possible alternative assumption was calculated. For that purpose, significance shall be judged with respect to profit or loss, and total assets or total liabilities, or, when changes in fair value are recognised in other comprehensive income, total equity.

(i) for recurring and non-recurring fair value measurements, if the highest and best use of a non-financial asset differs from its current use, an entity shall disclose that fact and why the non-financial asset is being used in a manner that differs from its highest and best use.

9.6. Areas where business valuation is used

The key areas of business valuation are as under:

> - Valuation of equity shares in the primary, secondary as well as derivative markets
> - Private placement of equity shares
> - Securitisation and other debt instruments
> - Corporate restructuring – strategy mapping for the future
> - Valuation of verticals for divestment

> ➤ Demergers and reverse mergers
> ➤ Portfolio management – mutual fund, hedge fund, PE funding and professional investors
> ➤ Implementation of Basel II recommendation
> ➤ Long term and medium term investment decisions through merger & acquisition, divestment, disinvestment, venture capital investment, use of strategic investors, use of financial investors and so on
> ➤ Borrowing decisions
> ➤ Dividend decision
> ➤ Buy back of shares
> ➤ Financial risk management decisions
> ➤ Court case related decisions
> ➤ Transfer pricing and other tax related valuation issues
> ➤ Valuation of intangibles lying patent, copyright
> ➤ Forensic accounting and financial fraud investigation
> ➤ Development project valuation
> ➤ Property valuation
> ➤ Technology know how valuation for calculation of royalty
> ➤ Value based performance measurement
> ➤ Estate planning and financial planning
> ➤ Dissolution of firm, partner buy out and admission
> ➤ Valuation of insurance products
> ➤ Credit rating
> ➤ Fairness and solvency opinion
> ➤ Charitable donation
> ➤ Value based performance measurement specially for divisions / verticals and profit centres

9.7. Principles of valuation

The principles of valuation, which provide the foundation of various techniques of valuation are as under:

1. **Principle of substitution**: The risk averse investor would always compare and resist paying for businesses if a desirable substitute is available
2. **Principle of alternatives**: The investor would also look for alternatives and evaluate the quality of the target investment
3. **Principle of time value of money**: This is the genesis of valuation based on discounting future cash flows of a target enterprise being subjected to valuation by using appropriate discount rate
4. **Principle of risk and return**: As enunciated by Harry Markowitz, the father of modern finance, there are two assumptions based on which investor identifies an optimal portfolio. These are
   a) an investor is risk averse and
   b) given two portfolio investments have similar risk profile, one with the higher expected return will always be preferred by the investor as it drives higher wealth and higher consumption value.
   These two assumptions form integral part of valuation exercise
5. **Principle of expectation**: Future cash flows are based on business performance of an enterprise in the future and not the past. Depending on the tenure and maturity graph of the business under consideration, future expectations will be dialled in and this will form the basic tenet on which valuation will be carried out
6. **Principle of reasonableness and reconciliation**: Since we need to consider a lot of assumptions and parameters to value a business, we need to always keep in mind that these

are reasonable and open to reconciliation to ensure reliability, which may result in robust valuation results. Hence the following attributes deserve great attention:

a) Inconsistency in judgement and assumptions
b) Apparent flaws in concepts
c) Formula errors and flaws in modelling of projections

9.8. Determinants while carrying out valuation exercise

According to Revenue Ruling of 59 – 60 of USA, seven factors that must be considered in valuation exercise are:

1. The nature of business and the history of the enterprise from inception
2. Economic outlook in general and the industry in particular in which the enterprise belongs
3. The earnings and dividend paying capacity of the enterprise
4. The financial condition of the business and carrying value of assets
5. Whether the enterprise has intangible assets
6. Sale of equity and the size of the block of equity to be valued
7. The market value of enterprises engaged in similar business and their stocks are actively traded in the stock market.

9.9. Standards of value

Standard of value is defined as per the international glossary of business valuation as " identification of the type of value being utilised in a specific engagement e.g. fair market value, fair value or investment value. Five most common standards of value are:

1. **Fair market value**: Defined under International glossary of business valuation terms (IGBVT) as "The price expressed in terms of cash equivalents, at which property would change hands between a hypothetical willing and able buyer and a hypothetical willing and able seller, acting at arm's length in an open and unrestricted market, when neither is under compulsion to buy or sell when both have reasonable knowledge of the relevant facts.

2. **Investment value:** As defined by IGBVT, "it is the value to a particular investor based on individual investment requirements and expectations" In this case synergies are considered to be specific to purchaser and hence this value may be higher than FMV.

3. **Intrinsic value:** As per IGBVT, "it is the value that an investor considers, on the basis of an evaluation or available facts to be the "true" or "real" value that will become the market value when other investors reach the same conclusion". There are four major components of intrinsic value of a going concern:

   a) level of normal earning power and profitability in the employment of assets as distinguished from reported earnings
   b) dividends paid or the capacity to pay such dividends currently and in the future
   c) a realistic expectation about the trend line growth of earning power
   d) stability and predictability of those quantitative and qualitative projections of the future economic value of the enterprise

4. **Fair value**: As far as IFRSs, fair value is the amount for which an asset could be exchanged or liability settled between knowledgeable and willing parties in an arm's length transaction. According to US GAAP fair value is defined as "the price that would be received to sell an asset or paid to transfer a liability in an orderly transaction between market participants at the measurement date".

5. **Market value:** According to IVS Committee, the leading property valuation standard setting body, market value "is the estimated amount for which a property should exchange on the date of valuation between a willing buyer and a willing seller in an arm's length transaction after proper marketing wherein the parties had each acted knowledgeably, prudently and without compulsion."

9.10. Premises of business valuation

The premises of business valuation are twofold:

Liquidation basis	This premise assesses the value of a business as if it would cease operations and sell its individual assets. However, there is no consideration given to goodwill. Asset based lenders and banks tend to favour this basis.
	 The liquidation value per share would be:
	 (x-y)/Z,
	 Where, x = value realised from liquidating all the assets of the firm
	         Y = amount to be paid to all the creditors and preference share Holders
	         Z = Number of outstanding equity shares
	 Liquidation basis is not a standard of value but a premise since it is considered an attribute

Going concern basis	IGBVT defines going concern as " an ongoing operating business enterprise" and going concern value as" the value of a business enterprise that is expected to continue to operate into the future. The intangible elements of going concern value result from factors such as having a trained work force, an operational plan and the necessary licenses, system and procedures in place" Going concern value is not considered as standard of value but a premise of value since it is an attribute.

9.11. Steps to be carried out in business valuation

The sequential steps to be carried out in business valuation are:

Steps	Description
1	Determine the purpose of valuation
2	Define the standards of value
3	Select the premise of value
4	Carry out historical analysis
5	Carry out environment scan
6	Select appropriate valuation approaches
7	Select appropriate methods of valuation
8	Calculate value
9	Carry out reconciliation and reasonableness check
10	Conclude valuation

9.12. Valuation process

The valuation process to be followed comprises the following:

> ➢ Understanding the business, the industry in which it performs, the competitive scenario and the industrial environment in general
> ➢ Forecasting company performance, either top-down forecasting using macroeconomic analysis or bottom-up forecasting using individual company forecast and aggregate to industry forecast and macroeconomic forecast
> ➢ Selecting the appropriate valuation model, following the three broad criteria namely:
>   a) the valuation model should be consistent with the characteristics of the company being valued
>   b) the valuation model should be appropriate given the availability and quality of data
>   c) the valuation model should be consistent with the purpose of valuation,

> ➤ Converting forecasts into valuation
> ➤ Communicating valuation results – preparation of the report.

9.13. Approaches to valuation
General approaches to valuation incorporates three different types

a) Cost approach e.g. adjusted book value based on financial statements
b) Market approach e.g. comparables based on market parameters
c) Income approach e.g. discounted cash flow based on present value of future earnings expectations

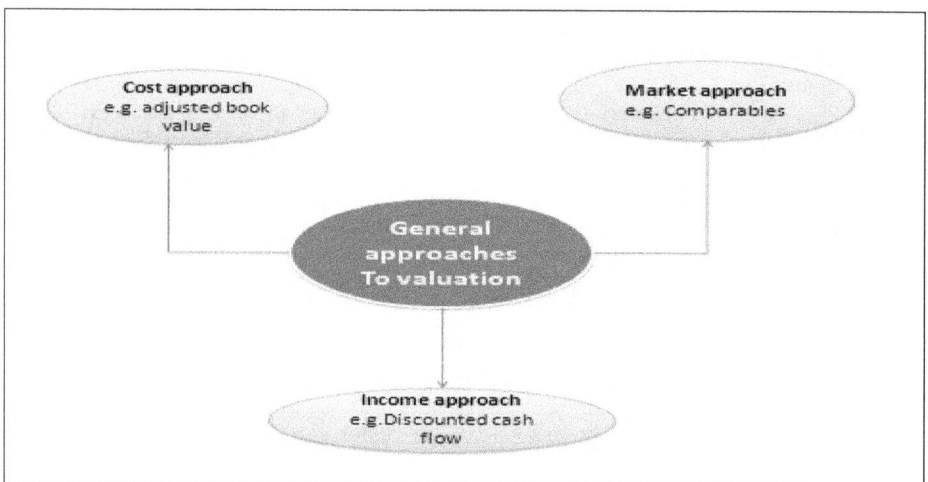

9.13.1. Cost approach:
This approach is also called Asset based approach, which is synonymous to asset accumulation approach, net asset value approach, the adjusted book value method and the asset build up method.

The objective of this method is to study and assess values to the company's assets and liabilities to generate value of the business. In this approach, the substance value, which assets minus liabilities must be positive. If however, liabilities are higher than assets, then this method loses its relevance.

The drawback of this approach is that, it uses balance sheet carrying values which are quite different from the real value, especially for assets when these are depreciated over their useful lives. In such cases the real value would represent the fair market value of the assets as ascertained in open market.

The two methods used are:

a) The liquidation value, being aggregate of estimated sales value of all the assets owned by the enterprise,
b) Replacement cost, being the current of replacing all the assets of an enterprise.

9.13.2. Market based approach:

This approach determines enterprise value by comparing one or more aspects of the subject enterprise to the similar aspects of other entities which have established market value

9.13.3. Income based approach:
This approach is commonly called Discounted Cash flow approach. It is universally accepted as by far the most appropriate method used for business valuations. According to the income based approach the business valuer must make estimation of the following elements highlighted below:
a) Estimation of business life expectancy
b) Estimation of future income flows that a business will generate during its life expectancy
c) Estimation of discount rate in order to calculate the present value of the estimated income flows.

9.14. Different valuation models
The models of valuation are highlighted as under:

9.14.1. Market based valuation model: This is the simplest way to value an enterprise traded publicly in a stock exchange. The company's stock can be bought and sold in that exchange. The value of a publicly traded enterprise is very simple to calculate. The formula is as under:

Equity market value (market capitalisation) = Price of a public traded share x No.of equity shares outstanding.

Illustration 9.1

Stock price of X Ltd is Rs.240 per share. Number of shares outstanding is 10 crores. What is the equity value of the enterprise.

Solution
Equity market value (market capitalisation) of X Ltd is as under:
= Market price per share x No. of shares outstanding
= Rs.240/- x 10 crores
= Rs.2400 crores.

9.14.2. Dividend Discount model: From the standpoint of the shareholder who buys and holds stocks, the cash flows received at any point in time, are the dividends paid on it and the market price of the share at that point. The present value of a share is nothing but the future value of dividends receivable on that share.
There are three versions of this model that are used to determine the intrinsic value of a share of stock:

i)   the constant (or no-growth) dividend model,

The formula is : P = Dt / Ke
Where, P = Intrinsic value
Dt = Expected dividend
Ke = Cost of equity or expected return

---

ii)   the constant dividend with growth model and

> **The formula is:**
> **P = Dt / (Ke – g)**
> **Where, P = Intrinsic value**
>   **Dt = Expected dividend**
>   **Ke = Cost of equity or expected return**
>   **g = constant dividend growth rate**

iii)   the two stage (or two phase) dividend growth model

> **The formula is:**
> **P = Sigma t=1 [Do (1+g1)t / (1 + Ke)t] + Dt (1+g2)t / (Ke – g2)**
> **[1 / (1 + Ke)t]**
> **Where, P = Intrinsic value = PV of dividends + PV of price**
>   **Dt = Expected dividend**
>   **Ke = Cost of equity or expected return**
>   **g 1= initial dividend growth rate**
>   **g 2= Steady dividend growth rate**

Two stage growth relates to high growth in the first stage followed by constant low growth till the end. This is ideally meant for firms which plough back more profit and pay only residual amount as dividend. Let us take an example as shown below.

Illustration 9.2: Dividend Discount model

Alpha Ltd is a company operating in a mature industry. Currently, its EPS is Rs.6.75. Alpha's dividend payout ratio is 60% and ROE IS 10% and both of these are expected to be the same in the near future. The beta of the company is 0.86. The treasury bill rate is 9.86% and the average return from the market is 15.26%.
Required:
Calculate the intrinsic value of Alpha Ltd using the Dividend Discount model.

Solution
To find out the intrinsic value we use the following formula:

        Po   = (Do (1 + g))/ k-g

a) EPSo   = Rs.6.75
    Dividend payout = 60%
                    = Rs.6.75 x 0.60
    Do   = Rs.4.05

b) Growth   = (1 – dividend payment) x ROE

	= (1 – 0.6) X 10%
	= 0.4 X 10%
	= 4%
c) K	= Rf + Beta (Rm – Rf) (using CAPM)
	= 0.986 + 0.86 (0.1526 – 0.986)
	= 14.504%

Now transposing all the values in the aforesaid formula,

Po = (4.05 x (1 + 0.04)) / (0.14504 – 0.04)

= **Rs.40.00**

9.14.3. Discounted cash flows valuation:

This method relates to the value of an asset to the present value of expected future cash flows on that asset. For details please refer 11.17.

9.14.4. Net Asset value method:

The net asset value method estimates value as the net cash remaining if all assets are disposed of to get the best possible price for each asset and all liabilities are paid with the proceeds. Assets and liabilities are adjusted to their individual appraised values. The net result is the value arrived at for the total enterprise.

Illustration 9.3: Net Asset Value method

Given below is the Balance Sheet of K Ltd as on 31.3.2013:   (Rs in lakhs)

Liabilities	Amount	Assets	Amount
Share capital (Share of Rs.10)	100	Land & Building	40
Reserves and surplus	40	Plant & Machinery	80
Creditors	30	Investments	10
		Stock	20
		Debtors	15
		Cash at bank	5
	170		170

You are required to work out the value of the company's shares on the basis of net assets method and profit earning capacity (capitalisation) method and arrive at the fair price of the shares, by considering the following information:

a) Profit for the current year Rs.64 lakhs includes Rs.4 lakhs extraordinary income and Rs. 1 lakh income from investments of surplus funds; such surplus funds are unlikely to recur,
b) In subsequent years, additional advertisement expenses of Rs.5 lakhs are expected to be incurred each year
c) Market value of land & building and Plant & Machinery has been ascertained at Rs.96 lakhs and Rs.100 lakhs respectively. This will entail additional depreciation of Rs.6 lakhs each year.
d) Effective income tax rate is 30%
e) The capitalisation rate applicable to similar business is 16%.

Solution

I) Net Assets method:

Net Assets	Rs in lakhs
Land & Building	96
Plant & Machinery	100

Investments	10
Stocks	20
Debtors	15
Cash at bank	5
Total Assets	246
Less: Creditors	30
Net Assets	216

Value per share

No. of shares = 100 lakhs / 10 = 10 lakhs

Value per share = Net Asset / no. of shares

= Rs.216 lakhs / 10 lakhs

= **Rs.21.60**

9.14.5. Earnings method:

The earnings method includes capitalisation of earnings, capitalisation of excess earnings and present value of future earnings. The capitalisation of earnings method is among one of the most popular methods of valuation approaches.

Illustration 9.4: Earnings method

Using the same example is in Illustration 2 above we would calculate the Profit earning capacity method:

Profit earning capacity method:

Particulars	Rs in lakhs
Profit before tax	64
Less: Extra-ordinary income	4
Less: Investment income not likely to recur	1
Less: Additional expenses for forthcoming years - advertisement	5
Less: Depreciation	6
Expected earnings before taxes	48
Less: Income taxes @ 30%	14.4
Future maintainable profits	33.6

Value of business = Future maintainable profit / Capitalisation factor

= 33.6 / 0.16

= Rs.210 lakhs

Value per share = **Rs.21.00**

9.14.6. Relative valuation:

This method estimates the value of an asset by looking at the pricing of comparable assets relative to a common variable such as earnings, cash flows, book value or sales.

Some of the important relative valuation matrix is as under:

Quantity	X	Multiple	Value
Cash flow	X	Firm value / Cash flow of firm	Cash flow multiple = Value of firm
EBITDA	X	Firm value / EBITDA of firm	EBITDA multiple = Value of firm
Sales	X	Firm value / Sales value of firm	Sales multiple = Value of firm
Customers	X	Firm value / Customers	Customer multiple = Value of firm

Earnings	X	Price per share / earnings	Price earnings ratio = share price

Multiples as highlighted above can be derived either by using fundamentals or comparable factors of firms or time and make explicit or implicit assumptions about how firms are similar or vary on fundamentals. Under comparable method, a firm is valued in lines with valuation of similar firms operating in the same industry or in instances comparable prior periods. Let us take an example as shown below.

Illustration 9.5: Relative valuation

A start-up health care company X is planning to go public. The financials of X along with similar Companies in the same industry are as under:

Company	Value (Market cap) Rs lakhs	Sales Rs lakhs	EBITDA Rs lakhs	Earnings Rs lakhs	Sales multiple (Market cap / sales)
X	?	100	20	10	?
Y	2100	70	17	12	30
Z	3000	75	18	8	40

Since the three companies are similar and operate in the same industry, the company X can be valued at comparable multiples of Y and Z.

Accordingly, drawing from comparable multiples of Y and Z, the value of Company X would be anywhere between: 30 x 100 = Rs.3000 lakhs to 40 x 100 = Rs.4000 lakhs. Investors and bankers would value the company within this range of Rs.30 crores and Rs.40 crores.

9.14.7. Economic Value Added (EVA):

It is a performance metric that calculates the creation of shareholder value. It distinguishes itself from traditional financial performance metrics such as net profit and EPS. EVA is the calculation of what profits remain after the cost of company's capital – both debt and equity – is deducted from operating profit. Let us use a simple example to explain EVA.

Say C Ltd earned Rs.10 million on a capital of Rs.100 million. According to traditional accounting methods C Ltd has achieved a return of 10% on capital. However, if we go by C Ltd's debt obligations plus the rate of return which the investors demand, it works out to 14%, which happens to be the cost of capital. If we use this benchmark and apply on the capital base of Rs.100 million, the company should have earned Rs.14 million. Hence it has achieved Rs.4 million short for the shareholders. Now if C Ltd would have earned say Rs. 20 million which is 20% return, it would have earn an EVA of Rs.6 million.

The steps in calculation of EVA are:

a) Calculate Net Operating Profit after Tax (NOPAT)
b) Calculate Total Invested Capital (TC)
c) Determine Weighted Average Cost of Capital (WACC)
d) Calculate EVA = NOPAT – CT X WACC

Illustration 9.6: Economic Value Added

Calculate EVA for Ram Ltd using the following information:

Particulars	Rs.
Revenues	3000000
Cost of goods sold	2000000
Operating expenses	700000
Cost of capital	8%
Short term and long term capital employed	1500000

Solution

EVA = NOPAT – WACC X Invested capital

= (3000000 – 2000000 – 700000) – 0.08 x 1500000

= Rs.1,80,000

9.14.8. Contingent claim valuation:

This is a revolutionary valuation model used to value assets the cash flows of which are contingent on occurrence of a future event. The examples are, an unknown oil rig, development of pharmaceutical drug, development of new product, innovation. In each of these cases there is high risk and uncertainty involved.

This method uses option pricing models to measure the value of assets that have share option characteristics also. Some of these assets are traded financial assets like warrants and some of these options are not traded and are based on real assets e.g. projects, patents and oil reserves as mentioned above.

The benefits of carrying out earnings based valuation and /or contingent valuations are:

a) They allow firms that are going concerns to value their ability to generate free cash flows in the near and far term,

b) They make an estimate of the WACC and the ability of future free cash flows to create wealth

c) They estimate terminal value of the enterprise and capture the effect of enterprise's intangible assets like intellectual capital, branding etc

d) They provide the owners an intelligent exit route out of the business

A few areas are highlighted as important cases of contingent claim valuation. These are:

1) **Real options valuation**

These options are valued as managerial rights and not obligations connected with projects to ensure that grow and expand with time and also abandon projects or assets after the investments are made.

2) **Valuations of intangibles and brands**

These valuations presuppose Identifiability and being separable. The three main approaches are:

a) Cost

b) Market value

c) Economic value

3) **Valuation of Warrants**

A warrant represents an option issued by a company to buy a stated number of shares of stock at a specified price. Warrants are generally distributed with debt or preferred stock to induce investors to buy those securities at lower cost. Most warrants are detachable – this signifies that these can be detached from the underlying security and traded separately.

What is the difference between convertible security and warrants?

Convertible securities	Warrants
Convertible securities are debentures or preferred stock which is converted to equity at a future date at the discretion of the owner.	A warrant is a long term right given to the owner to purchase common stock at a stated price
When conversion is exercised by the owner it is exchanged directly for common stock	With respect to warrants, both money and the warrant are exchanged for the common stock
Convertible securities have a face value and a coupon rate	Minimum price of a warrant is equal to zero until the price of the stock rises above the warrant's exercise price. After that warrant's minimum price shows positive values. The degree to which the warrant price rises with increases in the common stock price depends on the exercise ratio.

The formula is as under:

Minimum price = (Market price of common stock – Exercise price) x Exercise ratio

Warrant premium = Market price of warrant – Minimum price of warrant

The factors that affect the warrant premium are:

1. The stock price / exercise price ratio – as the ratio of stock price to exercise price rises, the warrant premium falls, as the leverage effect of warrants declines
2. As the warrant expiry date approaches near, the size of premium goes down
3. If investors feel strongly about the stock, the warrant premium goes up
4. The more volatile the common stock the higher the warrant premium.

Illustration 9.7: Contingent claim valuation - Valuation of Warrants

Alpha Ltd has announced issue of warrants on 1:1 basis for its equity shareholders. The current price of stock is Rs.10 and warrants are convertible at an exercise price of Rs.1.71 per share. Warrants are detachable and are trading at Rs.3.

What is the minimum price of the warrant? What is the warrant premium? Now had the current price been Rs.16.375, what is the minimum price and warrant premium? Consider warrants are tradable at Rs.9.75.

Solution

A. **At current price of Rs.10**

1. **Statement of calculation of minimum price**

    Minimum price = (Market price of common stock – Exercise price) x Exercise ratio

    = (Rs.10.00 – Rs.11.71) x 1.0

    = - Rs.1.71

    Since minimum price is negative it is considered as zero as one cannot sell at negative prices.

2. **Statement of calculation of warrant premium**
   Warrant premium = Market price of warrant – Minimum price of warrant
   $$= Rs.3.0 - 0$$
   $$= Rs.3.0$$

B. **At market price of Rs.16.375**
   Statement of calculation of minimum price
   Minimum price = (Market price of common stock – Exercise price) x Exercise ratio
   $$= (Rs.16.375 - Rs.11.71) \times 1.0$$
   $$= - Rs.4.665$$
   Statement of calculation of warrant premium
   Warrant premium = Market price of warrant – Minimum price of warrant
   $$= Rs.9.75 - Rs.4.665$$
   $$= Rs.5.085$$

4) **Valuation of preferred stock**

A preferred stock has the characteristics of both equity as well as debt. Preferred stock holders have preferential rights over common stock holders in right to dividend, and advantages in the event of dissolution, liquidation or bankruptcy. Since preference shares generally pay a constant dividend over its life time the value of a preferred stock is equivalent to

Value of preferred stock = Preference dividend / Required rate of return.

Of all types of preference shares, convertible preference shares are popular with equity investors, as these can be exchanged for a predetermined number of the enterprise common stock. The basic characteristics of preferred stock vis-à-vis its movement in value are highlighted in the chart below:

Characteristic	Increase in value	Decrease in value
Cumulative or non-cumulative	Cumulative	Non-cumulative
Convertible or non-convertible	Convertible	Non-convertible
Put option	Yes	No
Participating vs non-participating	Participating	Non-participating
Voting vs Non-voting	Voting	Non-voting
Redeemable vs irredeemable	Call price high	Call price low

The formulae on convertible preference shares are as under:

a) **Conversion ratio = Par value of convertible security / conversion price**
b) **Conversion value = Conversion ratio x Market value per share of common stock**
c) **Value of preferred stock = Preference dividend / expected rate of return**
d) **Conversion premium (in absolute terms) = Market price of convertible preferred stock – higher of the security value and conversion value**

Illustration 9.8: Valuation of preferred stock

Alpha Ltd is issuing 5% Rs.25 preference shares at par that would be convertible after three years to equity shares at Rs.27. If the current market price of equity shares is Rs.13.25, what is the conversion value and conversion premium? The convertibles are trading at Rs.17.75 in the market. Assume expected rate of return as 8%.

Solution

a) Conversion ratio = Par value of convertible security / conversion price

   = Rs.25 / Rs.27 = 0.9259

b) Conversion value = Conversion ratio x Market value per share of common stock

   = 0.9259 x Rs.13.25 = Rs.12.27

c) Value of preferred stock = Preference dividend / expected rate of return

   = (Rs.25 x 0.05)/ 0.08

   = 1.25 / 0.08

   = Rs.15.625

d) Conversion premium (in absolute terms) = Market price of convertible preferred stock – higher of the security value and conversion value

   = Rs.17.75 – Rs.15.625

   = Rs.2.125

9.15. Factors that affect valuation

The factors that affect formation of valuation are:

Internal factors	External factors
1.Market for the products	1. Competition
2. Market values of assets / liabilities	2. Technology development
3. Goodwill	3. Relations with Government agencies
4. Rate of dividend declared	4.Import / export policies
5. Industrial relations with employees	5. Taxation matters
6. Nature of plant / machinery	6. Current state of economy
7. Expansion policies of the company	7. Stability of Government in power
8. Reputation of management	

9.16. Difference between equity value and enterprise value

The principal difference between equity value and enterprise value is as under:

Equity value	Enterprise value	
The equity value of an entity is the value of the shareholders' claims in the company. The value of a share is arrived at by dividing the value of the company's equity as accounted in the Balance Sheet by the total number of equity shares outstanding. When a company is publicly traded, the value of the equity equals the market capitalisation of the company.	The enterprise value of a company stands for the value of the entire company to all its claimholders shown as under:	
	Enterprise value equals	Equity value
		Market value of debt
		Minority interest
		Pension and other benefits
		Other claims

9.17. Difference between fundamental valuation and relative valuation

The difference between fundamental valuation and relative valuation is as under:

Fundamental valuation	Relative valuation
Fundamental valuations are calculated based on a company's fundamental economic parameters relevant to the company and its future. These are also alluded to as "standalone valuations". Under this method the principal determinants are: a) cash flows : the cash flow to equity shareholders (dividends) or to both the equity shareholders and debtors (related to free cash flow) b) Returns : the difference between company's return on net assets and weighted average cost of capital c) Operational variables: Installed capacity, sales volume linked to capacity utilisation, projected market price in various verticals, cost structure etc.	Relative valuations are evidenced by relative multiples which apply to a relation between specific financial or operational characteristic from a similar enterprise or an industry in which it belongs and is being valued. This method expresses the value of a company as a multiple of a specific statistic or a metrix

General Illustrations
Illustration 9.9 : Dividend discount model

Information on two stocks A and B are given. Compare the intrinsic values of both the stocks.

	Stock A	Stock B
Dividend payout ratio	50%	60%
Cost of capital	10%	12%
ROE	14%	15%
EPS	Rs.2	Rs.3

Solution

Intrinsic value of Stock A:

$$P_{stockA} = D_1 / (k - g)$$
$$= D_1 / (k - (b \times ROE))$$
$$= 1 / (0.10 - (0.50 \times 0.14))$$
$$= Rs.33.33$$

$$P_{stockB} = D_1 / (k - g)$$
$$= D_1 / (k - (b \times ROE))$$
$$= 1 / (0.12 - (0.40 \times 0.15))$$
$$= Rs.16.67$$

Illustration 9.10: Dividend discount model

XYZ Ltd is expected to pay Re.0.60 dividend next year. The dividend is expected to grow at 50% per annum in the second and third year, at 20% premium in the fourth and fifth year and at 5% per annum thereafter. If the required rate of return is 12%, what is the value per share?

Solution:

The present value table is calculated below using the Gordon Growth model

Time	Value	Calculation	Dt or Vt	Present values
1	D1	0.60	0.60	0.536
2	D2	0.60 x 1.50	0.90	0.717
3	D3	0.90 x 1.50	1.35	0.961
4	D4	1.35 x 1.20	1.62	1.030
5	D5	1.62 x 1.20	1.944	1.103
5	Terminal value	(1.944 x1.05)/(0.12-0.05)	29.16	16.546
TOTAL				20.893

Hence the total present value of the dividend of this stock is Rs.20.893

Illustration 9.11: Economic Value Added

	Orange	Grape	Apple
Total Invested capital	100000	100000	100000
Debt / Assets ratio	0.8	0.5	0.2
Shares outstanding	6,100	8,300	10,000
Pre-tax cost of debt	16%	13%	15%
Cost of equity	26%	22%	20%
Operating Income (EBIT)	25,000	25,000	25,000
Net Income	8970	12350	14950

The tax rate 25% in all the cases above.
Required:
Compute the following:
a) Weighted average cost of capital for each company
b) Economic Value Added (EVA) for each company
c) Based on EVA which company would be considered for best investment? Give reasons
d) If the industry PE ratio is 11x, estimate the price for the share of each company
e) Estimated market capitalisation for each of the companies.

Solution
Calculation of WACC

Item	Orange	Grape	Apple
Wd	0.8	0.5	0.2
Kd	10.4	8.45	9.75
We	0.2	0.5	0.8
Ke	26%	22%	20%
WACC	13.52%	15.225%	17.95%

Calculation of EVA

Item	Orange	Grape	Apple
Invested capital	100000	100000	100000
WACC	13.52%	15.225%	17.95%
WACC X Invested capital (B)	13520	15225	17950
EBIT	25,000	25,000	25,000
NOPAT (A)	16250	16250	16250
EVA (A – B)	2730		1025

- 1700

Calculation of estimated market capitalisation

Item	Orange	Grape	Apple
Shares outstanding	6,100	8,300	10,000
Net Income	8970	12350	14950
EPS	1.47	1.49	1.50
P / E	16.18	16.37	16.45
Market capitalisation	98670	135850	164450

Illustration 9.12: Economic Value Added

A firm has assets in place in which it has capital investment of Rs.100 crores. The other facts are as under:

1. The after-tax operating income on assets in place is Rs.15 crores. This return on capital of 15% is expected to be sustained in the future, and the company has a cost of capital of 10%
2. At the beginning of each of the next 5 years, the firm is expected to make investments of Rs.10 crores each.
3. These investments are also expected to earn 15% as a return on capital and the cost of capital is expected to remain 10%
4. After year 5, the company will continue to make investments and earnings will grow at 5% per annum, but the new investments will have a return on capital of only 10%, which is also the cost of capital.
5. All assets and investments are expected to have infinite lives. Thus, the assets in place and the investments made in the first five years will make 15% a year in perpetuity, with no growth.
   Please value the firm.

Solution

The value of the firm is worked out as under:

Firm value = Capital invested in assets in place + (EVA t, assets in place) / (1+WACC)t
+ (EVA t, future assets) / (1 + WACC)t

I)   Capital invested in assets in place = **Rs.100 crores**

II)   EVA t, for assets in place   = ((0.15 – 0.10) x 100)/0.10
     = 0.05 x 100 / 0.10
     = **Rs.50 crores**

III)   EVA for future assets is as under:

Year (investment Beginning of year)	Formula for EVA = ((RONA – WACC) X Value of asset)/WACC	EVA Value Rs crores	Discount factor at 10%	DCE Amount Rs crores
1	(0.15-0.10) x Rs.10 crores / 0.10	5.0	1.0	5.00
2	(0.15-0.10) x Rs.10 crores / 0.10	5.0	0.909	4.55
3	(0.15-0.10) x Rs.10 crores / 0.10	5.0	0.826	4.13
4	(0.15-0.10) x Rs.10 crores / 0.10	5.0	0.751	3.76
5	(0.15-0.10) x Rs.10 crores / 0.10	5.0	0.683	3.42
	Total	25.0		**20.86**

Hence the value of firm would be (I + II + III) = (Rs.100 crores + Rs.50 crores + Rs.20.86 crores)
= Rs.170.86 crores, say rounded off to Rs.170 crores

Illustration 9.13: P/E for a high growth firm

Assume that you have been asked to estimate PE ratio for a firm which has the following characteristics:

Item	High growth phase	Stable growth phase
Expected growth rate	25%	8%
Payout ratio	20%	50%
Beta	1.00	1.00
Number of years	5 years	Forever

Risk free rate = Treasury bond rate = 6%

Risk premium = 5.5%

Solution

a) Statement of calculation of required rate of return

Required rate of return = Risk free rate + beta (risk premium)

$$= 6\% + 1.00 \times 5.5\%$$

$$= 11.5\%$$

b) Statement of calculation of P/E

P/E = $(0.2 \times 1.25 \times (1 - ((1.25)_5 / (1.115)_5))/(0.115 - 0.25)$

$+ (0.5 \times (1.25)_5 \times 1.08)/((0.115 - 0.08) \times (1.115)_5)$

$= 28.75$

Thus, for a firm with these characteristics the PE would be 28.75.

Similar results will emanate if dividend discounting model is used as well.

Illustration 9.14: PE for a high growth firm

Calculate the PE ratio for a firm which has the following characteristics:

Item	High growth phase	Stable growth phase
Expected growth rate	13.63%	66.67%
Cost of equity	10.85%	10.00%
Payout ratio	36.00%	?
Number of years	5 years	Forever

Return on equity based on industry average = 15%

Solution

a) Statement of calculation of payout ratio for stable growth phase:

Stable period payout ratio = (1- growth rate) / Return on equity

$$= (1 - 5\%) / 15\%$$

$$= 66.67\%$$

b) Statement of calculation of P/E

P/E = $(0.36 \times 1.1363 \times (1 - ((1.363)_5 / (1.1085)_5))/(0.1085 - 0.1363)$

$+ (0.67 \times (1.363)_5 \times 1.05)/ ((0.10 - 0.05) \times (1.1085)_5)$

$= 17.79$

Thus, for a firm with these characteristics the PE would be 17.79

Illustration 9.15: Relative valuation

We need to value a company A in the Auto component sector. Its financial parameters are as under:

a) Annual sales Rs.180 crores

b) Net debt   Rs.100 crores

c) EBITDA   Rs.70 crores

d) Earnings   Rs. 40 crores

Companies in this industry will be valued with sales, EBITDA and earnings multiples. The other companies in the Auto component sector are as under:

Company	Sales	EBITDA	Earnings	Market cap
W	220	115	82	900
X	190	90	60	700
Y	280	68	42	650
Z	150	45	26	320

Requirement:

Value the company A based on

a) Sales multiples

b) EBITDA multiples

c) Price to earnings multiples.

Solution

Company	Sales Multiples (Market cap / sales)	EBITDA Multiples (Market cap / EBITDA)	Price to earnings Multiples (Market cap / Earnings)
W	4.1	7.8	11.0
X	3.7	7.8	11.7
Y	2.3	9.6	15.5
Z	2.1	7.1	12.3
AVERAGE	**3.1**	**8.1**	**12.6**

Tutorial note: Enterprise value (market capitalisation) is divided by Sales and EBITDA to ascertain Sales and EBITDA multiples, but Equity value is divided by Earnings to ascertain Price to earnings multiples. Here in the absence of debt figures for these companies enterprise value is treated as synonymous to equity value.

Using the average values we can now work out the values of Company A as under:

Company	Sales Multiples (Market cap / sales)	EBITDA Multiples (Market cap / EBITDA)
Sales & EBITDA Co A (a)	Rs.180 crores	Rs.70 crores
Average of multiples (b)	3.1	8.1
Enterprise value (a x b=c)	Rs.558 crores	Rs. 565 crores
Debt value (d)	Rs.100 crores	Rs.100 crores
Equity value (c – d)	Rs.458 crores	Rs.465 crores

Company	Price to Earnings Multiples (Market cap / sales)
Earnings of Co A (a)	Rs.40 crores
Average of multiples (b)	12.6
Equity value (a x b=c)	Rs.505 crores
Debt value (d)	Rs.100 crores
Equity value (c + d)	Rs.605 crores

Tutorial note: In case of Price earnings multiple Earnings multiplied by average would give the equity value. When debt value is added to equity value it would generate enterprise value. Hence, based on above the equity value of Company A would range between Rs.458 crores and Rs.505 crores, whereas the enterprise value would range between Rs.558 crores and Rs.605 crores.

9.18. Discounted cash flow method of valuation

Discounted Cash Flow method has its foundation in the present value concept and the time value of money. In this method the value of any asset is the present value of expected future cash flows that the asset generates. To carry out valuation in this method, we need to
   a) Estimate the life of the asset
   b) Estimate the cash flows during the life of the asset
   c) Estimate the discount rate to apply to these cash flows to get present value
The formula is as under:

Value = Sigma t=n (CFt / (1+r)t)
Where,
n = life of the asset
CF = Cash flow in period t
r = Discount rate reflecting the riskiness of the estimated cash flows.

The cash flows vary from asset to asset. For example, with respect to stocks it will be linked to dividends, coupon rate of interest or implicit rate of interest on face value of bonds, and after tax cash flows for a real project.

Discount rates will vary depending on riskiness of the project, riskier the assets higher the rate and vice versa. Discount rate for a Government security would be its coupon rate, of a corporate bond would be its default risk, for zero coupon bonds would be zero.

9.18.1. Underlying bases of discounted cash flow method

Discounted cash flow models have three distinct underlying approaches. These are:

   a) Going concern vs asset valuation
   The value of an asset in the discounted cash flow method, is the present value of expected cash flows generated out of that asset. The value of a business is the sum total of values of individual assets owned by the business. Theoretically, this concept may be right but from practical perspective there is always variance between valuing a collection of assets and that of a business.
   Valuation of business is done based on going concern, which is based on financial statements of an entity. In going concern valuation, best judgement is applied not only on existing investments but also on expected future investments and their profitability as well.
   On the other hand on asset based valuation the focus is primarily on the assets in place and value of each asset is estimated separately. For entities with lucrative growth opportunities, asset based valuation will yield lower values whereas based on going concern the values will be higher.

b) Equity valuation vs firm valuation

The cash flows which remain after debt payments and reinvestment needs are called free cash flows and this relates to equity holders. The discount rate that reflects just the cost of equity financing is called the cost of equity. Hence valuation of equity stake in the business is referred to as equity valuation.

Whereas, the firm valuation comprises discounting of future cash flows approach generated from both the assets-in-place and growth assets. The discount rate is the weighted average cost of equity and debt which is called the weighted average cost of capital (WACC).

c) Variations on Discounted Cash flow models

There are couple of widely used variants to the above model we have explained, whereby future cash flows are discounted as risk adjusted rate.

In the first scenario, we bifurcate the cash flows into normal return scenario and excess return cash flows. Earning the risk-adjusted required return (measured through weighted average cost of capital or equity) is considered normal return cash flows. But any cash flow above or below this return would be treated as excess or short return. Accordingly the value of business would be:

Value of business = cash flow from existing business + present value of excess return cash Flows from both existing and future projects

---

In the second scenario, called adjusted present value (APV) approach, we segregate the effects on value of debt financing from the value of the assets of a business. Using debt to fund a firm's operations creates tax benefits (as interest expenses are net of tax) on the plus side and increases in bankruptcy risks (and expected bankruptcy costs) on the minus side. In this approach, the value of a firm would be as under:

Value of business = value of business with 100% equity financing + present value of expected tax benefits of debt – expected bankruptcy costs

---

9.18.2. Input to discounted cash flow models

The inputs to discounted cash flow models are as under:

a) Discount rates :

In general the weighted average cost of capital comprising both cost of equity and debt (net of tax) are used. However, riskier the business higher would be the discount rate. There are two ways to use discount rates to value under DCF method:

Weighted Average Cost of Capital (WACC) method
Adjusted Present Value (APV) Method

These methods will be explained later in pages that follow.

b) **Expected growth :**
   Expected future growth needs to be estimated taking into account the past trend as well as future business scenario both external and internal in nature

c) **Expected cash flows :**
   The cash flow accruing to the firm is the cumulative cash flow to all claimholders in the firm. This is derived by obtaining cash flows prior to debt and preferred dividend payments, by subtracting from the after-tax operating income the net investment needs to sustain growth. This cash flow is called the free cash flow to the firm (FCFF) and the models that use these cash flows are called FCFF Models. Free cash flow to equity model is called FCFE Model.

9.18.3. Net Present Value

The concept of Net Present Value centres around the time value of money. In simple words it states that the value of Rupee today is worth more than value of Rupee say a year from now. The basic reason is that a Rupee today can be invested in risk-free interest like Government securities and can earn a return. A rupee a year down the road is worth less today as it has not earned interest it would have earned had it been invested today. Hence the value of NPV is as under:

> **Present Value = Future value / (1 + Rd)n**
> **Where, Rd = the discount rate and**
> **n = Number of years in the future**

The concept of NPV uses discount rates based on whether APV method or WACC method is used, and the formula is as under:

> **NPV = FCF$_1$ / (1+Rd)$_1$ + FCF$_2$ / (1+Rd)$_2$ + FCF$_3$ / (1+Rd)$_3$ + ...**
> **+ FCF$_{10}$ / (1+Rd)$_{10}$**
>
> **or**
>
> **= Sigma n = FCFi / (1+Rd)i**
> **i = 1**
> **Where, FCF1 = Free Cash flow for year 1 and so on**
> **Rd = Discount rate**

Thus Net Present Value (NPV) is calculated by applying appropriate discount rate using either the APV method or the WACC method on future cash flows to determine the present values of future cash flows and the sum-total of all those values is termed as Net Present Value (NPV) of the business / enterprise.

9.18.4. FCFF and FCFE models

Definition of FCFF model is

> **FCFF = NOP – Taxes – Net Investment – Net change in Working Capital**
> Or
> **FCFF = Net Income + Non-cash charges + Interest (I-T) – Net investment – Net change in working capital**

Specimen format of FCFF model is as under:

Specimen format of calculation of free cash flows (FCFF)

Year	0	1	2	3	4	5	Remarks
Revenue	X	X	X	X	X	X	
Costs	X	X	X	X	X	X	
Depreciation on assets	X	X	X	X	X	X	Non-cash item
Profit before tax	X	X	X	X	X	X	
Taxation	(x)	(x)	(x)	(x)	(x)	(x)	
Net operating profit after tax (NOPAT)	X	X	X	X	X	X	
Add: Depreciation	X	X	X	X	X	X	Adjustment of non-cash item
Operating cash flow	X	X	X	X	X	X	
Add: Capital expenditure	X	X	X	X	X	X	
Add: Change in working capital	X	X	X	X	X	X	
Free cash flow to Firm	X	X	X	X	X	X	

Illustration 9.16

Please calculate Free Cash Flow to Firm from the following:
Sales : Rs.100000, Costs : Rs.75000, Depreciation : Rs.20000, Tax : 35%, Change in working capital Rs.1000, Capital expenditure Rs.10000.

Particulars	Amount Rs
Sales	100000
Less: Costs	75000
Depreciation	20000
Profit before tax	5000
Less: Tax @ 35%	1750
Profit after tax	3250
Add: Depreciation	20000
Less: Capital expenditure	10000
Less: Change in working capital	1000
Free Cash Flow to Firm (FCFF)	12250

Free cash flow to Equity model is a variant of the same which measure how much cash can be paid to the equity shareholders of the company after all expenses, reinvestment and debt repayment. Free cash flows to equity represents cash flow a company generates after necessary expenses and after satisfaction of claims of debt holders. It is derived out of Free Cash flow to the Firm (FCFF) as under:

FCFE = FCFF – After tax interest expenses + Net borrowing

If the company borrows more in a year than it repays it will have additional funds that could be distributed to shareholders, hence net borrowing has been added to FCFF in order to arrive at FCFE.

Specimen format of FCFE model is shown as under:

Specimen format of calculation of free cash flows (FCFE)

Year	0	1	2	3	4	5	Remarks
Revenue	X	X	X	X	X	X	
Costs	X	X	X	X	X	X	
Depreciation on assets	X	X	X	X	X	X	Non-cash item
Profit before tax	X	X	X	X	X	X	
Taxation	(x)	(x)	(x)	(x)	(x)	(x)	
Net operating profit after tax (NOPAT)	X	X	X	X	X	X	
Add: Depreciation	X	X	X	X	X	X	Adjustment of non-cash item
Operating cash flow	X	X	X	X	X	X	
Add: Capital expenditure	X	X	X	X	X	X	
Add: Change in working capital	X	X	X	X	X	X	
Free cash flow to firm	X	X	X	X	X	X	
Less: After tax interest expense $(I \times (1 - T))$	X	X	X	X	X	X	
Add: Net borrowing	X	X	X	X	X	X	
Free Cash Flow to Equity (FCFE)	X	X	X	X	X	X	

Illustration 9.17

Please calculate Free Cash Flow to Equity from the following:
Sales: Rs.100000, Costs: Rs.75000, Depreciation: Rs.20000, Tax : 35%, Change in working capital Rs.1000, Capital expenditure Rs.10000. Interest Rs.1000.
The company resorts to net borrowing of 6000.

Particulars	Amount Rs
Sales	100000
Less: Costs	75000
Depreciation	20000

Interest	1000
Profit before tax	4000
Less: Tax @ 35%	1400
Profit after tax	2600
Add: Depreciation	20000
Less: Capital expenditure	10000
Less: Change in working capital	1000
Free Cash Flow to Firm (FCFF)	11600
Less: After tax interest expense i.e.(1000 X (1-0.35)	650
Add: Net borrowing	6000
Free Cash Flow to Equity (FCFE)	16950

Once the free cash flows have been estimated as above, the value of the firm is the sum of the present values of the free cash flows for a planning period plus the present value of the cash flows beyond the planning horizon i.e. terminal value.

9.18.5. Capital Asset Pricing Model (CAPM)

This is a model used to calculate expected return on investment also referred to as the expected return on equity. This is a linear model with one independent variable called Beta.
Beta represents relative volatility of the investment in question vis-à-vis the market. This means if Beta is 1, it means the degree of volatility of the investment is identical to that of the market returns. If Beta is less than 1 then the return on the investment (say an utility company), is less volatile than the market. Conversely, if Beta is greater than 1, then the return on the target investment (say a dot.com company) is more volatile than that of the market.
The CAPM formula is as under:

$$Ke = Rf + Beta\ (Rm - Rf)$$

Where Ke = Discount rate for an all equity firm
Rf = Risk free rate (e.g. Government securities)
Rm = Market return
Rm-Rf = Risk premium being excess market return
Beta = Equity Beta

We need to be careful to use Equity Beta value as opposed to Asset Beta value. If we have information related to Beta Assets and not Beta equity, then we need to convert Beta asset to Beta equity using the following formula:

$$Be = Ba \times (D + E) / E$$

Where, Be = Beta equity
Ba = Beta assets
D = Market value of debt (assumed as zero)
E = Market value of equity (market capitalisation e.g. market price x no. of shares outstanding)

9.18.6. Steps followed for calculating FCFE valuation

The steps followed are as under:

Step I: Estimate free cash flow to equity.

> **Free cash flow to equity = Net Income – Capital expenditure + Depreciation – Working capital accruals + New debt issued – debt repayment**

Step II

Calculate the PV of equity cash flows by using cost of equity (Ke) as discounting rate.

Step III

Cost of Equity can be calculated using CAPM (Capital Asset Pricing Model) approach as mentioned in 9.18.5 above.

9.18.7. What is stable growth FCFE model

The value of equity under stable growth FCFF model is a function of the following:
a) expected FCFE in the next period
b) the stable growth rate
c) the required rate of return

and the formula is

> **Po = FCFE1 / (r – gn)**
> *where,* **Po** = Value of stock today
> **FCFE** = Expected FCFE next year
> **r** = Cost of equity of the firm
> **gn** = Growth rate in FCFE for the firm forever.

Illustration 9.18

Earnings per share	= Rs.3.15
Capital expenditure per share	= Rs.3.15
Depreciation per share	= Rs.2.78
Change in working capital per share	= Rs.0.50
Debt financing ratio	= 25%

Earnings, capital expenditure, depreciation and working capital are all expected to grow at 6% per year.
The beta for stock is 0.90. Treasury bond rate is 7.5%. Rate of return for common stocks 12%
Calculate value of stock.

Solution

As per CAPM approach cost of equity would be as follows:	
Cost of equity	= 7.5% + 0.90 (12% -7.5%)
	= 7.5% + 0.90 x 4.5%
	= 7.5% + 4.05%
	= 11.55%
Expected growth rate = 6%	
Base year FCFE	= Rs.3.15 – (Rs.3.15 – Rs.2.78) (1 – 0.25) – 0.50 (1 – 0.25)
	=2.4975
Value per share	= (2.4975 x 1.06 / (0.1155 – 0.06)
	= 2.4975 x 19.0991
	= 47.70

9.18.8. Two stage and three stage FCFE model

a) Two stage FCFE model:

In the two stage FCFE model, the value of stock would comprise:

i)   The present value of the FCFE per year for the extra-ordinary growth period and

ii)   Terminal value at the end of the period

Hence, Value of stock = PV of FCFE + PV of Terminal price

$$= \text{Sigma t=n FCFEt (1+r) t + Pn (1+r) n}$$

Where, FCFEt = FCFE in year t

Pn = Price at the end of extra ordinary growth period

r = Required rate of return to equity investors in high growth period.

The terminal value is calculated using the infinite growth rate model:

Pn = FCFE n+1 (rn – gn)

Where, gn = Growth rate after the terminal year forever

rn = Required rate of return to equity investors in stable growth period

---

b) Three stage FCFE model – E model:

The three stage FCFE model – called the E model – is designed to value firms that are expected to go through three stages of growth, namely,

i)   An initial phase of high growth,

ii)   A transitional period where growth rate declines and

iii)   A steady state where growth rate is stable.

The formula is as under:

Po = Sigma t=n1 = FCFEt / (1 +r) t + Sigma t = 2 FCFE1 / (1 +r) t + Pn2 / (1+r) 2

Where Po = Value of stock today

FCFEt = FCFE in year t

---

t = Cost of equity
r = required rate of return
Pn2 = Terminal value at the end of transition period
= FCFEn2 + 1 / (r – gn)
n1 = End of initial high growth period
n2 = End of transition period

9.18.9. How do we calculate the appropriate discount rate

There are two ways to use discount rates to value under DCF method:

a) Weighted Average Cost of Capital (WACC) method

b) Adjusted Present Value (APV) Method

The difference between the above methods is mainly the use of discount rate.

a) **Weighted Average Cost of Capital (WACC) method**
For WACC, the discount rate is calculated as under:

WACC = (E / (D + E)) X Re(leveraged) + (E / (D + E)) X (1 – t) x Rd
Where, D = Market value of debt
E = Market value of equity
Rd = Discount rate for rate (average long term debt)
Re (leveraged) = Discount rate for leveraged equity (calculated using CAPM)

We know CAPM formula is revisited as under:

CAPM = Rf + Beta L (Rm – Rf)
Where, Rf = Risk free rate
Rm = Market rate of return
Rm – Rf = Excess Market return - risk premium
Beta L = Leveraged Beta

The value of leveraged beta can be derived out of unlevered beta based on the equation below, a process which is called unlevering of beta.

Beta L = Beta u x [(1 + (1- t) D) / E]
Where, Beta u = Unlevered Beta
D = Market value of debt
E = Market value of equity

231

b) **Adjusted Present Value (APV) Method:**
In case of APV approach the CAPM formula undergoes a change as we can see in the following formula:

$$
\begin{aligned}
&\textbf{CAPM = Rf + Beta u (Rm – Rf)}\\
&\textbf{Where, Rf = Risk free rate}\\
&\textbf{Rm = Market rate of return}\\
&\textbf{Rm – Rf = Excess Market return - risk premium}\\
&\textbf{Beta}_u\textbf{ = Unleveraged Beta}
\end{aligned}
$$

This signifies that in case of APV approach we assume the unlevered beta approach, which assumes unleveraged equity discount rate, meaning that debt is zero. On the other hand WACC approach assumes leveraged beta, which signifies leveraged (historical) discount rate. Now the question arises, as to what happens in case the company has debt, as APV does not capture the real value of the enterprise. Hence in such cases we need to add the value of Debt Tax Shield or the amount the company saves by not having to pay interest on debt. To adjust this difference a value of Debt Tax Shield (DTS) is added to the overall value of the enterprise. The formula of Debt Tax Shield is as under:

$$
\begin{aligned}
&\textbf{DTS = D X Rd x t}\\
&\textbf{Where, D = Total debt of the company in the period under consideration}\\
&\textbf{Rd = Weighted average rate of interest}\\
&\textbf{t = Corporate tax rate}
\end{aligned}
$$

To bring this concept in perspective, this principle happens to be the principle reason for leveraged buy-out. We need to keep in mind that the discount rate to be used for DTS would be the one which best represents the risk associated with the DTS in question.

The difference between WACC and APV approach is as under:

WACC Approach	APV Approach
WACC considers the target debt equity ratio to calculate the discount rate. However, we need to consider that target debt equity ratio is reached when the company is matured until some time period is elapsed. Hence it may not be considered practically complete.	APV approach considers an all equity valuation, debt being considered as zero.

9.18.10. Terminal value
The terminal value calculation is based on the premise that the cash flows of final year of projection (usually year 10 in a ten year projection) will keep growing at a particular rate of growth. The rate of growth would not be as high as the growth in the first ten years, as it is expected that the enterprise growth has stabilised in the first ten years. Hence a reasonable estimate of growth may be considered. The terminal value is calculated as under:

> **Terminal value = (Terminal year FCF $_{10}$ X (1+g)) / (Rd – g)**

This is discounted as under:

> **Present value of Terminal Value**
> **= (FCF $_{10}$ X (1 + g) / ((1 + Rd)$_{10}$ x (Rd – g))**

Finally, the present value of Free cash flows of each year are aggregated with the present value of terminal value at the final year of projection to arrive at the final enterprise valuation.

9.18.11. Situations when FCFE models and dividend discount valuation models provide similar as well as dissimilar results

We know that FCFE model is an alternative to dividend discounting model. However, at times they provide the same results. Let us see which the similar results are.

Similar results
a) Where dividends are equal to FCFE
b) Where FCFE is greater than dividends but excess cash (FCFE – Dividends) is invested in projects with NPV = 0 (investments are fairly priced)

Dissimilar results
a) When FCFE is greater than dividends and excess cash earns interest below market rates or invested in negative NPV – value projects, the value from FCFE will be greater than the value from discount model,
b) When dividends are greater than FCFE, the firm will have to issue either new stock or go for fresh debts to pay the dividend,

20.18.12. Step by step build-up of Discounted cash flows

The steps followed in building up a discounted cash flow are as under:

Step 1	Estimate free cash flows for the explicit forecast period
Step 2	Eliminate a suitable discount rate for the acquisition
Step 3	Calculate the present value of cash flows for the explicit forecast period
Step 4	Estimate the terminal value
Step 5	Determine the value of the firm
Step 6	Subtract the value of debt
Step 7	Calculate intrinsic value of shares

Let us build the steps through an example.

Illustration 9.19

Step 1: Say, we estimate the free cash flows of an organisation K Ltd for the next five years which is shown as under: (Rs.lakhs)

Particulars	Y1	Y2	Y3	Y4	Y5

Revenues	15400	18700	23300	27900	33500
Expenses	11300	13500	17100	20500	24600
EBITDA	4100	5200	6200	7400	8900
Depreciation	500	550	600	700	900
EBIT	3600	4650	5600	6700	8000
Tax 30%	1080	1395	1680	2010	2400
PAT	2520	3255	3920	4690	5600
Add: Depreciation	500	550	600	700	900
Less: Capex	(1500)	(1500)	(1600)	(2000)	(2500)
Less: Change in Net working capital	(100)	(155)	(220)	(290)	(300)
Free Cash flow (FCF)	1420	2200	2700	3100	3700

In the above chart explicit forecast period is from year 1 to year 5

Step 2: Estimate a suitable discount rate
This step involves computation of cost of capital to the firm. The cost of capital is nothing but the cost of funds and represents the rate at which the enterprise borrows funds both through the routes of equity and debt. This rate is used to discount the future free cash flows to arrive at their present values. The cost of capital is to be computed as the weighted average of the cost of all sources of funds, which are based on the market value of each component of the capital.

The formula of weighted average cost of capital is as under:
Ko = Ke (S / V) + Kp (P / V) + Kd (1-t) (B / V)
Where, V = Market value of the firm
       S = Market value of equity
       P = Market value of preference capital
       B = Market value of debt
       Ko = Weighted average cost of capital
       Ke = Cost of equity capital
       Kp = Cost of preference capital
       Kd = Cost of debt and (1 – t) represents after tax cost of debt
Continuing with the above example let us assume
       Ke = 15%
       Kd = 8% and after tax at 30% would be 10% x (1 -0.3) = 7%
Debt / equity ratio is 1: 1
Hence Ko (WACC) = 0.5 X 0.15 + 0.5 X 0.07
       Ko = 0.075 + 0.035
       Ko = 11%

Step 3: Calculate the present value of cash flows for the explicit forecast period
Based on free cash flow calculated in step 1, we now proceed to determine the present value of future free cash flows for the explicit forecast period, which is assumed as five years in foreseeable future.
The calculation is as under: (Rs lakhs)

Particulars	Y1	Y2	Y3	Y4	Y5
Revenues	15400	18700	23300	27900	33500
Expenses	11300	13500	17100	20500	24600
EBITDA	4100	5200	6200	7400	8900
Depreciation	500	550	600	700	900
EBIT	3600	4650	5600	6700	8000

Tax 30%	1080	1395	1680	2010	2400
PAT	2520	3255	3920	4690	5600
Add: Depreciation	500	550	600	700	900
Less: Capex	(1500)	(1500)	(1600)	(2000)	(2500)
Less: Change in Net working capital	(100)	(155)	(220)	(290)	(300)
Free Cash flow (FCFF)	1420	2200	2700	3100	3700
WACC = 11%	0.9009	0.8116	0.7312	0.6587	0.5934
Present value of FCFF	1279	1785	1974	2042	2196

Hence the total present value of FCFF for the five years aggregate to Rs. 9276 lakhs

Step 4: Estimate the terminal value
Terminal value of the enterprise is calculated based on the free cash flow of the fifth year. The formula is as under:

Terminal value = (CF1 (1+g))/k-g

Where, CF1 = Cash flow of the last year

         g = constant growth rate (here growth rate is assumed at 2%)

         k = discount rate

Tranposing the values we get the following:

            = (3700 x 1.02)/ (0.11-0.02) x (1/1.11$_5$)

            = 3774 / 0.09 x 0.5934

            = Rs 24883 lakhs

Step 5: Determine the value of the firm
Now in order to arrive at the value of the firm we have add the following:

Present value of FCFF for five years (Step 3)   = Rs.9276 lakhs (A)

Present value of Terminal value at the end of five years (Step 4) = Rs.24883 lakhs (B)

Total value of firm (A + B)   = Rs.34159 lakhs

Step 6: Subtract the value of debt
From the value arrived at in Step 5 we now need to deduct the debt and other obligations assumed by the acquirer to ascertain the value of equity. Say the debt component of K Ltd is Rs.100.00 crores. Hence the value of equity would be Rs.341.59 crores – Rs.100 crores = Rs.241.59 crores.

Step 7: Calculate the intrinsic value of shares
Say, the equity share capital is Rs.100 crores at Rs.10 each per equity share.

Therefore intrinsic value of one equity share would be as under:

Value of equity (Step 6)   Rs.2415900000 (X)

No. of equity shares   100000000 (Y)

Intrinsic value per equity share (X/Y) = Rs.24.159

Illustration 9.20
You are given the following information for Company Alpha you are valuing:

Item	Year 1	Year 2	Year 3	Year 4
EBIT	7.0	7.5	7.9	8.4
Depreciation	2.9	2.7	2.7	2.6
Capital expenditure	1.5	2.5	2.5	3.0
Increase in working capital	0.8	1.5	1.5	0.9

The other information is as under:	
Tax rate t	35%
Book value debt (D)	7.0
Book value equity (E book)	10.0
Market value equity (E market)	15.0
Beta (historical)BL	1.5
Long term treasury bond Rf	10.0%
Long term debt rate Rd	12.0%
Long term growth rate (g)	6.0%
Long term risk premium (Rm – Rf)	8.0%
Debt Equity ratio	2:3

Required : Value of the company.

Solution

1. **Statement of cash flows**

Item	Year 1	Year 2	Year 3	Year 4
EBIT	7.00	7.50	7.90	8.40
Tax rate 35%	2.45	2.62	2.76	2.94
Earnings after tax	4.55	4.88	5.14	5.46
Depreciation	2.90	2.70	2.70	2.60
Capital expenditure	(1.50)	(2.50)	(2.50)	(3.00)
Increase in working capital	(0.80)	(1.50)	(1.50)	(0.90)
Free Cash Flow	5.15	3.58	3.84	4.16

2. **Calculation of APV Analysis**

$$\text{Beta L} = \text{Beta u} \times [(1 + (1- t)\, D) / E]$$
   Where, Beta u = Unlevered Beta
   D = Market value of debt
   E = Market value of equity
   Or, Beta u = Beta L / [(1 + (1-t) D)/E]
   Or, Beta u = 1.5 / (1 + (1-0.35)x7.0/15.0)
   Or, Beta u = 1.15

Using the same in CAPM:

CAPM = Rf + Beta u (Rm – Rf)
Where, Rf = Risk free rate
   Rm = Market rate of return
   Rm – Rf = Excess Market return - risk premium
   Beta u = Unleveraged Beta
CAPM = 0.10 + 1.15 (0.08) = 0.0192
   = **19.2%**

3. **Calculation of WACC**

$$\text{Beta L} = \text{Beta u} \times [(1 + (1- t)\, D) / E]$$
Where, Beta u = Unlevered Beta
D = Market value of debt
E = Market value of equity
Beta L = 1.15 X (1 + (1 - 0.35) 0.4/0.6)
   = 1.64

Using the same in CAPM:
   CAPM = Rf + Beta L (Rm – Rf)

Where, Rf = Risk free rate

Rm = Market rate of return

Rm – Rf = Excess Market return - risk premium

Beta L = leveraged Beta

CAPM = 0.10 + 1.64 (0.08) = 0.2312

= 23.12%

WACC = 0.6 X 0.2312 + 0.4 X (1- 0.35) X 0.12

= 16.99%

= rounded off to 17%

4. **Calculation of terminal value**

Based on four years cash flow, year 4 cash flow works out to 4.16 (1)above

APV = Terminal value = (Terminal year FCF $_4$ X (1+g)) / (Rd – g)

= 4.16 (1 + 0.05) / (0.192 – 0.05)

= 30.76

WACC = Terminal value = (Terminal year FCF $_4$ X (1+g)) / (Rd – g)

= 4.16 (1 + 0.05) / (0.17 – 0.05)

= 35.51

5. **Statement of calculation of NPV (APV method)**

Item	Year 1	Year 2	Year 3	Year 4
Free Cash Flow	5.15	3.58	3.84	4.16
Terminal value				30.76
Total	5.15	3.58	3.84	34.92
Present value = 19.2%	0.839	0.704	0.590	0.495
Net Present Value = **26.41**	4.32	2.52	2.27	17.30

NPV as above	**= 26.41**
Add: Debt Tax Shield = (26.41 X 0.4 x 0.35)	**= 3.70**
Total value	**= 30 .11**

6. **Statement of calculation of NPV (WACC method)**

Item	Year 1	Year 2	Year 3	Year 4
Free Cash Flow	5.15	3.58	3.84	4.16
Terminal value				35.51
Total	5.15	3.58	3.84	39.67
Present value = 17%	0.855	0.731	0.624	0.534
Net Present Value = **30.57**	4.4	2.6	2.4	21.17

Hence in both the methods the value of the enterprise ranges between 30.11 and 30.57

Illustration 9.21

XYZ Ltd has FCFF of Rs.170 crores and FCFE of Rs.130 crores. XYZ Ltd's WACC is 13% and its cost of equity is 15%. FCFF is expected to grow forever at 7% and FCFE is expected to grow forever at 7.5%. XYZ Ltd has debt outstanding at Rs.1500 crores. Find the value of XYZ Ltd using FCFF approach and FCFE approach

Solution
a)FCFF approach (discount rate = WACC)
The value of firm is the present value of FCFF discounted at the weighted average cost of capital
(WACC) = FCFF$_t$ / (k-g)
$\qquad$ = (Rs.170 crores x 1.07)/(0.13 – 0.07)
$\qquad$ = Rs.3031.67 crores (A)
Less: Value of debt Rs.1500 crores (B)
Market value of equity (A – B) = **Rs.1531.67 crores**

b)FCFE approach (discount rate = cost of equity)
The present value of FCFE, discounted at cost of equity
= FCFE$_t$ / (k-g)
= Rs.130 crores x 1.075 / (0.15 – 0.075)
= **Rs.1863.33 crores**

Illustration 9.22

Alpha Ltd currently sells for Rs.32.50 per share. In an attempt to determine if Alpha Ltd is fairly priced, an analyst has assembled the following information.
a)The before tax required rates of return on Alpha Ltd's debt, preference shares and equity capital are 7%, 6.8% and 11% respectively.
b)The enterprise's target capital structure is 30 % debt, 20% preference shares and 50% equity capital.
c) The market value of debt of the enterprise amounted to Rs.145 million and its preference share is valued at Rs.65 million.
d) Alpha Ltd's FCFF for the year just ended is Rs.28 million. FCFF is expected to grow at a constant rate of 4% for the foreseeable future.
e)The tax rate is 35%
f) Alpha Ltd has 8 million outstanding common shares.
What is Alpha Ltd's estimated value per share? Is Alpha Ltd's share under-priced ?

Solution
a)Weighted Average Cost of Capital (WACC) of Alpha Ltd is as under
$\quad$ WACC $\qquad$ = 0.30 (7%) (1-0.35) + 0.20 (6.8%) + 0.50 (11%)
$\qquad\qquad\qquad$ = 8.225%
$\quad$ Firm value $\quad$ = FCFF$_0$ (1+g) / (WACC – g)
$\qquad\qquad\qquad$ = 28 x (1 + 0.04)/ (0.08225-0.04)
$\qquad\qquad\qquad$ = 29.12 / 0.04225
$\qquad\qquad\qquad$ = Rs.689.23 million (A)
Less: Debt $\qquad$ = Rs.145.00 million (B)
Less: Pref.shares = Rs.65.00 million (C)
Value of equity
(A – B – C) $\qquad$ = Rs.479.23 million (D)
No of shares $\quad$ = 8 million (E)
Value per share
(D / E) $\qquad\qquad$ = Rs.59.90
Current price $\quad$ = Rs.32.50
Hence Alpha Ltd's share appears to be undervalued.

Illustration 9.23

Beta Ltd, being a dairy company is financed by debt and equity to the extent of 3 : 7, with total debt of Rs.10.82 million. The company's debt is valued at 8%. The beta of the company's equity is known to be 1.5. The company generates a free cash flow of Rs.2 million with the known growth projection of 5% to perpetuity. If it is known that the market risk premium is 6% and the risk free rate is 5% what is the value of each equity share for the 1 million shareholders of the company? Assume that the company is in the 40% tax bracket.

Solution

In the instant case the Beta Ltd's FCF = Rs.2.0 million with growth rate of 5% to perpetuity.

FCF_1 = 2.00 (1.05) = Rs.2.1 million

Beta = 1.5

Risk free rate = 5%

Risk premium = 6%

Cost of debt = 8%

W_d = 30%

Tax rate = 40%

Ke	= r_{rf} + r_{rp} (Beta)
	= 5%+ 6%(1.5)
	= 14%
WACC	= 0.7 x 0.14 + 0.3 x (0.08)(1-0.40)
	= 11.24%
Value of firm	= FCFE (1+g)/(WACC – g)
	= 2.1 / (0.1124 - 0.05)
	= Rs.33.65 million (A)

Value of debt = Rs.10.82 million (B)

Value of equity = Rs.22.83 million (A – B) = (C)

No. of shares = 1 million (D)

Value of equity share = C/ D = **Rs.22.83** per share

Illustration 9.24

Continuing with the above illustration, the following scenarios are observed:

Free cash flow for year 1 = Rs.2.5 million,

Year 2 = Rs.2.9 million,

Year 3 = Rs.3.4 million

Year 4 onwards growth = 5%

Tax shield available each year on interest of Rs.1.5 million for years 1 to 3. With all the other information remaining same please find the value per equity share?

Solution

Working Notes:

1.WACC = 11.24%

2. Statement of calculation of terminal value:

= FCF3 (1+g)/ (WACC – g)

= 3.4 (1.05) / 0.1124 – 0.05), WACC being 11.24% as per previous example

= **Rs.57.21 million**

Item	Year 1	Year 2	Year 3	Year 4
Free cash flow	2.5	2.9	3.4	3.57
Add: tax shield on interest@ 40%	0.6	0.6	0.6	0.6

	Total	3.1	3.5	4.0	
Terminal value					57.21(2)
Total		3.1	3.5	4.0	61.38

Since tax shield has been considered, WACC needs to be recalculated gross of tax on debt as under:

K = WgKd + WeKe

  = 0.3 x 0.08 + 0.7 x 0.14

  =12.20%

Value of the firm will be calculated as under:

V_{firm} = (3.1/(1.122)) + (3.5/(1.122)$_2$) + (4.0 / (1.122)$_3$)

  = Rs.51.80 million. (A)

Value of debt = Rs.10.82 million (B)

Value of equity = (A – B) = Rs.40.98 million

No.of shares = 1 million

Value per share = **Rs.40.98**

Illustration 9.25

The free cash flow of Sunrise Ltd is projected to grow at a compound annual average rate of 35% for the next five years. Growth is then expected to slow down to a normal 5% annual growth rate. The current year's cash flow of Sunrise Ltd is Rs.4 lakhs. Sunrise Ltd's cost of capital during high growth period is 18% and 12% beyond the fifth year, as growth stabilises. Calculate the value of Sunrise Ltd.

Solution

1.Statement of calculation of present value of cash flows during the forecast period

PV $_{1-t}$ = $FCFE_0$ x (1+gt)$_t$ / (1+WACC)$_t$

PV_{1-5} = [(4 X 1.35)/1.18 +(4 X 1.35$_2$)/1.18$_2$ + (4 X 1.35$_3$)/1.18$_3$ +(4 X 1.35$_4$)/1.18$_4$ + (4 X 1.35$_5$)/1.18$_5$]

    = 5.4/1.18 + 7.29/1.39 + 9.84 /1.64   + 13.29/1.94   + 17.93/2.29

    = 4.58 + 5.24 + 5.99 + 6.85 +7.84

    = Rs.30.50 lakhs

2.Statement of calculation of terminal value

  Pn = FCFn x (1+g) / (Ke – g)

    = (17.93 x 1.05) / (0.12-0.05)

    = 18.83 / 0.07

    = Rs.269 lakhs

Present value of terminal value of Rs.269 lakhs would be : Rs.269 lakhs / (1.18)$_5$ = Rs.117.58 lakhs

Value of firm = PV $_{1-5}$ + Pn

        = Rs.30.50 lakhs + Rs.117.58 lakhs

        = Rs.148.08 lakhs

Illustration 9.26

XYZ Ltd is considering going public, but is unsure of a fair offering price for the company. Before hiring an investment banker to assist in making the public offering, managers of XYZ Ltd have decided to make their own estimate of the firm's common stock value. The firm's CFO has gathered data for performing the valuation using the free cash flow valuation model. The firm's weighted average cost of capital is 12 % and it has Rs.14 lakhs of debt at market value and Rs.5 lakhs of preferred stock at its assumed market value. The estimated free cash flows over the next five years, 2009 through 2013, are given below. Beyond 2013 to infinity, the firm expects its free cash flow to grow at 4 % annually.

Year	Free Cash Flow
2009	Rs.2,50,000

2010	Rs.2,90,000
2011	Rs.3,20,000
2012	Rs.3,60,000
2013	Rs.4,00,000

a) Estimate the value of XYZ Ltd's entire company by using the free cash flow approach.
b) Using (a), along with the data provided above, find XYZ's equity share value.
c) If the firm plans to issue 2, 00, 000 shares of equity, what is its estimated value per share?

Solution

a)The value of the firm is as under:

= (250000 / 1.12) + (290000/1.12_2) + (320000 / 1.12_3) + (360000 / 1.12_4) + {(400000 / (0.12-0.04) X 1 / 1.12_5)

= **Rs.40,88.547**

b)Value of equity = Rs.40,88,547 – Rs.14,00,000 –Rs 5,00,000 = **Rs.21,88,547**

c) Based on 2,00,000 shares, the price per share would be Rs.21,88,547 / 2,00,000
  = **Rs.10.94**

Illustration 9.27

From the given financial statement of XYZ Ltd find the Free Cash Flows to Firm (FCFF) and Free Cash Flows to Equity (FCFE)?

Balance Sheet of XYZ Ltd	(Rs in Crores)	
Assets	**31.3.2012**	**31.3.2013**
Cash	210	248
Accounts Receivable	474	513
Inventory	520	564
Total current assets	1204	1325
Gross Fixed Assets	2501	2850
Accumulated Depreciation	(604)	(784)
Net Fixed Assets	1897	2066
Total assets	**3101**	**3391**
Equity and Liabilities		
Current Liabilities		
Accounts payable	295	317
Notes payable	300	310
Accrued taxes and expenses	76	99
Total current liabilities	671	726
Long term debt	1010	1050
Share capital	50	50
Additional paid in capital	300	300
Retained earnings	1070	1265
Total Shareholders' equity	1420	1615
Total Liabilities	**3101**	**3391**

Statement of Income – XYZ Ltd for the year ended 31.3.2013	(Rs in crores)
Total revenues	2215
Operating costs and expenses	1430
EBITDA	785
Depreciation	180
EBIT	605

Interest expense	130
PBT	475
Tax @ 40%	190
Net Income	285
Dividends	90
Transfer to retained earnings	195

Statement of cash flows – XYZ Ltd for the year ended 31.3.2013	(Rs in crores)
Operating activities	
Net Income	285
Adjustments	
Depreciation	180
Change in working capital	
Accounts receivable	(39)
Inventories	(44)
Accounts payable	22
Accrued taxes and expenses	23
Cash provided by operating activities	**427**
Investing activities	
Purchase of fixed assets	349
Cash used for investing activities	**349**
Financing activities	
Notes payable	(10)
Long term debt	(40)
Dividends	90
Cash used for financing activities	**40**
Cash and equivalents increase	38
Cash – at the beginning of the year	210
Cash – at the end of the year	248
Additional disclosures	
Interest paid	130
Income taxes paid	190

Solution

A) Free Cash flow to the firm:

FCFF = NI + Non-cash charges + Interest (1-T) – Net Investment – Net change in working capital

Transposing values:

FCFF = 285 + 180 + 130(1-0.40) – 349* - (39 + 44 – 22 - 23)

*Net investment in 2013 = Change in gross fixed assets = 2850 – 2501 = 349

FCFF = 285 + 180 + 78 -349 – 38

   = Rs.156 million

B) Free cash flow to equity is given by:

FCFE = FCFF – Interest (1 – T) + Net borrowing

Transposing values:

FCFE = 156 – 130 (1-0.40) + (10+40)

FCFE = 156 – 78 + 50

   = Rs.128 million

Control:

FCFE = NI + Non-cash charges – Net investment – Net change in working capital + Net borrowing

Transposing values:
FCFE = 285 + 180 − 349 − 38 + 50
    = **Rs.128 million**

9.19. Value of firm

Enterprise valuation is a method of valuation which includes all stakeholders e.g. equity, preference shareholders and debt holders. The value of the firm is obtained by discounting expected cash flows to the firm i.e. the residual cash flows after meeting all operating expenses, reinvestment needs and taxes, but before payment to either debt or equity holders. The discounting is done at the weighted average cost of capital, which is the cost of the different components of financing used by the firm, weighted by their market value proportions.

Value of firm is as under:

> Value of firm = Sigma t=n (CF to Equity − 1) / (1 + WACC)t
> Where, CF to firm = Expected cash flows to firm in period 1
> and WACC = Weighted average cost of capital.

Let us go through the following example which will explain how firm is valued along with equity.

Illustration 9.28

Year-wise cash flows to equity and cash flows to firm are mentioned below:

Year	Cash flow to equity	Interest (1 − t)	Cash flow to firm
1	50	40	90
2	60	40	100
3	68	40	108
4	76.2	40	116.2
5	83.49	40	123.49
Terminal value	1603.008		2363.008

Cost of equity is 13.625% and the firm can borrow long term at 10%.
Tax rate of the firm 50%.
The value of debt outstanding is Rs 800 million.
   a) Calculate value of equity
   b) Calculate value of firm
   c) Calculate Weighted average cost of capital

Solution
   a) PV of equity = 50 / (1.13625)+ 60 / (1.13625)2 + 68 / (1.13625)3 + 76.2 / (1.13625)4 + (83.49 + 1603) / (1.13625)4
        = Rs. 1073 million.
      Hence value of equity is Rs.1073 million
   1) Value of debt = Rs.800 million.
   b) PV of firm   = (Rs.1073 million + Rs.800 million) = Rs.1873 million.

Hence value of firm is Rs.1873 million

c) WACC = Cost of equity (Equity / (Debt + Equity) + Cost of debt (Debt / (Debt + Equity))
= 0.13625 x (1073 / 1873) + 0.05 x (800 / 1873)
= 9.94%

Control : Value of firm

a) PV of firm = 90 / (1.0994)+ 100 / (1.0994)$_2$ + 108 / (1.0994)$_3$ + 116.2 / (1.0994)$_4$ + (123.49 + 2363) / (1.13625)$_4$
= Rs. 1873 million.

b) PV of equity = Rs.1873 million – Rs.800 million = Rs.1073 million

Illustration 9.29

A task has been assigned to a research analyst in a fund house to find out at what price the fund should subscribe to an IPO issue (through book building) of a transformer company A Ltd. The following details of the company from Annual Report as on 31.3.2013 are as under:

Particulars	Rs lakhs
Revenues	248.79
Operating expenses	214.41
EBITDA	34.38
Other income	3.84
Interest expense	1.01
Preliminary expenses w/o	0.00
Depreciation	1.92
Profit before taxes	35.30
Income tax @ 35%	12.27
Profit after tax	23.03

To calculate future cash flows, the following projections for the financial year ended 31.3.2014 till 31.3.2018 is available:

Item	Fy 14	Fy 15	Fy 16	Fy 17	Fy 18
Revenue growth	55%	50%	28%	20%	14%
Operating exp / Income	87%	87%	87%	88%	88%
Other Income	2.5	2.2	2.5	2.5	2.5
Interest expense	2.0	3.0	3.0	3.0	3.0
Preliminary expenses w/o	-	-	-	-	-
Depreciation	2.6	3.5	4.1	3.9	3.7
Capital spending	2.0	5.0	5.0	2.0	2.0
Working capital	2.0	5.0	5.0	2.0	2.0

It is given that revenues would grow at 0% after the explicit forecast period. A Ltd's total assets of Rs.219.98 lakhs are financed with equity of Rs.208.66 lakhs and balance debts sourced at 8% p.a. Assume risk free rate of 7.5%, market risk of 15% and beta of stock as 1.07.

The firm falls in the 35% tax bracket. The company including the shares floated in this issue would have issued a total of 1.02 lakhs shares. Find out the intrinsic value of share using Discounted Cash Flow analysis. If the price band announced by A Ltd stands at Rs.345 to Rs.365, should his fund subscribe to this book building issue and at which end of the price band?

Solution
Working Notes:
1. **Statement of calculation of cost of equity using CAPM approach:**
   Cost of equity = Rf + Beta (Rm - Rf)

= 7.5% + 1.07 x (15% - 7.5%)

= 7.5% + 1.07 x 7.5%

=7.5% + 8.025%

= 15.525%

Cost of debt = 8%

WACC = (208.66 / 219.98) X 0.15525 + (11.32 / 219.98) X 0.08

= 15%

2. Statement of calculation of Future Free Cash Flows for the explicit period of 5 years (Rs in lakhs)

Particulars	31.03.14	31.03.15	31.03.16	31.03.17	31.03.18
Revenues	385.63	578.44	740.41	888.49	1012.88
Operating expenses	335.50	503.25	644.15	781.87	891.33
EBITDA	50.13	75.20	96.25	106.62	121.55
Other income	2.5	2.2	2.5	2.5	2.5
Interest expense	2.00	3.0	3.0	3.0	3.0
Preliminary expenses w/o	-	-	-	-	-
Depreciation	2.6	3.5	4.1	3.9	3.7
Profit before taxes	48.03	70.90	91.65	102.22	117.35
Income tax @ 35%	16.81	24.81	32.08	35.78	41.07
Profit after tax	31.22	46.08	59.57	66.45	76.27
Add: Depreciation	2.60	3.5	4.1	3.9	3.7
Less: Capital spending	2.00	5.0	5.0	2.0	2.0
Less: Working capital	2.00	5.0	5.0	2.0	2.0
Free Cash Flow to the firm	29.82	39.58	53.67	66.34	75.97

3. Statement of calculation of value of firm: (Rs in lakhs)

Particulars	Cash flows	DCF 15%	PV of cash Flows
2013 – 14	29.82	0.870	25.93
2014 – 15	39.58	0.756	29.93
2015 – 16	53.67	0.658	35.29
2016 – 17	66.34	0.572	37.93
2017 – 18	75.97	0.497	37.77
Terminal value	506.50*	0.496	251.44
Value of firm (A)			418.30
Value of debt (B)			11.32
Value of equity (A – B = C)			406.98
Equity shares outstanding			1.02
Share price in Rs.			399.00

*Calculation of terminal value:

Terminal value = (75.97 (1+0%)) / (15% - 0%)

= 506.50

Conclusion

Since the price band is Rs.345 to Rs.365 and the intrinsic value is Rs.399, there is scope for appreciation and hence the fund can subscribe to these shares at the upper band of Rs.365.

Illustration 9.30

An unlisted company ABC Ltd manufacturing electronic equipment is currently in the expansion mode and is expected to be a good investment keeping in mind the expected sales and profits over the next five years. The projected statement of free cash flows is given below for the period 2009 – 2013. The shares are likely to be listed after an initial public offer in the foreseeable future.

(Rs in lakhs)

Particulars	31.03.09	31.03.10	31.03.11	31.03.12	31.03.13
Income	99.58	121.48	151.91	189.76	231.40
Expenditure	87.63	106.29	132.16	164.15	199.01
Operating profit (EBITDA)	11.95	15.18	19.75	25.62	32.40
Depreciation	3.23	9.29	9.63	9.63	9.31
Interest	0.85	0.67	0.39	0.12	0.00
PBT	7.87	5.23	9.73	15.87	23.08
Provision for taxation	2.60	1.72	3.21	5.24	7.62
Profit after taxation	5.28	3.50	6.52	10.64	15.47

Some Balance Sheet related information is as under:

(Rs in lakhs)

Particulars	31.03.09	31.03.10	31.03.11	31.03.12	31.03.13
Capital expenditure	14.57	30.30	1.70	0.00	0.00
Working capital change	17.09	22.59	12.59	12.00	12.00

This is a company with similar risk characteristics that of XYZ Lt which is listed and whose average beta is 0.85. The risk free rate and the market risk premium are 7% and the company is funded with 93% equity and 7 % debt, whose cost is 9.25%. A 5% growth is projected beyond 5 years till perpetuity. The firm falls in the 33% tax bracket. The total of 1.06 crores shares would be outstanding. Find out the intrinsic value of share using Discounted Cash Flow Analysis.

Solution
1. Statement of calculation of Free cash flows   (Rs in lakhs)

2. Particulars	31.03.09	31.03.10	31.03.11	31.03.12	31.03.13
Income	99.58	121.48	151.91	189.76	231.40
Expenditure	87.63	106.29	132.16	164.15	199.01
Operating profit (EBITDA)	11.95	15.18	19.75	25.62	32.40
Depreciation	3.23	9.29	9.63	9.63	9.31
Interest	0.85	0.67	0.39	0.12	0.00
PBT	7.87	5.23	9.73	15.87	23.08
Provision for taxation	2.60	1.72	3.21	5.24	7.62
Profit after taxation	5.28	3.50	6.52	10.64	15.47

Add: Depreciation	3.23	9.29	9.63	9.63	9.31
Less: Capital expenditure	14.57	30.30	1.70	0.00	0.00
Less: Working capital change	17.09	22.59	12.59	12.00	12.00
Free cash flow to the firm	-23.16	-40.10	1.85	20.26	24.78

2. Statement of calculation of Weighted Average Cost of Capital (WACC)
a) Calculation of cost of equity using CAPM approach:
    Cost of equity = Rf + Beta (Rm – Rf)
                = 0.07 + 0.85 x 0.07

= 12.95%
Cost of debt = 9.25%
WACC = 0.93 X 0.1295 + 0.07 X 0.0925 X (1 – 0.33)
= 12.48%

3. Statement of calculation of value of firm: (Rs in lakhs)

Particulars	Cash flows	DCF 12.48%	PV of cash Flows
2008 – 09	-23.16	0.889	-20.59
2009 – 10	-40.10	0.790	-31.69
2010 – 11	1.85	0.703	1.30
2011 – 12	20.26	0.625	12.66
2012 – 13	24.78	0.555	13.76
Terminal value	347.84*	0.555	193.18
Value of firm			168.61
Equity shares outstanding			1.06
Share price in Rs.			159.07

*Calculation of terminal value:
Terminal value = (24.78 (1+5%)) / (12.48% - 5%)
= 347.84
Hence the intrinsic value of share amounts to **Rs.159.07**

9.20. Valuation of a business

Valuation of business is carried out in two fold ways:

a) Liquidation basis
b) Going concern basis

Bases of valuation on going concern basis are	i)	Historical cost valuation method (historical cost of assets + value of goodwill)
	ii)	Current cost valuation method
	iii)	Economic valuation method (sum of discounted value of future earnings or cash flows)
	iv)	Average value method
	v)	Book value method
	vi)	Fair value method
	vii)	Earning based valuation method
	viii)	Market value method
	ix)	Asset valuation method

Valuation of business is summarised in the following table:

i)Historical cost method	Value of business = Carrying value of all assets + value of goodwill
ii)Current cost	Value of business = Current cost of all assets

valuation method	
iii)Economic valuation method	Value of business is calculated by any one of the following: a)Capitalisation of future maintainable profit or b)Sum of present value of future earnings or c)Sum of present value of future cash flows
iv)Average value method	Valuation of business = (Current cost of all assets + Net realisable value of all assets) / 2
v)Book value method	Value of business = Balance Sheet values of all assets – Balance Sheet values of all third party liabilities
vi) Fair value method	Valuation of business = Fair value of all assets – Fair value of all third party liabilities
vii)Earnings based valuation method	This is determined based on a)(Earnings capacity value per share) X (number of equity shares) b) + book value of preference share capital c) + book value of debt capital). In carrying out this calculation book values of Preference capital and debt capital should be considered.

viii)Market value method	This is calculated based on
	    a) aggregate of market capitalization (market value of equity X number of equity shares) and
	    b) Market value of preference and
	    c) Market value of debt capital

ix)Asset valuation method	Valuation of business computed based on upper and lower limit: Upper limit = Current cost of all assets Lower limit = Net realisable value of all assets

Illustration 9.31: Determination of value of business

Kay Limited gives the following cash flows estimate:

Year 2003	Rs.20 lakhs
Year 2004 – 2006	Compound growth rate 6.5%
Year 2007 – 2010	Compound growth rate 9.5%

Apply 20% discount rate and determine the value of business.

Solution
Statement of cash flows

Year	Cash flows Rs Lakhs	Discount factor 20%	DCF (Rs Lakhs)
2003	20.0000	0.8333	16.6660
2004	21.3000	0.6944	14.7907
2005	22.6845	0.5787	13.1275
2006	24.1590	0.4823	11.6519
2007	26.4541	0.4019	10.6319
2008	28.9672	0.3349	9.7011
2009	31.7191	0.2791	8.8528

2010	34.7324	0.2326	8.0788
			93.5007

As per discounted cash flows for the eight years till 2010 the value of business would be Rs.93.5007 lakhs.

Illustration 9.32: Valuation of business

The Balance Sheets of R Ltd for the years ended 31.3.2008; 31.3.2009 and 31.3.2010 are as follows: (Rs)

Liabilities	31.03.2008	31.03.2009	31.03.2010
320000 equity shares of Rs.10 each fully paid	3200000	3200000	3200000
General reserve	2400000	2800000	3200000
Profit & Loss Account	280000	320000	480000
Sundry creditors	1200000	1600000	2000000
	7080000	7920000	8880000
Assets			
Goodwill	2000000	1600000	1200000
Building and Machinery(less depreciation)	2800000	3200000	3200000
Inventories	2000000	2400000	2800000
Sundry debtors	40000	320000	880000
Cash and bank	240000	400000	800000
	7080000	7920000	8880000

Actual valuation was as under:

Item	31.03.2008	31.3.2009	31.3.2010
Building & Machinery	3600000	4000000	4400000
Inventories	2400000	2800000	3200000
Net profit (including opening balance) after writing of depreciation and goodwill, tax provision and transfer to general reserve	840000	1240000	1640000

Capital employed in the business at market values at the beginning of 2007-08 was Rs.7320000, which included the cost of goodwill. The normal annual return on Average capital employed in the line of business engaged by R Ltd is 12.5 %.
The balance in General Reserve account on 1st April 2007 was Rs.20 lakhs.
The goodwill shown on 31.3.2008 was purchased on 1.4.2007 for Rs.20 lakhs on which date the balance in the Profit and Loss Account was Rs.240000. Find out the average capital

employed each year.

Goodwill is valued at 5 years purchase of super profits (simple average method). Also find out the total value of the business as on 31.3.2010.

Solution

1. **Statement of calculation of average capital employed (Rs'000)**

Item	31.3.2008	31.3.2009	31.3.2010
Goodwill (since goodwill has paid for, it is included)	2000	1600	1200
Building & Machinery (revalued assumed after depreciation)	3600	4000	4400
Inventories (revalued)	2400	2800	3200
Sundry debtors	40	320	880
Cash and bank	240	400	800
Total Assets	8280	9120	10480
Less: Sundry creditors	1200	1600	2000
Closing capital employed (A)	7080	7520	8480
Opening capital employed (B)	7320	7080	7520
Average capital employed (A+B)/2	**7200**	**7300**	**8000**

2. **Statement of calculation of super profit: (Rs'000)**

Item	31.3.2008	31.3.2009	31.3.2010
Net profit per question	840	1240	1640
Less: opening balance	240	280	320
	600	960	1320
Adjustments			
Add: undervaluation of stock	400	400	400
Less: Adjustment for valuation in opening stock	-	-400	-400
Add: Goodwill written off	-	400	400
Add: Transfer to reserves	400	400	400
Maintainable profit (A)	1400	1760	2120
Less: Normal return (12.5% on average capital) (B)	900	912.5	1000
Super profit (A – B)	500	847.5	1120
Average super profit (500+847.5+1120)/3= 822.5			

3. **Statement of valuation of goodwill**

   Goodwill = 5 years purchase of super profit as in 2 above.

   = 5 x Rs.822500

   = Rs.4112500/-

4. **Statement of valuation of business (Rs'000)**

   Total net assets (31.3.2010)   8480

Less: Goodwill	1200
	7280
Add: Goodwill as in 3 above	4112.5
Value of business	11392.5

Hence value of business works out to Rs.11392500/-

Illustration 9.33: Valuation of business

S Garments Ltd is a company which produces and sells to retailers a certain range of fashion garments. They have made the following estimates of potential cash flows for the next 10 years.

Year	1	2	3	4	5	6	7	8	9	10
Cash-flows (Rs lakhs)	1500	1700	2000	2500	3000	3400	3800	4500	5000	6000

K Garments Ltd is a company which owns a chain of boutiques in a certain locality. The boutiques buy clothes from various suppliers and retail them. Each boutique has a manager and an assistant but all purchasing and policy decisions are taken centrally. Independent cash flow estimates of K Garments Ltd were as follows:

Year	1	2	3	4	5	6	7	8	9	10
Cash-flows (Rs lakhs)	120	160	200	280	340	460	520	600	660	800

S Garments Ltd is interested in acquiring K Garments Ltd in order to get some additional retail outlets. They make the following cost-benefit calculations:

1) Net value of assets of K Garments Ltd:

	Rs Lakhs
Sundry fixed assets	800
Investments	200
Stock	400
	1400
Less: Sundry creditors	400
Net assets	1000

2) Sundry fixed assets amounting to Rs.50 lakhs cannot be used and their net realisable value is Rs.45 lakhs.
3) Stock can be realised immediately at Rs.470 lakhs
4) Investments can be disposed off for Rs.212 lakhs
5) Some workers of K Garments Ltd are to be retrenched for which estimated compensation is Rs.130 lakhs
6) Sundry creditors are to be discharged immediately.

7) Liabilities on account of retirement benefits not accounted for in the balance sheet by K Garments Ltd is Rs. 48 lakhs.

8) Expected cash flows of the combined business will be as follows:

Year	1	2	3	4	5	6	7	8	9	10
Cash-flows (Rs lakhs)	1800	1900	2300	2950	3500	4000	4500	5300	5800	6900

Find out the maximum value of K Garments Ltd which S Garments Ltd can quote. Also show the difference in valuation had there been no merger. Use 20% as discount factor.

Solution

1. Statement of valuation of K Garments Ltd had there been no merger

Year	1	2	3	4	5	6	7	8	9	10
Cash-flows (Rs lakhs)	120	160	200	280	340	460	520	600	660	800
Discount Factor 20%	0.8333	0.6944	0.5787	0.4823	0.4019	0.3349	0.2791	0.2326	0.1938	0.1615
DCF (Rs Lakhs)	99.996	111.104	115.740	135.044	136.646	154.054	145.132	139.560	127.908	129.200

= **Rs. 1294.384 lakhs.**

2. Statement of calculation of S Garments Ltd in the combined scenario (Rs Lakhs)

Year	1	2	3	4	5	6	7	8	9	10
Cash-flows	1800	1900	2300	2950	3500	4000	4500	5300	5800	6900
Less: Projected Cash Flows of S Garment Ltd without Merger	1500	1700	2000	2500	3000	3400	3800	4500	5000	6000
	300	200	300	450	500	600	700	800	800	900

Discount

Factor										
20%	0.8333	0.6944	0.5787	0.4823	0.4019	0.3349	0.2791	0.2326	0.1938	0.1615
DCF (Rs/L)	249.99	138.88	173.61	217.03	200.95	200.94	195.37	186.08	155.04	145.35

= **Rs.1863.245 lakhs**

3. **Statement of maximum value to be quoted**

Item	Rs Lakhs	Rs Lakhs
Value as per discounted cash flows from combined operations		1863.24
Add: Cash to be collected immediately by disposal of assets:		
Sundry fixed assets	45.00	
Investments	212.00	
Stock	470.00	727.00
		2590.24
Less: Sundry creditors	400.00	
Provision for retirement benefits	48.00	
Retrenchment compensation	130.00	578.00
		2012.24

Conclusion

From the foregoing it is evident that the stand-alone value of K Garments Ltd is Rs.1294.384 Lakhs whereas based on incremental cash flows the value of K Garments merged with S Garments Ltd goes up to Rs.2012.24 lakhs. Hence S Garments can quote a figure of Rs.2012 .24 lakhs for acquisition of K Garments Ltd.

Illustration 9.34: Valuation of business

T Inc is in the business of making sports equipment. The Company operates from Singapore. To globalise its operations T has identified FT Ltd an Indian Company, as a potential take-over candidate. After due diligence of FT Ltd the following information is available:
a) Cash flow forecasts (Rs crores)

Year	10	9	8	7	6	5	4	3	2	1
FT Ltd	24	21	15	16	15	12	10	8	6	3
T Ltd	108	70	55	60	52	44	32	30	20	16

b) The net worth of FT Ltd after considering certain adjustments suggested by the due diligence team read as under: Rs Lakhs
   Tangible fixed assets   750
   Inventories   145

Receivables		75
Total		970
Less: Creditors	165	
Bank loans	250	(415)
Represented by equity shares of Rs.1000 each		555

Talks for takeover have crystallised on the following:

1. T Ltd will not be able to use machinery worth Rs.75 lakhs which will be disposed of by them subsequent to take over. The expected realisation will be Rs.50 lakhs.
2. The inventories and receivables are agreed for takeover at values of Rs.100 and Rs.50 lakhs respectively which is the price they will realize on disposal.
3. The liabilities of FT Ltd will be discharged in full on takeover along with an employee settlement of Rs.90 lakhs for the employees who are not interested in continuing under the new management.
4. T Ltd will invest a sum of Rs.150 lakhs for upgrading the Plant of FT Ltd on takeover. A further sum of Rs.50 lakhs will also be incurred in the second year to revamp the machine shop floor of FT Ltd.
5. The anticipated cash flows (Rs/crores) post takeover are as follows:

Year	1	2	3	4	5	6	7	8	9	10
Cash-flows (Rs lakhs)	18	24	36	44	60	80	96	100	140	200

You are required to advise the management the maximum price which they can pay per share of FT Ltd if a discount factor of 20% is considered appropriate.

Solution

1. **Statement of present value of incremental cash flows (Rs crores)**

Year	1	2	3	4	5	6	7	8	9	10
Cash-flows Post take Over	18	24	36	44	60	80	96	100	140	200
Less: Cash flows Pre take Over	16	20	30	32	44	52	60	55	70	108
Incremental Cash flows	2	4	6	12	16	28	36	45	70	92
DF=20%	0.8333	0.6944	0.5787	0.4823	0.4019	0.3349	0.2791	0.2326	0.1938	0.1615
DCF	1.67	2.78	3.47	5.79	6.43	9.38	10.05	10.47	13.56	14.86

254

= **Rs. 78.45 crores**

2. **Statement of calculation of maximum price that can be quoted for takeover of FT Ltd**

Item	Rs Crores	Rs Crores
Present Value of incremental cash flows from operations (refer statement 1 above)		78.45
Add: Cash to be collected immediately by disposal of assets:		
Sundry fixed assets	0.50	
Proceeds from disposal of inventories	1.00	
Receipts from debtors	0.50	2.00
		80.45
Less: Sundry creditors	1.65	
Bank loan	2.50	
Employee settlement	0.90	
Renovation of plant	1.50	
Revamp of machine shop floor (Rs.50 lakhs x 0.6944)*	0.35	6.90
Maximum price that can be offered		**73.55**

*Discount factor of year 2 @ 20%

Hence maximum price per share of FT Ltd would be:

= Rs.73.55 crores / 55500 shares

= **Rs.13252.79**

Illustration 9.35: Valuation of cash flows and business

S Ltd is considering buying the business of R Ltd, the final accounts of which for the last three years were as follows:

Profit and Loss Accounts for the three years ended December 31st

	2007 Rs.	2008 Rs.	2009 Rs.
Sales	200000	190000	224000
Material consumed	100000	95000	112000
Business expenses	80000	80000	82000
Depreciation	12000	13000	14000
Net Profit	8000	2000	16000

Balance Sheets as at 31st December

	2006 Rs.	2007 Rs.	2008 Rs.	2009 Rs.

Fixed Assets (at cost)	100000	120000	140000	180000
Less: Depreciation	70000	82000	85000	109000
	30000	38000	45000	71000
Stock-in-trade	16000	17000	18500	21000
Sundry debtors	21000	24000	26000	28000
Cash in hand and at bank	32000	11000	28000	13200
Prepaid expenses	1000	500	2000	1000
Total	100000	90500	119500	134200
Share capital	50000	50000	70000	70000
Share premium	-	-	5000	5000
General reserve	16000	24000	26000	42000
Debentures	20000			
Sundry creditors	11000	13000	14000	14000
Accrued expenses	3000	3500	4500	3200
Total	100000	90500	119500	134200

S Ltd wishes the offer to be based upon trading cash flows rather than book profits. By trading cash flow is meant cash received from debtors less cash paid to creditors and for business expenses (excluding depreciation), together with an allowance for average annual expenditure on fixed assets of Rs.15000 per year.
The actual expenditure on fixed assets is to be ignored, as is any cash received or paid out on the issue or redemption of shares or debentures.

S Ltd wishes the trading cash flow to be calculated for each of the years 2007, 2008 and 2009 and for these to be combined using weighting of 20% for 2007, 30% for 2008 and 50% for 2009 to give an average annual trading cash flow.

S Ltd considers that the average annual trading cash flow should show a return of 10% on its investment.

You are required to calculate:
a) The trading cash flow for each of the years 2007, 2008 and 2009.
b) The weighted average annual trading cash flow
c) The price which S Ltd should offer for the business. *(CA Final : Nov 2010)*

Solution
a) **Statement of computation of trading cash flows of R Ltd for 2007, 2008 ,2009**

Particulars	2007	2008	2009
	Rs.	Rs.	Rs.
Net profit	8000	2000	16000
Add: depreciation	12000	13000	14000
Add: Opening balance:			
Stock-in-trade	16000	17000	18500
Sundry debtors	21000	24000	26000
Prepaid expenses	1000	500	2000
	58000	56500	76500
Less: Opening balance			

Sundry creditors	(11000)	(13000)	(14000)
Accrued expenses	(3000)	(3500)	(4500)
	44000	40000	58000
Less: Closing balance			
Stock-in-trade	(17000)	(18500)	(21000)
Sundry debtors	(24000)	(26000)	(28000)
Prepaid expenses	(500)	(2000)	(1000)
	2500	(6500)	8000
Add: Closing balance			
Sundry creditors	13000	14000	14000
Accrued expenses	3500	4500	3200
Less: Allowance for Annual expenditure on fixed			
Assets	(15000)	(15000)	(15000)
Trading cash flows	4000	(3000)	10200

b) Statement of weighted average annual trading cash flow

Year	Trading cash flow Rs.	Weights	Product Rs.
2007	4000	20%	800
2008	(3000)	30%	(900)
2009	10200	50%	5100
			5000

Therefore the weighted average annual trading cash flow amounts to Rs.5000

c) Price S Ltd should offer for the business is as under:
Expected return on investment   =   10%
Offer price (5000 / 10%)   =   Rs.50000

Illustration 9.36: Valuation of business through DCF method : APV as well as WACC

You are given the following information for Company Glenworks India Ltd, which is in the FMCG space. You need to value the enterprise based on the details given below:

Item	Year 1	Year 2	Year 3	Year 4
EBIT	480.0	530.0	580.0	605.0
Depreciation	145.0	130.0	110.0	100.0
Capital expenditure	160.0	140.0	130.0	110.0
Increase in working capital	25.0	20.0	15.0	12.0

The other information is as under:

Tax rate t	40%
Book value debt (D)	1200.0
Book value equity (E$_{book}$)	1500.0
Market value equity (E$_{market}$)	1800.0
Beta (historical)B$_L$	1.1
Long term treasury bond Rf	8.0%
Long term debt rate Rd	10.0%

Long term growth rate (g)			4.0%
Long term risk premium (Rm – Rf)			6.0%
Debt Equity ratio			3:7

Solution

1. **Statement of cash flows**

Item	Year 1	Year 2	Year 3	Year 4
EBIT	480.0	530.0	580.0	605.0
Tax rate 40%	192.0	212.0	232.0	242.0
Earnings after tax	288.0	318.0	348.0	363.0
Depreciation	145.0	130.0	110.0	100.0
Capital expenditure	(160.0)	(140.0)	(130.0)	(110.0)
Increase in working capital	(25.0)	(20.0)	(15.0)	(12.0)
Free Cash Flow	248.0	288.0	313.0	341.0

2. **Calculation of APV Analysis**

Beta L = Beta u x [(1 + (1- t) D) / E]

Where, Beta u = Unlevered Beta

D = Market value of debt

E = Market value of equity

Or, Beta u = Beta L / [(1 + (1-t) D)/E]

Or, Beta u = 1.1 / (1 + (1 - 0.4)x1200.0/1800.0)

Or, Beta u = 0.79

Using the same in CAPM:

CAPM = Rf + Beta u (Rm – Rf)

Where, Rf = Risk free rate

Rm = Market rate of return

Rm – Rf = Excess Market return - risk premium

Beta u = Unleveraged Beta

CAPM = 0.08 + 0.79 (0.06) = 0.0192

= **12.7%**

3. **Calculation of WACC**

Beta L = Beta u x [(1 + (1- t) D) / E]

Where, Beta u = Unlevered Beta

D = Market value of debt

E = Market value of equity

Beta L = 0.79 X (1 + (1 - 0.4) 0.3/0.7)

= 0.993

Using the same in CAPM:

CAPM = Rf + Beta L (Rm – Rf)

Where, Rf = Risk free rate

Rm = Market rate of return

Rm – Rf = Excess Market return - risk premium

Beta L = leveraged Beta

CAPM = 0.08 + 0.993 (0.06) = 0.1395

= **13.95%**

WACC = 0.7 X 0.1395 + 0.3 X (1- 0.4) X 0.1

= **11.53%**

4. **Calculation of terminal value**

Based on four years cash flow, year 4 cash flow works out to 4.16 (1)above

APV = Terminal value = (Terminal year FCF $_4$ X (1+g)) / (Rd – g)

= 341 (1 + 0.05) / (0.127 – 0.05)

= **4650**

WACC = Terminal value = (Terminal year FCF $_4$ X (1+g)) / (Rd – g)

= 341 (1 + 0.05) / (0.1153 – 0.05)

= **5483**

5. **Statement of calculation of NPV (APV method)**

Item	Year 1	Year 2	Year 3	Year 4
Free Cash Flow	248.0	288.0	313.0	341.0
Terminal value				4650.0
Total	248.0	288.0	313.0	4991.0
Present value = 12.7%	0.887	0.787	0.699	0.620
Net Present Value = **3759**	220.0	226.7	218.66	3093.8

NPV as above	=	**3759**
Add: Debt Tax Shield = (3759 X 0.4 x 0.3)	=	**451**
Total value	=	**4210**

6. **Statement of calculation of NPV (WACC method)**

Item	Year 1	Year 2	Year 3	Year 4
Free Cash Flow	248.0	288.0	313.0	341.0
Terminal value				5483.0
Total	248.0	288.0	313.0	5824.0
Present value = 11.53%	0.855	0.804	0.721	0.646
Net Present Value = **4443.62**	222.36	231.53	225.6	3764.1

Hence in both the methods the value of the enterprise ranges between 4210 and 4444.

Illustration 9.37: Valuation of business

NRPL (Nuclear Reactors Private Ltd) is engaged in the business of design and construction of nuclear reactors that are supplied exclusively to the Atomic Energy Department. The core component of such reactors is outsourced by NRPL from FIL (Fusions Industrials Ltd) the sole manufacturer of this item. NRPL wants to gain leadership in this industry and seeks to takeover FIL. NRPL estimates that its goodwill in the industry will increase by a minimum of Rs.300 crores consequent on the acquisition. NRPL has made the following calculation of the economic benefits presently available and that foreseen as a result of acquisition.

(i) Projected cash flows of NRPL in the next five years:

Year	1	2	3	4	5

Cash flow (Rs crores)	1000	1500	2000	2500	3000

(ii) Projected cash flows of FIL in the next five years:

Year	1	2	3	4	5
Cash flow (Rs crores)	400	400	600	800	1000

(iii) Audited net worth of FIL

	Rs
Fixed Assets	2000
Investments (non-trade)	1000
Current Assets	1000
TOTAL	4000
Current Liabilities	1000
Net worth	3000

(iv) Other information:

a) 10% of the Fixed Assets of FIL will not be required in the event of the acquisition and the same has ready buyers for Rs.100 crores

b) Current assets include surplus stocks of Rs.20 crores that can realise Rs.30 crores

c) Investments have a ready market for Rs.1500 crores

d) The current liabilities are to be paid off immediately ; Rs.510 crores are payable on account of a compensation claim awarded against FIL, which has been treated as a contingent liability in the Accounts on which 20% was provided for.

(v) NRPL has estimated the combined cash flows post-merger as under:

Year	1	2	3	4	5
Cash flow (Rs crores)	1500	2000	2500	3000	3500

You are required to advise NRPL the maximum value it can pay for takeover of FIL; also show the current valuation of of FIL as a standalone entity. The discount rate of 15% is advised appropriate, values for which are given below:

Year	PV
1	0.870
2	0.756
3	0.658
4	0.572
5	0.497

Solution

1. Statement of valuation of FIL had there been no merger (Rs lakhs)

Year	Cash flows	PV at 15%	DCF
1	400	0.870	348.0
2	400	0.756	302.4
3	600	0.658	394.8
4	800	0.572	457.6
5	1000	0.497	497.0

TOTAL	3200		1999.8

2. Statement of combined valuation of NRPL (Rs Lakhs)

Year	Combined Cash flows	Cash flows before acquisition	Incremental Cash flows	PV at 15%	DCF
1	1500	1000	500	0.870	435
2	2000	1500	500	0.756	378
3	2500	2000	500	0.658	329
4	3000	2500	500	0.572	286
5	3500	3000	500	0.497	248.5
TOTAL					1676.5

3. Statement of computation of maximum value that can be quoted

Particulars	Rs.crores	Rs.crores
Value as per discounted cash flows		1676.5
Add: cash collected on disposal of assets		
Fixed assets	100.0	
Investments – market value	1500.0	
Stock	30.0	1630.0
Total of above		3306.5
Less: Current liabilities paid	1000.0	
Contingent liability (Rs.510 crores x 80%)	408.0	1408.0
Valuation of business on standalone basis		1898.5
Add: Goodwill on takeover		300.0
Maximum value to be quoted		2198.5

Conclusion

From the foregoing it is evident that the standalone value of FIL is Rs.1999.8 crores whereas based on incremental cash flows the value of NRPL merged with FIL works out to Rs.2198.5 crores. Hence NRPL can quote a maximum amount of Rs.2198.5 crores for takeover of FIL.

Illustration 9.38 : Valuation of business

Acquiring Ltd is in the business of making bicycles. The company operates from North India. To diversify in operations Acquiring Ltd has identified Target Tyres Ltd, a South India based company, as a potential takeover candidate. After due diligence the following information is available:

(i) Cash flow forecast   (Rs lakhs)

Year	1	2	3	4	5	6	7	8	9	10
Target Tyres Ltd	150	300	400	500	600	750	800	750	1050	1200
Acquiring Ltd	800	1000	1500	1600	2200	2600	3000	2750	3500	5400

(ii)Balance Sheet of Target Tyres Ltd as at 31st March 2013   (Rs lakhs)

Particulars	2013
EQUITY AND LIABILITIES	
Shareholders' funds	
Share capital (Face value of Rs.10)	100.00
Reserve and surplus	2170.95
	2270.95
Non-current liabilities	
Long term borrowing	565.00
Bank loan	78.50
	643.50
Current liabilities	
Trade payables	163.50
Other current liabilities	47.25
	210.75
TOTAL EQUITY AND LIABILITIES	3125.20

Particulars	2013
ASSETS	
Non-current Assets	
Fixed Assets:	
Tangible assets	1291.00
Intangible assets	120.20
	1411.20
Non-current investments	155.00
Other non-current assets	21.25
	1587.45
Current Assets	
Inventories	511.40
Trade Receivables	745.50
Cash & bank balances	268.50
Other current assets	12.35
	1537.75
TOTAL ASSETS	3125.20

(iii) Talks for the takeover have crystallised the following:
- (a) Acquiring Ltd will not be able to use Machinery worth Rs.175 lakhs which will be disposed off by them subsequent to take over. The expected realisation will be Rs.150 lakhs.
- (b) The inventories and trade receivables are agreed for take over value of Rs.400 and Rs.700 lakhs respectively, which is the price they will realise on disposal
- (c) The liabilities of Target Tyres Ltd will be discharged in full on take over along with an employee settlement of Rs.129 lakhs for the employees who are not interested in continuing under the new management.
- (d) Acquiring Ltd will invest a sum of Rs.250 lakhs for upgrading the Plant of Target Tyres Ltd on takeover. A further sum of Rs.250 lakhs will be incurred to revamp the machine shop floor of Target Tyres Ltd
- (e) The estimated cash flows of the combined business post take over are as follows: (Rs lakhs)

Year	1	2	3	4	5	6	7	8	9	10
Cash flows	900	1200	1800	2200	3000	4000	4800	5000	7000	10000

The management of Target Ltd is not ready to accept its present standalone value as consideration for the take-over. Acquiring Ltd wishes to know up to what extent they can quote higher price, without suffering any loss in value post-merger.

You are required to advise the management the upper limit price which they can pay per share of Target Tyres Ltd , if a discount factor of 15% is considered appropriate.

Use the following discount table:

Year	1	2	3	4	5	6	7	8	9	10
Discount factor at 15%	0.8696	0.7561	0.6575	0.5718	0.4972	0.4323	0.3759	0.3269	0.2843	0.2472

Solution

1. **Statement of present value of incremental cash flows**

Year	1	2	3	4	5	6	7	8	9	10
Cash flow post take over	900	1200	1800	2200	3000	4000	4800	5000	7000	10000
Less: Cash flow pre take over	800	1000	1500	1600	2200	2600	3000	2750	3500	5400
Incremental cash flows	100	200	300	600	800	1400	1800	2250	3500	4600
Discounted cash flow 15%	0.8696	0.7561	0.6575	0.5718	0.4972	0.4323	0.3759	0.3269	0.2843	0.2472
Discounted cash flow	86.96	151.22	197.25	343.08	397.76	605.22	676.62	735.525	995.05	1137.12

Rs/lakhs 5325.805

2. **Statement of calculation of maximum price that can be quoted for takeover of Target Tyres Ltd**

Item	Rs lakhs	Rs lakhs
Present Value of incremental cash flows from operations (refer statement 1 above)		5325.80
Add: Cash to be collected immediately by disposal of assets:		
Tangible assets	150.00	
Proceeds from disposal of inventories	400.00	
Receipts from Trade receivables	700.00	1250.00
		6575.80
Less: Long term borrowing	565.00	
Bank loan	78.50	
Trade payables	163.50	
Other current liabilities	47.25	
Employee settlement	129.00	
Renovation of plant	250.00	
Revamp of machine shop floor (Rs.250 lakhs x 0.7561)*	189.02	1422.27
		5153.53

*Discount factor of year 2 @ 20%

Hence maximum price per share of Target Tyres Ltd would be:

=   Rs.5153.53 lakhs / 10, 00,000 shares

=   **Rs.515.353**

Illustration 9.39: Valuation of business

The Balance Sheets of Resurgent Ltd for the years ended 31.03.2011; 31.03.2012 and 31.03.2013 are as follows:

Liabilities	31.03.2011 Rs	31.03.2012 Rs	31.03.2013 Rs
3,20,000 equity shares of Rs.10 fully paid up	32,00,000	32,00,000	32,00,000
General reserve	24,00,000	28,00,000	32,00,000
Profit & Loss Account	2,80,000	3,20,000	4,80,000
Creditors	12,00,000	16,00,000	20,00,000
Total	70,80,000	79,20,000	88,80,000

Assets	31.03.2011 Rs	31.03.2012 Rs	31.03.2013 Rs
Goodwill	20,00,000	16,00,000	12,00,000
Building & Machinery (less depreciation)	28,00,000	32,00,000	32,00,000
Stock	20,00,000	24,00,000	28,00,000
Debtors	40,000	3,20,000	8,80,000
Bank balance	2,40,000	4,00,000	8,00,000
Total	70,80,000	79,20,000	88,80,000

Actual valuations were as under:

Particulars	31.03.2011 Rs	31.03.2012 Rs	31.03.2013 Rs
Building & Machinery	36,00,000	40,00,000	44,00,000
Stock	24,00,000	28,00,000	32,00,000
Net Profit (including opening balance) after writing off depreciation and goodwill , tax provision and transfer to general reserve	8,40,000	12,40,000	16,40,000

Capital employed in the business at market values at the beginning of 2010-11 was Rs.73,20, 000, which included the cost of goodwill. The normal annual return on average capital employed in the line of business engaged by Resurgent Ltd is 12.5%.

The balance in the general reserve account on 1st April 2010 was Rs.20 lakhs.

The goodwill shown on 31.3.2011 was purchased on 1.4.2010 for Rs.20 lakhs on which date the balance of Profit & Loss Account was Rs.2, 40,000. Find out the average capital employed each year. Goodwill is to be valued at five years purchase of super profits (simple average method). Also find out the total value of the business as on 31.03.2013.

Solution

1. **Statement of computation of average capital employed**

Particulars	31.03.2011 Rs	31.03.2012 Rs	31.03.2013 Rs
Goodwill	20,00,000	16,00,000	12,00,000
Building & Machinery (revalued)	36,00,000	40,00,000	44,00,000

Stock (revalued)	24,00,000	28,00,000	32,00,000
Debtors	40,000	3,20,000	8,80,000
Bank balance	2,40,000	4,00,000	8,00,000
Total assets	82,80,000	91,20,000	1,04,80,000
Less: Creditors	12,00,000	16,00,000	20,00,000
Closing capital employed	70,80,000	75,20,000	84,80,000
Opening capital employed	73,20,000	70,80,000	75,20,000
	1,44,00,000	1,46,00,000	1,60,00,000
Average capital employed	72,00,000	73,00,000	80,00,000
Normal return on capital employed at 12.5%	9,00,000	9,12,500	10,00,000

Note

Since goodwill has been paid for, it is considered part of capital employed. Capital employed at the end of each year has been worked out as above.

It has been assumed that building & machinery has been revalued after considering depreciation.

2. Statement of computation of maintainable profit

Particulars	31.03.2011	31.03.2012	31.03.2013
	Rs	Rs	Rs
Net profit as given	8,40,000	12,40,000	16,40,000
Less: Opening balance	2,40,000	2,80,000	3,20,000
	6,00,000	9,60,000	13,20,000
Add: Undervaluation of closing stock	4,00,000	4,00,000	4,00,000
	10,00,000	13,60,000	17,20,000
Less: Adjustment in valuation of opening stock	-	4,00,000	4,00,000
	10,00,000	9,60,000	13,20,000
Add: Goodwill written off		4,00,000	4,00,000
Transfer to reserves	4,00,000	4,00,000	4,00,000
	14,60,000	17,60,000	21,20,000
Normal return on capital employed at 12.5%	9,00,000	9,12,500	10,00,000
Super profit	5,00,000	8,47,500	11,20,000

3. Statement of computation of goodwill

Particulars	Rs.
Average super profit (5,00,000 + 8,47,500 + 11,20,000)/3	8,22,500
Goodwill (five years purchase) – (Rs.8,22,500 x 5)	41,12,500

4. Statement of computation of valuation of business

Particulars	Rs.
Total net assets	84,80,000
Less: Goodwill	12,00,000
	72,80,000
Add: Goodwill (five years purchase) – (Rs.8,22,500 x 5)	41,12,500
Valuation of business	**1,13.92,500**

9.21. Valuation of brand

In modern competitive world, the corporate value and earning power are decided and generated by intangible assets more than tangible assets. In highly competitive marketing environment, brand endorses great competitive advantage to corporate entities. Today, instead of product selling by itself, it is the brand that initiates the sale of the product. Massive sums of money are spent by today's corporate world to build, propagate and accentuate brand identity among product or service community at large. Hence brands become strategic assets which hold on their own in today's complex competitive business environment.

According to American Marketing Association, brand identifies a name, term, sign, symbol or design or a combination of these intended to identify the goods or services of one seller or group of sellers and to differentiate them from those of competitors.

9.21.1. Objectives of corporate branding

The critical objectives of corporate branding are:	a) Corporate identity b) Practice of nurturing and building Total Quality Management and garnering of best practices c) Trigger customer preferences d) Market segmentation e) Build-up of strong market

9.21.2. Brands identified as an asset

We know an asset as a concept would be characterized by the following features:

a) to be an asset there must exist some specific right to future benefits or service potential
b) rights over assets must accrue to a specific individual or firm
c) there must be a legally enforceable claim to the rights or services over the asset
d) the asset must be the result of a past transaction or event.

Based on the above characteristics, brand would be treated as an asset. The principal objective of establishing brand names is to incur future economic benefits through increase in sale to willing customers or through increased sales of the brand itself or the business that owns the brand.

9.21.3. Features of valuation of brand

Salient features of valuation of brand	• No valuation shall be made for internally generated brand • When the brand is acquired separately, the valuation would be made at initial cost of acquisition (with subsequent addition to cost , if any)

	• All identifiable intangible assets including patents, copyrights, know-how and designs which are acquired separately, valuation would be made at initial cost of acquisition (with subsequent addition to cost, if any). • The depreciable amount of an intangible asset should be allocated on a systematic basis over the best estimate of its useful life. There is a rebuttable presumption that the useful life of an intangible asset will not exceed ten years from the date when the asset is available for use. • Amortization should commence when the asset is available for use.

9.21.4. Models used in valuation of brand
The models used in valuation of brand are enumerated as under:

9.21.4.1. Acquired brands

Value at price paid	When a brand is acquired, then the excess of purchase consideration over the net assets taken over is considered as representing goodwill. This includes various factors like brands, locational advantage, raw material availability at competitive prices, however, it is difficult to segregate value of brand from other factors.

9.21.4.2. Self-generated brands

1.Historical cost model	Brand is valued at the costs incurred for developing and maintaining it. Brand value is the sum of: a)brand development cost b)brand marketing and distribution cost c)brand promotion cost It is easy to calculate the value of brand, but does not consider the impact of the brand on the profitability of the firm.
2.Replacement cost model	Brand is valued at the costs which would be incurred if an existing brand is recreated. This model assumes that existing brand can be replaced exactly by new brands, which is impracticable. Also the value becomes subjective
3.Market price model	Model is valued at net realisable value from sale. However, there is no active market for sale of brands. Brands are not ordinarily traded asset. In reality the valuation is done from buyers viewpoint, based on expected benefits from purchase.

4.Current cost model	Brand is valued at current cost to the enterprise. It is revalued annually and hence no amortisation. The model ignores alternative uses of the brand and changes in the range of branded products and increase in the value of brand due to special circumstances
5.Present value model	Brand value is the sum-total of present value of expected future brand revenues for the economic life of the brand and the residual value of the brand at the end of that period. The discount rate is weighted average cost of capital added by a suitable risk premium. The residual value is estimated assuming a perpetual stream of revenue, which is constant or which increases at a constant rate. However, it is always difficult to build future cash flows out of projected brand revenues, discount rate etc.
6.Potential earning model	In this model, the potential earnings of a brand (i.e. net brand revenue) is estimated and capitalised using an appropriate rate to determine the brand value. This is calculated as under: (Brand units x Unit brand price) – (brand units x unit brand cost)(Marketing cost + research and development cost + taxes) However, difficulties may arise while calculating marketing cost of brand and the capitalisation rate
7.Sensitivity model	Brand revenues are assumed as dependent on various market factors as under: a) awareness of brand (AB) b) level of customer influence (BI) c) level of brand autonomy (BA) with different levels of sensitivity. The formula is as under: (Brand units x unit brand price) x AB x BI x BA – (BDC+BMDC+BPC), where, BDC = Brand development cost BMDC = Brand marketing and distribution cost BPC = Brand Promotion cost As is evident from above formula, there are too many variables and hence the results may be theoretical.
8.Life cycle model	In this model, brand values build up over a period of the brand's life, forming an "S" shaped curve, just like the product life cycle. This model uses this curve to explain the level and behaviour of the brand value at different stages of brand's life. However, this model gives only theoretical pictorial results of brand value over a period of time and it is always difficult to quantify.
9.Incremental model	Brand value is measured as the incremental benefits expected to be achieved as a result of acquisition or revaluation of brands.

10.Market oriented approach model	This model calculates brand value based on environmental factors such as market size, market share, competition and the formula is as under: Discount factor x enterprise profitability ratio x (cumulative market size in next 10 years – cumulative total market share of other branded and non-branded products over the next 10 years) However, the model presupposes thorough understanding of the market variables to make it effective.
11.Value chain approach Model	An enterprise consists of a stream of value drivers, which add value to the products from the input stage to output stage and this is called value chain approach. In this model, the contribution from each value driver is aggregated and then deducted from the total contribution of the enterprise to arrive at a surplus, which is contributed by the enterprise's brand. The surplus is estimated for a certain period and then discounted to arrive at brand value.
12.Whole organisation as a brand model	In this model the entire organisation is regarded as a brand. Accordingly the brand value is determined as under: Intrinsic value of an enterprise – net asset value of an enterprise, where intrinsic value is arrived by the valuation of enterprise as a whole including brands and net asset value is arrived at based on individual
13.Human resources as a brand	As we know key executives of an enterprise may also work as a brand for the enterprise as a whole. Some of the basic approaches are: a)Cost approach – where cost of development of key executives are factored b)Compensation approach – worked out based on present value of total future compensation payable to employees c)Intrinsic approach– worked out as present value of total future compensation payable to employees as adjusted with key performance indicators within the enterprise d)remainder approach – formula is as under: Discount factor x (total profits of the organisation with branded employees for next 10 years – total profits of the organisation without branded employees for next 10 years)

Illustration.9.40: Valuation of brand under potential earning model

From the following information, determine the possible value of brand as per potential earning model:

	Rs in lakhs
a) Profit after tax (PAT)	2500
b) Tangible fixed assets	10000
c) Identifiable intangible other than brand	1500

d) Weighted average cost of capital %   14%
e) Expected normal return on tangible assets
   Weighted average cost (14%) + normal spread 4%   18%
f) Appropriate capitalization factor for intangibles   25%

Solution

Statement of calculation of possible value of brand   **Rs in lakhs**

Item	Amount
Profit after tax (PAT)	2500
Less: Profit allocated to tangible assets (18% of Rs.10000)	1800
Profit allocated to intangible assets including brand	700
Capitalization factor	25%
Capitalized value of intangibles including brand ((700 x 1/25) x 100)	2800
Less: Identifiable intangibles other than brand	1500
Brand value	1300

Illustration 9.41: Valuation of brand under potential earnings model:

From the following information determine the possible value of brand under the Potential Earning Model:

S/L	Particulars	Rs in lakhs
1.	Profit before tax	13.00
2.	Income tax	3.00
3.	Tangible fixed asset	20.00
4.	Identifiable intangible other than brand model	10.00
5.	Expected return on tangible fixed assets	6.00

Appropriate capitalization factor for intangibles is 25% (*CA Final May 2011*)

Solution

Statement of valuation of brand: potential earnings model

S/L	Particulars	Rs in lakhs
1.	Profit before tax	13.0
2.	Tax	(3.0)
3.	Profit after tax	10.0
4.	Expected return on tangible fixed assets	(6.0)
5.	Return due to intangibles (including brand) (3-4)	4.0
6.	Capitalisation factor for intangibles	25%
7.	Total value of intangibles (5/6)	16.0
8.	Identifiable intangibles other than brand	10.0
9.	Value of brand (7 – 8)	6.0

Illustration 9.42: Value of brand under present value model

ABC Ltd provides the following estimated cash flow of the enterprise as on 1.4.2013:

Rs lakhs

Year	2013-14	2014-15	2015-16	2016-17	2017-18
Cash flow of the enterprise	4000	6000	6000	8000	4000

Residual value at the end of year 2017-18 = Rs.1000 lakhs
Useful life of the brand = 5 years
Weighted average cost of capital = 15%
Present value factor at 15%

Year	1	2	3	4	5
	0.870	0.756	0.658	0.572	0.497

Calculate value of brand under Present value model.

Solution

Year	Cash flow of enterprise (A)	PV @ 15% (B)	Present value ((AX B) = C)
2013-14	4000	0.870	3480
2014-15	6000	0.756	4536
2015-16	6000	0.658	3948
2016-17	8000	0.572	4576
2017-18	4000	0.497	1988
2017-18	1000	0.497	497

Value of brand under present value model (3480+4536+3948+4576+1988+497) = 19025

Illustration.9.43: Value of brand under Super profits model

ABC Ltd provides the following estimates of profit of an enterprise as on 1.4.2013:

Rs lakhs

Year	2013-14	2014-15	2015-16	2016-17	2017-18
Total profit of an enterprise	4000	6000	6000	8000	4000
Total profit of an enterprise without the brand	1000	2000	3000	4000	1000

Useful life of the brand = 5 years
Weighted average cost of capital = 15%
Present value factor at 15%

Year	1	2	3	4	5
	0.870	0.756	0.658	0.572	0.497

Calculate value of brand under Super profit model.

Solution

Year	Total profit of enterprise (A)	Total profit of enterprise Without brand (B)	Profit of enterprise attributable to brand((A-B)=C)	PV @ 15% (D)	Present value ((C X D) = E)
2013-14	4000	1000	3000	0.870	2610
2014-15	6000	2000	4000	0.756	3024
2015-16	6000	3000	3000	0.658	1974
2016-17	8000	4000	4000	0.572	2288
2017-18	4000	1000	3000	0.497	1491

Value of brand under super profit model (2610+3024+1974+2288+1491) = 11387

Illustration.9.44: What is corporate brand strength?

Solution

Corporate brand strength / value can be viewed as the sum-total of all benefits flowing from different dimensions of brand such as market leadership (ML), stability of market (SM), market share (MS)of the brand, levels of international acceptance (IA) , ability of the brand to meet the changing modern marketing trends (MT), the extent of strategic support (SS) provided by the brand, competitive strength (CS) offered by the brand and last but not the least all the legal and social brand protection (BP).

Accordingly, the brand value would be the sum-total as under:

Brand value = (ML + SM + MS + IA + MT + SS + CS + BP)

Illustration 9.45: Valuation of brand under earnings multiple method

Zed Ltd is an FMCG player in the range of men's cosmetics and deals in both branded and unbranded products. The branded products are sold under the brand of "ZED" and are fully outsourced to third party manufacturers. The company's unbranded products are manufactured at the company's own manufacturing units. The earnings for the last three years (Rs lakhs) are furnished below:

	Year 1	Year 2	Year 3
Earnings before interest and tax (EBIT) from sale of products	5,100	7,500	9,900
Other income – royalty for partial usage of ZED brand	90	135	225

The details of fixed assets employed at the company's manufacturing units are given below:

	Year 1	Year 2	Year 3
Tangible fixed assets employed (Rs lakhs)	9,000	10,800	13,500
Return (before interest and tax) on cost of tangible assets	14%	12%	14%
Spread over return	2%	3%	4%

The average annual funds used in the company's operations are Rs.5,200 lakhs of which Rs.2,800 lakhs is in respect of the branded business. The company's tax rate is 33.33% and has an average cost of funds of 17% after considering tax shelter on cost of borrowed funds. You are required to determine the value of Brand ZED considering a capitalisation rate of 20%. *(CA Final Nov 2013)*

Solution

1. Computation of Brand value under earning multiple model (Rs lakhs)

	Year 1	Year 2	Year 3
Earnings before interest and tax (EBIT) from sale of products (A)**	5,100	7,500	9,900
EBIT from non-branded products (Tangible assets employed for non-branded products x (return (before interest and tax)on cost of tangible assets + spread over return) (B)	1440* *(9000 x 16%)	1620* *(10800 x 15%)	2430* *(13500 x 18%)
Past EBIT on branded products ((A-B)=C)	3660	5880	7470

**Since other income is attributable to royalty for partial usage of ZED brand, it is not deducted from EBIT

Average EBIT	= (3660+5880+7470)/3
	= 5670
Less tax 33.33%	= 1890
Average EAT	= 3780
Brand earnings	= Average EAT – weighted average cost of funds x funds used for branded activities
Brand earnings	= 3780 – 17% x Rs.2800 lakhs
	= 3780 – 476
	= 3304

Brand Value
(Brand earnings/
Capitalisation rate) = 3304 / 0.20
= **Rs. 16520 lakhs**

Illustration: 9.46

RS Ltd furnishes the following information relating to the previous three years, and requests you to compute the value of the brand of the Company — [Rs. in Lakhs]

Particulars	2011	2012	2013
Profit before interest and tax	75.00	85.25	150.00
Loss on sale of assets	3.00	-	18.00
Non-operating income	12.00	7.25	8.00

Inflation was 9% for 2012 and 15% for 2013. If the capitalization factor considering internal and external value drivers to the brand is 14, determine the brand value. Assume an all inclusive future tax rate of 35%.

Solution

Particulars	2011	2012	2013
Profit before interest and tax	75.00	85.25	150.00
Add: Loss on sale of assets	3.00	-	18.00
Less: Non-operating income	(12.00)	(7.25)	(8.00)
Branded earnings	66.00	78.00	160.00
Inflation adjustment factor	1.09 x 1.15 = 1.25	1.15	1.00

Inflation adjusted earnings as at 31.03.2013	82.50	89.70	160.00
Weights	1	2	3
Product	82.50	179.40	480.00
Weighted average earnings before tax: =(82.50+179.40+480.00)/(1+2+3)			123.65
Less: taxes @ 35%			(43.28)
Weighted average brand earnings after tax			80.37
Capitalisation factor			14
Brand value			Rs.1125.18 lakhs

Illustration: 9.47

The following financial share data pertaining to Infotech Ltd an IT Company are made available to you: (Rs crores)

Year ended March 31st	2012	2011	2010
EBIT	696.03	325.65	155.86
Non-branded income	53.43	35.23	3.46
Inflation compounded factor @ 8%	1.000	1.087	1.181

Remuneration of capital	5% average capital employed
Average capital employed	Rs.1112.0 crores
Corporate tax rate	35%
Capitalisation factor	16%

You are required to calculate Brand value of Infotech Ltd.

Solution

Statement of computation of brand value of Infotech Ltd   **Rs crores**

Year ended March 31st		2012	2011	2010
EBIT		696.03	325.65	155.86
Non-branded income		53.43	35.23	3.46
Adjusted profit		642.60	290.42	152.40
Inflation compounded factor @ 8%		1.000	1.087	1.181
Present value of profits for the brand		642.60	315.69	179.98
Weightage factor		3	2	1
Weightage profit		1927.80	631.38	179.98
Profits=(1927.80+631.38+179.98)6	(A)	456.53		
Less: Remuneration of capital at 5% of average capital employed (1112.0 X 5%)	(B)	55.60		
Brand related profits	(A-B)=(C)	400.93		
Corporate tax @ 35%	(D)	140.33		
Brand earnings	(C – D) = (E)	260.60		
Capitalisation factor	(F)	16%		
Brand value	(E / F = G)	1628.75		

Illustration: 9.48

From the following information determine the Possible Value of Brand as per Potential Earning Model – (Rs.Lakhs)

Particulars	Case A	Case B
(i)Profit before tax (PBT)	-	15.00
(ii)Income tax	-	3.00
(iii)Profit after tax (PAT)	2,700	
(iv) Tangible fixed assets	10,000	20.00
(v)Identifiable Intangible other than brand	1,500	
(vi)Weighted average cost of capital (%)	15%	-
(vii)Expected normal return on tangible assets		
Weighted average capital cost + normal spread	20%	6.00
5%	25%	25%
(viii)Appropriate capitalisation factor for intangibles		

Solution

Statement of brand valuation of Case A

Particulars	Rs lakhs	Rs lakhs
(i)Profit after tax (PAT)	2,700	2,700
Less: Normal return from tangible assets (Rs.10,000	(2,000)	(2,000)
lakhs x 20%)	(375)	(375)
Less: Normal return from other tangible assets		
(Rs.1, 500 lakhs x 25%)	325	325
Brand earnings	25%	15%
Capitalisation factor – WACC	Rs.1,300 lakhs	Rs.2,166.67 lakhs
Value of brand		

Statement of brand valuation of Case B

Particulars	Rs lakhs
(i)Profit before tax (PBT)	15.00
(II)Income tax	(3.00)
(III)Profit after tax (PAT)	12.00
Less: Normal return from tangible assets	(6.00)
Less: Normal return from other tangible assets	
(Rs.10 lakhs x 25%)	(2.50)
Brand earnings	3.50
Capitalisation factor	25%
Value of brand (Rs.3.50 lakhs / 25%)	Rs.14 lakhs

Chapter 10: Economic Value Added

10.1. *Economic Value Added* as a residual income measure of financial performance is simply the operating profit after tax less a charge for the capital equity as well as debt, used in the business. The components of EVA are explained below:

Components of EVA

- NOPAT
  - Net operating profit after tax
- Invested capital (net operating assets)
  - Net operating working capital, net PP&E, goodwill, and other operating assets
- Cost of capital
  - Weighted average cost of capital %
- Capital charge
  - Cost of capital % * Invested capital
- Economic value added
  - NOPAT less the capital charge.

10.1.1. The steps in calculation of EVA revisited as under:

e) Calculate Net Operating Profit after Tax (NOPAT)
f) Calculate Total Invested Capital (TC)
g) Determine Weighted Average Cost of Capital (WACC)
h) Calculate EVA = NOPAT – TC X WACC

EVA helps to	- Measure the financial performance
	- Take important managerial decision
	- Equate managerial incentives with shareholder interests
	- Improve financial and business literacy throughout the firm

The steps are explained in the charts below

Step A. Calculate Net Operating Profit after Tax (NOPAT)

NOPAT is calculated as shown in the chart below:

NOPAT

Net sales	150,000
Cost of sales	135,000
Depreciation	2,000
SG&A	7,000
Net Operating profit	6,000
Taxes @ 40%	2,400
NOPAT	3,600

Excludes financing charges

From the above chart it is clear that Net Operating Profit after TAX (NOPAT) is calculated after deducting Cost of sales, depreciation and Selling, General and Administrative overheads and arrive at Net Operating profit. Then tax is calculated and deducted from net operating profit to work out NOPAT.

Step B. Calculate total invested capital (IC)

Invested Capital

- Capital: Net operating assets adjusted for certain accounting distortions
  - Asset write-downs, restructuring charges, ...
- Net operating assets:
  - Cash, receivables, inventory, prepaids
  - Trade payable, accruals, deferred taxes
  - Net property, plant, and equipment
- Exclude non-operating assets:
  - Marketable securities, investments,...

As explained in the Chart, Invested Capital is comprised of net operating assets after deducting asset write-downs, restructuring charges and non-operating assets like marketable securities etc.

Step C: Weighted Average cost of capital (WACC)

Weighted average cost of capital is calculated as under:

Weighted Average Cost of Capital

- **Weighted average cost of capital consists of:**

  Cost of debt after taxes

  = Market interest rate x (1 − tax rate)

  Cost of equity

  = Risk-free rate + beta x (market risk premium)

  WACC

  = Cost of debt after taxes x % debt + cost of equity x % equity

  where % debt + % equity = 100%.

10.1.2. Constituents of Weighted Average cost of capital

Cost of capital	This means the cost of long term funds of a company. It is the multiple of capital employed and weighted average of cost of debt capital, cost of equity capital and cost of preference shares capital. Accordingly it is known as Weighted Average cost of capital (WACC). WACC is post tax.
Capital employed	Capital employed signifies (Debt capital + equity capital + preference share capital)
Cost of debt capital	It is the discount rate that equates the present value of after tax interest payment cash outflows to the current market value of the debt capital. Due to the tax benefit on interest payment on debt capital, cost of debt is , generally , lower than the cost of equity capital
Cost of equity capital	It is the market expected rate of return. Equity capital and accumulated reserves and surpluses which are free to equity shareholders carry the same cost.
Cost of preference capital	It is the discount rate that equates the present value of after tax interest payment cash outflows to the current market value of the preference share capital

10.1.3. Factors involved in calculation of EVA

Factors involved in calculating EVA	• Cost of debt capital (Kd) (Interest on long term borrowings (1-Tax rate) / Long term

	borrowings)x 100 • Cost of equity (Ke) Risk free rate (Rf) + Beta (Market rate (Rm) – Risk free rate(Rf)) • Cost of preference (Kp) (Preference dividend / Preference share capital) x 100 • Cost of retained earnings (Kr) • Overall cost of capital (Kd x (debt / total funds)) + (Kp x (PSC / Total funds)) + (Ke x (equity / total funds)) • Total funds = Debt + preference capital + equity capital

10.1.4. Capital Asset Pricing Model (revisited)

Capital Asset Pricing Model (CAPM)	• is the most widely used method of calculating the cost of equity capital. This is expressed as : = Risk free rate + Specific risk premium = Risk free rate + Beta x Equity risk premium = Risk free rate + Beta x (market rate (Rm) – risk free rate(Rf)) Specific risk premium is a multiple of Beta and Equity Risk premium
Beta	• is a relative measure of volatility that is determined by comparing the return on a share to the return on the stock market. Which means greater the volatility, the more risky the share and higher the beta. • For the companies, which are not listed in stock exchanges, beta of similar industry may be considered after transforming it to un-geared beta and then re- gearing it according to the debt equity ratio of the company. Ungeared data = Industry beta / (1 + (1- tax rate)(industry debt equity ratio) Geared data = Ungeared data / (1 = (1 – tax rate) (Debt Equity ratio)
Equity risk premium	Equity risk premium is the excess return above the risk free rate that investors demand for holding risky securities. It is calculated as "market rate of return (MRR)" Minus Risk Free Rate ". Market rate may be calculated from the movement of share Market indices over a period of an economic cycle basing on moving average to smooth out abnormalities. Many of them do not calculate the MRR but on an ad-hoc basis they assume 8% to 12 % as the equity risk premium.

Step D Calculating EVA.

This is essentially in two parts.

In the first part we determine Capital charge. This is done as under:

Capital Charge

- Represents a rental charge for the use of the invested capital (net operating assets as above)
- Minimum rate of return the operating capital should earn
- Calculated as the firm's weighted average cost of capital % x invested capital.

In the second part we ascertain the Economic Value Added (EVA). This is shown as under:

Calculating EVA

Net operating profit after tax (NOPAT)

- Capital charge (WACC * Capital)

= Economic value added (EVA)

10.1.5. Value drivers of EVA

Now we need to understand what are the value drivers that impact EVA. Please refer the chart below:

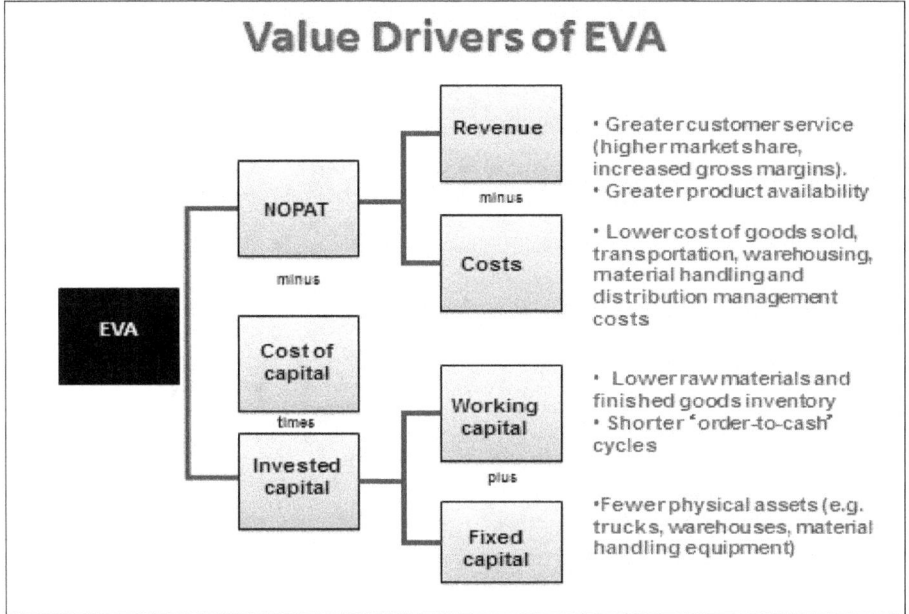

From the above chart it is clear that, the value drivers are:
   a) revenue, based on improved customer service, greater product availability in the market,
   b) Variable and fixed costs, lower and more competitive the cost structure, better the net operating profit
   c) Working capital, lower receivables and inventories, shorter purchase to payables and order to cash cycle
   d) Fixed assets, which are productive operating assets utilised for generation of revenue.

Hence to optimise EVA the fundamental strategy for business should be to
   a) improve NOPAT by increasing revenue and reducing costs and
   b) reduce capital charge by optimising invested capital and restructuring weighted average cost of capital by minimising cost of borrowing.

As long as returns on investment exceed cost of capital one needs to continue to invest in the business. However, if the cost of capital exceeds returns then this should be considered as wake-up call to "harvest" by re-deploying capital elsewhere.

This is explained in the chart below:

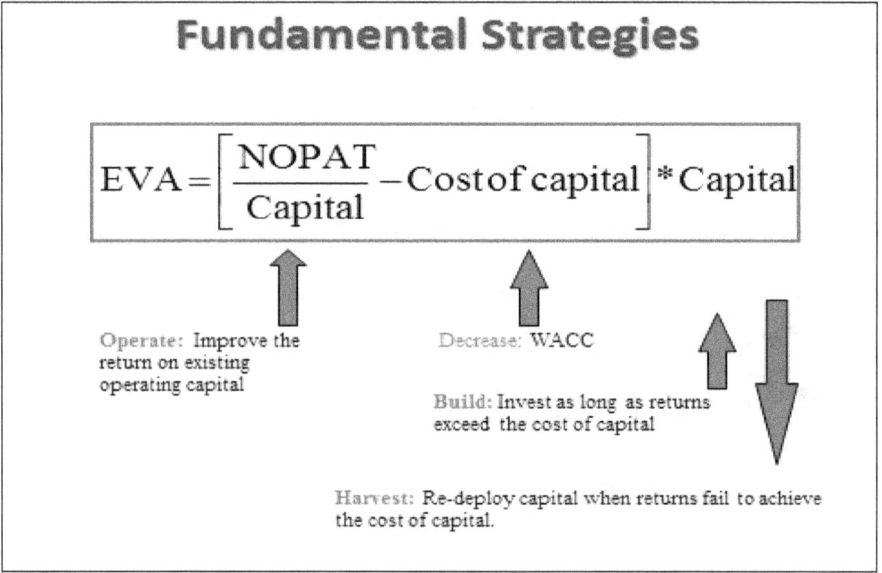

10.2. Market Value Added (MVA)

It is the difference between the current market value of a firm and the capital contributed by Investors.

If MVA is positive the firm has added value. If it is negative the Firm has destroyed value.

MVA = Market value of capital – Capital employed

Key elements of MVA are:
   a) Market value of equity

   b) Market value of debt

   c) Calculation of capital invested

This is further explained in the chart below:

MVA

- MVA = Market value of capital
  - book value of capital
- Key elements:
  - Calculation of market value of capital
    - Market value of debt + market value of equity
  - Calculation of capital invested
    - Accounting adjustments necessary
- MVA ➜ Related to EVA.

The concept of market value added is further explained diagrammatically as under:

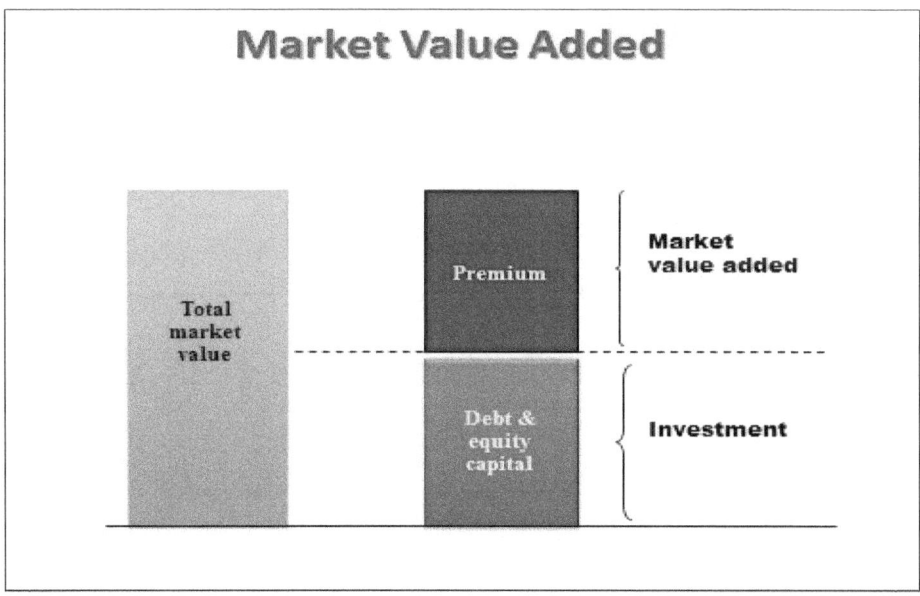

Now we need to understand the relationship between MVA and EVA. Companies which consistently earn profits in excess of their weighted average cost of capital, which in other words is the required rate of return, eventually generate total market value which is much higher than the capital employed. And that is Market Value Added (MVA) in the long run.

Market value of a company reflects:
a) Value of ongoing operations
b) Value of invested capital
c) Present value of expected future economic profits, wherein it captures improvement in operating performance.

At the same time EVA Is related to MVA
- Measuring all the capital
- Seeing what the firm is going to do with the capital
- Turn FCF forecasts into EVA forecasts
- Discount EVA.

This is further explained in the chart below:

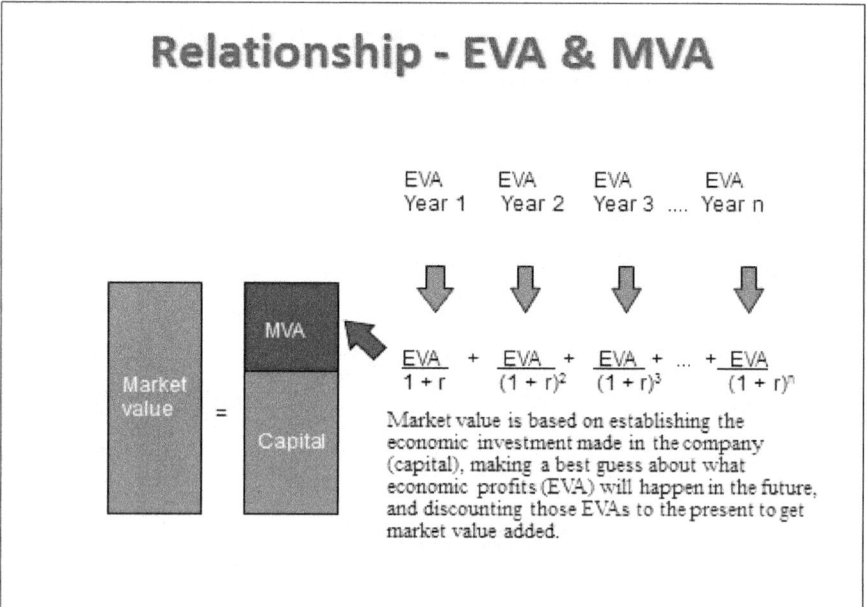

10.3. Shareholders Value Added

Shareholders Value Added is a value-based performance measure of a company's worth to shareholders.

The basic calculation is as under:

Net Operating profit after tax **(NOPAT)**

minus

Weighted Average cost of capital **(WACC)**

10.4. Relation between NPV and EVA

Let us explain the relation between Net Present Value (NPV) and Economic Value Added (EVA) with the help of an example as provided below.

Illustration

A)Computation of NPV

Let us consider the following data points:

Investment   : Rs.1000
Annual cash flow: Rs.350
Annual ATOI   : Rs.150
Investment's life: 5 years
Cost of capital   : 12%
Assume straight line depreciation.

Answer:
NPV = 3.605 X 350 – Rs.1000 = Rs.262/-

B)Computation of EVA and present value of total EVA

On the same data mentioned above

Item	1	2	3	4	5
ATOI	150	150	150	150	150
Capital charge	120	96	72	48	24
EVA	30	54	78	102	126
PV factor	0.893	0.797	0.712	0.636	0.567
Present value	26.8	43.0	55.5	64.9	71.4

Total PV of EVA = Rs.262/- ; NPV = Rs.262/-

The above example clearly shows how NPV discounted over five years is equal to the present value of EVA over the same period. This is where EVA proves its superiority and becomes an overriding metric to measure creation and value and wealth in an organisation.

10.5. Benefits of EVA

The benefits of EVA may be summarised as under:
   a) Common language and focus for planning and managing
   b) More accountability for delivering value
   c) Greater concern for managing assets
   d) Stronger emphasis on continuous improvement
   e) Greater willingness to rationalise and redirect resources
   f) Better bridge linking operations and strategy with financial results
   g) Higher market value

Illustration 10.1: Economic Value Added

Calculate EVA for Ram Ltd using the following information:	
Particulars	**Rs.**

Revenues	3000000
Cost of goods sold	2000000
Operating expenses	700000
Cost of capital	8%
Short term and long term capital employed	1500000

Solution

EVA = NOPAT – WACC X Invested capital

= (3000000 – 2000000 – 700000) – 0.08 x 1500000

= Rs.1,80,000

Illustration 10.2: Economic Value Added

The following information is available of a concern:

Debt capital 12%	Rs.2000 crores
Equity capital	Rs.500 crores
Reserves & Surplus	Rs.7500 crores
Capital employed	Rs.10000 crores
Risk free rate	
9%	
Beta factor	1.05
Market rate of return	19%
Equity (market) risk premium	10%
Operating profit after tax	Rs.2100 crores
Tax rate	30%
Calculate E.V.A	

Solution

The base definitions that will help solve the problem are given below:

E.V.A.	=	NOPAT – COCE
NOPAT	=	Net Operating Profit after tax
COCE	=	Cost of capital employed
	=	Weighted average costs of capita x average capital employed
	=	WACC X Capital employed

Accordingly the calculations are as under:

Debt capital 12%	=	Rs.2000 crores	
Equity capital	=	(Rs.500 crores + Rs.7500 crores) = Rs.8000 crores	
Capital employed	=	(Rs.2000 crores + Rs.8000 crores)	=
	=	Rs.10000 crores	
Debt to capital			
Employed	=	2000 / 10000 = 0.20	
Equity to capital			

Employed	=	8000 / 10000 = 0.80
Debt cost (gross)	=	12 %
Less tax (30% x12%)	=	3.6%
Debt cost (net of tax)	=	8.4%

Statement of Cost of equity capital

According to Capital Asset Pricing Model (CAPM)		
Cost of Equity capital	=	Risk free rate + Beta x Equity risk premium
	=	Risk free rate + Beta (Market rate – risk free rate)
	=	9 + 1.05 x (19-9)
	=	9 + 1.05 x 10
	=	19.5 %

Statement of WACC and EVA

WACC	=	Equity to C.E. X Cost of equity capital
		+ Debt to C.E. X Cost of debt
	=	0.8 x 19.5% + 0.2 x 8.4%
	=	15.6 % + 1.68 %
	=	17.28%
COCE	=	WACC X Capital employed
	=	17.28 % x Rs.10000 crores
	=	Rs.1728 crores
E.V.A.	=	NOPAT – COCE
	=	Rs. 2100 – Rs. 1728
	=	Rs.372 crores

Illustration 10.3: Economic Value Added (EVA)

P Ltd supplies the following information using which you are required to calculate the Economic value added.

- Financial leverage   1.4 times
- Capital (equity and debt)   Equity shares of 34000 (number) of Rs.1000 each
  Accumulated profit   : Rs.260 lakhs
  10% debentures 80 lakhs (number) of Rs.10 each
  Dividend expectation of equity shareholders :17.5%
  Prevailing corporate tax rate :   30%

(CA Final: June 2009)

Solution
Statement of computation of EVA

Computation of EVA	Rs Lakhs
Net profit after tax (Working note 1)	140
Add: Interest adjusted for tax effect (800 x 10% x 0.70)	56
Return to providers of funds	196
Less: Cost of capital (Working note 2)	161
Economic value added (EVA)	35

Working Notes

1. **Interest and net profit**

Financial leverage   =   Profit before interest and tax (PBIT) / PBT
Interest on borrowings =   Rs.800, 00, 000 x 10% = Rs.80 lakhs
Therefore   1.40   =   PBIT / (PBIT – Interest)
                 1.40   =   PBIT / (PBIT – 80)
            1.40(PBIT-80) =   PBIT
            1.40 PBIT – 112 =   PBIT
          1.40 (PBIT-PBIT) =   112
              0.40 PBIT   =   112
                 PBIT   =   112 / 0.40
                 PBIT   =   Rs.280 lakhs
                  PBT =   Rs.280 lakhs – Rs.80 lakhs = Rs.200 lakhs
             Tax 30%   =   Rs. 200 lakhs x 30% = Rs.60 lakhs
             NOPAT   =   PBT – Tax = **Rs.140 lakhs**

2. **Statement of cost of capital**

Item	Rs Lakhs	Weights	Cost %	WACC %
Equity shareholder funds	600	0.4286	17.5%	7.50%
10% debenture holders funds	800	0.5714	7.0%	4.00 %
Total	1400	1.0000		11.50%

Cost of capital = Average capital employed x WACC
              = Rs.1400 lakhs x 11.5%
              = **Rs. 161 lakhs**

Illustration 10.4: Economic Value Added (EVA)

From the following information of V Ltd, compute the economic value added:

i) Share capital	Rs.2000 lakhs
ii) Reserves and surplus	Rs.4000 lakhs
iii) Long term debt	Rs.400 lakhs
iv) Tax rate	30%
v) Risk free rate	9%
vi) Market rate of return	16%
vii) Interest	Rs.40 lakhs
viii) Beta factor	1.05
ix) Profit before interest and tax	Rs.2000 lakhs

(CA Final: June 2009)

Solution
The base definitions that will help solve the problem are given below:

E.V.A.	=	NOPAT – COCE
NOPAT	=	Net Operating Profit after tax
COCE	=	Cost of capital employed
	=	Weighted average costs of capita x average capital employed
	=	WACC X Capital employed

Accordingly the calculations are as under:

Debt capital	=	Rs.400 crores
Equity capital	=	(Rs.2000 crores + Rs.4000 crores) = Rs.6000 crores
Capital employed	=	(Rs.400 crores + Rs.6000 crores)
	=	Rs.6400 crores
Debt to capital		
Employed	=	400 / 6400 = 0.0625
Equity to capital		
Employed	=	6000 / 6400 = 0.9375
Debt cost (gross)	=	Interest / Long term debt
	=	Rs.40 lakhs x Rs.400 lakhs = 10 %
Less tax (30% x10%)	=	3.0%
Debt cost (net of tax)	=	7.0%

Statement of Cost of equity capital

According to Capital Asset Pricing Model (CAPM)		
Cost of Equity capital	=	Risk free rate + Beta x Equity risk premium
	=	Risk free rate + Beta (Market rate – risk free rate)
	=	9 + 1.05 x (16-9)
	=	9 + 1.05 x 7
	=	16.35 %

Statement of WACC and EVA

WACC	=	Equity to C.E. X Cost of equity capital
		+ Debt to C.E. X Cost of debt
	=	0.9375 x 16.35% + 0.0625 x 7.0%
	=	15.328 % + 0.4375 %
	=	15.7655%
COCE	=	WACC X Capital employed
	=	15.7655 % x Rs.6400 crores
	=	Rs.1009 crores
NOPAT	=	PBIT X (1-30%)
	=	Rs.1400 crores
E.V.A.	=	NOPAT – COCE
	=	Rs. 1400 – Rs. 1009
	=	Rs.391 crores

Illustration 10.5: Economic Value Added (EVA)

From the following data compute the Economic Value Added:

Share capital	:	Rs.1600 crores
Long term debt	:	Rs. 320 crores
Interest	:	RS.32 crores
Reserve & Surplus	:	Rs. 3200 crores
Profit before interest & tax	:	Rs.1432 crores
Tax rate	:	30%
Beta factor	:	1.05
Market rate of return	:	14%
Risk free rate	:	10%

(CA Final: May 2010)

Solution

1. Statement of Capital employed

Item	Rs in crores
Share capital	1600.00
Reserves & surplus	3200.00
Shareholders' funds	4800.00
Debt fund – long term debt	320.00
Capital employed	5120.00

2. Statement of calculation of cost of debt (post tax)

Item	Rs in crores
Total debt	320.00
Interest @ 10%	32.00
Less: Tax rate	30%
Post tax cost of debt	
= (1 - 0.30) x 32 /320	**7%**

3. Statement of calculation of cost of equity

Item	%
Cost of equity = Risk free rate + Beta x (market rate of return – risk free rate)	
= 10% + 1.05 (14 -10)	**14.2%**

4. Statement of calculation of WACC (weighted average cost of capital)

Item	Rs in crores
Total shareholders' funds	4800
Cost of equity	14.2%
Total debt	320
Cost of debt (net of tax)	7%
Weighted average cost of capital (WACC)	
= ((4800 X 14.2)+(320 X 7)) / (4800 + 320)	13.75%

5. Statement of calculation of Economic Value Added:

Item	Rs in crores
Profit before interest and tax	1432.00
Tax @ 30%	429.60
Net Operating Profit After Tax (A)	1002.40
Capital employed x WACC = (5120 X 13.75%) (B)	704.00
Economic value added (A − B)	**298.40**

Illustration 10.6: Economic Value Added (EVA)

Prosperous Bank has a criterion that it will give loans to companies that have an "Economic Value Added" greater than zero for the past three years on an average. The bank is considering lending money to a small company that has the economic value characteristics shown below. The data relating to the company is as follows:

i) average operating income after tax equals Rs.2500000 per year for the last three years.
ii) average total assets over the last three years equals Rs.7500000.
iii) weighted average cost of capital appropriate for the company is 10% which is applicable for all three years.
iv) The company's average current liabilities over the last three years are Rs.1500000.

Does the company meet the bank's criterion for a positive economic value added?
(*CA Final May 2011*)

Solution
Statement of computation of Economic Value Added

S/L	Particulars	Amount Rs.
1.	Net Operating Profit after Taxes (NOPAT)(WN1)	2500000
2.	Less Cost of capital (WN2)	600000
3.	**Economic Value Added (1-2)**	**1900000**

Therefore, the company qualifies for loan as it has a positive economic value added.

Working Notes:
1. Statement of Net Operating Profit after taxes (NOPAT)

S/L	Particulars	Amount Rs.
1.	Average operating income after tax equals	2500000

2. Statement of Capital Employed

S/L	Particulars	Amount Rs.
1.	Average total assets for the last three years	7500000
2.	Less: average current liabilities for the last three years	1500000
3.	Total Capital employed (1 - 2)	6000000
4.	Weighted average cost of capital for last three years	10%
5.	Cost of capital (3 x 4)	600000

Illustration 10.7: Economic Value Added (EVA)

LG and Co provides you with the following as at 31st March 2004: (Rs/Lakhs)

Liabilities	Amount	Assets	Amount
Share capital	1000	Fixed Assets (net)	3000
Reserves and surplus	2000	Investments	150
Long term debt	200	Current Assets	100
Sundry creditors	50		
	3250		3250

Additional information provided is as follows:
 a) Profit before interest and tax is Rs.1000 (Rs in lakhs)
 b) Interest Rs 20 lakhs
 c) Tax 35.875%
 d) Risk free rate – 10%
 e) Market rate – 15%
 f) Beta factor   - 1.4

Compute economic value added.

Solution
Working Notes:
  1. **Statement of cost of equity**

Cost of equity = risk free rate + beta factor x (market rate – risk free rate)
= 10% + 1.4 (15% - 10%)
= 10% + 7%
= 17%

  2. **Statement of cost of debt (net of tax)**

Particulars	Rs in lakhs
Interest	20.000
Less: Tax savings (20 x 35.875%)	(7.175)
Interest after tax savings	12.825
Cost of debt = (Interest on long term borrowing) / Long term borrowing x 100 = 12.825 / 200.000 x 100 = 6.4125%	

3. Statement of weighted average cost of capital (WACC)

Particulars	Rs in Lakhs
Cost of equity 3000 x 17% (WN1)	510.000
Cost of debt 200 x 6.4125 % (WN2)	12.825
Total	522.825
WACC = 522.825 / 3200 = 16.34%	

4. Statement of profit after tax

Particulars	Rs in lakhs	Rs in lakhs
Profit before interest and tax	1000	
Less: Interest	(20)	980.000
Less: Tax (980 x 35.875%)		351.575
Profit after tax		628.425

5. Statement of capital employed

Particulars	Rs in lakhs	Rs in lakhs
Share capital	1000	
Reserves and surplus	2000	3000
Long term debt		200
Capital employed		3200

Statement of computation of Economic Value Added

Particulars	Rs in lakhs
Profit after taxes (WN4)	628.425
Add: Interest on long term borrowings adjusted for tax	12.825
NOPAT	641.250
Less: Cost of capital (3200 x 16.34%) (WN3)	522.880
Economic value added	118.370

Illustration 10.8 : Economic Value Added and Market Value Added

Life Industries Ltd (LIL) furnishes the following information from which you are required to calculate prevailing Economic Value Added of the company and also explain the difference, if any, of the EVA as calculated by you and the MVA (Market Value Added) of LIL amounting to Rs.14005 crores.

Common shares of Rs.1000 face value	158200
12% debentures Rs.10 face value	5000000
Current tax rate	30%
Financial leverage	1.1
Share premium Account (Lakh rupees)	155
Free reserves (Lakh rupees)	154

Capital reserve (Lakh rupees)	109

It is a prevailing practice for companies in the industry to which LIL belongs to pay at least a dividend of 15% p.a. to its common shareholders.(*CA Final Nov 2011*)

Solution
Statement of computation of EVA

Computation of EVA	Rs Lakhs
Net profit after tax (Working note 1)	420
Add: Interest adjusted for tax effect (500 x 12% x 0.70)	42
Return to providers of funds	462
Less: Cost of capital (Working note 2)	
342	
Economic value added (EVA)	120

Market Value Added (MVA) It is the difference between the current market value of a firm and the capital contributed by Investors. This is shown as below.

MVA = Market value of capital – Capital employed
Since the MVA (Rs.14005 crores) is positive being much greater than capital employed it demonstrates that the company has created value.

Working Notes

2. **Interest and net profit**

Financial leverage	= Profit before interest and tax (PBIT) / PBT
Interest on borrowings	= (5000000 x Rs.10) x 12% = Rs.60 lakhs
Therefore 1.10	= PBIT / (PBIT – Interest)
1.10	= PBIT / (PBIT – 60)
1.10(PBIT-60) = PBIT	
1.10 PBIT – 66 = PBIT	
1.10 (PBIT-PBIT) = 66	
0.10 PBIT = 66	
PBIT = 66 / 0.10	
PBIT = Rs.660 lakhs	
PBT = Rs.660 lakhs – Rs.60 lakhs = Rs.600 lakhs	
Tax 30% = Rs. 600 lakhs x 30% = Rs.180 lakhs	
NOPAT = PBT – Tax = **Rs.420 lakhs**	

3. **Statement of cost of capital**

Item	Rs Lakhs	Weights	Cost %	WACC %
Equity shareholder funds	2000	0.8000	15.0%	12.00%
12% debenture holders funds	500	0.2000	8.4%	1.68 %
Total	2500	1.0000		13.68%

Cost of capital = Average capital employed x WACC
                = Rs.2500 lakhs x 13.68%
                = **Rs. 342 lakhs**

Note: Equity shareholders' funds: Rs/Lakhs
      Equity share capital (158200 x Rs.1000)   =   1582
      Share premium   =   155
      Free reserves   =   154
      Capital reserve   =   109
      Total   2000

Illustration 10.9 : Economic Value Added

The following information (as of 31.03.2012) is supplied to you by M/s Fox Ltd:

		Rs crores	Rs.crores
(i)	Profit after tax (PAT)		205.90
(ii)	Interest		4.85
(iii)	Equity share capital	40.00	
	Accumulated surplus	700.00	
	Shareholders' funds	740.00	
	Loans (long term)	37.00	
	Total long term funds		777.00
(iv)	Market capitalisation		2892.00

Additional information:
a) Risk free rate   12.0%
b) Long term market rate (based on BSE index)   15.5%
c) Effective tax rate for the company   25.0%
d) Beta for last few years

Year	
1	0.48
2	0.52
3	0.60
4	1.10
5	0.99

Using the above data you are requested to calculate the Economic Value Added of Fox Ltd as on 31st March 2012. (*CA Final: May 2012*)

Solution

1. Statement of capital employed

Item	Rs crores
Equity Share capital	40.00
Accumulated surplus	700.00

Shareholders' funds	740.00
Long term debt	37.00
Capital employed	777.00

2. Statement of cost of debt

Item	Rs. Crores
Long term debt	37.00
Interest	4.85
Interest rate (4.85 / 37.00 x 100)	**13.11%**
Post tax cost of debt (1 – 0.25)	**9.83%**

3. Statement of calculation of equity

Item	%
Cost of equity = risk free rate + beta x (market rate of return – risk free rate) = 12% + 0.99 x (15.5% - 12%) =	**15.465**
Note: Assumed beta for year five as the current beta to measure the degree of volatility, alternatively average beta for the last five years could be considered – but that would significantly reduce the degree of volatility	

4. Statement of calculation of WACC (weighted average cost of capital)

Item	%
Total shareholders' funds = 740.00 x 15.465% = 114.44 Total debt funds = 37.00 x 9.83% = 3.64 Weighted average cost of capital = ((740 x 15.465%)+(37 x 9.83%)) / (740 + 37) = (114.44 + 3.64) / 777	**15.197**

5. Statement of calculation of Economic Value Added

Item	Rs crores
Profit after tax	205.90
Add: Interest	4.85
Net Operating Profit After tax (NOPAT) (A)	210.75
Capital employed x WACC = 777 X 15.197% (B)	118.08
Economic Value Added (A –B)	92.67

Illustration 10.10: Economic Value Added

	Orange	Grape	Apple
Total Invested capital	100000	100000	100000
Debt / Assets ratio	0.8	0.5	0.2
Shares outstanding	6,100	8,300	10,000
Pre-tax cost of debt	16%	13%	15%
Cost of equity	26%	22%	20%
Operating Income (EBIT)	25,000	25,000	25,000
Net Income	8970	12350	14950

The tax rate 25% in all the cases above.

Required:

Compute the following:

a) Weighted average cost of capital for each company

b) Economic Value Added (EVA) for each company

c) Based on EVA which company would be considered for best investment? Give reasons

d) If the industry PE ratio is 11x, estimate the price for the share of each company

e) Estimated market capitalisation for each of the companies.

Solution

Calculation of WACC

Item	Orange	Grape	Apple
Wd	0.8	0.5	0.2
Kd	10.4	8.45	9.75
We	0.2	0.5	0.8
Ke	26%	22%	20%
WACC	13.52%	15.225%	17.95%

Calculation of EVA

Item	Orange	Grape	Apple
Invested capital	100000	100000	100000
WACC	13.52%	15.225%	17.95%
WACC X Invested capital (B)	13520	15225	17950
EBIT	25,000	25,000	25,000
NOPAT (A)	16250	16250	16250

EVA (A – B)   2730   1025
- 1700

Calculation of estimated market capitalisation

Item	Orange	Grape	Apple
Shares outstanding	6,100	8,300	10,000
Net Income	8970	12350	14950
EPS	1.47	1.49	1.50
P / E	16.18	16.37	16.45
Market capitalisation	98670	135850	164450

Illustration 10.11: Economic Value Added

A firm has assets in place in which it has capital investment of Rs.100 crores. The other facts are as under:

6. The after-tax operating income on assets in place is Rs.15 crores. This return on capital of 15% is expected to be sustained in the future, and the company has a cost of capital of 10%.

7. At the beginning of each of the next 5 years, the firm is expected to make investments of Rs.10 crores each.

8. These investments are also expected to earn 15% as a return on capital and the cost of capital is expected to remain 10%

9. After year 5, the company will continue to make investments and earnings will grow at 5% per annum, but the new investments will have a return on capital of only 10%, which is also the cost of capital.

10. All assets and investments are expected to have infinite lives. Thus, the assets in place and

297

the investments made in the first five years will make 15% a year in perpetuity, with no growth.
Please value the firm.

Solution

The value of the firm is worked out as under:

Firm value = Capital invested in assets in place + (EVA t, assets in place) / (1+WACC)t

+ (EVA t, future assets) / (1 + WACC)t)

IV)   Capital invested in assets in place = **Rs.100 crores**

V)   EVA t, for assets in place   = ((0.15 − 0.10) x 100)/0.10

= 0.05 x 100 / 0.10

= **Rs.50 crores**

VI)   EVA for future assets is as under:

Year (investment Beginning of year)	Formula for EVA = ((RONA − WACC) X Value of asset)/WACC	EVA Value Rs crores	Discount factor at 10%	DCE Amount Rs crores
1	(0.15-0.10) x Rs.10 crores / 0.10	5.0	1.0	5.00
2	(0.15-0.10) x Rs.10 crores / 0.10	5.0	0.909	4.55
3	(0.15-0.10) x Rs.10 crores / 0.10	5.0	0.826	4.13
4	(0.15-0.10) x Rs.10 crores / 0.10	5.0	0.751	3.76
5	(0.15-0.10) x Rs.10 crores / 0.10	5.0	0.683	3.42
	Total	25.0		**20.86**

Hence the value of firm would be (I + II + III) = (Rs.100 crores + Rs.50 crores + Rs.20.86 crores)

= Rs.170.86 crores, say rounded off to Rs.170 crores

Chapter 11: Merger & Acquisition

11.1. Types of Merger & Acquisition

11.1.1. Amalgamation

Amalgamation is an arrangement and a legal process by which two or more companies are to be merged or blended with another. As a result, the amalgamating company loses its existence and its shareholders become shareholders of new company or the amalgamated company. In case of amalgamation a new company may come into existence or an old company may survive while amalgamating company may lose its existence. There may be amalgamation by transfer of one or more undertaking to a new company or transfer of one or more undertaking to an existing company. Amalgamation signifies the transfer of all or some part of assets and liabilities of one or more than one existing company or two or more companies to a new company.

11.1.2. Types of Amalgamation

The Accounting Standard, AS-14, issued by the Institute of Chartered Accountants of India has defined the term amalgamation by classifying

(i)   Amalgamation in the nature of merger, and

(ii)   Amalgamation in the nature of purchase.

11.1.3. Amalgamation in the nature of merger:

As per AS-14, an amalgamation is called in the nature of merger if it satisfies all the following condition:

- All the assets and liabilities of the transferor company should become, after amalgamation; the assets and liabilities of the other company.

- Shareholders holding not less than 90% of the face value of the equity shares of the transferor company (other than the equity shares already held therein, immediately before the amalgamation, by the transferee company or its subsidiaries or their nominees) become equity shareholders of the transferee company by virtue of the amalgamation.

- The consideration for the amalgamation receivable by those equity shareholders of the transferor company who agree to become equity shareholders of the transferee company is discharged by the transferee company wholly by the issue of equity share in the transferee company, except that cash may be paid in respect of any fractional shares.

- The business of the transferor company is intended to be carried on, after the amalgamation, by the transferee company.

- No adjustment is intended to be made in the book values of the assets and liabilities of the transferor company when they are incorporated in the financial statements of the transfere company except to ensure uniformity of accounting policies.

Amalgamation in the nature of merger is an organic unification of two or more entities or undertaking or fusion of one with another. It is defined as an amalgamation which satisfies the above conditions.

As per Income Tax Act 1961, merger is defined as amalgamation under Sec. 2(1B) with the following three conditions to be satisfied.

a) All the properties of amalgamating company(s) should vest with the amalgamated company after amalgamation.

b) All the liabilities of the amalgamating company(s) should vest with the amalgamated company after amalgamation.

c) Shareholders holding not less than 75% in value or voting power in amalgamating company(s) should become shareholders of amalgamated companies after amalgamation. Amalgamation does not mean acquisition of a company by purchasing its property and resulting in its winding up. According to Income tax Act, exchange of shares with 90%of shareholders of amalgamating company is required.

11.1.4. Amalgamation in the nature of purchase:

Amalgamation in the nature of purchase is where one company's assets and liabilities are taken over by another and lump sum is paid by the latter to the former. It is defined as the one which does not satisfy any one or more of the conditions satisfied above.

11.1.5. Acquisition

Acquisition refers to the acquiring of ownership right in the property and asset without any combination of companies. Thus in acquisition two or more companies may remain independent, separate legal entity, but there may be change in control of companies. Acquisition results when one company purchase the controlling interest in the share capital of another existing company in any of the following ways:

(a) By controlling interest in the other company. By entering into an agreement with a person or persons holding shares of other company.

(b) By subscribing new shares being issued by the other company.

(c) By purchasing shares of the other company at a stock exchange, and

(d) By making an offer to buy the shares of other company, to the existing shareholders of that company.

11.1.6. Demerger

It has been defined as a split or division. As the name suggests, it denotes a situation opposite to that of merger. Demerger or spin-off, as called in US involves splitting up of conglomerate (multi-division) of company into separate companies.

This occurs in cases where dissimilar business are carried on within the same company, thus becoming unwieldy and cyclical almost resulting in a loss situation. Corporate restructuring in such situation in the form of demerger becomes inevitable.

Demerger also occurs due to reasons almost the same as mergers i.e.

a) the desire to perform better,
b) strengthen efficiency, business interest and longevity and
c) to curb losses, wastage and competition.

Undertakings demerge to delineate businesses and fix responsibility, liability and management so as to ensure improved results from each of the demerged unit.

Demerged Company, according to Section (19AA) of Income Tax Act, 1961 means the company whose undertaking is transferred, pursuant to a demerger to a resulting company.

Resulting company, according to Section2(47A) of Income Tax Act,1961 means one or more company, (including a wholly owned subsidiary thereof) to which the undertaking of the demerged company is transferred in a demerger, and the resulting company in consideration of such transfer of undertaking issues shares to the shareholders of the demerged company and include any authority or body or local authority or public sector company or a company established, constituted or formed as a result of demerger.

A part from core competencies being main reason for demerging companies according to their nature of business, in some cases, restructuring in the form of demerger was undertaken for splitting up the family owned large business empires into smaller companies.

11.1.7. Reverse Merger

Normally, a small company merges with large company or a sick company with healthy company. However in some cases, reverse merger is done. When a healthy company merges with a sick or a small company is called reverse merger. This may be for various reasons. Some reasons for reverse merger are:

(a) The transferee company is a sick company and has carry forward losses and Transferor Company is profit making company. If Transferor Company merges with the sick transferee company, it gets advantage of setting off carry forward losses without any conditions. If sick company merges with healthy company, many restrictions are applicable for allowing set off.

(b) The transferee company may be listed company. In such case, if Transferor Company merges with the listed company, it gets advantages of listed company, without following strict norms of listing of stock exchanges.

In such cases, it is provided that on date of merger, name of Transferee Company will be changed to that of Transferor Company. Thus, outside people even may not know that the transferor company with which they are dealing after merger is not the same as earlier one.

11.1.8. Diversification

Diversification into new areas and new products can also be a motive for a firm to merge another with it. For instance a firm operating in Eastern India, if merges with another firm operating primarily in North India, can definitely cover broader economic areas. Individually these firms could serve only a limited area. Moreover, products diversification resulting from merger can also help the new firm fighting the cyclical/ seasonal fluctuations.

11.2. Factors that favour external growth and diversification through Mergers and Acquisitions

(i) Some goals and objectives may be achieved more speedily through an external acquisition.

(ii) The cost of building an organization internally may exceed cost of an acquisition.

(iii) There may be fewer risks, lower costs, or shorter time requirements involved in achieving an economically feasible market share by the external route.

(iv) The firm may not be utilizing their assets or arrangement as effectively as they could be utilized by the acquiring firm.

(v) The firm may be able to use securities in obtaining other companies, where as it might not be able to finance the acquisition of equivalent assets and capabilities internally.

(vi) There may be tax advantages.

(vii) There may be opportunities to complement capabilities of other firms.

11.3. Basic rationale for Mergers and Acquisitions

The most common reasons for Mergers and Acquisitions are:
a) Consolidation of production capacities
b) Increasing marketing reach
c) Enhancement of brand value

d) Synergistic operating economies
e) Diversification
f) Taxation benefits
g) Inorganic growth

11.4. Types of mergers

a) Horizontal merger:	The two companies which are in the process of merger belong to the same industry, normally the market share of the new consolidated company would be larger and it is possible that it may move closer to being a monopoly or a near monopoly.
b) Vertical merger:	Merger of two companies which are in different field altogether, the coming together of two concerns may give rise to a situation similar to a monopoly
c) Reverse merger:	Where, in order to avail benefit of carry forward of losses which are available according to tax law only to the company which had incurred them, the profit making company is merged with companies which have accumulated losses
d) Conglomerate merger:	These relate to merger of firms engaged in unrelated business operations. This signifies that the two companies are neither related horizontally nor vertically. In a pure conglomerate merger, there are no common indicators between the companies in production, marketing, research, development and technology.
e) Co-generic merger:	In this type of merger, the acquirer and the target companies are related through basic technologies, production processes or markets. These mergers represent an outward movement by the acquirer from its current business scenario to other related business activities.

11.5. Concepts of value in Mergers & Acquisition

Intrinsic Value: This is based on the net present value of expected future cash flows completely independent of any acquisition.

Market Value: Commonly known as 'current market capitalization', it is the same as share price. It reflects the market's valuation of a company.

Purchase Price: It is the price that a bidder anticipates having to pay to be accepted by the target company's shareholders.

Synergy Value: It is the net present value of expected future cash flows that will result from the combined operations and additional benefits expected to accrue.

Value Gap: The difference between the intrinsic value and the purchase price.

11.6. Principal steps involved in a successful Merger & Acquisition program
a) Manage the pre-acquisition phase
b) Screening of target corporates on basis of motives

c) Eliminate those who do not meet the criteria and value the rest
d) Calculate the value of synergies and analyse the advantages of acquisition
e) Decide about accounting method – is the deal consummated at large premium
f) Decide about payments whether in cash or in stock
g) Enter into negotiations and
h) Launch into post-merger integration
i) Analyse the post financial performance after acquisitions

11.7. The process of Merger & Acquisition

The process of merger can be summarised under the following three phases:

Phases	Description
Pre-merger phase	• Due diligence process on the target company • Financial position of transferor company • Market Value • Brand Value • Communication Issues • Share Holders & other stake holders' view • Assets & Liabilities
Acquisition phase	• Cost of merger & acquisition • Maintenance of customer relationships during integration phase • Knowledge transfer among units that are to be integrated • Overcoming of staff's suspiciousness of the other organization ('Us vs. Them' syndrome)
Post-merger phase	• Corporate culture • Synchronisation of existing value systems • Staff qualification • Change Management • Manage disparity in Salary • Manage and integrate diverse Technology • Usher in integrated HR Policy • Synthesise leadership styles • Proper utilisation of existing core competencies and fill up shortages if any • Post Integration – delegation of authority and allocation of responsibility • Language barriers and country specific cultural differences.

11.8. People involved in Merger & Acquisition process

(a)Investment Bankers	Investment bankers offer strategic and tactical advice, screen potential buyers and sellers, make initial contact with a seller and buyer and provide negotiation support, valuation exercise and deal structuring.
(b) Lawyers	The legal framework surrounding a typical transaction has become so complicated that no one individual can have sufficient expertise to address all the issues. So, legal teams consisting of lawyers each of whom represents a specialised aspect of the law are used to carry out legal due diligence.
(c) Accountants	Accountants perform the role of auditors by reviewing the target's

	financial statements and operations through a series of interviews with senior and middle level managers as a part of financial due diligence.
(d) Valuation Experts	They build models that incorporate various assumptions such as costs or revenues growth rate.
(e) Institutional Investors	Institutional investors can announce how they intend to vote on a matter and advertise their position in order to seek support and have more influence.
(f) Arbitrageurs	Arbitrageurs provide market liquidity during transactions. With the number of merger arbitrageurs increasing, they are becoming more proactive in trying to anticipate takeover situations. Their objective is to identify the target before the potential acquirer is required by law to announce its intentions.

11.9. Due Diligence process in Merger & Acquisition

A summary check-list of due diligence process applied in Merger & Acquisition is reproduced as under:

A. General company data	1. A list of each direct or indirect subsidiary of the Company.
	2. Capitalization of the Company showing the number of authorized shares of each class or series of capital stock, the number of issued and outstanding shares of such stock, and the record owners of such shares. Certificate or articles of incorporation and bylaws of the Company, or articles of organization and operating agreement in effect.
	3. Minutes of meetings of the Company's stockholders or members, board of directors, or any committee thereof, for the last 3 years.
	4. All agreements among stockholders or members of the Company relating to management, ownership, or control of the Company.
	5. All documents entered into with respect to or related to any prior financings or equity issuances of the Company, including, but not limited to, Stock Purchase Agreements, Stockholders Agreements and Registration Rights Agreements.
	6. All correspondence and agreements between or among the Company and the directors or officers of the Company relating to indemnity, employment, loans, or advances.
	7. Stock books, stock transfer ledgers, and other stock records of the Company.
	8. A list of options, purchase rights, and warrants issued by the Company specifying the name of the holder, the number of options, rights or warrants issued, the date

	granted, the option or purchase price, and the position of the holder with the Company, together with copies of option, right or warrant agreements.
	9. An address list of the locations of all land, buildings, and other improvements either leased or owned by the Company.
	10. All material governmental permits, licenses or authorizations, and related correspondence, of the Company.
	11. Other than customer contracts, any agreements with any federal, state, or local regulatory authorities to which the Company is a party.
B. Financial information	1. Audited financial statements for each of the Company for the last three fiscal years, with the auditor's opinion and all footnotes.
	2. Un-audited financial statements for each of the Company for the most recent month or quarter end.
	3. Comparison of last two (2) years forecasted budgets compared to actual performance.
	4. Copies of the financial packages delivered to management and the Board of Directors of the Company during the past three (3) years.
	5. Detail of capital expenditures for the last three (3) calendar years. Receivables aging schedule.
	6. All correspondence between the Company and the Company's auditors for the last three (3) years.
	7. The Company's forecast projections for performance for the next three years.
C. Corporate agreements	1. All agreements or documents relating to or evidencing borrowings (other than accounts payable incurred in the ordinary course) of the Company or any Subsidiary, whether secured or unsecured, including credit agreements, other senior debt agreements and instruments, surplus or other subordinated debt agreements and instruments, hedging or derivative agreements, guarantees and letters of credit.

2. Bank letters or agreements confirming any other lines of credit in favor of the Company or any <u>Subsidiary</u>.

3. All documents and agreements evidencing other financing arrangements to which the Company or any Subsidiary is a party or under which the Company or any Subsidiary is otherwise obligated, including sale and leaseback arrangements, capitalized leases, real estate and other instalment purchases, make-whole agreements (or covenants) and guarantees.

4. All acquisition agreements and related documents and schedules regarding the Company's acquisition of its Subsidiaries.

5. All documents relating to any material acquisition or disposition of assets by the Company or any Subsidiary in the last ten years (whether or not the Company or any Subsidiary retains the related property or assets).

6. All material agreements encumbering real or personal property owned by the Company or any Subsidiary, including all mortgages, deeds of trust, and security agreements.

7. All real estate contracts of the Company and each Subsidiary.
Deeds and title policies relating to any real property owned by the Company or any Subsidiary.

8. All leases of real or material personal property (including computer leasing agreements) to which the Company or any Subsidiary is lessee or lessor or to which the Company or any Subsidiary proposes to become a lessee or lessor.

9. All joint venture, partnership, or other management, operating, or consulting agreements relating to the Company or any <u>Subsidiary</u>.

10. All franchise, conditional sales contracts and consignment agreements to which the Company or any Subsidiary is a party.

11. All agreements between the Company and its 20 largest customers, and a form (or forms) of any agreement typically used by the Company in provided goods or services to its customers, together with copies or descriptions of significant variations from such form

	(or forms) in the case of particular customers. All material customer purchaser orders. **12.** To the extent not duplicative of L, all agreements related to the distribution by the Company or its Subsidiaries of products in the ordinary course of business. **13.** All contracts under which the Company (or any of its Subsidiaries) has agreed to refrain from competing with any other person or entity or otherwise to refrain from engaging in any particular business activity (whether in a particular geographic area or otherwise). **14.** All contracts between the Company (or any of its Subsidiaries) and any affiliate. A written description of any oral agreement between the Company (or any of its Subsidiaries) and any affiliate. **15.** Any agreement providing for participation in the Company's equity, other than options, rights or warrants. **16.** A list of any agreements to which the Company or any Subsidiary is a party that cannot be disclosed due to any non-disclosure covenant or agreement. relating to the Company or any Subsidiary, not otherwise described above, to which the Company or any Subsidiary is a party. **17.** All material contracts **18.** A list of the Company's 20 largest customers and vendors, determined by annual revenues and expenditures, respectively. **19.** Other than customer contracts, any agreements with any federal, state, or local regulatory authorities to which the Company is a party.
D.Legal documents	**1.** A list of each direct or indirect subsidiary of the Company. **2.** Capitalization of the Company showing the number of authorized shares of each class or series of capital stock, the number of issued and outstanding shares of such stock, and the record owners of such shares. Certificate or articles of incorporation and bylaws of the Company, or articles of organization and operating agreement in effect.

	3. Minutes of meetings of the Company's stockholders or members, board of directors, or any committee thereof, for the last 3 years.
	4. All agreements among stockholders or members of the Company relating to management, ownership, or control of the Company.
	5. All documents entered into with respect to or related to any prior financings or equity issuances of the Company, including, but not limited to, Stock Purchase Agreements, Stockholders Agreements and Registration Rights Agreements.
	6. All correspondence and agreements between or among the Company and the directors or officers of the Company relating to indemnity, employment, loans, or advances.
	7. Stock books, stock transfer ledgers, and other stock records of the Company.
	8. A list of options, purchase rights, and warrants issued by the Company specifying the name of the holder, the number of options, rights or warrants issued, the date granted, the option or purchase price, and the position of the holder with the Company, together with copies of option, right or warrant agreements.
	9. An address list of the locations of all land, buildings, and other improvements either leased or owned by the Company.
	10. All material governmental permits, licenses or authorizations, and related correspondence, of the Company.
	11. Other than customer contracts, any agreements with any federal, state, or local regulatory authorities to which the Company is a party.
E. Intellectual property rights and product information	1. Schedule of all trademarks, service marks, trade names, copyrights and patents that relate to the products, services, operations or names of the Company.
	2. For each product presently or previously marketed, or presently being developed, by the Company or its Subsidiaries:

a) the name of each individual who performed work on the product, its documentation, and/or its enhancements and modifications;

b) the status of each such individual when the work on the product was performed and whether such individual signed an agreement with the Company assigning all rights in such work to the Company;

c) any and all information concerning the development of the product, including whether the product is based, in whole or in part, on any other product, public domain, open source or otherwise; and

d) any reviews or critiques of the product.

3. All agreements concerning confidentiality, nondisclosure and assignment of inventions with employees, contractors, visitors or other parties.

4. Date of first use of all unregistered trademarks, and date on which copies of any material copyright first released to the public.

5. All documents concerning registration of trademarks and service marks, including registration certificates, applications, correspondence and searches, and the results of any trademark or service mark searches conducted by the Company.

6. All documents concerning registration of patents, patent applications, and the results of any patent searches conducted by the Company.

7. All R & D agreements, including agreements with independent contractors who participated in development of any product.

8. All agreements and documents concerning assignment, purchase, sale or license of proprietary rights, royalties or maintenance, including patents, copyrights, trade secrets, and trademarks.

9. Manual or other written documents detailing the procedures for maintaining the secrecy of trade secrets.

10. Copies of all "End User License Agreements" associated with any products delivered.

11. Copies of all escrow agreements or descriptions of

	escrow agreements relating to any computer source code. **12.** Blank form of end user agreements. **13.** Documents relating to claims or disputes concerning products, services or proprietary rights owned or used by the Company. **14.** Product literature distributed to the public over the last 2 years. **15.** Product maintenance logs and error reports for the last 12 months. **16.** A schedule of any exclusive rights granted by the Company. **17.** All agreements with computer on-line service providers and internet access providers relating to services or data provided by or to the Company. **18.** Copies of all agreements with third parties relating to the development of company products and software.
F.Insurance coverage	Description of each property, general liability, automobile, worker's compensation, and umbrella liability insurance policy issued to the Company, specifying: • Name of insurance carrier(s) • Annual Premium • Coverage • Claims within the last 3 years • Self-insured retention, co-payment, or deductible • Whether the policies are "occurrence" or "claims made" policies.
G.Litigation history and documents	• A list of any litigation or judgments settled within the last 5 years in which the company was involved either directly or indirectly. • A list of all pending or threatened litigation or administrative proceedings, inquiries, or investigations, including copies of petitions or complaints. • A list of names and addresses of all legal counsel who are currently acting on behalf of the Company. • A list of all consent decrees, judgments, injunctions, other decrees, orders, settlement agreements, arbitrations, and arbitration findings to which the Company is subject or

	bound

H. Employees and Human Resources	• All management employment contracts, "golden parachute agreements," severance agreements, consulting agreements, "stay" agreements, and agreements not to compete to which the Company is a party.
	
	• All labour contracts, collective bargaining agreements, union agreements, and any consents, waivers or amendments.
	
	• An organizational chart which lists the name and title of each divisional Vice President and Director. Include the number of direct reports by functional area under each Manager.
	
	• A list of the executive employees of the Company, and employees of the Company whose total annual compensation is in excess of $100,000, including the dollar amount of each such employee's total annual compensation.
	
	• With respect to each employee benefit plan:
	
	    a) copies of such Employee Benefit Plan and any related trust, insurance policy, annuity contract, or other funding vehicle;
	
	    b) the most recent favorable determination letter or tax exemption letter issued by the Internal Revenue Service ("IRS");
	
	    c) all applications for IRS determination or tax-exemption with respect to which a favorable determination letter has not yet been received;
	
	    d) the most recent summary plan description and any subsequent summaries of material modifications;
	
	    e) the three most recently filed Forms 5500, including all attached schedules;
	
	    f) a description of the funding status and non-funded liability of each Employee Benefit Plan, including but not limited to executive compensation, severance pay, and retiree medical plans; and
	
	    g) all actuarial and financial reports prepared during the last three years with respect to such Employee Benefit Plans.

	• A summary of liability for termination payments to employees. Copies of all bonus, severance, employee option and employee equity participation plans or agreements. • Details of all other employee plans and arrangements that do not constitute Employee Benefit Plans. • List of employees including both active and inactive employees employed by the company for the last three years. • A description of any order or decree to which any senior executive of the Company is subject that does or could impact the business or the Company as currently conducted or contemplated to be conducted in the future. • Discuss number of employees and average tenure.
I.Environmental matters	• A list of all environmental permits under which any facilities owned or leased by the Company operate. • All written reports made in the last five years regarding any environmental testing or environmental matters affecting the operations or properties of the Company. • All written estimates prepared in the last five years concerning future expenditures for environmental programs relating to the operations or properties of the Company. • All notices and demands of environmental authorities relating to the operations or properties of the Company. • All records regarding compliance history with environmental permits including air, water, waste, and sewer permits under federal, state, and local rules and regulations. • Locations of any on-site hazardous waste disposal sites. • Locations of any underground tanks and lines including those no longer used, specifying any history of spillage or leakage.
J.Tax filings and documents	• All federal, state, local, and other tax returns and reports filed by or on behalf of the Company for the last three fiscal years and for all open years.

	• All information related to any audit of any return or report filed by or on behalf of the Company for the last five fiscal years or related to any pending audits or administrative or judicial disputes relating to taxes for any open periods.
	• All tax allocation, sharing, or preparation agreements involving the Company
	• Agreements which waive or extend the period for assessment or collection of any federal, state, local or other taxes.
	• All ruling requests filed with the Internal Revenue Service relating to the Company.
	• Any tax elections which may have a material effect on the Company.
H.Marketing and customer information	• Total customer counts by major product year for each of the last 3 years.2. Listing of any customer that constituted more than 1% of total sales during the last three years.
	• Total number of web site visitors by month for the last 2 years
	• Total number of product evaluation requests by month for the last 2 years.
	• Discuss primary sales channels including Internet and reseller, as it pertains to the following:
	• For each of the Company's products, discuss target customer and marketing strategy. How are sales efforts organized?
	a) Internet sales as a percentage of total sales, currently and over time
	b) Resellers as a percentage of total sales, currently and over time
	c) Number of resellers
	d) Structure of reseller agreements

	e) Resellers by geography
	• Describe how new business is generated and the process of entering into arrangements with the customer.
	• Absent any significant sales expenditures, how does the Company drive:
	• Discuss the importance of individual customer relationships in the business; how are purchase orders processed (i.e., via the web/fax/mail)?
	• Regarding market share, discuss the size of both the international and domestic market segments for which the company's products are sold.
	a) Brand awareness
	b) Product upgrades
	c) New product introductions
	• List the company's top competitors, their market share and how the company differentiates itself from each of these competitors including competitor products, market focus and pricing.
	• How does the Company's customer base differ from its competitors?
	• Who are the Company's primary competitors?
	• Does the Company have any strategic alliances or business relationships with other industry participants? How are they structured.
I.Internal control and information systems	• Generally describe the information systems used by the Company and how they compare with industry standards and the Company's direct competition.
	• Complete List of all Hardware and Software used to manage the business Quantify the dollar investment made by the Company over the past three years with regard to its technology.
	• Describe the Company's accounting and financial controls and MIS functions. What MIS and technology expenditures will be needed in the future?

	• Generally describe the IT physical security as well as Internet IT security.
	• Determine how many security breaches the company has had as a result of hackers within the last 24 months and the extend of information lost or compromised.
	• Identify What remote locations have secured or non-secured internet access to servers which contain corporate information.
	• Identify which employees have "administrative" or "super-user" access to critical company files and databases. How many of those employees were terminated within the last 24 months.
	• What is the backup procedure to secure critical business electronic records and databases.
	• Are any records secured in an offsite or third party location?
	• Does the company have a disaster recovery plan?
J. Sales operation information	1. Breakdown of sales by channel (distributors, direct, e-commerce) by month for the last 3 years.
	2. Listing of top 20 resellers or distributors and revenue by reseller for the last 3 years.
	3. Written statement of annual revenue derived from new customers verses existing customers as well as revenue from new product sales verses recurring maintenance contracts for the last 3 years.
	4. If any revenue was a result of international sales include a written statement detailing the amount of annual revenue by country for the top 10 countries placing orders for each of the last 3 years.
	5. Provide information related to the Company's planned new product releases (i.e., expected timing of release, related product and service margins and markets targeted).
	6. Discuss any new business the Company might have been awarded and comment on any business which may have been recently lost.

	7. Are there particular areas of the Industry that the Company would identify as significant growth opportunities?
	8. Discuss the Company's major partnerships, if any, and how these help drive revenue growth.
K. Support services and product servicing	1. Discuss the economics behind (1) Product fees, (1) license fees and (2) maintenance fees, (3) other revenue producing fees.
	2. Discuss current margins and growth in margins for (a) Products and (b) maintenance services.
	3. What pricing advantages does the Company have versus its competitors?
	4. Discuss the Company's pricing strategy and contract terms.
	5. Describe the Company's proprietary products, systems and technologies with specific reference to economics underlying the offering.
	6. How are upgrades delivered to the customer?
	a) Are customers charged for upgrades or are this tied to a maintenance contract?
	b) Are upgrades made available via the web, on a CD or both?
	7. Does the Company perform any product customization? If so, discuss the economics behind this offering.
	8. Describe the Company's support function. Is this 24/7?

11.10: Some illustrations of high profile mergers and acquisitions that happened in the last twenty years world-wide

Please find below a summary of top ten mergers and acquisitions that have changed the world in the last twenty years.

LIST OF TOP MERGERS AND ACQUISITIONS IN THE LAST TWENTY YEARS

1. Travelers Group's acquisition of Citicorp
   Deal worth: $72.6 billion

Year: 1998

The merger of US financial conglomerate Travelers Group and fellow banking giant Citicorp created the world's largest financial services company. After the merger, it was called Citigoup and offered banking, insurance and investment operations in 140 countries. A decade after the merger, the bank was caught up in a credit crisis and went to the US authorities seeking help.

2. **AT&T acquired BellSouth Corporation**
   Deal worth: $72.7 billion
   Year: 2006

Already a major player in the US telecom market at the time, AT&T's acquisition of America's third largest phone company, BellSouth, gave it access to a total of 22 states and 70 million local customers.

3. **Royal Dutch Petroleum Corporation's acquisition of Shell Transport and Trading Company**
   Deal worth: $74.6 billion
   Year: 2004

Before the merger, Shell had dual ownership with 60% being owned by Royal Dutch Petroleum and 40% by Shell Transport & Trading. Royal Dutch Shell is one of the largest energy firms in the world, with a market cap larger than that of its UK peer, BP.

4. **Glaxo Wellcome's acquisition of SmithKline Beecham**
   Deal worth: $76 billion
   Year: 2000

The merger between the two European pharmaceutical firms resulted in the largest drug company in the world, GlaxoSmithKline (GSK). One of two drugs giants listed in the UK, it remains a pick for investors in that country.

5. **Exxon Corporation's acquisition of Mobil Corp**
   Deal worth: $78.9 billion
   Year: 1998

The partnership between the two oil firms formed the multinational oil and gas giant Exxon Mobil Corporation – the largest company in market cap. The merger was unique because it reunited the two largest firms of John D. Rockefeller's Standard Oil trust, Standard Oil Company of New Jersey/Exxon and Standard Oil Company of New York/Mobil, which had been separated by a government order about a 100 years ago.

6. **Pfizer's acquisition of Pharmacia Corporation**
   Deal worth: $ 89.2 billion
   Year: 2003

Pharma giant Pfizer bought Pharmacia Corporation for $89.2bn in 2003 in an attempt to expand its product base and develop new medicines. They forged one of the world's fastest growing and highly valued pharmaceutical firms, making Pfizer a world leader.

7. **RBS' acquisition of ABN-AMRO**
   Deal worth: $98.5 billion
   Year: 2007

The Royal Bank of Scotland proposed a deal in 2007 which was to become infamous across the world. Leading a consortium which included Belgium's Fortis bank and Spain's Banco Santander, RBS edged out rival Barclays, which was also eyeing ABN. However, the takeover turned sour a year later as the credit crunch hit home and RBS was forced to turn to the UK taxpayer to prevent its collapse.

8. **Shareholders' acquisition of Philip Morris International**
   Deal worth: $107.6 billion
   Year: 2008

US cigarette company Philip Morris International was an operating company of Altria Group until its spin-off in March 2008. Altria said Philip Morris would have more 'freedom' outside the constraints of US corporate ownership in terms of potential litigation and legislative restrictions to develop sales in emerging markets. The move saw Altria shareholders being given Philip Morris shares, which were listed on the London Stock Exchange and other markets.

9. **America Online's acquisition of Time Warner**
   Deal worth: $164.7 billion
   Year: 2000

The deal was described as the 'deal of the millennium' at that time. The two companies hoped to become the largest media company in the world. However, the partnership was hit hard when the dotcom bubble burst and subsequently they broke up.

10. **Vodafone Air Touch's acquisition of Mannesmann AG**
    Deal worth: $202.8 billion
    Year: 1999

Vodafone became Vodafone Air touch after it bought Air Touch Communications. It again reverted to its original name, Vodafone Group in 2001. Vodafone Air touch tried to take over German mobile network provider Mannesmann, which was seen as a hostile one, drawing a protest from the Germans. They were upset that a UK firm was taking a dominant role in its domestic market. Later the conglomerate broke up.

11.11. Indian scenario with respect to evolution of takeovers, principles and enforcements

There are typically two major modes of takeover which are prevalent in India, namely,
   a) takeover through direct negotiations with financial institutions and
   b) takeover by acquisition of adequate shareholding.

This process may be by way of:
   a) Acquisition of company's shares
   b) Acquisition of business assets (ABOs)
   c) Acquisition of brands
   d) Acquisition of companies by friendly or hostile takeover
   e) Reverse acquisition

Some of the high profile mergers and acquisitions – specially overseas acquisitions - that have happened in India are highlighted below:

Top overseas acquisitions by Indian Conglomerates
Mittal Steel-Arcelor

Mittal Steel, owned by Lakshmi Mittal, bought Arcelor, a Luxembourg-based company, for $33 billion in 2006. The new entity, which went by the name ArcelorMittal S.A., became the world's largest steel producer with an annual crude steel production of 97.2 million tonnes as of 2011.

Bharti-Zain

Bharti Airtel completed its $9-billion acquisition of African operations from Kuwait's Zain, making the Indian firm the world's fifth biggest cell phone company in terms of number of subscribers. Bharti's plan was to have 100 million subscribers in Africa. Then, Zain Africa had 42 million subscribers.

Tatas-Corus

Tata Steel acquiring Anglo-Dutch firm Corus Group in 2006 is one of the biggest by an Indian firm. Tatas' acquisition created the largest steel maker in the world. The deal was worth $7.6 billion.

Hindalco-Novalis

Hindalco Industries, an Aditya Birla Group company, bought Canada-based firm, Novalis, in 2007 in an all-cash transaction for $6 billion. Hindalco is the country's largest non-ferrous metals company.

Sterlite-Asarco

Sterlite Industries, a part of the Vedanta Group, acquired copper mining company Asarco for $2.6 billion in 2008. After finalisation of the deal, Sterlite became third largest copper mining company in the world.

Tatas-Jaguar & Land Rover

Tatas acquired UK's most famous carmaker Jaguar & Land Rover in a $2.3- billion deal with Ford, its American owners, in 2008. At that time, it was the most talked-about deals across the world.

ONGC-Imperial Energy

Oil & Natural Gas Corporation, India's biggest exploration firm, agreed to buy Imperial Energy Plc, a UK-based petroleum exploration and production company, for $2.58 billion in 2008. ONGC acquired the company to tap Siberian deposits and make up for the dwindling output at home.

Tanti Group-Honiton Energy

Tanti group of companies, the promoters of Suzlon Energy Ltd, along with Bahrain-based Arcapita Bank, acquired Honiton Energy Holdings, a Chinese wind energy firm, for an undisclosed sum. The partners will invest $2 billion to develop a 1,650-MW portfolio of wind farms in the Inner Mongolia region of China.

Adani-Abbot Point Coal Terminal

Adani Enterprises bought Abbot Point Coal Terminal in Australia for $2 billion in 2011. Adani group runs the country's biggest private port and India's largest coal importer. The deal will help the company ship out coal from an Australian mine it acquired in 2010.

Essar-Algoma Steel

Essar Steel acquired Canada-based Algoma Steel in a $1.58-billion all-cash deal in 2007. Algoma is a steel producer based in Sault Ste Marie, Ontario, with steel shipments of 2.4 million tonnes in 2006.

Reliance-Atlas Energy

Reliance Industries bought a $1.7 billion stake in natural-gas properties from US-based Atlas Energy in 2010, to bet on growing fuel output in US shale formations. Reliance paid $340 million upfront and funded $1.36 billion of Atlas's drilling costs in a joint venture in Marcellus Shale of Pennsylvania.

Tata-Tetley

Tetley Group, the maker of second-biggest brand of tea bags in the world, has been acquired by Tata Tea for $433.6 million. The two companies were already working together through a joint venture, Tata Tetley, which manufactures tea bags in India.

Essel Packaging-Propack

Subhash Chandra's Essel Packaging Ltd announces a merger of Swiss tube packaging major, Propack, with itself in 2000. Propack, then the fourth largest laminated tube producer, held 22 per cent stake in the merged entity. The new entity became the world's manufacturer of laminated tubes.

Ranbaxy-Allen SpA

Ranbaxy Laboratories acquired the unbranded generics business of Allen SpA, a division of GlaxoSmithKline, in Italy, for an undisclosed sum. In the same week, Ranbaxy bought Romania's largest independent generic drug producer, Terapia, and Belgium's drug maker Ethimed NV.

11.12. General Illustrations

Illustration 1:

Alpha Company is planning an acquisition of Beta Company which has 1.5 crores shares outstanding and issued. The market price per share is Rs.400 at present. Alpha Company's average cost of capital is 12%. Available information from Beta Company indicates its expected cash accruals for the next three years as under:

Year	Rs crore
1	250
2	300
3	400

Calculate the range of valuation that Alpha Company has to consider. (PV factors at 12% for years 1 to 3 respectively: 0.893, 0.797 and 0.712)

Solution

Calculation of range of valuation of Beta Company is as under:

Valuation based on market price

Market price per share (A)		Rs.400/-
Number of shares outstanding and issued (B)		1.5 crores
Valuation of total business (A X B = C)		Rs.600 crores

Valuation based on discounted cash flow

Year	Expected cash accruals	Discount factor	Value in crores
1	250	0.893	223.25
2	300	0.797	239.10
3	400	0.712	284.80
Total			747.15

Number of shares outstanding and issued	1.5 crores
Value per share (Rs.747.15 crores / 1.5 crores)	Rs.498.10 per share

Statement of range of valuation

Item	Total Value in crores	Value per share Rs.
Maximum	600.00	400.00
Minimum	747.15	498.10

Illustration 2

Alpha Limited is a highly successful company and wishes to expand inorganically by acquiring other firms. Its expected high growth in earnings and dividends is reflected in its PE ratio of 17. The Board of Directors of Alpha Ltd has been advised that if it were to take over firms with a lower PE ratio than its own, using a share-for-share exchange, then it could increase its reported earnings earnings per share. Delta Ltd has been suggested as a possible target for a takeover, which has a PE ratio of 10 and 100000 shares in issue with a share price of Rs.15. Alpha Ltd has 500000 shares in issue with a share price of Rs.12.

Calculate the change in earnings per share of Alpha Ltd if it acquires the whole of Delta Ltd by issuing shares at its market price of Rs.12. Assume price of Alpha Ltd shares remain constant.

Solution

Total Market value of Delta Ltd

No of shares	(A)	100000
Share price	(B)	Rs.15
Total market value	((AXB) = C)	Rs.1500000
PE ratio (per problem)	(D)	10
Earnings	((C / D) = E)	Rs.150000

Total Market value of Alpha Ltd

No of shares	(A)	500000
Share price	(B)	Rs.12
Total market value	((AXB) = C)	Rs.6000000
PE ratio (per problem)	(D)	17
Earnings	((C / D) = E)	Rs.352941
EPS	(E/A) = F)	**Re.0.71**

The number of shares to be issued by Alpha Ltd as a result of merger:

Total market value of Delta Ltd as above	Rs.1500000
Share price of Delta Ltd	Rs.12
Total number of shares issued by	
Alpha Ltd as a result of merger (Rs.1500000 / Rs.12) =	125000
Total number of shares of Alpha Ltd (500000 + 125000) =	625000 (X)
Total earnings of the merged Company =	(Rs.150000+ Rs.352941)
=	Rs.502941 (Y)

The EPS of the merged Company ((Y / X) = Z) = **Re.0.80**
Hence the EPS of Alpha Ltd increases from Re.0.71 to Re.0.80 as an outcome of merger.

Illustration 3

XYZ Ltd is considering acquiring ABC Ltd and following information is available:

Entity	Profit after tax (PAT) Rs.	No. of equity shares	Market value per share Rs.
XYZ Ltd	6000000	1200000	200.00
ABC Ltd	1800000	300000	160.00

Exchange of equity shares for acquisition is based on current market value as above. There is no synergy advantage available.

a) Find the earnings per share of XYZ Ltd post-merger and

b) Find the exchange ratio so that shareholders of ABC Ltd would not be at a loss. *(Adapted from CA)*

Solution

a) **Earnings per share of XYZ Ltd post-merger is as under**:

Exchange ratio = (160:200) = 4:5

This means 4 shares of XYZ Ltd for every 5 shares of ABC Ltd.

Hence total number of shares to be issued in XYZ Ltd on acquisition = 4/5 x 300000 = 240000

Total number of shares = 1200000 (XYZ Ltd) + 240000 (ABC Ltd) = 1440000 shares (A)

Total profit after tax (Rs.600000 (XYZ Ltd) + Rs.1800000 (ABC Ltd) = Rs.7800000 (B)

Earnings per share post-merger (B / A) = Rs.5.42 per share

b) **To find the exchange ratio so that shareholders of ABC Ltd would not be at a loss**

Present earnings per share of XYZ Ltd = (Rs.6000000 / 1200000) = Rs.5.00

Present earnings per share of ABC Ltd = (Rs.1800000 / 300000) = Rs.6.00

Exchange ratio would be 6 shares of XYZ Ltd for every 5 shares of ABC Ltd.

Hence shares to be issued to ABC Ltd would be (300000 x 6/5) = 360000 shares

Total number of shares in XYZ Ltd post-merger = (1200000 (XYZ Ltd) +360000 (ABC Ltd)

= 1560000 shares

Hence EPS post-merger would be = (Rs.7800000 / 1560000) = Rs.5.00 per share

Total earnings available to shareholders of ABC Ltd post-merger would be = 360000 x Rs.5

= Rs.1800000

This is equivalent to earnings prior to merger of ABC Ltd.

Hence exchange ratio on the basis of earnings per share is recommended.

Illustration 4

A Ltd wants to acquire B Ltd and has offered a swap ratio of 1:2(0.5 share for every one share of B Ltd). Following information is provided:

Item	A Ltd	B Ltd
Profit after tax	Rs.1800000	Rs.360000
Equity shares outstanding (nos)	600000	180000
EPS	Rs.3	Rs.2
PE Ratio	10 times	7 times
Market price per share	Rs.30	Rs.14

Required:

i)   The number of equity shares to be issued by A Ltd for acquisition of B Ltd

ii) What is the EPS of A Ltd after acquisition?

iii) Determine the equivalent earnings per share of B Ltd

iv) What is the expected market price per share of A Ltd after the acquisition, assuming its PE multiple remains unchanged?

v)   Determine the market value of the merged firm.

Solution

i)   The number of equity shares to be issued by A Ltd for acquisition of B Ltd

The exchange ratio is 0.5

Hence, new shares = 180000 x0.5 = 90000 shares

ii) EPS of A Ltd after acquisition is as under:

Total earnings = (Rs.1800000 + Rs.360000) = Rs.2160000

No. of shares = (600000 + 90000) = 690000
EPS = (Rs.2160000 / 690000) = Rs.3.13

iii) Equivalent earnings per share of B Ltd
No. of new shares   0.5
EPS as above   Rs.3.13
Equivalent EPS (0.5 X Rs.3.13) Rs.1.57

iv) Expected market price per share of A Ltd after the acquisition, assuming its PE multiple remains unchanged:
Present P/E ratio of A Ltd   10 times
Expected EPS post-merger   Rs.3.13
Expected market price (10 x Rs.3.13) = Rs.31.30
v) Expected market value of the merged firm
Total number of shares   690000
Expected market price (Rs.31.30 x 690000) = Rs.21597000

Illustration 5

Alpha Ltd is intending to acquire Beta Ltd by merger and the following information is available in respect of the companies:

	Alpha Ltd	Beta Ltd
Number of equity shares	1000000	600000
Earnings after tax (Rs)	5000000	1800000
Market value per share (Rs)	42	28

Required:
i)   What is the present EPS of both the companies?
ii) If the proposed merger takes place, what would be the new earning per share for Alpha Ltd? Assume that the merger takes place by exchange of equity shares and the exchange ratio is based on the current market price.
iii) What should be the exchange ratio, if Beta Ltd wants to ensure the earnings to members are as before the merger takes place?

Solution
i)   What is the present EPS of both the companies?
EPS = Earnings after tax / number of equity shares
Alpha Ltd = Rs.5000000 / 1000000 = Rs.5.00
Beta Ltd = Rs.1800000 / 600000 = Rs.3.00

ii) If the proposed merger takes place, what would be the new earning per share for Alpha Ltd assuming that the merger takes place by exchange of equity shares and the exchange ratio is based on the current market price?
No. of shares shareholders of Beta Ltd will get in Alpha Ltd based on current market value per share = Rs.28 / Rs.42 x 600000 shares = 400000 shares
Total no. of equity shares post-merger = 1000000 + 400000 = 1400000 shares
EPS post-merger = (Rs.5000000 + Rs.1800000) / 1400000 shares = Rs.4.86

iii) What should be the exchange ratio, if Beta Ltd wants to ensure the earnings to members are as before the merger takes place?
Shares to be exchanged based on EPS = (Rs.3/Rs.5) x 600000 = 360000 shares
Total no. of equity shares post-merger = 1000000 + 360000 = 1360000 shares

EPS post-merger = (Rs.5000000 + Rs.1800000) / 1360000 shares = Rs.5.00
Total earnings in Alpha Ltd available to shareholders of Beta Ltd = 360000 x Rs.5
= Rs.1800000
Hence to ensure that earnings to members are same as before, the ratio of exchange
should be Rs.3 / Rs.5 i.e. Re.0.60: Re.1.00.

Illustration 6

Alpha Ltd is considering merger with Beta Ltd. Alpha Ltd shares are currently traded at Rs.20. It has 250000 shares outstanding and its earnings after tax amount to Rs.500000. Beta Ltd has 125000 shares outstanding ; its current market price is Rs.10 and its EAT are Rs.125000. The merger will be effected by means of a stock swap (exchange). Beta Ltd has agreed to a plan under which Alpha Ltd will offer the current market value of Beta Ltd's shares:

i)   What is the pre-merger earnings per share (EPS) and P/E ratios of both the companies?
ii)   If Beta Ltd's PE ratio is 6.4, what is the current market price? What is the exchange ratio? What will Alpha Ltd's post-merger EPS be?
iii) What should be the exchange ratio; if Alpha Ltd's pre-merger and post-merger EPS are to be the same?

Solution

i)   What is the pre-merger earnings per share (EPS) and P/E ratios of both the companies?

Particulars	Alpha Ltd	Beta Ltd
Earnings after taxes (A)	500000	125000
Number of shares outstanding (B)	250000	125000
EPS ((A/B) = C)	2	1
Market price per share (D)	20	10
PE ratio (times) (D/C = E)	10	10

ii)   If Beta Ltd's PE ratio is 6.4, what is the current market price? What is the exchange ratio? What will Alpha Ltd's post-merger EPS be?
Current market price of Beta Ltd = 6.4 x Rs.1 = **Rs.6.40**
Exchange ratio = Rs.20 / Rs.6.40 = **3.125**
Post-merger EPS would be:

$$= \frac{(Rs.500000 + Rs.125000)}{(250000 + (125000/3.125))}$$

$$= \frac{Rs.625000}{290000}$$

$$= \textbf{2.16}$$

iii) What should be the exchange ratio; if Alpha Ltd's pre-merger and post-merger EPS are to be the same?
Total number of shares in post-merged company

$$= \frac{Post\text{-}merged\ earnings}{Pre\text{-}merger\ EPS\ of\ Alpha\ Ltd}$$

$$= \frac{Rs.625000}{2}$$

$$= \text{Rs. } 312500$$

Number of shares required to be issued
= 312500 – 250000 = 62500

Hence the desired exchange ratio is:
= 62500:125000
= **0.50**

Illustration 7

X Ltd is studying the possible acquisition of Y Ltd by way of merger. The following data are available in respect of the companies:

Particulars	X Ltd	Y Ltd
Earnings after tax (Rs)	8000000	2400000
No. of equity shares	1600000	400000
Market value per share (Rs)	200	160

i)   If the merger goes through by exchange of equity and the exchange ratio is based on the current market price, what is the new earning per share for X Ltd?

ii) Y Ltd wants to be sure that the earnings available to its shareholders will not be diminished by the merger. What would be the exchange ratio in that case?

Solution

i)   If the merger goes through by exchange of equity and the exchange ratio is based on the current market price, what is the new earning per share for X Ltd?
No of equity shares to be issued by X Ltd to Y Ltd
= 400000 shares x Rs.160 / Rs.200
= 320000 shares
Total no. of equity shares in X Ltd post-acquisition of Y Ltd
= 1600000 + 320000
= 1920000
Total earnings after tax post-acquisition
= (Rs.8000000 + Rs.2400000)
= Rs.10400000
EPS = (Rs.10400000 / 1920000 equity shares)
= **Rs.5.42**

ii) Calculation of exchange ratio which would not diminish the EPS of Y Ltd post-merger with X Ltd:
Current EPS:
X Ltd = Rs.8000000 / 1600000 equity shares = Rs.5.00
Y Ltd = Rs.2400000 / 400000 equity shares = Rs.6.00
Exchange ratio = 6/5 = 1.20
No. of new equity shares to be issued by X Ltd to Y Ltd
= 400000 x 1.20
= 480000 shares
Total no. of equity shares in X Ltd post-acquisition of Y Ltd

= 1600000 + 480000

= 2080000

Total earnings after tax post-acquisition

= (Rs.8000000 + Rs.2400000)

= Rs.10400000

EPS = (Rs.10400000 / 2080000 equity shares)

= **Rs.5.00**

Hence total earnings available to new equity shareholders in X Ltd will be

= 480000 X Rs.5.00

= Rs.2400000

Therefore, it is recommended that exchange ratio (6:5) based on EPS is beneficial to shareholders of Y Ltd.

Illustration 8

A Ltd is considering acquiring B Ltd and the following information is available:

Company	Profit after tax	Number of equity shares	Market value per share
A Ltd	5000000	1000000	200.00
B Ltd	1500000	250000	160.00

Exchange of equity shares for acquisition is based on current market value as above. There is no synergy advantage available:

i)   Find the earning per share for A Ltd after merger

ii)   Find the exchange ratio so that shareholders of B Ltd would not be at a loss.

Solution

i)   **Calculation of EPS for A Ltd after merger**

Exchange ratio 160:200 = 4:5

Thus 4 shares of A Ltd would be exchanged for 5 shares of B Ltd.

No of equity shares to be issued by A Ltd to B Ltd

= 250000 shares x 4 / 5

= 200000 shares

Total no. of equity shares in A Ltd post-merger of B Ltd

= 1000000 + 200000

= 1200000

Total Profit after tax post-merger

= (Rs.5000000 + Rs.1500000)

= Rs.6500000

EPS = (Rs.6500000 / 1200000 equity shares)

= **Rs.5.42 per share**

ii)   **Calculation of exchange ratio so that shareholders of B Ltd would not be at a loss.**

Current EPS:

A Ltd = Rs.5000000 / 1000000 equity shares = Rs.5.00

B Ltd = Rs.1500000 / 250000 equity shares = Rs.6.00

Exchange ratio = 6/5 = 1.20

No. of new equity shares to be issued by A Ltd to B Ltd

= 250000 x 1.20

= 300000 shares

Total no. of equity shares in A Ltd post-acquisition of B Ltd

= 1000000 + 300000

= 1300000

Total earnings after tax post-acquisition
= (Rs.5000000 + Rs.1500000)
= Rs.6500000
EPS = (Rs.6500000 / 1300000 equity shares)
= **Rs.5.00**
Hence total earnings available to new equity shareholders in B Ltd will be
= 300000 X Rs.5.00
= Rs.1500000
This is equal to earnings prior merger for B Ltd
Therefore, it is recommended that exchange ratio (6:5) based on EPS is beneficial to shareholders of B Ltd.

Illustration 9

Alpha Ltd is contemplating the purchase of Beta Ltd. Alpha Ltd has 300000 shares having a market price of Rs.30 per share, while Beta Ltd has 200000 shares selling at Rs.20 per share. The EPS are Rs. 4.00 and Rs.2.25 for X Ltd and Y Ltd respectively. Managements of both the companies are discussing two alternative proposals for exchange of shares as indicated below:
i)   In proportion to the relative earnings per share of two companies
ii)   0.5 share of Alpha Ltd for one share of Beta Ltd (0.5 : 1)

Required:
i)   Calculate the EPS after merger under two alternatives and
ii)   Show the impact of EPS for the shareholders of two companies under both the alternatives

Solution
i)   **Calculation the EPS after merger under two alternatives**

a)   **In proportion to the relative earnings per share of two companies (Rs)**

Company	Existing no. of shares	EPS	Total earnings
A Ltd	300000	4.00	1200000
B Ltd	200000	2.25	450000
		Total Earnings	1650000

Shares to be delivered post-merger to shareholders of B Ltd = (200000 x 2.25/4.00) = 112500
No. of shares post-merger = (300000 + 112500) = 412500
Hence EPS of A Ltd post-merger = (1650000 / 412500) = Rs.4.00
Equivalent EPS of B Ltd:
EPS Pre-merger = Rs.2.25
Post-merger (Rs.2.25 / (2.25/4.00)) = Rs.4.00

b)   **0.5 share of Alpha Ltd for one share of Beta Ltd (0.5: 1)**
Total earnings post-merger: Rs. 1650000
No. of shares post-merger ((300000 + (0.5 x 200000))   400000
Resultant EPS (Rs.1650000 / 400000)   4.125

ii)   **Impact of EPS for the shareholders of two companies under both the alternatives**

A Ltd	Rs.
EPS before merger	4.000
EPS after merger i.e.(1650000 / 400000)	4.125
Increase in EPS	0.125

B Ltd	Rs.
Equivalent EPS before merger (2.25 / 0.5)	4.500
EPS after merger i.e.(1650000 / 400000)	4.125
Decrease in EPS	0.375

Illustration 10

The following information is provided related to the acquiring Firm Mark Limited and the target Firm Mask Limited:

Particulars	Firm Mark Limited	Firm Mask Limited
Earnings after tax (Rs lakhs)	2000	400
No of shares outstanding (lakhs)	200	100
PE ratio (times)	10	5

Required:

i)   What is the SWAP Ratio on current market prices?

ii)   What is the EPS of Firm Mark Limited after acquisition?

iii)   What is the expected market price per share of Firm Mark Limited after acquisition, assuming PE ratio of Mark Limited remains unchanged?

iv)   Determine the market value of the merged firm

v)   Calculate gain / loss for shareholders of the two independent companies after acquisition.

Solution

Particulars	Firm Mark Limited	Firm Mask Limited
EPS (Rs)	2000 / 200 = 10.00	400 / 100 = 4.00
Market price	Rs.10.00 x 10 times= Rs.100	Rs.4.00 x 5 times = Rs.20

i)   **SWAP Ratio on current market prices**

Rs.20 / Rs.100 = 0.2 or one share of Firm Mark Ltd for five shares of Firm Mask Limited

No. of shares to be issued = 100 lakhs x 0.2 = 20 lakhs

ii)   **EPS of Firm Mark Limited after acquisition**

$$= \frac{(Rs.2000\ lakhs + Rs.400\ lakhs)}{(200\ lakhs + 20\ lakhs)} = Rs.10.91$$

iii)   **Expected market price per share of Firm Mark Limited after acquisition, assuming PE ratio of Mark Limited remains unchanged**

= Rs.10.91 x 10

= Rs.109.10

iv)   **The market value of the merged firm**

= Rs.109.10 x 220 lakhs = Rs.240.02 crores

v)   **Calculation of gain / loss for shareholders of the two independent companies after acquisition**

Particulars		Rs. crores
Post-merger market value of the merged firm		240.02
Less: Pre-merger market value		
Firm Mark Ltd 200 lakhs x Rs.100 =	Rs.200 crores	

Firm Mask Ltd 100 lakhs x Rs.20 =	Rs.20 crores	220.00
Gain from merger		20.02

Appropriation among shareholders: Firm Mark Ltd (Rs.218.20-Rs.200) 18.02
Firm Mask Ltd (Rs.21.82-Rs.20.00) 1.82
Total 20.02

Illustration 11

Following information is provided relating to the acquiring company M Ltd and the target company R Ltd:

Particulars	M Ltd	R Ltd
Earnings after tax (Rs lakhs)	2000	4000
No. of shares outstandings (lakhs)	200	1000
PE ratio (no. of times)	10	5

Required:
i)   What is the swap ratio based on current market prices?
ii)   What is the EPS of M Ltd after the acquisition?
iii)   What is the expected market price per share of M Ltd after the acquisition, assuming its PE ratio is adversely affected by 10%?
iv)   Determine the market value of the merged co.
v)   Calculate gain / loss for the shareholders of the two independent entities, due to merger.

Solution

i)   **Swap ratio based on current market prices**

Particulars	M Ltd	R Ltd
Earnings after tax (Rs lakhs)	2000	4000
No. of shares outstandings (lakhs)	200	1000
EPS (A)	Rs.10	Rs.4
PE ratio (no. of times) (B)	10	5
Market price before acquisition (A X B)	Rs.100	Rs.20
Swap ratio: 20 / 100 = 1/5 = 0.20		

ii)   **EPS of M Ltd after the acquisition**
(Rs.2000 lakhs + Rs.4000 lakhs) / (200 + 200*) lakhs = Rs.6000 lakhs / 400 lakhs
= **Rs.15.00**
(* 1000 x 0.20 = 200)

iii)   **Expected market price per share of M Ltd after the acquisition, assuming its PE ratio is adversely affected by 10%**

Particulars	M ltd
EPS after acquisition (ii)	Rs.15.00
PE ratio after acquisition (10 times x 90%)	9
Market price per share (Rs.15.00 x 9)	**Rs.135.00**

iv)   **Market value of the merged company M Ltd**
No. of shares   = 400 lakhs
Market price per share = Rs.135.00
Market value of the merged company M Ltd = 400 x Rs.135.00 = **Rs.540.00 crores.**

v) Calculation of gain / loss for the shareholders of the two independent entities, due to merger. (Rs. crore)

Particulars	M Ltd	R Ltd
Total value before acquisition	100	200
Total value after acquisition	270	270
Gain (total)	70	70
No. of shares pre-merger (lakhs)	200	1000
Gain per share (Rs)	35	7

Illustration 12

P Ltd is considering take-over of R Ltd by the exchange of four new shares in P Ltd for every five shares in R Ltd. The relevant financial details of the two companies prior to merger announcement are as under:

Particulars	P Ltd	R Ltd
Profit before tax (Rs crores)	15	13.50
No. of shares outstandings (crores)	25	15
PE ratio (no. of times)	12	9

Corporate tax rate: 30%.

Required:

i) Market value of both the companies
ii) Value of original shareholders
iii) Price per share after merger.
iv) Effect on share price of both the companies if the directors of P Ltd expect their own pre-merger PE ratio to be applied to the combined earnings.

Solution

i)   Market value of both the companies

Particulars	P Ltd	R Ltd
Profit before tax (Rs crores)	15.00	13.50
Less Tax @ 30%	4.50	4.05
Profit after tax (Rs crores) (A)	10.50	9.45
No. of shares outstandings (crores) (B)	25	15
EPS (Rs) (A / B = C)	Re.0.42	Re.0.63
PE ratio (no. of times) (D)	12	9
Share price before merger (C X D = E)	Rs.5.04	Rs.5.67
Market value of company (B X E = F)	**Rs.126.00 crores**	**Rs.85.05 crores**
Combined (Rs.126.00 cr + Rs.85.05 cr) = Rs.211.05 crores		
ii) Value of original shareholders		
Post-merger No. of shares (crores) Combined = (25+12) = 37	25	(15x 4/5) = 12
% of Combined equity (A)	25 / 37 x 100 = 67.57%	12 / 37 x 100 32.43%
Share of combined value = Rs.211.05 crores	Rs.211.05 x 67.57% = **Rs.142.61 crores**	Rs.211.05 x 32.43% = **Rs.68.44 crores**
iii) Price per share post-merger		
		Combined P Ltd

EPS = (Rs.10.50 crores + Rs.9.45 crores)/(25 + 12)	
= Rs.19.95 crores / 37 crores	Re.0.539 per share
PE Ratio	12
Market value per share (Re.0.539 per share x 12)	Rs.6.47
No. of combined shares	37
Total market value (Rs.6.47 x 37 crores)	Rs.239.39 crores
Price per share = (Rs.239.39 crores / 37 crores)	**Rs.6.47**

iv) **Effect on share price of both the companies if the directors of P Ltd expect their own pre-merger PE ratio to be applied to the combined earnings**

Particulars	P Ltd	R Ltd
Price per share (Rs)	6.47	6.47
For R Ltd (Rs) = (4/5 x Rs.6.47)		5.18
Price per share pre-merger (Rs)	5.04	5.67
Gain / loss per share (Rs)	1.43	(0.49)
Gain / loss % on price per share pre-merger	1.43 / 5.04 x 100 = 28.4%	(0.49) / 5.67 x 100 = (8.64%)

Illustration 13

Simple Ltd and Dimple Ltd are planning to merge. The total values of the companies are dependent on the fluctuating business conditions. The following information is given for the total value (debt + equity) structure of each of the two companies:

Business condition	Probability	Simple Ltd Rs.lakhs	Dimple Ltd Rs.Lakhs
High growth	0.20	820	1050
Medium growth	0.60	550	825
Slow growth	0.20	410	590

The current debt of Dimple Ltd is Rs.65 lakhs and of Simple Ltd is Rs.460 lakhs.
Calculate the expected value of debt and equity separately for the merged entity.

Solution
Computation of value of equity:
Simple Ltd (Rs lakhs)

Particulars	High growth	Medium growth	Slow growth
Debt + Equity	820	550	410
Less: Debt	460	460	460
Equity	360	90	-50

Since the company has limited liability the value of equity cannot be negative, therefore the value of equity under slow growth will be considered as zero because of insolvency risk and the value of debt is taken as Rs.410 lakhs. The expected value of debt and equity can then be calculated as under:

Simple Ltd (Rs lakhs)

Particulars	High growth		Medium growth		Slow growth		Expected values
	Prob.	Value	Prob.	Value	Prob.	Value	
Debt	0.20	460	0.60	460	0.20	410	450
Equity	0.20	360	0.60	90	0.20	0	126
Total		820		550		410	576

Dimple Ltd (Rs lakhs)

Particulars	High growth		Medium growth		Slow growth		Expected values
	Prob.	Value	Prob.	Value	Prob.	Value	
Debt	0.20	985	0.60	760	0.20	525	758
Equity	0.20	65	0.60	65	0.20	65	65
Total		1050		825		590	823

Expected values

Equity	Rs lakhs	Debt	Rs lakhs
Simple Ltd	126	Simple Ltd	450
Dimple Ltd	758	Dimple Ltd	65
	884		515

Illustration 14

The following information is provided relating to the acquiring company Efficient Ltd and the target company Healthy Ltd.

Particulars	Efficient Ltd	Healthy Ltd
No. of shares (F.V. Rs.10 each)	10.00 lakhs	7.5 lakhs
Market capitalisation	500.00 lakhs	750.00 lakhs
PE Ratio (times)	10.00	5.00
Reserves and surplus	300.00 lakhs	165.00 lakhs
Promoters holding (no of shares)	4.75 lakhs	5.00 lakhs

Board of Directors of both the companies have decided to give a fair deal to the shareholders and accordingly for swap ratio the weights are decided as 40%, 25% and 35% respectively for Earning, book value and market price of share of each company:

i) Calculate the swap ratio and also calculate promoters holding % after acquisition
ii) What is the EPS of Efficient Ltd after acquisition of Health Ltd?
iii) What is the expected market price per share and market capitalisation of Efficient Ltd after acquisition, assuming PE ratio of Firm Efficient Ltd remains unchanged.
iv) Calculate free float market capitalisation of the merged firm.

Solution

Swap ratio		Efficient Ltd	Healthy Ltd
Market capitalisation		500 lakhs	750 lakhs
No. of shares		10 lakhs	7.5 lakhs
Market price per share		Rs.50	Rs.100
PE Ratio		10	5
EPS		Rs.5	Rs.20
Profit (Rs lakhs)		50	150
Share capital (Rs lakhs)		100	75
Reserve and surplus (Rs lakhs)		300	165
	Total	400	240
Book value per share		Rs.40	Rs.32
i) Calculation of swap ratio			
EPS (Rs.5 : Rs.20) = 1:4 = 4.0 x 40%			1.6
Book value (Rs.40 : Rs.32) = 1:08 = 0.8 x 25%			0.2
Market price (Rs.50 : Rs.100) = 1 : 2 = 2.0 x 35%			0.7
	Total		2.5
Hence for every one share of Health Ltd to be issued			

2.5 shares of Efficient Ltd. Total no. of shares would be = (7.5 lakh shares x 2.5)		18.75 lakh shares	
Total no. of combined shares for merged entity (10 lakhs + 18.75 lakhs) shares =		28.75 lakh shares (A)	
Promoters' holdings			
Efficient Ltd :	4.75 lakhs		
Healthy Ltd : 5.0 Lakh x 2.5 =	12.50 lakhs	17.25 lakh shares (B)	
Promoters holding %	((B/A) X 100)	60%	

ii) **Calculation of EPS**

Total no. of shares	= (10 lakhs + 18.75 lakhs) = 28.75 lakhs
EPS = Total profit/ no. of shares	= (Rs.50 lakhs+Rs.150 lakhs) /28.75 lakh shares = 200 / 28.75 lakh shares = Rs.6.956

iii) **Expected market price per share and market capitalisation of Efficient Ltd after acquisition, assuming PE ratio of Firm Efficient Ltd remains unchanged**

EPS as above	Rs.6.956
P/E Ratio	10
Expected market price	Rs.69.56
No. of shares	28.75 lakhs shares
Market capitalisation	Rs.69.56 x 28.75 lakh shares = Rs.1999.85 lakh

iv) **Free float of market capitalisation**

Market capitalisation (as above)	Rs.1999.85 lakhs
No. of shares	28.75 lakhs
Free float no. of shares = 28.75 x 40%	11.50 lakhs
Expected market price (as above)	Rs.69.56
Free float of market capitalisation	Rs.799.94 lakhs
Free float of market capitalisation (control)	Rs.1999.85 lakhs x 40% = Rs.799.94 lakhs

Illustration 15

Abhiman Ltd is a subsidiary of Janam Ltd and is acquiring Swabhiman Ltd which is also a subsidiary of Janam Ltd.

The following information is given:

Particulars	Abhiman Ltd	Swabhiman Ltd
Percentage shareholding of promoter	50%	60%
Share capital	Rs.200 lakhs	Rs.100 lakhs
Free reserves and surplus	Rs.900 lakhs	Rs.600 lakhs
Paid up value per share	Rs.100	Rs.10
Free float market capitalisation	Rs.500 lakhs	Rs.156 lakhs
P/E Ratio (times)	10	4

Janam Ltd is interested in doing justice to both companies. The following parameters have been assigned by the board of Janam Ltd, for determining the swap ratio:

Book value	25%
Earnings per share	50%
Market price	25%

Required:

i)   Compute the swap ratio
ii)   The Book value, Earnings per share and Expected market value of Swabhiman Ltd. (assuming P/E Ratio of Abhiman ratio remains the same and all assets and liabilities of Swabhiman Ltd are taken over at book value).

Solution

i)   **Swap ratio**

Particulars		Abhiman Ltd Rs/lakhs	Swabhiman Ltd Rs/lakhs
Share capital		200	100
Reserves and surplus		900	600
	Total	1100	700
No. of shares		2 lakhs	10 lakhs
Book value per share (Rs)		550	70
Promoters holding		50%	60%
Non-promoters holding		50%	40%
Free float market capitalisation (public)		500	156
Total market capitalisation		(500/50%) = 1000	(156/40%) = 390
No. of shares		2 lakhs	10 lakhs
Market price		Rs.500	Rs.39
P/E Ratio		10	4
EPS		Rs.50	Rs.9.75
Total profit		(200000 x Rs.50) = Rs.100 lakhs	(1000000 x Rs.9.75) = 97.50 lakhs

Calculation of Swap ratio

Particulars	Swap ratio	Weightage	Resultant
Book value per share	550 : 70 = 1 : 0.1273	0.1273 x 25%	0.031825
EPS	50 : 9.75 = 1 : 0.195	0.195 x 50%	0.097500
Market price	500 : 39 = 1 : 0.078	0.078 x 25%	0.019500
Total			0.148825

Hence Swap ratio is **0.148825** shares of Abhiman Ltd for every share of Swabhiman Ltd
Total no. of shares to be issued = 10 lakhs x 0.148825 = **148825 shares**

ii)   **Calculation of Book value, EPS and Expected Market price**

Particulars	Rs lakhs
Total capital = (Rs.200 lakhs + Rs.148.825 lakhs)	348.825
Total reserves = (Rs.900 lakhs + Rs.551.175 lakhs*)	1451.175
* (Rs.600 lakhs – Rs.148.825 lakhs)	
Total shareholders funds	1800.000 (A)
No. of shares (200000 + 148825)	348825 (B)
Book value per share = (1800.000 (A) / 348825 (B))	Rs.516.02
EPS = (Total profit / no. of shares) = (Rs.100 lakhs + Rs.97.50 lakhs)/348825	**Rs.56.62**
Expected market price = (EPS X P/E Ratio) = Rs.56.62 x 10	**Rs.566.20**

Illustration 16

The following information relating to the acquiring company Abhiman Ltd and the target company Abhishek Ltd are available. Both the companies are promoted by Multinational Company Trident Ltd. The promoters' holding are 50% and 60% respectively in Abhiman Ltd and Abhishek Ltd:

Particulars	Abhiman Ltd	Abhishek Ltd
Share capital (Rs/lakhs)	200	100
Free reserve and surplus (Rs/lakhs)	800	500
Paid up value per share (Rs)	100	10
Free float market capitalisation (Rs/lakhs)	400	128
P/E Ratio (times)	10	4

Trident Ltd is interested to do justice to the shareholders of both the companies. For the swap ratio weights are assigned to different parameters by the Board of Directors as follows:

Book value   25%
Earnings per share   50%
Market price   25%

Required:

a) What is the swap ratio based on above weights?

b) What is the book value, EPS and expected market price of Abhiman Ltd after acquisition of Abhishek Ltd (assuming P/E Ratio of Abhiman Ltd remains unchanged and all assets and liabilities of Abhishek Ltd are taken over at book value)

c) Calculate:

   i)   Promoters revised holding in the Abhiman Ltd

   ii)   Free float market capitalisation

   iii)   Also calculate no. of shares, Earnings per share (EPS) and book value if after acquisition of Abhishek Ltd , Abhiman Ltd decided to:

      a) Issued bonus shares in the ratio of 1:2 and

      b) Split the stock (share) as Rs.5 each fully paid.

Solution

a) Swap ratio

Particulars		Abhiman Ltd Rs/lakhs	Abhishek Ltd Rs/lakhs
Share capital		200	100
Free Reserves and surplus		800	500
	Total	1000	600
No. of shares		2 lakhs	10 lakhs
Book value per share (Rs)		500	60
Promoters holding		50%	60%
Non-promoters holding		50%	40%
Free float market capitalisation (public)		400	128
Total market capitalisation		(400/50%) = 800	(128/40%) = 320
No. of shares		2 lakhs	10 lakhs
Market price		Rs.400	Rs.32
P/E Ratio		10	4
EPS		Rs.40	Rs.8
Total profit		(200000 x Rs.40) = Rs.80 lakhs	(1000000 x Rs.8) = 80 lakhs

Calculation of Swap ratio

Particulars	Swap ratio	Weightage	Resultant
Book value per share	500 : 60 = 1 : 0.12	0.12 x 25%	0.03
EPS	40 : 8 = 1 : 0.2	0.2 x 50%	0.10
Market price	400 : 32 = 1 : 0.08	0.08 x 25%	0.02
Total			0.15

Hence Swap ratio is **0.15** shares of Abhiman Ltd for every one share of Abhishek Ltd
Total no. of shares to be issued = 10 lakhs x 0.15 = **150000 shares**

b) **Calculation of Book value, EPS and Expected Market price**

Particulars	Rs lakhs
Total capital = (Rs.200 lakhs + Rs.150 lakhs)	350.0
Total reserves = (Rs.800 lakhs + Rs.350 lakhs*) *(Rs.500 lakhs – Rs.150 lakhs)	1250.0
Total shareholders' funds	1600.000 (A)
No. of shares (200000 + 150000)	350000 (B)
Book value per share = (1600.000 (A) / 350000 (B))	Rs.457.14
EPS = (Total profit / no. of shares) = (Rs.80 lakhs + Rs.80 lakhs)/350000	Rs.45.71
Expected market price = (EPS X P/E Ratio) = Rs.45.71 x 10	Rs.457.10

c) **Promoters revised holding, free float capitalisation and revised capital**

Particulars	Rs lakhs
i)**Promoters revised holding:** Abhiman 50% Abhishek 60%	 1.00 lakh shares 0.90 lakh shares
Total revised holding	1.90 lakh shares
Promoters' revised holding % = (1.90 /3.50) x 100	54.29%
ii)**Free float market capitalisation** Free float market capitalisation = (3.5 lakh – 1.9 lakh) x Rs.457.10	 731.36
iii)**Revised capital in Abhiman Ltd** Bonus issue 1: 2 = Rs.350 lakhs + Rs.175 lakhs = Rs.525 lakhs No. of shares before split: Rs.525 lakhs / Rs.100 No. of shares after split (Rs.5 each fully paid up: (Rs.525 lakhs / Rs.5) EPS = (Total profit / no. of shares) = (Rs.80 lakhs + Rs.80 lakhs)/105 lakh Book value = (Cap.Rs.525 lakhs + Res. Rs.1075 lakhs*) / 105 lakh shares = *(1250 – 175) = 1075 **Book value based on original shareholders' funds** = (Cap.Rs.525 lakhs + Rs.1125 lakhs) / 105 lakh shares =	 5.25 lakhs 105 lakhs Rs.1.523 Rs.15.238 per share Rs.15.714 per share

Illustration 17

You have been provided the following financial data of two companies:

Particulars	Krishna Ltd	Rama Ltd
Earnings after taxes (Rs)	700000	1000000
Equity shares (outstanding)	200000	400000
EPS	3.5	2.5
P/E Ratio	10 times	14 times

Market price per share	Rs.35	Rs.35

Company Rama Ltd is acquiring the company Krishna Ltd, exchanging its shares on a one-to-one basis for company Krishna Ltd. The exchange ratio is based on the market prices of the shares of the two companies.

Required:
- i)   What will be the EPS subsequent to the merger?
- ii)   What is the change in EPS for the shareholders of companies Rama Ltd and Krishna Ltd?
- iii)   Determine the market value of the post-merger firm. P/E ratio is likely to remain the same.
- iv)   Ascertain the profits accruing to shareholders of both the companies.

Solution

i)   Calculation of EPS subsequent to merger

Particulars	Rs.
Exchange ratio	1 : 1
Total shares outstanding (400000 + 200000)	600000
Total earnings after tax (Rs.1000000 + Rs.700000)	1700000
New EPS subsequent to merger (1700000 / 600000)	Rs.2.83

ii)   Change in EPS for the shareholders of companies Rama Ltd and Krishna Ltd

Particulars	Rs.
Rama Ltd	
Existing EPS of Rama Ltd	2.50
New EPS on merger	2.83
Increase in EPS of Rama Ltd	0.33
Krishna Ltd	
Existing EPS of Krishna Ltd	3.50
New EPS on merger	2.83
Decrease in EPS of Krishna Ltd	0.67

iii)   Determination of the market value of the post-merger firm - P/E ratio is likely to remain the same

Particulars	Rs.
P/E Ratio in the new firm (expect to remain same)	14 times
EPS	2.83
New market price (14 times x Rs.2.83)	39.62
Total No. of shares (200000 + 400000)	600000
Total market capitalisation (Rs.39.62 x 600000)	23772000
Existing market capitalisation (700000 x 10) + (1000000 x 14)	21000000
Net gain	2772000

iv)   Ascertainment of the profits accruing to shareholders of both the companies

Particulars	Rama Ltd	Krishna Ltd	Total
No. of shares post-merger	400000	200000	600000
Market price post-merger	Rs.39.62	Rs.39.62	Rs.39.62
Total market values	15848000	7924000	23772000
Existing market values	14000000	7000000	21000000
Net gain to shareholders	1848000	924000	2772000

Hence, the gain of Rs.27.72 lakhs has been shared between Rama Ltd and Krishna Ltd in the ratio of 2:1.

Illustration 18

T Ltd and E Ltd are in the same industry. The former is in negotiation for acquisition of the latter. Important information about the two companies as per their latest financial statements is given below:

Particulars	T Ltd	E Ltd
Rs.10 equity shares outstanding	12 lakhs	6 lakhs
Debt:		
10 % debentures (Rs lakhs)	580	-
12.5 % institutional loan (Rs lakhs)	-	240
Earnings before interest, depreciation and tax (EBIDAT)	Rs.400.86 lakhs	Rs.115.71 lakhs
Market price per share (Rs)	220.00	110.00

T Ltd plans to offer a price for E Ltd, business as a whole which will be 7 times EBIDAT reduced by outstanding debt, to be discharged by own shares at market price.

E Ltd is planning to seek one share in T Ltd for every two shares in E Ltd based on the market price. Tax rate for the two companies may be assumed as 30%.

Calculate and show the following under both alternatives – T Ltd's offer and E Ltd's plan:

- i) Net consideration payable
- ii) No. of shares to be issued by T Ltd
- iii) EPS of T Ltd after acquisition
- iv) Expected market price per share of T Ltd after acquisition
- v) State briefly the advantages to T Ltd from the acquisition.

Calculations (except EPS) may be rounded off to 2 decimals in lakhs.

Solution

As per T Ltd's offer

Particulars		Rs in lakhs	Rs in lakhs
i)	**Net consideration payable**		
	7 times EBIDAT X Rs.115.71 lakhs	809.97	
	Less: Debt (12.5% institutional loan)	240.00	569.97
ii)	**No. of shares to be issued by T Ltd**		
	(Rs.569.97 / Rs.220/-) nos		259000
iii)	**EPS of T Ltd after acquisition**		
	Total EBIDAT (Rs.400.86 lakhs + Rs.115.71 lakhs)	516.57	
	Less: Interest (Rs.580 lakhs x 10%)+(Rs.240 lakhs x		
	12.5%)	88.00	428.57
	Less 30% tax		128.57
	Total earnings (NPAT)		300.00 (A)
	Total no. of shares outstanding		14.59 lakhs (B)
	(12 lakhs + 2.59lakhs)		
	EPS of T Ltd after merger (A / B)		Rs.20.56
iv)	**Expected market price per share of T Ltd after**		

	acquisition		
	Pre-merger P/E Multiple:		
	EBIDAT	400.86	
	Less: Interest (580 x 10/100)	58.00	
		342.86	
	Less: 30% tax	102.86	
	NPAT	240.00	
	No. of shares (lakhs)	12	
	EPS (pre-acquisition) (240.0/12)	Rs.20.00	
	Hence P/E Multiple:	(Rs.220 /Rs.20)	11
	Expected market price after acquisition	(Rs.20.56 x 11)	Rs.226.16

As per E Ltd's plan

Particulars		Rs in lakhs	Rs in lakhs
i)	**Net consideration payable**		
	6 lakhs shares x Rs.110		660
ii)	**No. of shares to be issued by T Ltd**		
	(Rs.660 / Rs.220/-) nos		300000
iii)	**EPS of T Ltd after acquisition**	516.57	
	Total EBIDAT (Rs.400.86 lakhs + Rs.115.71 lakhs)		
	Less: Interest (Rs.580 lakhs x 10%)+(Rs.240 lakhs x	88.00	
	12.5%)		428.57
	Less 30% tax		128.57
			300.00 (A)
	Total no. of shares outstanding		
	(12 lakhs + 3 lakhs)		15.00 lakhs (B)
	EPS of T Ltd after merger (A / B)		Rs.20.00
iv)	**Expected market price per share of T Ltd after**		
	acquisition		
	Pre-merger P/E Multiple:		
	EBIDAT	400.86	
	Less: Interest (580 x 10/100)	58.00	
		342.86	
	Less: 30% tax	102.86	
		240.00	
	No. of shares (lakhs)	12	
	EPS (pre-acquisition) (240.0/12)	Rs.20.00	
	Hence P/E Multiple:	(Rs.220 /Rs.20)	11
	Expected market price after acquisition	(Rs.20.00 x 11)	Rs.220.00

Illustration 19

The following information is relating to Fortune India Ltd having two divisions, viz, Pharma division and Fast Moving Consumer Goods Division (FMCG). Paid up share capital of Fortune India Ltd is consisting of 3000 lakhs equity shares of Re.1 each. Fortune India Ltd decided to de-merge Pharma division as Fortune Pharma Ltd w.e.f 1.4.2009. Details of Fortune India Ltd as on 31.3.2009 and of Fortune Pharma Ltd as on 1.4.2009 are given below:

Particulars	Fortune Pharma Ltd	Fortune India Ltd
	Rs/lakhs.	Rs/lakhs.
Outside liabilities		
Secured loans	400	3000
Unsecured loans	2400	800
Current liabilities & provisions	1300	21200
Assets		
Fixed Assets	7740	20400
Investments	7600	12300
Current Assets	8800	30200
Loans & Advances	900	7300
Deferred tax / misc. expenses	60	(200)

Board of Directors of the company have decided to issue necessary equity shares of Fortune Pharma Ltd of Re.1 each, without any consideration to the shareholders of Fortune India Ltd. For that purpose the following points are to be considered:
  i)   Transfer of liabilities and assets at book value
  ii)   Estimated profit for the year 2009-10 is Rs.11400 lakh for Fortune India Ltd and Rs.1470 lakhs for Fortune Pharma Ltd
  iii) Estimated market price of Fortune Pharma Ltd is Rs.24.50 per share
  iv)   Average P/E Ratio of FMCG sector is 42 and Pharma sector is 25, which is to be expected for both the companies.

Calculate:
  1. The ratio in which shares of Fortune Pharma are to be issued to the shareholders of Fortune India Ltd.
  2. Expected Market price of Fortune India Ltd
  3. Book value per share of both the companies immediately after Demerger.

Solution

  1. **The ratio in which shares of Fortune Pharma are to be issued to the shareholders of Fortune India Ltd.**

Particulars	Fortune Pharma Ltd
Estimated profit (Rs lakhs) (given)	1470
Estimated market price per share(Rs) (given)	24.50
Estimate P/E ratio (given)	25
Estimate EPS (Rs.24.50 / 25)	0.98
No. of shares – lakhs	1500
Hence ratio would be (3000 : 1500) = (2 : 1) i.e. one share of Fortune Pharma for 2 shares of Fortune India Limited	

  2. **Expected Market price of Fortune India Ltd**

Particulars	Fortune India (FMCG) Ltd
Estimated profit (Rs lakhs) (given)	11400
No. of equity shares (given)	3000
Estimate EPS Rs. (Rs.lakhs 11400 / 3000)	3.8
Estimated P/E ratio	42
Estimate Market price (Rs.3.8 x 42)	Rs.159.60

3. Book value per share

Particulars	Fortune India Ltd Rs lakhs	Fortune Pharma Ltd Rs lakhs	Fortune India(FMCG) Ltd Rs lakhs
Assets	70000	25100	44900
Less outside liabilities	25000	4100	20900
Net worth	45000	21000	24000
No. of shares (lakhs)		1500	3000
Book value of shares		Rs.14	Rs.8

Illustration 20

Reliable Industries Ltd (RIL) is considering a takeover of Sunflower Industries Ltd. The particulars of 2 companies are as under:

Particulars	Reliance Industries Ltd Rs.	Sunflower Industries Ltd Rs.
Earnings after tax (EAT)	2000000	1000000
Equity shares o/s	1000000	1000000
Earnings per share (EPS)	2	1
PE Ratio (times)	10	5

Required:
i) What is the market value of each company before merger?
ii) Assume that the management of RIL estimates that the shareholders of SIL will accept an offer of one share of RIL for four shares of SIL. If there are no synergic effects, what is the market value of the post-merger of RIL? What is the new price per share? Are the shareholders of RIL better or worse off than they were before the merger?
iii) Due to synergic effects, the management of RIL estimates that the earnings will increase by 20%. What are the new post-merger EPS and price per share? Will the shareholders be better off or worse off than before the merger?

Solution
i) Market value of each company before merger

Particulars	Reliance Industries Ltd Rs.	Sunflower Industries Ltd Rs.
Equity shares o/s (A)	1000000	1000000
Earnings per share (EPS) (B)	2	1
PE Ratio (times) (C)	10	5
Total market value (A X B X C)	2,00,00,000	50,00,000

ii) Post-merger effects on RIL

Particulars	Rs.
Post-merger earnings (Rs.2000000 + Rs.1000000) (A)	3000000
Exchange ratio (1: 4)	
No. of equity shares o/s (1000000 + 1000000 x ¼) = (B)	1250000
EPS = (A / B)	2.4
P/E Ratio (times)	10
Market value per share (10 x 2.4) = (C)	24.0
Total value post-merger ((B X C) = D)	3,00,00,000
Less: Pre-merger market value (E)	
RIL : (Rs.2000000 x 10) = 2.00.00.000	
SIL : (Rs.1000000 x 5) = 50.00.000	2,50,00,000
Total gain from merger (D – E)	50,00,000

Apportionment of gain between shareholders

Particulars	RIL (Rs.)	SIL (Rs.)
Post-merger market value -		
RIL – 1000000 X Rs.24/-	2,40,00,000	
SIL - 250000 X Rs. 24/-		60,00,000
Less pre-merger value	2,00,00,000	50,00,000
Gain from merger	40,00,000	10,00,000

iii) **Post-merger scenario with 20% increase in earnings owing to synergic effects**

Particulars	Rs.
Increase in earnings post-merger =(30,00,000 x 1.20)	36,00,000
No. of equity shares outstanding	12,50,000
EPS = (Rs.36,00,000 / 12,50,000) =	Rs.2.88
P/E Ratio	10
Market price per share (Rs.2.88 x 10)	Rs.28.80
Hence shareholders will be better off with increase of market price per share by 20% post-merger owing to synergic effects.	

Illustration 21

A valuation done of an established company by a well-known analyst has estimated a value of Rs.500 lakhs, based on the expected free cash flow for next year of Rs.20 lakhs and an expected growth rate of 5%.

While going through the valuation procedure, you found that the analyst has made the mistake of using the book values of debt and equity in his calculation. While you do not know the book value weights he used, you have been provided with the following information:

   i)   Company has a cost of equity of 12%
   ii)   After tax cost of debt is 6%
   iii)   The market value of equity is three times the book value of equity, while the market value of debt is equal to the book value of the debt.
You are required to estimate the correct value of the company.

Solution

The value of the firm
$= V_0 = FCFF_1 / (Kc – Gn)$
Where,
$FCFF_1 =$ Expected FCFF for year 1
Kc = Cost of capital
Gn = Growth rate forever
Thus value of firm having been calculated at Rs.500 lakhs, free cash flow at Rs.20 lakhs and growth rate is 5%, the equation is as under:
Rs.500 lakhs = Rs.20 lakhs / (Kc – g)
or 500 (Kc – g) = 20
or 500 x Kc – 500 x 5% = Rs.20 lakhs
or 500 x Kc = Rs.20 lakhs + Rs.25 lakhs
or Kc = Rs.45 lakhs / Rs.500 lakhs
or Kc = 9%

Now let us calculate the weight of debt, which may be taken as X.
Cost of equity = 12%
Cost of debt = 6%

Or 12% (1-X) + 6% X = 9%
Or 12% - 12%X + 6% X = 9%
Or 12% - 9% = 12%X – 6% X
Or 3% = 6% X
Or 3%/6% = X
Or 0.5 = X
Hence weight of debt is 0.5, so book value weight of debt is 50%
Correct weight should be 75% equity and 25% debt
Hence, Kc = 12% x 0.75 + 6% x 0.25
Kc = 9% + 1.5%
Kc = 10.5 %
Correct value of the firm would be Rs.20 lakhs / (10.5% – 5.0%)
= Rs.20 lakhs / 5.5%
= **Rs. 363.64 lakhs**

Illustration 22
Following information are available in respect of XYZ Ltd which is expected to grow at a higher rate
for 4 years after which growth rate will stabilize at a lower level:
Base year information:
Revenue   :   Rs.2000 crores
EBIT   :   Rs.300 crores
Capital expenditure: Rs.280 crores
Depreciation   :   Rs.200 crores

Information for high growth and stable growth period are as follows:

Particulars	High growth	Stable growth
Growth in revenue and EBIT	20%	10%
Growth in capital expenditure and depreciation	20%	Capital expenditure are offset by depreciation
Risk free rate	10%	9%
Equity beta	1.15	1
Market risk premium	6%	5%
Pre-tax cost of debt	13%	12.86%
Debt equity ratio	1 : 1	2 : 3

For all time, working capital is 25% of revenue and corporate tax rate is 30%.
What is the value of the firm?

Solution
Calculation of cost of capital:
  a) **High growth phase:**
     Ke = Risk free rate + equity beta x market risk premium = 0.10 +1.15 x 0.06 = 16.9%
     Kd = 0.13 x (1 – 0.3) = 0.091 = 9.1%
     Cost of capital = 0.5 x 0.169 + 0.5 x 0.091 = 13%
  b) **Stable growth phase:**
     Ke = Risk free rate + equity beta x market risk premium = 0.09 +1.0 x 0.05 = 14%
     Kd = 0.1286 x (1 – 0.3) = 0.091 = 9%
     Cost of capital = 0.6 x 0.14 + 0.4 x 0.09 = 12%
     Determination of forecasted free cash flow of the firm (FCFF)

Particulars	Yr1	Yr2	Yr3	Yr4	Terminal year
Revenue (GR:20%)	2400	2880	3456	4147.20	4561.92

EBIT (GR: 20%)	360	432	518.40	622.08	684.29
EAT (GR: 20%)	252	302.40	362.88	435.46	479.00
Capital net of depreciation (GR: 20%)	(96)	(115.20)	(138.24)	(165.89)	0
Incremental working capital: (25% of base revenue x 20% growth)	(100)	(120)	(144)	(172.80)	(103.68)
Free cash flow(FCF)	56.00	67.20	80.64	96.77	375.32

Calculation of present value of FCFF during the explicit forecast period:

FCFF (Rs crores)	PV : 13%	PV (Rs crores)
56.00	0.885	49.56
67.20	0.783	52.62
80.64	0.693	55.88
96.77	0.613	59.32
		217.38

Calculation of terminal value:
RS 375.32 Lakhs / (0.12 − 0.09) = Rs.12510.67 crores
Present value of the terminal value = Rs.12510.67 crores x 0.613 = Rs. 7673.02 crores

The value of the firm:
= Rs.217.38 + Rs7673.02 crores
= **Rs.7890.40 crores**

Illustration 23

ADC Ltd wishes to acquire BDC Ltd. The shares issued by the two companies are 10, 00,000 and 5, 00,000 respectively:

i) Calculate the increase in the total value of BDC Ltd, resulting from the acquisition on the basis of the following conditions:

Current expected growth rate of BDC Ltd	7%
Expected growth rate under control of ADC Ltd (without any Additional capital investment and without any change in risk of operations)	8%
Current market price per share of ADC Ltd	Rs. 100/-
Current market price per share of BDC Ltd	Rs.20/-
Current dividend per share of BDC Ltd	Re.0.60

ii) On the basis of aforesaid conditions calculate gain or loss to shareholders of both the companies, if ADC Ltd were to offer one of its shares for every four shares of BDC Ltd

iii) Calculate the gain of the shareholders of both the companies, if ADC Ltd pays Rs.22 for each share of BDC Ltd assuming the P/E Ratio of ADC Ltd does not change after the merger. EPS of ADC Ltd is Rs.8 and that of BDC Ltd is Rs.2.50. It is assumed that ADC Ltd invests its cash to earn 10%.

Solution

i) **For BDC Ltd, pre-acquisition:**
The cost of capital of BDC Ltd may be calculated by using the following formula:
(Dividend / Price) + Growth %
Hence, Cost of capital is determined as:
= (Re.0.60 / Rs.20) + 0.07
= 0.10
Post-acquisition the growth rate becomes 8%.

Hence cost of capital would work out to
Ke = Re.0.60/ (0.10 – 0.08) = Rs.30/-
The increase in value thereof is (Rs.30 – Rs.20) x 5, 00,000 = Rs.50, 00,000.

ii) **Calculation of gain to the shareholders of both the companies**
   If ADC Ltd were to offer one of its shares for every four share of BDC Ltd
   BDC Ltd:
   (Rs.100 – (Rs.20 x 4))= Rs.20 per share. This may be higher if price of ADC Ltd rises
   following merger which they should go ahead with.
   ADC Ltd:

Value of company now (10, 00,000 x Rs.100)	Rs.1000 lakhs
Value of BDC Ltd (5, 00,000 x Rs.30)	Rs. 150 lakhs
	Rs.1150 lakhs
No. of shares (10, 00,000 + 5, 00,000 x 1/4)	11, 25,000
EPS (Rs.1150 lakhs / 11.25 lakhs shares)	Rs.102.22
Hence,	
Gain to shareholders of BDC Ltd (Rs.102.22 – (Rs.20 x 4))	= Rs.20.22
Gain to shareholders of ADC Ltd (Rs.102.22 – Rs.100)	= Rs.2.22

iii) **Calculation of the gain of the shareholders of both the companies, if ADC Ltd pays**
   Rs.22 for each share of BDC Ltd assuming the P/E Ratio of ADC Ltd does not change
   after the merger:

Gains to shareholders of ADC Ltd:	
Earnings of BDC Ltd (5, 00,000 x Rs.2.50)	Rs.12, 50,000
Less: Loss of earning in cash (5, 00,000 x Rs.22 x 0.10)	Rs.11, 00,000
Net earnings	Rs.1.50, 000
No of shares	10, 00,000
Net increase in earnings per share	Re.0.15
P/E Ratio of ADC Ltd = (Rs.100 / Rs.8) =	12.50
Hence, gain per share of shareholders of ADC Ltd = (0.15 x 12.50) =	Rs.1.88
Gain to the shareholders of BDC Ltd (Rs.22 – Rs.20) =	Rs.2 per share

Illustration 24

AB Ltd is planning to acquire and absorb the running business of XY Ltd. The valuation is to be based on the recommendation of merchant bankers and the consideration is to be discharged in the form of equity shares to be issued by AB Ltd. As on 31.3.2006, the paid up capital of AB Ltd consists of 80 lakh shares of Rs.10 each. The highest and the lowest market quotation during the last six months were Rs.570 and Rs.430. For the purpose of the exchange, the price per share is to be reckoned as the average of the highest and lowest market price during the last six months ended 31.3.06.

XY Ltd's Balance Sheet as at 31.3.2006 is summarised below:

	(Rs lakhs)
Sources	
Share capital	
20 lakhs equity shares of Rs.10 each fully paid	200.00
10 lakhs equity shares of Rs.10 each Rs. Paid	50.00
Loans	100.00
Total	350.00
Uses	150.00
Fixed Assets (net)	200.00
Net current assets	350.00

An independent firm of merchant bankers engaged for the negotiation, have produced the following estimates of cash flows from the business of XY Ltd:

Year ended	By way of	Rs lakhs
31.3.07	After tax earnings for equity	105
31.3.08	After tax earnings for equity	120
31.3.09	After tax earnings for equity	125
31.3.10	After tax earnings for equity	120
31.3.11	After tax earnings for equity	100
	Terminal value estimate	200

It is the recommendation of the merchant banker that the business of XY Ltd may be valued on the basis of the average of (i) aggregate of discounted cash flows at 8% and (ii) net assets value. Present value factors at 8% for years

1 – 5	0.93	0.86	0.79	0.74	0.68

You are required to:
  i)   Calculate the total value of business of XY Ltd
  ii) Calculate the number of shares to be issued by AB Ltd and
  iii) The basis of allocation of the shares among the shareholders of XY Ltd

Solution

  i)   **Calculation of the total value of business of XY Ltd**

Particulars	Rs/lakhs
Price per share of AB Ltd for determination of number of shares to be issued: (Rs.570 + Rs.430) /2	Rs.500 (A)

Value of XY Ltd based on future cash flows:

Year ended	After tax earnings Rs lakhs	Present value factors at 8%	DCF Rs lakhs
31.3.07	105	0.93	97.65
31.3.08	120	0.86	103.20
31.3.09	125	0.79	98.75
31.3.10	120	0.74	88.80
31.3.11	100	0.68	68.00
	200	0.68	136.00
Total			592.40 (B)

Value of XY Ltd based on net assets (Rs.200 lakhs + Rs.50 lakhs)	Rs.250 lakhs (C)
Average value (B + C)/2	Rs.421.20 (D)
ii) **No. of shares in AB Ltd to be issued** (D / A) =	84240 nos

iii) Basis of allocation of the shares among the shareholders of XY Ltd

Fully paid equivalent shares in XY Ltd (20 + 5) lakhs	2500000
Distribution to fully paid shareholders (84240 x 20/25) =	67392
Balance distribution to partly paid shareholders (84240 – 67392) =	16848

Illustration 25

BA Ltd and DA Ltd both the companies operate in the same industry. The financial statements of both the companies for the current financial year are as follows:

Balance Sheet

Particulars		BA Ltd	DA Ltd
		Rs	Rs
Current assets		14,00,000	10,00,000
Fixed Assets (net)		10,00,000	5,00,000
	Total	24,00,000	15,00,000
Equity capital (Rs.10 each)		10,00,000	8,00,000
Retained earnings		2,00,000	-
14% long-term debt		5,00,000	3,00,000
Current liabilities		7,00,000	4,00,000
	Total	24,00,000	15,00,000

Income Statement

Particulars	BA Ltd	DA Ltd
	Rs	Rs
Net sales	34,50,000	17,00,000
Cost of goods sold	27,60,000	13,60,000
Gross Profit	6,90,000	3,40,000
Operating expenses	2,00,000	1,00,000
Interest	70,000	42,000
Earnings before taxes	4,20,000	1,98,000
Taxes @ 50%	2,10,000	99,000
Earnings after taxes (EAT)	2,10,000	99,000
Additional information:		
No. of equity shares	1,00,000	80,000
Dividend payout ratio (D/P)	40%	60%
Market price per share	Rs.40	Rs.15

Assume that both companies are in the process of negotiating a merger through an exchange of equity shares. You have been asked to assist in establishing equitable exchange terms and are required to:

i) Decompose the share price of both the companies into EPS and P/E components and also segregate their EPS figures into Return on Equity (ROE) and book value / intrinsic value per share components

ii) Estimate future EPS growth rates for each company

iii) Based on expected operating synergies BA Ltd estimates that the intrinsic value of DA's equity share would be Rs.20 per share on its acquisition. You are required to develop a range of justifiable equity share exchange ratios that can be offered by BA Ltd to the shareholders of DA Ltd. Based on your analysis in part (i) and (ii), would you expect the negotiated terms to be closer to the upper, or the lower exchange ratio limits and why?

iv) Calculate the post-merger EPS based on an exchange ratio of 0.4: 1 being offered by BA Ltd and indicate the immediate EPS accretion or dilution, if any, which will occur for each group of shareholders.

v) Based on a 0.4: 1 exchange ratio and assuming that BA Ltd's pre-merger P/E ratio will continue after the merger, estimate the post-merger market price. Also show the resulting accretion or dilution in pre-merger market prices.

Solution

Tutorial note:

Market price per share (MPS) = EPS X P/E ratio = P/E ratio = MPS / EPS

i) Determination of EPS and P/E components and also segregate their EPS figures into Return on Equity (ROE) and book value / intrinsic value per share components

Particulars	Formula	BA Ltd	DA Ltd
Earnings after tax	(A)	Rs.2,10,000	Rs.99,000
No. of shares	(B)	100,000	80,000
EPS	(A / B = C)	Rs.2.10	Rs.1.2375
Market price per share	(D)	Rs.40	Rs.15
P/E Ratio	(D / C = E)	19.05	12.12
Equity funds	(F)	Rs.12,00,000	Rs.8,00,000
Book value per share	(F / B = G)	Rs.12/-	Rs.10/-
ROE	(A / F = H)	17.5%	12.37%

ii) Estimation of future EPS growth rates for each company

Particulars	Formula	BA Ltd	DA Ltd
Retention ratio	(1 – D / P ratio)	0.6	0.4
Growth rate	(ROE X Retention ratio)	10.5%	4.95%

iii) Justifiable equity share exchange ratios that can be offered by BA Ltd to the shareholders of DA Ltd

Intrinsic value based	= Rs.20 / Rs.40	0.5 : 1 (upper limit)
Market price based = MPS DA / MPS BA	= Rs.15 / Rs.40	0.375 : 1(lower limit)

Since BA Ltd has a higher EPS, ROE, P/E ratio and even higher EPS growth expectations, the negotiable terms would be expected to be closer to the lower limit, based on the existing share prices.

iv) Calculation of post-merger EPS and its effects

Particulars	Formula	BA Ltd	DA Ltd	Combined
EAT (Rs)	(A)	2,10,000	99,000	3,09,000
Share outstanding	(B)	1,00,000	80,000	1,32,000*
EPS (Rs)	(A / B= C)	2.1	1.2375	2.341
EPS Accretion (Dilution) (Re)		(2.341-2.10)	(0.301**)	
		= 0.241		

*Shares outstanding (combined) = 100000 shares + 0.4 x 80000 = 132000 shares
**EPS claim per old share = Rs.2.341 x 0.4   = Rs.0.936
    EPS dilution   = Rs.1.2375 – Rs.0.936 = Rs.0.3015

v) Estimation of post-merger market price and other effects

Particulars	Formula	BA Ltd	DA Ltd	Combined
EPS (Rs)	(A)	2.10	1.2375	2.341
P/E Ratio	(B)	19.05	12.12	19.05
MPS (Rs)	(A X B)	40.0	15.0	44.6
MPS Accretion		4.6	2.84***	

***MPS claim per old share   = Rs.44.60 x 0.4 = Rs.17.84
    Less MPS per old share   = Rs.15.00
                                                            Rs.2.84

Illustration 26

ABC, a large business house is planning to sell its wholly owned subsidiary KLM. Another large business entity XYZ has expressed its interest in making a bid for KLM. XYZ expects that after acquisition the annual earning of KLM will increase by 10%.

Following information, ignoring any potential synergistic benefits arising out of possible acquisitions are available:

   i)   Profit after tax for KLM for the financial year which has just ended is estimated to be Rs.10 crore
   ii)   KLM's after tax profit has an increasing trend of 7% each year and the same is expected to continue
   iii)   Estimated post tax market return is 10% and risk free rate is 4%. These rates are expected to continue.
   iv)   Corporate tax rate is 30%.

Particulars	XYZ	ABC	Proxy entity for KLM in the same line of business
No. of shares	100 lakhs	80 lakhs	-
Current share price	Rs.287	Rs.375	-
Dividend payout	40%	50%	50%
Debt : Equity at market values	1:2	1:3	1:4
P/E Ratio	10	13	12
Equity beta	1	1.1	1.1

Assume gearing level of KLM to be the same as for ABC and a debt beta of zero.
You are required to calculate:
   a) Appropriate cost of equity for KLM based on the data available for the proxy entity
   b) A range of values for KLM both before and after any potential synergistic benefits to XYZ of the acquisition.

Solution

a) Beta equity ungeared for the proxy entity = 1.1 x 4 / (4 + (1-0.3)) = 0.9362
    0.9362 = Beta equity geared x 3 / (3 + (1-0.3))
    Beta equity geared = 1.1546
    Cost of equity =0.04 + 1.1546 x (0.1-0.04) = 10.93%

b) P/E Valuation – based on Rs.10 crore PAT

	Using Proxy entity's P/E	Using XYZ's P/E
Pre synergistic value	12 X Rs.10 crore = Rs.120 crore	10 x Rs.10 crore = Rs.100 crore
Post synergistic value	12 x Rs.10 crore x 1.1 = Rs.132 crore	10 x Rs.10 crore x 1.1 = Rs.110 crore

Dividend valuation model

	Based on 50% payout	Based on 40% payout
Pre synergistic value	$\dfrac{0.5 \times 10 \times 1.07}{0.1093 - 0.07}$ = Rs.136.13 crore	$\dfrac{0.4 \times 10 \times 1.07}{0.1093 - 0.07}$ = Rs.108.91 crore
Post synergistic value	$\dfrac{0.5 \times 10 \times 1.1 \times 1.07}{0.1093 - 0.07}$ = Rs.149.75 crore	$\dfrac{0.4 \times 10 \times 1.1 \times 1.07}{0.1093 - 0.07}$ = Rs.119.79 crore

Market price

It is possible to calculate a market value on proportion of earnings of ABC that is generated by KLM – though no specific information is available about the value of KLM.

Market value of ABC   = 80 lakh shares x Rs.375 = Rs.300 crore
Post tax earnings of ABC   = Rs.300 / 13   = Rs.23.08 crore

If market value of ABC is allocated to KLM in the proportion of relative earning of KLM to that of ABC, KLM would have a market value of Rs.300 crore x (10 / 23.08) = Rs.130 crore

KLM Post tax earnings   = Rs.10 crore

If ABC's P/E ratio is applied to it, the market value of KLM becomes Rs.10 crores x 13 = Rs.130 crore. Therefore, it assumes that KLM has the same P/E ratio as that of ABC.

Range of valuation

Pre synergistic	Rs.100 crore	Rs.136.13 crore
Post synergistic	Rs.110 crore	Rs.149.75 crore

Illustration 27

Using the chop-shop approach (or break-up value approach), assign a value for Cranberry Ltd whose stock is currently trading at a total market price of € 4 million. For Cranberry Ltd, the accounting data set forth three business segments: consumer wholesale, retail and general centres. Data for the firm's three segments are as follows:

Business segment	Segment sales	Segment assets	Segment operating income
Wholesale	€ 225,000	€ 600,000	€ 75,000
Retail	€ 720,000	€ 500,000	€ 150,000
General	€ 2,500,000	€ 4,000,000	€ 700,000

Industry data for "pure-play" firms have been compiled and are summarised as under:

Business segment	Capital-to-sales	Capitalisation / Assets	Capitalisation / Operating Income
Wholesale	0.85	0.7	9
Retail	1.2	0.7	8
General	0.8	0.7	4

Solution

Business segment	Capital-to-sales	Segment sales	Theoretical values
Wholesale	0.85	€ 225,000	€ 1,91,250
Retail	1.2	€ 720,000	€ 8,64,000
General	0.8	€ 2,500,000	€ 20,00,000
Total value			€ 30,55,250

Business segment	Capitalisation / Assets	Segment assets	Theoretical values
Wholesale	0.7	€ 600,000	€ 4,20,000
Retail	0.7	€ 500,000	€ 3,50,000
General	0.7	€ 4,000,000	€ 28,00,000
Total value			€ 35,70,000

Business segment	Capitalisation /	Segment operating	Theoretical values

	Operating Income	income	
Wholesale	9	€ 75,000	€ 6,75,000
Retail	8	€ 150,000	€ 12,00,000
General	4	€ 700,000	€ 28,00,000
Total value			€ 46,75,000

Average theoretical value = (€ 30, 55,250 + € 35, 70,000 + € 46, 75,000) /3 = € 37, 66,750
Hence average theoretical value of Cranberry Ltd = € 37, 66,750.

Illustration 28
The following is the Balance Sheet of Grape Fruit Company Ltd as at March 31st 2011:

Liabilities	Rs in lakhs	Assets	Rs in lakhs
Equity shares o Rs.100 each	600	Land & building	200
14% preference shares of Rs.100	200	Plant & Machinery	300
each		Furniture & fixtures	50
13% Debentures	200	Inventory	150
Debenture interest accrued and	26	Sundry debtors	70
payable		Cash at bank	130
Loan from bank	74	Preliminary expenses	10
Trade creditors	340	Cost of issue of debentures	5
		Profit & loss account	525
	1440		1440

The company did not perform well and has suffered sizeable losses during the last few years.
However, it is felt that the company could be nursed back to health by proper financial restructuring.
Consequently the following scheme of reconstruction has been drawn up:
  i)   Equity shares are to be reduced to Rs.25 per share, fully paid up;
  ii)   Preference shares are to be reduced (with a coupon rate of 10%) to equal number of
        shares of Rs.50 each fully paid up
  iii) Debenture holders have agreed to forego the accrued interest due to them. In the
        future, the rate of interest on debentures is to be reduced to 9 %
  iv)   Trade creditors will forego 25% of the amount due to them
  v)   The company issues 6 lakh equity shares at Rs.25 each and the entire sum was to be paid
        on application. The entire amount was fully subscribed by promoters.
  vi)   Land and Building was to be revalued at Rs.450 lakhs, Plant & Machinery was to be
        written down by Rs.120 lakhs and a provision of Rs.15 lakhs had to be made for bad and
        doubtful debts.

Required:
  i)   Show the impact of financial restructuring on the company's activities.
  ii)   Prepare the fresh Balance Sheet after the reconstruction is completed on the basis of
        the above proposals.

Solution

i)   Statement of impact of financial restructuring on the company's activities

Particulars	Rs in lakhs
i) Reduction of liabilities:	
- Reduction in equity share capital (6 lakh shares x Rs.75)	450
- Reduction in preference share capital (2 lakh shares x Rs.50)	100

	- Waiver of outstanding debenture interest	26
	- Waiver from trade creditors (Rs.340 lakhs x 0.25)	<u>85</u>
		661
ii)	Revaluation of assets	
	Appreciation of land and building (Rs.450 lakhs – Rs.200 lakhs)	<u>250</u>
	Total benefits from restructuring	<u>911 (A)</u>
iii)	Utilisation of funds to write off losses, fictitious and over-valued assets:	
	- Writing off profit and loss account	525
	- Cost of issue of debentures	5
	- Preliminary expenses	10
	- Provision for bad and doubtful debts	15
	- Revaluation of Plant & Machinery (Rs.300 lakhs – Rs.104 lakhs)	<u>120</u>
		<u>675 (B)</u>
iv)	Capital reserve ((A – B) = C)	<u>236</u>

ii)   Balance Sheet of Grape Fruit Ltd as at 31st March 2011 (after – reconstruction)

Liabilities	Amount Rs lakhs	Assets	Amount Rs lakhs
12 lakhs equity shares of Rs.25 each	300	Land & building	450
10% preference shares of Rs.50 each	100	Plant & Machinery	180
Capital reserve	236	Furnitures & fixtures	50
9% Debentures	200	Inventory	150
Loan from bank	74	Sundry debtors (70 – 15)	55
Trade creditors	255	Cash-at-bank (balancing fig)*	280
	1165		1165

*Opening balance of Rs.130 lakhs + sale proceeds from issue of new equity shares Rs.150 lakhs.

Chapter 12: Decision making through Strategic Cost Management

12.1. What is strategic cost management

According to Cooper and Slagmulder (1998) argued that strategic cost management is "the application of cost management techniques so that they simultaneously improve the strategic position of a firm and reduce costs". They suggest three sorts of cost management initiative, based on whether the impact on the organization's competitive position is positive, negative or neutral.

A few illustrations will help us understand what is strategic cost management.

Illustration 1
A hospital redesigns its patient admission procedure at the registration desk, so it becomes more efficient and easier for patients. The hospital will become known for its easy admission procedure so more people will come to that hospital if the patient has a choice. The strategic position of the hospital has just been increased over its competitors.

Illustration 2
A medical insurance company decides to re-evaluate its accounts payable system to make it more efficient. The evaluation has no positive benefits to the insurance company in the external market. The objective of the change is to make the organization more profitable. Since this is an internal back-office change it does not create any strategic impact to the world at large, except that internally it helps improves cash management.

Illustration 3
A large airline company only has two desks for administering and selling tickets. This set-up induces long queues for the airline customer which can ultimately result in high dissatisfaction and a bad reputation for the airline. This may reduce the amount of ticket sales when compared with the airline's competitors. Even though having only two desks available for customers may initially be cost effective, in the long run, it harms the company. This is a strategic intent which negatively impacts the organisation.

As it is clear from above, strategic cost management seeks to improve the strategic position of an organization and reduces costs at the same time and it is important because global competition means that firms must be constantly aware of their strategic position.
According to Porter, a firm has a choice of three generic strategies in order to achieve sustainable competitive advantage. They are cost leadership, differentiation, and focus. Where cost leadership is selected Porter advocates the use of strategic cost analysis.

Hence it is evident that an organization must compete in the areas of cost, quality, customer service, and flexibility with any cost reduction efforts contributing to an improved strategic position and here financial analytics plays a very critical role.

In the paragraphs we have tried to summarise the pillars of Strategic Cost Management which are:
  a) Conventional costing
  b) Activity based cost management
  c) Target costing
  d) Lifecycle costing
  e) Kaizen costing
  f) Total Quality Management techniques
  g) Use of marginal costing in decision making area

You'll note that in each of these pillars, financial analytics plays a very critical part.

12.2. Conventional costing

Conventional costing attempts to work out the cost of producing an item incorporating the costs of resources that are currently used or consumed. Therefore, for each unit made the classical variable costs of material, direct labour and variable overheads are included (the total of these is the marginal cost of production), together with a share of the fixed production costs. The fixed production costs can be included using a conventional overhead absorption rate or they can be accounted for using activity-based costing (ABC). ABC is more complex but almost certainly more accurate. However, whether conventional overhead treatment or ABC is used the overheads incorporated are usually based on the budgeted overheads for the current period.

Once the total absorption cost of units has been calculated, a mark-up (or gross profit percentage) is used to determine the selling price and the profit per unit. The mark-up is chosen so that if the budgeted sales are achieved, the organization should make a profit.

12.3. Activity based cost Management (ABM)

The use of ABC as a costing tool to manage costs at activity level is known as Activity Based Cost Management (ABM). It is a discipline that focuses on the efficient and effective management of activities as the route to continuously improving the value received by customers. ABM utilises cost information gathered through ABC. It determines what drives the activities of the organisation and how these activities can be improved to increase the profitability.

12.3.1. Key attributes in Activity Based Cost Management are:
   a) Cost object: It is an item for which cost measurement is required. e.g. a product or a customer
   b) Cost driver: It is a factor that causes a change in the cost of the activity. There are two categories of cost drivers:
      I)   Resource cost driver – it is a measure of the quantity of resources consumed by an activity. It is used to assign the cost of a resource to an activity or cost pool
      II)   Activity cost driver – It is a measure of the frequency and intensity of demand, placed on activities by cost objects. It is used to assign activity costs to cost objects

12.3.2. Stages of Activity based costing
The stages of activity based costing are:
   a) Identification of the activities that have taken place in the organisation
   b) Assigning costs to cost pool for each activity
   c) Spreading of support activities across primary activities
   d) Determining cost driver for each activity
   e) Assigning the costs of activities to products according to product demand for activities

12.3.3. Business Applications of Activities based cost management (ABM) are:
a) Cost reduction
b) Activity based budgeting
c) Business Process re-engineering
d) Benchmarking
e) Performance management

Examples of activity based cost management are as under:

Illustration1.

The budgeted overheads and cost driver volumes of XYZ are as follows.

Cost Pool	Budgeted Overheads Rs.	Cost Driver	Budgeted Volume
Material procurement	5,80,000	No. of orders	No. of orders
Material handling	2,50,000	No. of movements	No. of movements
Set-up	4,15,000	No. of set ups	No. of set ups
Maintenance	9,70,000	Maintenance hours	Maintenance hours
Quality control	1,76,000	No. of inspection	No. of inspection
Machinery	7,20,000	No. of machine hours	No. of machine hours

The company has produced a batch of 2,600 components of AX-15, its material cost was Rs. 1,30,000 and labour cost Rs. 2,45,000. The usage activities of the said batch are as follows.
Material orders – 26, maintenance hours – 690, material movements – 18, inspection – 28, set ups – 25, machine hours – 1,800
Calculate – cost driver rates that are used for tracing appropriate amount of overheads to the said batch and ascertain the cost of batch of components using activity Based Costing.

Solution
Statement of computation of cost driver rates

Particulars	Amount Rs.	Amount Rs.
Material procurement	580000/1100	527
Material handling	250000/680	368
Set-up	415000/520	798
Maintenance	970000/8400	115
Quality control		196
Machinery	720000/24000	30

Statement of computation of batch cost of 2600 units of AX – 15

Particulars	Amount Rs.	Amount Rs.
Material Cost		1,30,000
Labour cost		2,45,000
Prime cost		3,75,000
Add: Overheads		
Material orders (26 x 527)	13702	
Material handling (18 x 368)	6624	
Set-up (25 x 798)	19,950	
Maintenance (690 x 115)	79,350	
Quality control (28 x 196)	5,488	
Machinery (1800 x 30)	54,000	1,79,114
Total cost		5,54,114

Illustration 2
A company produces four products, viz. P, Q, R and S. The data relating to production activity are as under:

Product	Quality of	Material cost	Direct	Machine	Direct labour

	production	/ unit Rs.	labour hours /unit	hours /unit	cost / unit Rs.
P	1,000	10	1	0.5	6
Q	10,000	10	1	0.5	6
R	1,200	32	4	2.0	24
S	14,000	34	3	3.0	18

Production overheads are as under: Rs.
(i) Overheads applicable to machine oriented activity: 1,49,700
(ii) Overheads relating to ordering materials   7,680
(iii) Set up costs   17,400
(iv) Administration overheads for spare parts   34,380
(v) Material handling costs   30,294
The following further information have been compiled:

Product	No.of set up	No.of material order	No.of times material handled	No.of spare parts
P	3	3	6	6
Q	18	12	30	15
R	5	3	9	3
S	24	12	36	12

Required:

i) Select a suitable cost driver for each item of overhead expense and calculate the cost per unit of cost driver.

ii) Using the concept of activity based costing, compute the factory cost per unit of each product.

Solution:

Computation of Cost Driver Rates
1) Overheads relating to Machinery oriented activity
   Cost Driver at Machine Hour Rate
   (1000 x 0.5) + (1000 x 0.5) + (1200 x 2) + (14000 x 3)
   1, 49,700/49,900 = Rs. 3 per hour
2) Overheads relating to ordering materials
   Cost driver at No. of Material orders
   7680/30 = Rs. 256 per order
3) Set up costs
   Cost driver at No. of set ups
   17400/50 = Rs.348 per set up
4) Administrative Overheads for spare parts
   Cost driver at No. of spare parts
   34380/36 = Rs.955 per spare part.
5) Material Handling costs
   Cost driver at No. of times materials handled
   30294/81 = Rs. 374 per material handling

Computation of factory cost for each product

Particulars	P		Q		R		S	
Material		10		10		32		34
Labour		6		6		24		18
Overhead								
Machine activity	1.50		1.50		6.00		9.00	
Ordering of materials	0.768		0.31		0.64		0.22	
Set up costs	1.044		0.63		1.45		0.60	
Administrative spare parts	5.730		1.43		2.39		0.82	
Material handling	2.244	11.29	1.12	4.99	2.81	13.29	0.96	11.60
Factory cost (Rs)		27.29		20.99		69.29		63.60

12.4. Target costing

Target costing is defined as "a structured approach to determining the cost at which a proposed product with specified functionality and quality must be produced to generate a desired level of profitability at its anticipated selling price". It is an important part of a comprehensive management process aimed at helping an organisation to survive in an increasingly competitive environment.

There are certain shortcomings in conventional costing, which are highlighted below:

1. The product's price is based on its cost, but no one might want to buy at that price. The product might incorporate features which customers do not value and therefore do not want to pay for, and competitors' products might be cheaper, or at least offer better value for money. This flaw is addressed by *Target costing.*

1. The costs incorporated are the current costs only. They are the marginal costs plus a share of the fixed costs for the current accounting period. There may be other important costs which are not part of these categories, but without which the goods could not have been made. Examples include the research and development costs and any close down costs incurred at the end of the product's life. Why have these costs been excluded, particularly when selling prices have to be high enough to ensure that the product makes a profit. To make a profit, total revenue must exceed total costs in the long term. This flaw is addressed by *lifecycle costing.*

12.4.1. Features of Target costing

The features of target costing are as under:
1. Target costing is viewed as an integral part of the design and introduction of new products
2. For any given product, a target selling price is determined using various sales forecasting techniques
3. Integral to setting the target selling price is the establishment of target production volumes, given the relationship between price and volume
4. The next stage of the target costing process is to determine cost reduction targets
5. It should be noted that a fair degree of judgement is needed where the allowable cost and the target cost differ.
6. The total target is split into various components, each component is studied and opportunities for cost reductions are identified. These initiatives are often alluded to as *Value Engineering* and *Value Analysis.*

Target costing is marketing approach to costing.

The basic idea on product profitability is as under:

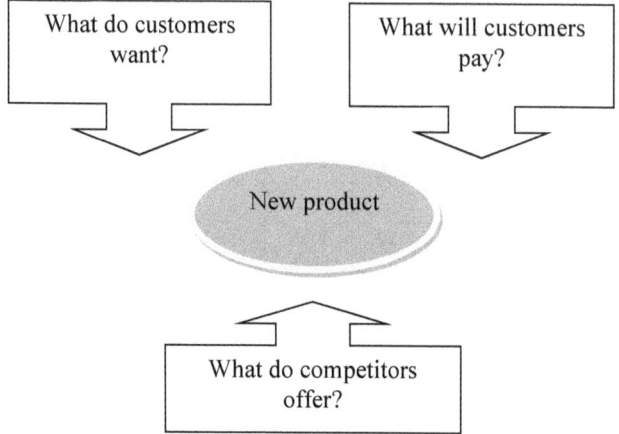

12.4.2. Target costing and impact on profitability
Target costing improves profitability in two ways:

a) It places such a detailed continuing emphasis on product costs throughout the life cycle of every product that it is unlikely that a company will experience runaway costs;

b) It improves profitability through precise targeting of the correct prices at which the company feels it can field a profitable product in the marketplace that will sell in a robust manner.

Instead of starting with the cost and working to the selling price by adding on the expected margin, target costing will start with the selling price of a particular product and work back to the cost by removing the profit element. This means that the company has to find ways of not exceeding that cost.

This is a powerful discipline imposed on the company. The main results are:

• The establishment of multifunctional teams consisting of marketing people, cost accountants, production managers, quality control professionals and others. These teams are vital to the design and manufacturing decisions required to determine the price and feature combinations that are most likely to appeal to potential buyers of products.

An emphasis on the planning and design stage. This becomes very important to the cost of the product because if something is designed such that it is needlessly expensive to make, it does not matter how efficient the production process is, it will always be a struggle to make satisfactory profits.

Here are some of the decisions, made at the design stage, which can affect the cost of a product:

• the features of the product.

- how to avoid 'over design'.
- the number of components needed.
- whether the components are standard or specialised.
- the complexity of machining and construction.
- where the product can be made.
- what to make in-house and what to sub-contract.
- the quality of the product.
- the batch size in which the product can be made.

You will see from this list that activity-based costing can also play an important part in target costing. By understanding the cost drivers (cost causers) a company can better control its costs. For example, costs could be driven down by increasing batch size, or reducing the number of components that have to be handled by stores.

12.5. Lifecycle costing

As mentioned above, target costing places great emphasis on controlling costs by good product design and production planning, but those up-front activities also cause costs. There might be other costs incurred after a product is sold such as warranty costs and plant decommissioning. When seeking to make a profit on a product it is essential that the total revenue arising from the product exceeds total costs, whether these costs are incurred before, during or after the product is produced. This is the concept of life cycle costing, and it is important to realise that target costs can be driven down by attacking any of the costs that relate to any part of a product's life. The cost phases of a product can be identified as:

Phase	Examples of types of cost
Design	Research, development, design and tooling
Manufacture	Material, labour, overheads, machine set up, inventory, training, production machine maintenance and depreciation
Operation	Distribution, advertising and warranty claims
End of life	Environmental clean-up, disposal and decommissioning

Principal lessons to be learned from lifecycle costing	1. All costs should be taken into account when working out the cost of a unit and its profitability.
	2. Attention to all costs will help to reduce the cost per unit and will help an organisation achieve its target cost.
	3. Many costs will be linked. For example, more attention to design can reduce manufacturing and warranty costs. More attention to training can machine maintenance costs. More attention to waste disposal during manufacturing can reduce end-of life costs.
	4. Costs are committed and incurred at very different times. A committed cost is a cost that will be incurred in the future because of decisions that have already been made. Costs are incurred only when a resource is used.

Illustration 1

A company is planning a new product. Market research information suggests that the product should sell 10,000 units at Rs.21.00/unit. The company seeks to make a mark-up of 40% product cost. It is estimated that the lifetime costs of the product will be as follows:

(i) Design and development costs Rs.50,000

(ii) Manufacturing costs Rs. 10/unit

(iii) End of life costs Rs.20,000

The company estimates that if it were to spend an additional ` 15,000 on design, manufacturing costs/ unit could be reduced.

Required

(a) What is the target cost of the product?

(b) What is the original lifecycle cost per unit and is the product worth making on that basis?

(c) If the additional amount were spent on design, what is the maximum manufacturing cost per unit that could be tolerated if the company is to earn its required mark-up?

Solution

The target cost of the product can be calculated as follows:

(a) Cost + Mark-up = Selling price

100%	40%	140%
Rs.15	Rs. 6	Rs.21

(b) The original life cycle cost per unit = (Rs.50,000 + (10,000 x Rs.10) + Rs.20,000)/10,000
=

Rs. 17

This cost/unit is above the target cost per unit, so the product is not worth making.

(c) Maximum total cost per unit = Rs.15. Some of this will be caused by the design and end of life costs:

(Rs.50,000 + Rs.15,000 + Rs.20,000)/10,000

= Rs.8.50

Therefore, the maximum manufacturing cost per unit would have to fall from Rs.10 to (Rs.15 – Rs.8.50) = Rs.6.50.

12.6. Kaizen costing

Kaizen costing is a process wherein a product undergoes cost reduction even when it is already on the production stage. The cost minimization can include strategies in effective waste management, continuous product improvement or better deals in the acquisition of raw materials.

Yashihuro Moden defines kaizen costing as "the maintenance of present cost levels for products currently being manufactured via systematic efforts to achieve the desired cost level." The word *kaizen* is a Japanese word meaning *continuous improvement*.

Moden has described two types of kaizen costing:

- Asset and organisation specific kaizen costing activities planned according to the exigencies of each deal
- Product model specific costing activities carried out in special projects with added emphasis on value analysis

Kaizen costing is applied to products that are already in production phase. Prior to kaizen costing, when the products are under development phase, target costing is applied.

'Kaizen costing is based on the belief that nothing is ever perfect, so improvements and reductions in the variable costs are always possible'

The cost-plus method is one of the most traditional and common pricing techniques. In fact, virtually all companies in the UK used cost-plus pricing until they started to realise that they were operating in price-competitive markets. Until then, they had naively assumed that consumers would be wiling to pay whatever price they arrived at by adding a percentage to the estimated cost of the product or service. This cost-plus approach has gradually been replaced by target costing. This addresses the pricing issue from the other direction. It must be accepted that in a competitive market a company has little influence over the selling price of its product.

12.7. Cost of quality and Quality Management

Total Quality Management is a systematic process for identifying and implementing solution and prioritised opportunities for improvement.

The TQM approach highlights the need for a customer oriented approach to management reporting, eliminating some of our more traditional reporting practices. Performance measurement and quality management are not the sole domain of manufacturing industry, but detailed applications of the new management accounting practices to the professional service environment.

12.7.1. Features of TQM

The features of TQM are:
  a) Commitment
  b) Culture
  c) Continuous improvement
  d) Co-operation
  e) Customer focus
  f) Control

Illustration 1.

A company manufactures a component on batches of 2,000 each. Each component is tested before being sent to the agents for sales. Each component can be tested at the factory at a cost of Rs.25. If any component is found to be defective, it can be rectified by spending Rs.200. In view of the large demand for the components and the sophisticated system of manufacture, a proposal came up that the practice of pre-testing of the components to be dispensed with to save costs. In that event, any defective component is received back from the customer under warranty, the cost of rectification and re-dispatch will be Rs.400 per component.

State at what percentage of manufacture of components, the company will find it cheaper to pre-test each component.

Solution:

Let the defectives be d

To set (2,000 × 25) + 200d

If defectives are rectified after return from customers from customers, the cost = 400d

At Cost indifference point:

(2,000 × 25) + 200d = 400d

or, 200d = 50,000

or, d=250

Percentage of defectives to total components = 250 ÷ 2,000 × 100 = 12.5%

If defectives are more than 12.5%, pre-testing is advised.

Illustration 2

Snacks Ltd. initiated a quality improvement program at the beginning of the year. Efforts were made to reduce the number of defective units produced. By the end of the year, reports from the production manager revealed that scrap and rework had both decreased. Though pleased with success, the CEO of the company wanted some assessment of the financial impact of the improvements. To make this assessment, the following financial data were collected for the current and preceding year:

Particulars	2011-12	2012-13
	Rs	Rs.
Sales	1,00,00,000	1,00,00,000
Scrap	4,00,000	3,00,000
Rework	6,00,000	4,00,000
Product inspection	1,00,000	1,25,000
Product warranty	8,00,000	6,00,000
Quality training	40,000	80,000
Material inspection	60,000	40,000

You are required to —

(i) Classify the cost as prevention, appraisal, internal failure, or external failure.

(ii) Compute the profit that has increased because of quality improvements?

Solution

(i)   **Statement of classification of costs**

Cost classification	Attributes
Prevention cost	Quality training
Appraisal cost	Product inspection
	Material inspection
Internal failure	Scrap and rework
External failure	Product warranty

(ii)   Computation of profit based on quality improvement

Particulars	Rs.
Total quality cost for the year 2011-12	20,00,000
Total quality cost for the year 2012-13	15,45,000
Cost savings	3,55,000

Illustration 3

A Company manufactures a single product, the estimated costs of which are as follows:

Direct material Rs.20 each

Direct Wages 10 hours at Re. 1.00 per hour

Overhead absorption rate Rs.2.00 per hour. (50% fixed overhead included)

During this period, 1,000 units will be produced and sold as follows:-

Particulars	Rs.
990 units of first at	60 each
50 units of second at	50 each
50 units of third at	30 each

Present information to management showing the loss due to the production of inferior units.

By reprocessing the inferior units, taking the full re-processing time of a further 5 hours and adding further materials, costing Rs.10 per unit, these 'seconds' and 'thirds' can be converted into 'firsts.' Present information to the Management.

Solution:

Present Position (Based on 1,000 units production)

Cost per unit:

Particulars	Rs.	Rs.
Direct material		20
Direct labour	10 hrs. @ Re.1.	10
Overhead	10 hrs. @ Rs.2.	20
Total		50

Statement of profit or loss:

Item	Sales price/unit Rs.	Cost price/unit Rs.	Profit / loss/unit Rs.	Units	Profit / Loss Rs.
Firsts	60	50	10	990	9,900
Seconds	50	50	0	50	0
Thirds	30	50	(20)	50	(1,000)
Total					8,900

Reprocessing of inferior units:

a) Additional cost of reprocessing of inferior units:

Particulars	Rs.
Direct Material	10
Direct Labour	5
Overhead	5
TOTAL	20

Total expenditure for 100 units x Rs.20 = Rs.2000

b) Incremental revenue post reprocessing:

Particulars	Rs.
Seconds (Rs.60 – Rs.50) = Rs.10 x 50	500
Thirds (Rs.60 – Rs.30) = Rs.30 x 50	1500

TOTAL	2000

Since incremental revenue equates additional cost, there is no change in profit.

12.8. Decision making and pricing strategies

Some of the areas where decision making on costing and pricing strategies are involved are:

1. Stock Management and Inventory Control Decisions,

2. Plant Location Decisions,

3. Machinery Replacement / Capital Budgeting Decisions,

4. Sale at Split-off or Further Processing Decisions,

5. Product Decisions - Dropping or adding a product line,

6. Marketing Decisions,

7. Submitting Tenders and Quotations for new jobs based on relevant cost analysis,

8. Acceptance of Incremental Orders in different situations like spare capacity, full capacity etc,

9. Make or Buy Decisions,

10. Operate or Shut Down Decisions,

11. Product Pricing Decisions - Reduction or maintenance of price,

12. Opening of new sales territory or branch,

13. Intra-Company Transfer Pricing Decisions,

14. Purchasing vs. Lease Financing Decisions.

The above areas involve the use of Marginal Costs, Relevant Costs and Differential Cost approaches.

12.9. Balance Score Card

Developed in the early 1990s by Robert Kaplan from the Harvard Business School and David Norton, the founder of an IT consulting firm, this management system has been applied to many organizations and across many industries with great success.

The original article in the Harvard Business Review ("The Balanced Scorecard – Measures that Drive Performance", Harvard Business Review, Jan/Feb 1992) starts with the adage we quoted at the start of this article, "What you measure is what you get". The whole system is based on this premise.

12.9.1. Balanced scorecard performance metrics

With the balanced scorecard, *objectives* address the issue of what is needed for strategies to be successful. **Performance metrics** or *balanced scorecard metrics* address the measuring and controlling of progress to ensure that everything stays on course to deliver the desired outcome in the future.

Balanced scorecard is a team effort both in decision making and responsibility. Participants within the different sectors, departments etc bear responsibility for some portion of the pie and know how their portion contributes to overall success. Generating willing participation is likely to produce better outcomes hence the appeal of the balanced scorecard approach for implementing change. Key to balanced scorecard implementation is the ability to manage performance and control progress by measuring and recording results on a regular basis which means that every scorecard objective needs to be measureable.

12.9.2. Adding measurements to scorecard objectives:

Consider a company whose *vision* is to be the largest national producer of their product. To realize this vision one strategy decided upon is to increase turnover. The basis of the balanced scorecard approach is that all aspects (perspectives) of the business are interconnected. Changes in perspectives don't happen in isolation but have ramifications throughout the organization. Changes in some perspectives will drive outcomes in others. In the usual four perspective model the drivers are the Process and Innovation perspectives and the outcomes appear in Customer and ultimately Financial perspectives.

This table shows examples of *Objectives* in each *Perspective* and the *performance metric* to measure progress towards success with the above strategy.

Balanced scorecard metrics

Perspective	Objective	Measure
Financial	Financial objective: Increase in turnover of 15% on last year	Monthly turnover
Customer	Customer objective: Customers must receive their deliveries in full and on time	What % of monthly deliveries reached desired destination in full and on time
Process	Process objectives: 1. Appoint a new sales person 2. Enter all orders into the production planning system promptly	1. Date salesman appointed 2. Number of orders entered within 24 hours.
Innovation	Innovation objective Change infrastructure - install a new XYZ widget maker	Installation date of new machinery

With performance metrics you take a measurement and rate it against a *Target* for comparison. The *Target* is usually graded into levels like Outstanding, above target, on Target and below target. In the presentation of results the target levels are usually colour coded so you can see at glance if you are on target, below target, above target etc

Other performance metrics examples

% decrease
% of achieved deliveries to planned
% of products released on due date
Availability of materials
Average age of application
Benchmarking data obtained

Client survey
Completion date 15 August
Cost of rework
Cost per desktop
Cost reduction achieved
Cost saving achieved
Deliveries on time as ordered
Deliveries on time to new markets
EVA / EVA by customer
Ec ROCE
Finished goods turnover
Help desk hours
Hours of education
Hours of skills training
Increase in sales value
Index of user satisfaction
Internet & WAN up-time
Lost staff hours
Market share
Markets at risk
NOPAT
No of People trained
No of seminars delivered
Number of hours billed
Number of projects held up
Number of quality customers
Number of repeat calls
Number of trained people in bar-coding
Number of training hours delivered
Percentage IRR
Percentage non-reworked jobs
Percentage of YTD expense budget
Percentage of on time delivery

Percentage of rejects from suppliers
Percentage of waste reduction
Printer up time
Projects on target
Raw materials dollars
Raw materials turnover
Revenue growth
Revenue growth – monthly
Staff feedback sessions per month
Survey response from customers
Surveyed satisfaction of IT staff
Waiting time for a call-back
Workstation hours
Worst case responses

www.ingramcontent.com/pod-product-compliance
Lightning Source LLC
Chambersburg PA
CBHW051623170526
45167CB00001B/44